Roman Finds: Context and Theory

Roman Finds: Context and Theory
Proceedings of a conference held
at the University of Durham

edited by

Richard Hingley and Steven Willis

CENTRE for ROMAN CULTURE
Durham University

 ROMAN
FINDS
GROUP

UNIVERSITY OF KENT

ENGLISH HERITAGE

ROMA

Oxbow Books

Published by
Oxbow Books, Oxford

© Oxbow Books and the individual authors, 2007

ISBN 978 1 84217 163 9

This book is available direct from

Oxbow Books
(*Phone:* 01865 241249; *Fax:* 01865 794449)

and

The David Brown Book Company
PC Box 511, Oakville, CT 06779, USA
(*Phone:* 860 945 9329; *Fax:* 860 945 9468)

or from our website

www.oxbowbooks.com

The front cover photograph was taken by Spencer Scott of the University of Kent.
The drawing on the back cover shows a near complete tile antefix with a design of a Medusa head; it was
recovered from a Roman deposit at The Gilberd School site, Colchester, in 1984. The illustration is by Terry Cook
of The Colchester Archaeological Trust and it appears in Colchester Archaeological Report 6. It is reproduced
here by kind permission of Philip Crummy, the director of the Trust.

Printed in Great Britain at
Hobbs the Printers
Southampton

Contents

Authors' Addresses

PROFESSOR DAVID BREEZE
Historic Scotland
Longmore House
Salisbury Place
Edinburgh
EH9 1SH

DR GILLY CARR
Department of Archaeology
University of Cambridge
Downing Street
Cambridge
CB2 3DZ

DR H. E. M. COOL
Barbican Research Associates
16, Lady Bay Road
West Bridgeford
Nottingham
NG2 5BJ

NICHOLAS J. COOPER
University of Leicester Archaeological Services
School of Archaeology and Ancient History
Leicester
LE1 7RH

NINA CRUMMY
2 Hall Road
Copford
Colchester
CO6 1BN

DR HELLA ECKARDT
Department of Archaeology
University of Reading
Reading
RG6 2AA

DR ANTON ERVYNCK
Flemish Heritage Institute
Phoenix-building
Kon. Albert II-laan 19 box 5, B-1210
Brussel
Belgium

DR IAIN FERRIS
Iain Ferris Archaeological Associates
80 Durley Dean Road
Selly Oak
Birmingham
B29 6RX

PROFESSOR MICHAEL FULFORD
Department of Archaeology
University of Reading
Reading
RG6 2AA

DR ANDREW GARDNER
Institute of Archaeology
University College London
31–34 Gordon Square
London
WC1H 0PY

DR IAN HAYNES
School of History, Classics and Archaeology
Birkbeck College
University of London
Malet Street
London
WC1E 7RH

DR RICHARD HINGLEY
Department of Archaeology
University of Durham
South Road
Durham
DH1 6LL

DR RICHARD HOBBS
The British Museum
Department of Prehistory and Europe
Great Russell Street
London
WC1B 3DG

DR FRASER HUNTER
National Museum of Scotland
Chambers Street
Edinburgh
EH1 1JF

RAPHAEL ISSERLIN
The Open University in the North
154 Otley Road
Leeds
LS16 5JX

DR SONJA JILEK
Simmeringerhauptstrasse 465
A1110 Vienna
Austria

DR CATHERINE JOHNS
The British Museum
Great Russell Street
London
WC1B 3DG

MARLEEN MARTENS
Stedelijk Museum 'het Toreke'
Grote Markt 6, B-3300
Tienen
Belgium

T. S. MARTIN
9 Campbell Avenue
Thurmaston
Leicester
LE4 8HD

PROFESSOR MARTIN MILLETT
Faculty of Classics
University of Cambridge
Sidgwick Avenue
Cambridge
CB3 9DA

DR ELLEN SWIFT
School of European Culture and Languages
University of Kent
Cornwallis Building, North-West
Canterbury
Kent
CT2 7NF

DR ROBIN SYMONDS
Base Archéologique INRAP
Rente du Bassin
Rue Aristide Berges
21800 Sennecey-Lès-Dijon
France

ALAIN VANDERHOEVEN
Flemish Heritage Institute
Jekerstraat 10
B-3700 Tongeren
Belgium

DR STEVEN WILLIS
School of European Culture and Languages
University of Kent
Cornwallis Building, North-West
Canterbury
Kent
CT2 7NF

Foreword

It is an enormous pleasure and privilege to write a forward to this collection of papers on the subject of Roman material culture. It is hard to grasp how far the subject has moved forward since the early days of typological study when the material was studied almost exclusively for its chronological potential. Even within the last thirty years or so we have seen a remarkable diversification of approaches which are partly reflected in the contents of this collection, but it is probably true to say that no single volume of essays can do justice to the way the subject has evolved. And it is not as if the subject has moved on to the point that we can dispense with established approaches such as developing new typologies or ignore the chronological issues. In some ways as we come to understand better individual categories of material the need to revisit them with regard to, say, typology, in order to understand the creation of form and the processes of manufacture in the context of the role, for example, of the individual craftsman, does not diminish.

Several key, strategic issues form the content of papers here, but where are the real pinch-points which are holding back the development of the subject area? Clearly resourcing the study of Roman material culture remains the biggest issue and there are concerns about the training and support of future generations of finds' specialists as the generation which benefited from a better resourced publicly funded archaeology of the 1960s to 1990s moves into senior roles or retires. While PPG16 has undoubtedly brought more resources into rescue archaeology as a whole since the mid 1990s, it has yet, through IFA and other appropriate public bodies, to create the support in the form of professional training and development which will foster the next generation of material culture specialists. As part of that planning there needs to be a more systematic review of the capacity to improve the infrastructure of material culture research, above all via developments linked to the web. Already there are subject areas with vast bibliographies where the profession is chasing too few specialists and where availability via the web for making identifications or understanding context would be immensely beneficial. Work has started here, but to take the case of the highly specialised field of samian/sigillata studies, how intimidating is the prospect of manually researching South Gaulish decorated sigillata through the 13 ring-bound volumes of *Gestempelte südgallische Reliefsigillata (Dragendorff 29) aus den Werkstätten von La Graufesenque* which is being published in conventional form in 2004 by the Römisch-Germanischen Zentralmuseums, Mainz? This, for just one decorated South Gaulish form! Progress in the field of digitised data, that can be made available via the web, with the support of bodies such as the ADS, offers enormous prospects where the benefits in some areas (such as sigillata studies) can be realised on a European-wide scale.

Then there are the issues of quality assurance – how can we be assured of the quality of identifications, or of finds reports in general? How do we know whether someone, competitive in cost though (s)he may be, is competent in a particular field? As far as I am aware there is no recognised HE course in the UK which provides training in Roman material culture studies. Certainly, there are undergraduates and post-graduates who are working on particular subjects under academic supervision with differing levels of academic expertise, but there is also an awful lot of scholarship and expertise in the private domain which is not being realised in a formal educational context. We need to capitalise on this in order to secure the future of the subject area.

There is one helpful new initiative. Taking its lead from a recommendation arising from the 2001 RAE, AHRB has ring-fenced a certain number of postgraduate studentships for material culture studies of any period. Fine, if a student knows that is what (s)he wants and can identify a supervisor, but what about the competent supervisors in departments where there is no graduate with a particular interest in this area? How do we get the students and the expertise properly matched and make real progress? How do we engage the expertise which is outside the HE system? Provision of courses which exploit the full potential of expertise within and outwith the HE sector and which are developed to meet the national need is a way forward, but to do this requires considerable organisation and may not be financially viable under the current financing regime of HE Certificate, Diploma and Masters' programmes. In the meanwhile, given the quality of digital photography now, validation might be conducted on a self-declaration basis whereby the consumer can satisfy her/himself by looking at visual images put up by the specialist of the key material categories of data as part of an electronic publication via the web which might or might not be complemented by a conventional printed publication. Indeed, robustly assured electronic publication has to be the solution for the publication of large datasets and archives which the subject generates.

How might we progress matters? Clearly issues relating to resourcing, enhancing the information base, training and quality assurance require both promotion and co-ordination. There has been a tendency for special interest groups to emerge and proliferate as the subject matter grows and diversifies. So, for example, there are generic groups for environmental archaeology and zooarchaeology and there are period-based groups in finds research, notably small finds and pottery. What is needed is to draw these small groups together under an appropriate banner as a Centre for Roman Archaeology, whether under the auspices of CBA, IFA, the Society for the Promotion of Roman Studies, or another organisation, to address common issues collectively and provide the focus for dissemination.

I have concentrated particularly on process and structure because it is important, but I should end with Roman material culture itself and its future study. A great deal of research is going on, both empirically and theoretically driven and, notwithstanding the early concerns that PPG 16 would kill off synthetic and fundamental research, this book is testimony to the vitality of Roman finds research at many levels. I have referred to the need to make more data easily accessible via the web and this leads on to thinking about how we might develop large datasets of material to explore relationships between different sets of material culture together. Ceramics, for example, and glass, too, are traditionally treated separately from the rest of the material finds' assemblage and then there is the question of relationships with animal bone and other environmental assemblages. With the growth of e-science it should be possible to develop methodologies to explore these relationships and so revisit issues surrounding regionality and identity, urban and rural, sacred and profane where our current understanding is so often based on a limited range of the available material and biological data.

There is much to do, but a priority must be to find a mechanism for concentrating our resources, ideally by developing in the first instance an umbrella organisation to coordinate, prioritise and promote the already excellent work which is being undertaken throughout the UK.

Michael Fulford
University of Reading
September 2004

Acknowledgements

The editors extend their thanks to the Durham students and others who helped at the conference, Teresa Gilmore, James Bruhn, Richard Jarrett, Laura Cripps, David Mein and David Allan. We would like to thank Dr Pete Wilson of English Heritage for general advice, Professors Malcolm Todd and Jennifer Price of the University of Durham, Lindsay Allison-Jones of Newcastle University and Dr J. D. Hill of the British Museum for chairing sessions and helping in other ways. Paul Booth, Dr Jane Webster, Dr Jerry Evans, Jane Evans and Dr David Petts provided helpful advice on the papers included in this volume, while Dr Ardle MacMahon created the website for the conference. St Johns College provided the venue and accommodation, while the Old Fulling Mill hosted the reception. Funds and support for the conference were provided by the Roman Society, English Heritage and the Centre for Roman Provincial Archaeology (University of Durham), while English Heritage and the Roman Finds Group provided funds for the editing and publication of this volume. Thanks also to Christina Unwin for assistance with the editing, index and illustrations and also general advice and support. John Harris and Spencer Scott of the University of Kent kindly assisted with the illustrations as well. The editors are most grateful to Tara Evans of Oxbow for her constructive input. A grant from Kenneth Arthur John enabled the inclusion of the colour prints.

The Context of Roman Finds Studies

1   Roman Finds: Context and Theory

Steven Willis and Richard Hingley

The Durham conference in perspective

Studies of the finds of Roman Britain and the Western Provinces have come to greater prominence in the literature on the period in recent years (*e.g.* Evans 1988; 1995a; 1995b; 2001; Snape 1993; Cool *et al.* 1995; Hoffmann 1995; Dungworth 1998; Price and Cottam 1998; Cool and Baxter 1999; Swift 2000; 2003; Allason-Jones 2001; Fulford 2001; Hunter 2001; Brickstock *et al.* 2002; Eckardt 2002a; and various papers in the TRAC proceedings). The quality and contribution of this work has begun to have a significant impact at several levels. The new work is theoretically informed, reflexive and uses rich data-sets (cf. James 2003).

Around us is an archaeology of the Roman era that is dense, complex and culturally encoded. Engaging with and interpreting this record of past communities in the Roman era is made possible through a number of characteristics of that record: the widespread and comparatively large material record of the period, the relative typological uniformity of much of the material of the era, the stratification of a large proportion of artefacts and the chronological refinements of the period. Synthetic and interpretative work with the finds from these sites and communities over the past twenty years (and particularly in the latter part of this period) has changed our understanding of the Roman era in fundamental ways, and hence work with finds is beginning to be accorded a greater recognition and standing within the domain of Roman studies (cf. James 2003, 182). At the same time, the often exciting and worthy results of research and publications, involving finds, has fuelled enthusiasm amongst other specialists dealing with the material fragments of the period. There has, however, been little in the way of a dedicated forum for the presentation and evaluation of current approaches to the study of material culture and its social interpretation (with the exception of the meetings of the Roman Finds Group).

The conference held in Durham over the weekend of 6th-7th July 2002 aimed to raise the profile of work on material culture of the Roman period in Britain and Europe and to advertise the strong potential of finds analysis for understanding many aspects of culture and practice during this period. In particular there was an emphasis upon theoretical approaches in finds work and examining new methodological approaches. Around 85 people from Britain and abroad attended the conference which was held in St John's College. A total of twenty-four papers were presented over the two days (see below), with extended discussions at the end of each day lead by J.D. Hill and Lindsay Allason-Jones. Sixteen of the papers from the conference have been written up by their authors for inclusion in this volume, while three additional submitted papers are also included, two written by delegates who attended the conference. These new papers likewise deal with finds and issues around finds and are consistent with the ethos of the conference.

This first paper provides an opportunity for the conference organizers (Richard Hingley and Steven Willis) to sketch out some important aspects of the present state of finds research and publication. We also take the opportunity to draw together recurring themes apparent amongst the papers and to examine theoretical and methodological issues and to consider work on material culture of the Roman era within the wider framework of current research.

The potential of Roman finds

The study of finds, including coins, pottery, glass, copper alloy objects, nails, shoes, and so forth, is often cast as a specialism. Perhaps, in past decades, reports and studies of such 'small things' were seen by too many scholars as just that, being cast as hermetically sealed specialized studies, not necessarily particularly germane for the understanding and interpretation of sites and landscapes. As a result consideration of the potential of finds for investigating the cultural and economic life and times of communities during the Roman era was circumscribed in scope. Viewing some older reports upon finds, it can appear that erstwhile 'finds specialists' were often accomplices to this situation, in so far as catalogues and reports/ discussions (where the latter appeared, which was far from invariably, as so frequently only catalogues were published) produced were very often not linked to the evidence of their find-spot nor to questions beyond those intrinsic to the specialism. Yet the role of finds work should be as much centre-stage as other categories of evidence (such as structural and environmental remains) given the potential of the information finds may yield (cf. Cool this volume; Casey 1974; Reece 1983; 1993a; 1995; Hunter 1998; Ferris 2000): the ostensibly mundane fragments recovered from countless soils are culturally loaded and encode information upon the societies that produced and consumed them. New work in the domain of finds study has emphasized how research upon the material culture of the period sheds vital light upon society. The conference and this proceedings volume show finds work to be, in the 21st century, not an ancillary field, but key to a vibrant informed understanding and interpretation of the archaeology of the Roman centuries.

Many of those working with finds from the Roman period have begun to employ this information to address a range of questions that focus around the use of artefacts in the Roman era, as work moves beyond the prerequisites of typology, dating and cataloguing. Papers in this volume testify to the breath of the subject and the potential for employing data acquired through the study of finds to engage with social, economic and metaphysical dimensions of the period. These articles are a snapshot of current methodologies and perspectives as the vast quantity of artefactual information recovered from sites is digested. Changes in understanding occur in the light of advances in knowledge of the period and its structures, unfolding theoretical approaches and more systematic finds processing procedures, as well as improved analytical tools and software. Many of the studies presented here are syntheses that harness the growing dataset of information upon categories of finds.

There has been a welcome trend in recent years toward the integration of information garnered from various categories of finds and, indeed, using this to categorize finds, particular areas within sites and whole classes of sites (Hoffmann 1995; Hunter 1998; Cool *et al.* 1995; Cool and Philo 1998; Evans 2001). This volume contains several papers which develop these themes (eg. Eckardt, looking at variations between different parts of the Colchester site and Isserlin in his detailed analysis of Bath). Examples from other cultural contexts attempt to rethink the standard categories in which finds are placed, attempting to think about the ways the artefacts were 'thought' and used in the everyday life of people (Barrett 1993; 1994; Hoskins 1998; Sharples 1998; Barrett *et al.* 2000; Hughes and Woodward forthcoming). Yet it should not be overlooked that this has been a trend within studies of the Roman material too (eg. Crummy 1983; Allason-Jones 1988; Clarke 2000; cf. Cool and Evans this volume). Many of the most useful studies of finds of the period, whether reports upon site assemblages or reviews of particular classes of artefacts, have combined these principles of synthesis and integration (eg. Hunter 1998; Mudd *et al.* 1999; Leach with Evans 2001). Nonetheless, the building blocks of these broader pictures must remain sound, standardized cataloguing, albeit that this is often routine and viewed as prosaic (Johns, this volume). Crummy's contribution to this volume stresses how such work should follow a structured framework if we are to order and make sense of the multifarious material fragments that are so regularly recovered from our sites.

On the other hand, attention to the particular, to groups of finds and to, crucially, context (that is, the nature of contexts) and site formation processes has produced dividends in much recent work involving pottery, glass and small finds (eg. Allason-Jones 1988; Clarke and Jones 1996; Clarke 1997; Fulford 2001). Linkage to other categories of information such as environmental/palaeobiological evidence can often generate a rounded picture, assisting interpretation of deposit formation. A pathfinding case in point is that of features F28 and F29 at 1–7 St Thomas' Street, Southwark (Dennis 1978) which yielded a wide ensemble of types of archaeological evidence, the analysis of which lead to the characterization of the filling of this pair of features if not a definitive interpretation as to their uses. Martin (this volume) reminds us how germane attention to such aspects can be in interpreting sites and their finds. As the historiography of Roman studies shows 'context', 'association of finds' and the nature of site formation processes (reasons behind group/assemblage formation) are long recognized elements in the archaeological equation, having preoccupied students of the period for decades (cf. Wheeler 1921; Kenyon 1948; Hull 1958; Millett 1980; 1987; Hodder 1989). Now, however, better all-round knowledge of the period, combined with appropriate methodologies and the drive to ask and address questions of the evidence has begun to bring forth nuanced pictures of the particular, the 'structured deposit' or 'group' which complement our more 'robust' definition of broad trends in artefact use, society and consumption. Work on structured deposition pursues earlier studies by J. D. Hill (1995) that used ideas derived from Neolithic and Bronze Age archaeology and applied them to the Iron Age (see papers by Martens and Millett, this volume). Some of this work, as illustrated here, has approached Cooper's ideal (Cooper, this volume) of the purpose of finds study, namely, re-constructing an: "intimate connection ... between the objects and the people who used them".

In promoting Roman finds and their study, this volume seeks to demonstrate that finds analysis, sound reporting and dissemination of information are vital for the overall health of studies of the Roman period and, indeed imperative, for exploring, addressing and informing upon the big questions which form the focus of attention of the mainstream of those within Roman studies. In this connexion it is worth noting that the Study Group for Roman Pottery in Britain produced a national and four regional research framework documents in 1997, these being updated in 2002 and 2004 (Willis 2004; www.sgrp.org). These frameworks outline the considered research aims and objectives of the Group. The Roman Finds Group in Britain operates through its meetings, newsletters and website as a platform for identification, discussion and research and has proved invaluable through its institution and membership in driving forward research in the period (www.romanfindsgroup.org.uk). The ethos of both of these organizations is closely articulated with wider priorities in the exploration of the Roman period (cf. James and Millett 2001); members of these Groups work with these directions in study and research in mind.

The contribution of work involving finds for engaging with knowledge of the period has been acknowledged in the various tiers of research assessment and regional and national research framework formation over the last ten years (eg. James and Millett 2001; C. J. Evans 2003). This 'pat-on-the-back' from the wider discipline has yet to be translated into a base of structured funding for Roman finds studies or a structured framework for training the next generation of archaeologists (Johns and Swift, this volume). The recent initiative of the Arts and Humanities Research Board to ring-fence funding for post-graduate studentships that focus upon 'ancient' finds should help with this problem (Lindsay Allason-Jones pers. comm.; James (2003)). Indeed, major contributions within the domain of finds analysis have come through to publication in recent years via the old 'route-one' of writing up detailed and dynamic theses (eg. Swift 2000; Eckardt 2002a), not through specific funding; or have been produced in the author's own time. A number of theses dealing with finds are nearing completion and will clearly be of great value, for instance, Gwladys Monteil's study of samian ware in London, Ester van der Linden's examination of the samian from the *canabae* and elsewhere at Nijmegen and Wim de Clercq's research on the handmade pottery tradition of the Roman period along the North Sea littoral of Belgium and The Netherlands. In addition, English Heritage has continued to provide a large proportion of funds for finds reports within specific site and grouped site publications (Wilson 2002; Cool 2004), as well as providing financial resources for a major new survey of the distribution of samian ware (Willis 1998; 2005; forthcoming a), for publications relating to mortaria, for database work relating to Roman coinage by Richard Brickstock, and for the exploration of database work and electronic publication of Roman pottery assemblages (Mills *et al.* forthcoming). This organization has also supported the Wroxeter Hinterlands Survey directed by Roger White and based at the University of Birmingham, with its important component relating to the analysis of surface collected artefacts.

There have been both practical and 'blue skies' aspects to these latter studies, and such elements are critical for developing understanding and sustaining vitality in finds work. Clearly research into finds has been strongly advanced by the commitment of a modest number of dedicated individuals motivated to a considerable degree by the sense of 'community' that exists between finds workers, and sheer intellectual curiosity (cf. Cooper and Swift, this volume). Gardner (this volume) has noted that finds research has been driven by "our interpretative ambition", in other words our need to 'find-out'. The 'discovery' of, for instance, 'sources', 'trends', 'patterns', etc. is the reward of such labour and can perhaps engender a sense of professional fulfilment for individual workers. Many of the papers given at TRAC are distinguished by an enthusiasm, expectation and desire to announce and disseminate the results of studies that relate finds and

material culture to society. The 'TRAC generation', indeed, includes a strong component who are familiar with finds and their use in constructing a social archaeology of the Roman era (cf. Laurence 1999; James and Millett 2001, 3; Mattingly 2002, 539; and see the various TRAC volumes). It should not be forgotten, of course, that work upon finds frequently generates surprises, as at Tongeren (Vanderhoeven and Ervynck this volume), Brougham (Cool 2004), Catterick (Wilson 2002), La Graufesenque (eg. Parca 2001, 69–70; Dannell 2002), Newstead (Clarke 1997), the lower Rhine valley (Derks and Roymans 2002) and Vindolanda (Bowman 1994).

The structure and content of this volume

The scope of the conference was wide and whilst the emphasis was upon new approaches to the study of finds in the fields of theory and methods, it was appropriate to consider issues around the study of finds, particularly the profile of the 'specialists' who undertake the work and issues around the future of artefact studies. Not surprisingly given the potential breath of the subject the conference attracted many offers of papers from a rich variety of workers dealing with diverse sites, materials and issues. Hence this volume provides a portmanteau of approaches, ideas and methods that reflect current ways of seeing and dealing with artefacts in the Roman West. We have divided the papers into three sections. The main separation is between those papers that outline approaches, methodological and theoretical, from those that on the whole deal with applications and case studies. The separation is ours and is not of a clear-cut nature as the content of papers can and does over-lap the section themes.

(I) Section one: the contemporary context of Roman finds studies

The first section includes four papers which discuss aspects of the contemporary context of Roman finds studies. These papers include the present article, Ellen Swift's benchmark survey of finds practitioners and perceptions of finds research, Catherine Johns' eloquent call for dedicated resourcing of finds studies, especially within the changing environment of the museum community, and Nick Cooper's rounded review of 'democratic' practice, information dissemination and analytical methods. These four papers are highly textured and political in so far as they relate closely to recent and present practice and experiences of working with finds, to finds specialists work circumstances (livelihoods, and, to use a sociological term, 'life/career chances'), to funding, and to the future of finds work. Perhaps these papers can be seen to weave and thread through issues, and ultimately present a somewhat ambivalent blend of actual circumstances, pessimism and optimism about the future. This mix may well reflect both the range of attitudes held by individuals and indeed the wider germane uncertainties about the future of this domain of archaeology. Yet ambiguity and uncertainty about the future of finds work and employment opportunities exists against a background of the acknowledged prospect of the material and of human abilities (of 'the specialists') to extract a meaning or narrative from the archaeological remains. Whilst there are concerns around the need to maintain standards, as to whether there are (and will be) sufficient competent personnel in this field of study to carry out the necessary work, and regarding funding, these exist in the context of the really exciting results coming from recent work and the strong potential for study, education and interpretation in this field.

(II) Section two: methodological and theoretical approaches

The second section groups papers that outline particular methodological and theoretical approaches. The section begins with Hilary Cool's essay evoking the value and insight of the finds specialist, drawing here particularly upon the experience of writing the publication report upon the Brougham cemetery, Cumbria (Cool 2004). Nina Crummy's contribution provides a template for approaching the categorization and study of small finds. This will doubtless prove to be a valuable reference tool for those working with finds, especially those new to finds study or with only moderate experience. The premise of the paper by Robin Symonds and Ian Haynes is the observation that it is of key importance that those working with material develop methods and record data in a manner which enables inter-site reference and inter-provincial comparisons, as this has been an Achilles heel to Roman pottery research across the empire and to attempts to engage with broad trends. They outline an approach to the comparison of pottery assemblages from different parts of the empire, based on the Museum of London recording system, giving concrete examples from recent projects. Precious metal hoards from across the empire and their values are then compared in an illuminating and original paper by Richard Hobbs. Hobbs examines ways of comparing the relative intrinsic values of deposits of silver and gold, especially of later Roman date, considering also the social control of these hoards. He takes into account other features with regard to hoarding apart from their bullion value, such as craftsmanship and portability.

Next follow two papers which consider various approaches to the analysis of the archaeological context of finds, and methods appropriate to extracting enhanced information in key areas of archaeological interest. Scott Martin's detailed examination of the character of deposits draws upon the evidence from sites in Essex, scrutinizing the relationships between site formation processes and chronology, and between feature type and the nature of deposits. The methical approach adopted by Martin produces illuminating results that will be helpful to

excavators and those writing up Roman period sites, as well as to pottery and other specialists. While Martin uses material already gathered from excavated sites and available at the post-excavation stage, Martin Millett's contribution demonstrates how straight-forward, but rarely employed, procedures on site, including volumetric recording and context-specific metal detector scanning, can, where systematically followed, yield dividends in establishing the anatomy of site use and in comparative site characterization. Gillian Carr examines the incidence of toilet instruments in southern Britain in the early Roman period. Carr argues that a case may be made for seeing some particular types and styles of instrument as indicators of a Creole style identity at a time of population flux (eg. Webster 2001).

The multiple roles of facsimiles of human body parts in the Roman era are examined by Iain Ferris. He shows how ancestor masks were used to maintain the memory of notable ancestors and as didactic tools for teaching to the young the moral qualities of earlier generations. Models of body parts were employed in processes seeking cures for ill-health. Ferris argues that such 'whole fragments', are typical of the Roman world, and might be seen as having served a symbolic function in (re-) incorporating individuals (the sick, the deviant, the young) into society. The stylised body fragment was thus an instrument for social cohesion. In his conference abstract he noted that: "in Roman art the fragmentation of the body when it occurred perhaps reflected the permeability of boundaries in Roman society ... The metaphor of containment or inclusion frequently used was basically an image of possession, of things taken from the world, dematerialised and made to belong to society itself. In some instances the corporeal body was reduced to the status of an artefact" (Ferris 2002).

Finally in this section, the paper by Andrew Gardner looks at artefacts and contexts at military sites in Britain and outlines how the evidence may be employed to develop an archaeology of social practice. Gardner shows how finds studies can play an important role in the integration of theory and practice in Roman archaeology. He outlines how detailed contextual analysis of artefacts is well-suited to engaging interpretative questions raised by the emergence of 'practice theories' in the social sciences. He employs the approach to define a series of activities which can be interpreted from the relationships between different kinds of finds and different kinds of contexts on archaeological sites. Thereby practice becomes a linking concept between the patterning of the archaeological record and past cultural life.

(III) Section three: applications of method and theory

Papers based around the archaeology of specific sites form the third Section, where these cases are used in an interpretative manner. Several use specific case studies, in turn articulating these with the evidence from more than one site and/or to extrapolate wider trends. Hella Eckardt examines the composition of finds assemblages from various locations around Colchester, finding 'contrasting contexts' in so far as contemporary assemblages from the different excavated areas show some marked differences. The author interprets these variations in terms of the structural morphology of the areas and, moreover, the likely nature of the social interactions at these localities and the identity and status of those living in and using these places. By contrast Marleen Martens presents the long and fascinating sequence recently excavated under her direction at the Grijpen industrial zone in the south-western suburb of the Roman 'Small Town' at Tienen, Flanders. A series of religious and ritual activities, along with other functions, occurred in this area, by the major east-west road from Tongeren and the German frontier in the east to Boulogne in the west. A rich, well-stratified, and very large finds assemblage was recovered and Martens has developed a 'state of the art' relational database system in order to house finds and contextual information, reflecting the detailed information collected in the course of the excavations. In the following paper the major civitas centre of the Tungri at Tongeren in eastern Belgium, west of Maastricht, is the focus. This centre has seen a series of important excavations in the past 15 years, and in their paper Alain Vanderhoeven and Anton Ervynck examine the evidence of an industry processing animal remains. Close attention is paid in this paper to contextual details and the context of the activities identified in terms of their urban social milieu. This contribution is particularly welcome as it considers technology and production; it is, of course, via these means that material culture comes into being, yet, so-often these have been areas that have, regrettably been 'Cinderella' subjects in Roman archaeology. John Evans' paper reports upon aspects of the incidence of finds at a Roman rural site in Hampshire, and in particular of field surface discovered pottery and other cultural material which he interpreted as a deliberate addition to the agricultural soil in order to 'culturally entexture' it (see below, this paper). Raphael Isserlin takes a fresh and nuanced look at the artefacts from the waters at Bath, considering both what has been recovered and what not and interpreting the evidence at more than face value. This will undoubtedly be an often referred to paper for a site with a complexity of evidence that requires detailed and thoughtful assessment. Sonja Jilek and David Breeze, in a comprehensive review, look at the finds assemblages from smaller military installations. This study fills a gap in our knowledge of the fortlets of the Limes, specifically on the German-Danubian frontier and in northern Britain. Their essay integrates the small finds from these sites with the structural evidence, sculpture and documentary/ literary sources, yielding a fuller picture of both cultural life on the frontiers and the 'identity' and functions of these sites and their garrisons. The final paper, by Fraser

Hunter, assesses the nature of *denarii* hoards around and beyond the frontiers of Rome's Northern provinces. Hunter takes the view that they relate to the Roman policy of payments to tribes beyond the imperial frontier. The uses of these coins within Roman Iron Age societies is re-considered, as is the question of hoard deposition within the context of local Iron Age hoarding traditions.

(IV) Papers presented at the conference not appearing in this volume

Eight papers presented at the conference were not submitted for publication in this volume either because their author had a prior arrangement to publish the work elsewhere, or because the work was still in progress during 2002–3. These papers are noted here both to complete the record of the content of the conference and to further highlight the range of dynamic work being undertaken with Roman period finds at the outset of the 21st century.

Mark Atkinson presented a paper on 'Special deposits' at Heybridge, Elms Farm, Essex, (1993–5) from where over 50 examples of 'special deposits' have been recognised. At this site they display considerable variation in the circumstance of their deposition and in their assemblage composition. Consideration of the composition of these deposits, Atkinson noted, reveals a surprisingly wide range of artefact types that seemingly had a significance that merited their inclusion. These extended from ceramic vessels to animal carcasses, tools to jewellery, coins to scrap metal and evidently industrial residues (see below). The results of the large scale excavations at Elms Farm are currently being processed for publication (Atkinson forthcoming).

Patricia Baker's paper assessed the deposition of Roman style medical instruments looking at evidence from the Roman provinces in modern day France, Germany, Switzerland, The Netherlands and Britain. She observed that Roman instruments have typically been viewed as having 'rational' functions because they are defined in the context of classical medical texts. Her aim was to establish, by developing a comparative approach, what might be understood about attitudes towards medical tools and possible taboos associated with them, particularly via studies of the deposition of instruments, and whether there were variations in the conceptualisation of illness and healing amongst people living in different areas of the empire. This paper has now appeared in the journal *Social History of Medicine* (Baker 2004).

Paul Bidwell gave a paper on the distribution of fourth-century coins in the fort at Newcastle upon Tyne. He discussed the question of whether the evidence indicated the existence of a market in the area of the *via praetoria* by the *principia*, which in later Roman forts seems usually to have been reserved for military ceremonies. He pointed out that Newcastle is an example of the difficulties and opportunities surrounding the proper understanding of context on Roman military sites, and raised questions that focused around our knowledge of how forts and fortresses functioned. This evidence and discussion is now published in the report upon the excavations in the fort at Newcastle (Snape and Bidwell 2002).

Ben Croxford presented the results of his study of the fragmentation of Romano-British statues, and this work has now appeared as an article in *Britannia* (Croxford 2003). He argued that there was a pattern to the incidence of pieces of statue encountered in deposits. His interpretation is that a process of 'body part' selection had occurred, suggesting that these images may have been deliberately fragmented with the resulting pieces retaining meaning, and receiving special treatment and deposition. Michael Erdrich spoke about the results arising from the 1991–3 excavations at Wijnaldum, in Frisia (The Netherlands), where a settlement existed in the Roman period (2nd and 3rd century) and again during the early medieval era (5th to 9th century). The analysis of the context of the Roman material lead to a quite surprising discovery: most of the samian and Roman copper alloy finds, which were well-dated in the 2nd and 3rd centuries, were found in clearly 5th to 8th century contexts. He stated that close attention to the Roman material, especially the metal finds, proved, that a selection process had occurred: they must be looked at as scrap collected and prepared for recycling and the production of early medieval artefacts, presumably brooches.

Daniel Keller spoke about the context of late Roman glass tableware from Petra (Jordan), specifically around the subject of late-antique dining in the Orient. His presentation related to a wider project on the site to which he is contributing and in which the content of this paper given at Durham will be located. Excavations between 1996 and 2001 by the University of Basel had investigated a large Roman period domestic building in the southern part of the city destroyed in an earthquake of AD 363. The sudden destruction of the building meant that the pottery and glass vessels were found in the location where they had been stored; it was therefore possible to show the spatial distribution of the glass vessels within the house and to distinguish different sets of glass tableware, as well as different kinds of glass lamps, used in this house at the time of its destruction. In combination with the architectural layout of the building and the quality of the interior stucco decoration of the different rooms, the glass finds provided evidence for the function and status of these rooms within the house: while the shapes of the good quality glass tableware with conical beakers and shallow bowls reflected typical late Roman dining customs of a high social status, the lower quality glass tableware showed differences in shapes with more hemispherical bowls and smaller beakers, thought by Keller as potentially indicating a local adaptation of these customs on a lower social level.

Steven Willis gave a paper in two parts looking at aspects of context. The first part presented some results of calibrating ratios of 'finds recovered to soil volume excavated' per context arising from his excavations at the Roman roadside settlement at Nettleton, on the Lincolnshire Wolds (Willis 2003). The results, together with the utility of the procedure, underscore the potential of this approach for characterizing sites, as discussed by Millett (this volume). The second part of his paper communicated some outcomes of a survey of samian ware distribution in Britain funded by English Heritage, and in particular the differential incidence of the ware by site type (cf. Willis 2005), and the specific case of the incidence of samian inkwells. The samian inkwell is a discrete type the distribution of which shows a remarkably close correlation with fortresses/forts and major civil centres and within those sites, at locations where written records were likely to have been generated (Willis forthcoming b).

A concluding paper was given at the conference by Richard Hingley, who summarized the themes of the meeting and assessed the prospects, signs and portents for the future. He considered work on finds within the framework of current trajectories and priorities for research in the Roman period, and argued that finds work needs to take on a more explicit role in the development of theory if it is going to appeal to the broader academic community.

Theory, method and finds research

The genesis and epistemology of finds studies is a subject little explored by archaeologists, except in the occasional text book, of which Tyers' consideration of the evolution of Roman pottery studies is an admirable case (Tyers 1996), and in distinct historiographical articles (Hodder 1989; Wallace 1990; Martin 2003). An empirical approach involving categorizing, cataloguing, counting, the use of statistical methods and a comparative perspective, has certainly been a cornerstone of work involving material culture of the period. This tradition has a long pedigree in British archaeology (eg. Hawkes and Hull 1947; Casey 1974; the applied studies of Roy Hodson (cf. Orton 1982); Shennan 1997). Behind this approach lies the belief that through categorizing artefacts, counting them and comparing incidence and composition, differences may be observed between deposits, areas or sites which are the product of archaeologically interesting phenomena, such as chronological variations, or factors of status, social identity, supply connections, consumption patterns and so forth. The 1970s and 1980s saw the development of means designed to make this approach more systematic and to explain its utility (eg. Casey 1974; 1984; Reece 1983; Orton 1978; 1989; Millett 1980; 1987; Creighton 1990). Recent years have seen the application of these methods in earnest. The work of Clive Orton and Richard Reece since the 1970s has been particularly influential in finds studies as they have pursued methodologies along these lines, generally, but not simply examining the pottery and coins, with which they are most closely associated. The impact of their work has influenced both method and archaeological outlook (eg. Orton 1982; Reece 1983; 1988). Students and practitioners were directly taught by them or learnt from their seminal publications, which involved empirical approaches. In particular, Richard Reece can now be seen to have been something of an 'epistemological god-father', with many of his students at The Institute of Archaeology (UCL) pursing methodological principles similar to his in numerous fields of artefact study, including pottery, coins and brooches. At Cardiff, Bill Manning supervised a number of post-graduate students studying a range of Roman finds types, resulting in a series of key studies and persons expert in the field of Roman find types. The professional and personal influence Bill Manning has had on research into Roman finds in Britain is demonstrated in cameo by the quality of work of his former students, and by the recent production of a Festschrift in his honor (Aldhouse-Green and Webster 2002). In a practical way the high regard in which his own research has been held, both at home and abroad, can be measured by the number of times he figures in bibliographies. The significance of Nina Crummy's volume on the Roman small finds from excavations in Colchester 1971–9 (Crummy 1983) also warrants highlighting as for the first time a substantive catalogue of Roman material items was ordered by function rather than its material composition, at once moving the conceptualization of Roman artefacts towards their social context in the hands and lives of past people.

All studies involve adopting a theoretical position whether acknowledged or tacit, and there can be no 'facts' established about the life and times of the Roman era that are independent of a theoretical view or framework of knowledge (cf. Johnson 1999). Perhaps this has been understated in Roman finds work in the past and thus it is important that Gardner (this volume) reminds us that: "Finds work involves a theoretical attitude". Recent work by, for example, Barrett (1993), Booth (1991), Cooper (1996; 2000), Crummy and Eckardt (2004), van Driel-Murray (1999), Eckardt (2000; 2002b), Evans (eg. 1988; 1995b), Gardner (2001; 2002), Going (1992), Meadows (1997) and Jane Webster (2001) has employed reference to finds in exploring theoretical approaches to the period (see also Hill 1995; 1997; 2001). Indeed, in their work finds studies are developed to construct social interpretations of the period, arguably the ultimate goal of labour in the domain of artefacts. Further, papers appearing in this volume show the impact of the new 'theoretically aware' spirit of the times (cf. Reece 1993b; Laurence 1999; James 2003), with post-processual and post-colonial approaches implicit and explicit in works here and elsewhere in contemporary Roman finds studies. Yet new ideas and directions have far from eclipsed the processualist, or more accurately empirical, approach to finds since certain elements of processual methodology help finds analysis to be rigorous and self-explicit (cf. Johnson 1999). There is a discernible methodological pluralism:

work with finds of the Roman period often has a foundation in traditional methods of classifying, cataloguing, quantifying and comparing, but often the most exciting work has, built from this base, a perspective and interpretation that owes much to TAG (the Theoretical Archaeology Group Conference) or TRAC and post-processual paradigms. From the 'secure', 'objective' platform of method and data synthesis have been flown some intellectual kites, for instance, considering subjectivities in the Roman world. We should not regard this intellectual development as problematic. Richard Bradley notes a similar wedding of convenience with regard to Geographic Information Systems which can be seen as a processualist technology that has been harnessed to post-processual agendas (Bradley 2002, 42). In a sense this is what Richard Reece and John Casey, might always have done with their coin studies: the normal pattern of coin loss is established and the incidence of Roman coins recovered per site is calibrated against this baseline to identify deviations from the normal pattern; what is deduced from this is a matter of interpretation. Perhaps in the round Reece's interpretations of coin assemblages (via this means) have been developed in more conventional terms than have some other areas of his output, but his work has always aimed to relate closely to past human perceptions and cultural practice (cf. Reece 1988).

Most of the papers in this volume are concerned with methods, procedures and good practice. Crummy outlines a guide to categorization, while Cool and Johns emphasize the rewards such methods may yield. Eckardt, Gardner, Hobbs and Symonds and Haynes (cf. Croxford 2003) follow what might be termed the Reecian line of placing (or advocating placing) material on a common base line, normally numeric, from which comparative analysis can proceed with differences and similarities observed and considered. From routine cataloguing and quantification, can come forth, on occasions, insightful interpretations that inspire. Scott Martin and Martin Millett deal with methods for capturing information from deposits and contexts through 'fine detail' and an analytical approach. These latter two contributions seem so near to the point of deposition and recovery that one might be reminded of the popular on-site witticism of the time-served field archaeologist: 'the answer lies in the soil'. There is an implicit *faith* in much of our work that attention to context and attention to details of deposition and assemblage composition will provide an access point to some worthwhile insights or inference upon past actions and attitudes to material culture and past materiality.

A new theoretical awareness in finds studies means that there are less purely functionalist views of finds and we are more imaginative and open to interpretative possibilities. Additionally, perhaps there is more of an obligation to interpret the results of study, where appropriate, rather than to just identify, list and produce the short summary.

New work on Roman finds might not be driven by post-processualist conceptions, but post-processualism resides in the way finds of the period are interpreted by those working with this evidence. That finds of material culture are to be understood by means of their past social context, which may have been highly specific and mutable, and that there may be no functional closure upon artefacts, meaning that their uses were open to interpretation and negotiation, are now long established maxims (cf. Shanks and Tilley 1987; 1992; Freeman 1993) that are perhaps to be considered axiomatic to those working with finds. Heterogeneity and the possibility of multiple definitions and meanings to 'things' is recognized (eg. Willis 1994; Eckardt 2000; cf. Mattingly 2002, 540).

Actuality can confound prospect. Unsurprisingly work in this area is confronted by the often complex nature of the archaeological record of the period. Roman finds studies have moved well beyond any view that the material culture recovered from sites represents a fossil of 'what was used'; the fossil at best is distorted and incomplete. Taphonomic factors, for instance, evidently skew the nature of the artefact assemblages that come down to us via fieldwork, 'over-representing' some activities and milieu and under-representing others (cf. Cooper this volume). Residuality (cf. Evans and Millett 1992) and the sheer partial nature of the record that is collected archaeologically (cf. Haselgrove 1985) are endemic challenges to finds study. These issues are consequently also considered in papers in this volume (eg. the papers by Martin and Isserlin; cf. Croxford 2003).

Finds, society and social practice

The papers in this volume demonstrate how emphatically those undertaking the study of finds now attempt to use these fragments from everyday lives in the past as a point of articulation with cultural practices, life-ways, belief systems, and perceptions of social relations in the Roman world (cf. papers by Carr, Ferris and Martens this volume). The study of material culture is "about social worlds" (Gardner, this volume), their 'reconstruction' and interpretation. To study finds is to attempt to reconstruct the 'small worlds' (cf. Goffman 1963; 1978) that the majority of past communities and peoples established and inhabited for most of the time of their lives. In the study of finds of the Roman era, as this is conducted these days, workers look for patterning, variation and trends and attempt to understand the variables by which the artefacts and assemblages recovered archaeologically were 'selected' in the past by human agency. Woven through this is a growing interest in the actions and experiences relating to the artefacts: their social context. In this way finds studies, as Pitt Rivers recognized, are the balance to the pictures of the 'big stage' presented by such indices as the histories, the synthetic narratives and town plans of the period, that focus upon dates, events, named people and the grand structures. Groups of artefacts, associations, assemblages and contexts (in their broadest sense) improve the possibil-

ity of generating textured accounts of past social practice, or what might be termed "thick description" (cf. Eckardt this volume; cf. Courtney 1996; 1997; Deetz 1996).

There is a new recognition and interest in the cultural heterogeneity of the empire. Variation was enormous, being temporal, geographical and social; it is ever more clear that every site is marked by its own 'individuality'. Artefacts were, of course, a key element in this variation. Syntheses of material culture help us to identify broad trends and identify levels of homogeneity, but also those domains of cultural variation that require different qualitative approaches in artefact studies (eg. because of low frequency of finds, such as some sites in the south-west peninsula of Britain or in northern Britain). Further, refinement in our methods (and thinking) may be particularly apposite given the observation by Eckardt (this volume) that *small* differences in assemblage composition must not be overlooked as these might actually reflect important social differences in status and identity. This suggests that the method of volumetric recording and calibration outlined by Millett (this volume) may prove to be all the more vital.

The Roman era engendered unprecedented changes in social life and brought forth opportunities and variety in cultural lives. Arguably it resulted in greater social differentiation through trade, consumption and wealth generation, the acquiring and production of materials and material culture, which brought forward greater difference in the life opportunities and pathways of individuals in the area of the western empire (cf. Cool and Eckardt this volume; Hingley 2005). Accordingly Carr, Cool, Eckardt, Evans, Gardner, and, in a manner, Hobbs have considered finds as a means of establishing and characterizing 'social identities'. This follows speculative studies along similar lines in recent years (Meadows 1994; Jones 1997; Rippengal 1995; Revell 1999; Webster 2001).

Current directions in finds analysis

(I) Attention to Space

The examination of the use of space, particularly domestic space, and the distribution of artefacts within such environs has become more common in the past decade or so. This can hardly be considered a novel archaeological approach; yet while this has been a longstanding and frequent feature of the reporting of sites of other periods and cultural settings (eg. Steer and Keeney 1947; Clarke 1972; Hodder 1978; Sharples 1991, especially 243–6; Hingley *et al.* 1997) such plotting and consideration has only recently begun to be featured with any regularity in the reporting of sites of the Roman period or in synthetic reviews. For decades this means of examining sites was not a part of Roman studies, despite, of course, the exceptional studies of locations such as Pompeii. This must reflect what archaeologists of the Roman era were and were not interested in through the 20th century, and what they saw as 'problematic'. At best one might say that this lack of attention to the use of space was a distinctive aspect, and a product of the prevailing culture in Roman archaeology until recent times. Functional and status variations across space were perhaps thought to be apparent from site type and building type, architecture, and building elaboration. The diversity of site types and buildings in itself suggested differentiation and seems not to have been a matter for standard investigation via close analysis of finds in a way that was, and is, more common for those cultures with less variation in building types and site morphology (eg. with the roundhouse in Britain). In other words archaeologies looking at other periods had long tended to press finds assemblages for greater degrees of information to do with spatial variations because the nature of the structural and site morphological remains was in itself less differentiated, whereas sites of Roman date lacked this tradition of spatial scrutiny of finds simply because variation was suggested by the nature of the site and/or its associated building types.

Latterly the comparatively large and varied assemblages of pottery and other finds from sites of the Roman era have come under closer attention, driven by the realisation that such studies can be illuminating, extending, enhancing or contrasting with the evidence as suggested by the structural record. An often cited study of this type by Martin Millett, albeit of a non-Roman site, pointed the way that others in Roman studies were to follow (Millett 1979; cf. 1987, 106). In this study Millett had examined the functional composition of pottery groups recovered from specific rooms at the Mycean site at Zagora on Andros, where sudden destruction had fossilized what presumably approximated to 'in-use' assemblages within a series of contemporary defined spatial locations ('rooms'). Latterly a series of exemplary studies were produced: Lindsay Allason-Jones examined the finds assemblages from the turrets on Hadrian's Wall, deducing a range of interesting patterns (Allason-Jones 1988); Simon Clarke developed a quantitative approach to the analysis of finds from areas in and around the fort at Newstead (Clarke 1994), while Birgitta Hoffmann (as a post-graduate student at Durham, supervised by Millett) undertook a revealing study of legionary centurions quarters, examining recovered finds by area/room (Hoffmann 1995). A further landmark was the study of finds from the fortress at York (Cool *et al.* 1995). Attention to the evidence that finds can reveal regarding space, status and function has now become an important element in some recent excavation reports, including the reports on: the 1990 excavations at the roadside settlement at Shepton Mallet, Somerset (Leach with Evans 2001), where 3–D recording was conducted for all finds including pottery; the *canabae* at Caerleon (Evans 2000); and the settlement at Birdlip Quarry, Gloucestershire (Mudd *et al.* 1999). Some thesis studies are also attending to questions of spatial variation in assemblages from

sites (eg. van der Linden forthcoming), while the *Londinium* Project is aiming to map the incidence of recorded finds types across the geography of Roman London (pers. comm. Angela Wardle).

In addition to questions of functional use and the status and identity of specific social places, finds can inform upon changes through time in these respects. The papers by Gardner, Eckardt and Martens in this volume, plus the two aforementioned papers by Keller and Bidwell presented to the conference, show how spatial studies, with attention to status, functional use and 'the identity of place' can develop to provide fruitful results, patterns of variation – and further questions (cf. Cooper forthcoming). Bidwell's paper had highlighted change in the function of areas within the fort at Newcastle, and he emphasized how limited our knowledge is of the use of space within forts, with old assumptions needing verification (cf. Gardner this volume). Hence even in those environs such as fort interiors where there had been erstwhile ideas and 'consensus' over the use of space, questions now arise which finds assemblages can help address, most appropriately site by site, area by area (von Schnurbein 2003). Research in this domain will doubtless become more popular in studies of the Roman period, and this is vital as we seek to characterize sites, buildings and places and the social definitions and interactions that passed within them.

(II) Attention to place

Many of the contributions to this volume, and to the conference in 2002, consider places of artefact deposition (eg. papers by Evans, Hunter, Isserlin and Martens; cf. Croxford 2003; Atkinson forthcoming). This is also an aspect, of course, of the insightful depositional studies by Millett and Martin (this volume). Attention to the place of deposition and in 'placed deposits' are a matter of growing interest in Roman archaeology (cf. Clarke 1997; 2000; Fulford 2001).

In his paper abstract for the conference, Atkinson noted that recognition of placed or structured deposits was far from straight-forward and implied that we are on a learning curve with such deposits. He observes that: "only the most obvious of these deposits were recognised for what they were in the field and ...the majority have been identified during subsequent analysis of the various assemblages and their 'host' features. Awareness and *acceptance* of structured deposition in the late Iron Age and Roman periods has clearly grown in recent years. However, it is apparent that there is still much room for both the excavator and the finds specialist to develop a greater awareness/appreciation of this use and meaning of artefacts in order that we can gain a fuller understanding of the role of religion, magic and superstition in everyday life. While we are developing a good overview of this aspect of depositional practice it seems evident that we are all too often missing the detail" (Atkinson

2002). In his paper to the conference Atkinson highlighted the ritualized disposal of waste, including industrial waste residues, such as slag seemingly placed in deposits. The challenge, of course, is to find means of differentiating between ritual and waste (cf. Hingley 1990, 104–5; Chapman 2000; Croxford 2003).

(III) Attention to context and site formation

Context type is consistently identified amongst the papers as a strong determinate of the assemblage type likely to be recovered, and this gives rise to questions of sampling strategy on site during excavation. The fills in ditches, for instance, may change along their course as they are punctuated with particular depositional events and tipping, while proximity to domestic occupation is also likely to be a key determinate of the character of their filling. All of us need to be more aware of such subtleties. It is implicit that we need to think more about the types of deposits we are working with and how they came into being. As Martens states: "The interpretation of the genesis of a context is as important as the identification of the material in it. By producing lists of categories and types of ceramics and other objects in archaeological features only a part of the research potential of a pit is used. The analysis of the formation process of many archaeological records can provide information on behaviour patterns of Gallo-Romans. This subject has rarely been thoroughly examined in past archaeological studies" (Martens, this volume).

As Martin points out periods of substantial deposition in the formation of sites are spasmodic, occurring particularly at times of new processes and of change, such as episodes of construction, destruction, site re-modelling, ditching or abandonment; the sequence at the Tienen site reported by Martens (this volume) is a clear example of such sequencing. Equally several papers point out the importance of the invisible processes, for instance of cleaning and removal of material, as at Bath (Isserlin's paper), as with ditches (Martin) and with fortlet interiors (Jilek and Breeze).

As to what is typically found deposited at sites in terms of small finds, Cooper's work (this volume) identifies the dominant element in 'rubbish' as personal everyday items including brooches, toilet instruments, jewellery, hairpins, etc. *Independent of site type* it is these items, which are 'domestic' and relate to personal adornment, that prevail: "rather than agricultural, commercial, industrial or military [finds]... There are clearly taphonomic factors (both behavioural and related to preservation) which are dominating the formation of assemblages and masking what must have been a more varied set of activities".

Vanderhoeven and Ervynk's paper identifies an important industrial activity in central Tongeren, with the siting of this noisome process in the midst of town life something of a surprise. The archaeological record has a delightful habit of throwing up such surprises. An interesting range of finds was recovered from pits cut into the street between the frontage of two barracks at the Gilberd School site, Colchester, during the short-lived fortress phase; it seems that some had been used as makeshift ovens for food preparation, while the street may have been covered at one stage and used as a workshop (Crummy 1992; pers. comm. Philip Crummy and Don Shimmin); such activities will have hindered movement in the congested fortress and are not consistent with the stereo-typical image of an orderly military environment. Clearly the context and place of activity is mutable: finds of material culture might not necessarily occur where one might predict.

Manufacturing places through material culture

Material culture is an active element in the human use of space and hence the nature of finds assemblages from particular environments is often key in their characterization and interpretation. It has long been recognized that 'places and spaces' may be just as fully manufactured and manipulated by human actions and definitions as are material artefacts and the small fashioned attributes of cultural life. As can be seen in a number of papers in this volume, material culture and its use in particular milieu assists in the ascription of meaning to places and spaces, reinforcing cultural definitions and appropriate normative actions. Hence it is not surprising that the archaeology of the Roman era often reveals marked continuity in the use of space over time. Attention to the specifics of the archaeological record reveal that this is often not a one-dimensional repetition of actions and processes, but a nuanced sequence of events occurring within an enduring cultural structure or 'idea' of what may be appropriate to a specific location. At Bath, Isserlin outlines the enduring use of the baths as a locus for types of deposition (and likely periodic clearance), while at Tienen, the Grijpen zone on the south-west side of the 'Small Town' was found to have been used through the Roman era as a place for religious or similar activities and burial (Martens, this volume; cf. Vanderhoeven *et al.* 2001). John Evans' distinctive paper in this volume brings a stimulating approach to this matter. He argues that in the case of the valley he studied by fieldwork, the Roman era saw an 'entexturing' of the land through its 'seeding' with the fragmented material culture of (evidently) the local community. This might be cast as a 'signing of the land' via the systematic introduction of artefactual remains to arable fields that would visually impact upon observers (particularly during the seasons when the land was not veiled in crops). From one perspective this might be understood as a visual Romanization of the landscape and agriculture, or one connecting material manufacture, the consumption of material culture and the agricultural cycle. Such phenomenological views of past understanding of place and landscape are familiar for those working in prehistoric archaeology but the approach is more novel in a Roman context (although see Witcher 1998). It might be suggested that these spreads represent disturbed midden or 'manuring'; however, the specific nature of some of the material as specified by Evans is not 'normal' fragmented domestic detritus but includes reconstructable pots and sawn amphora sherds. Whatever actually occurred in the past in this case (and this, of course, we will never know for certain) the interpretation advanced by Evans is stimulating, and encourages fresh thinking about perceptions of landscape and material culture and their potential connections, that may particularly impact upon the interpretation of surface gathered assemblages of this period and others.

Site type (and the identities and activities of those people who lived and interacted at such sites) is evidently an important variable in the composition of finds assemblages. In the countryside, where the vast majority of people lived and working during the Roman era greater attention needs to be paid to differentiating site functions and activities for rural sites are far from being a uniform category (cf. Hingley 1989; Taylor 2001) and in this finds may play a key role. A significant observation in this respect lies in the fact that differing material cultural items are likely to have been in use at specific times in the year relating to seasons and agricultural cycles, while different times of the year are likely to have been associated with the manufacture of particular artefacts (not simply pottery). Evidently there were many seasonally occupied sites in Roman Britain and the North-West provinces relating to altitude, dampness, resource procurement and perhaps transhumance. Such sites might yield modest groups of finds, as at the British upland sites at Roxby on the North York Moors (Inman *et al.* 1985) and Forcegarth Pasture South (Fairless and Coggins 1986), or distinctive assemblages, as that from the industrial saltern site complex at Shell Bridge, Holbeach St Johns (Gurney 1999). Whilst these sites may be characterized by meagre finds assemblages implying a lack of wealth we need to be wary of assumptions. Recovered finds may be unrepresentative of the actual wealth and status of the inhabitants of these sites, reflecting rather their attitudes to material items, a lack of need for coinage in such mileux and/or deposition practice. Season and the relationship of a site to agriculture and other productive activities may have been key to determining its finds assemblage.

Finds assemblages of the Roman era have traditionally been associated with buildings and occupied sites, but more recently increasing attention has come to be paid to finds from non-domestic localities. 'Off-site' deposition has more commonly been considered in studies of prehistoric societies (cf. Foley 1981). However, it is clear that the Roman period in Britain saw much marking of the landscape through the deposition of artefacts, and perhaps much of this activity had a symbolic dimension (cf. Evans, this volume; Croxford 2002).

Conclusion: the context of the present, and the Context of the past revisited

That finds studies make a vast contribution to understanding Roman archaeology is not in doubt. The papers by Cool, Crummy and Eckardt in this volume emphasize this and stress that finds research is central to the wider archaeological project.

Various issues relating to finds are considered through this volume. Many remain open to on-going debate, such as questions over the accessibility of finds information at various levels and the impact of the Portable Antiquities Scheme (cf. Worrall 2007. Recent developments, especially PPG16, mean that we are now examining sites in an altogether different configuration of places than previously. The archaeology being explored is different. This has impacts upon the nature of finds work and uncertain implications for the future. Large scale excavations in major towns are now uncommon; the 'Big Dig' in Canterbury at Whitefriars was a recent exception and it is appropriate that its finds assemblage is being examined by Mark Houliston employing innovative analytical approaches.

Turning to the structural problems in the world of Roman finds, there exist challenges on many fronts, the potential significance of which is outlined by Johns, Cool and Cooper in their papers. These circumstances are of considerable concern. Clearly there is much work to be undertaken if Roman finds studies are to maintain the vibrancy and momentum of recent years. Eckardt (2002b) has argued, for instance, that there is a need for new corpora of Roman finds, as existing typologies date (have dated) and are often housed within more than one volume, or, as in the case of some types, modern corpora have never been produced (eg. with brooches). More pressingly, the question of the continuing flow of keen people into the career of 'finds specialist' remains far from certain, while the demographic 'time-bomb' ticks on, which is particularly acute with some specialisms, such as the study of samian ware and mortaria (cf. Swift, this volume). The implications, or 'threat' as some see it, from commercial, cost led, archaeology, as several papers note, is still in the process of unfolding, potential impacts lying in the domain of full reporting, standards and adequate funding. Indeed, funding will doubtless remain an issue in the immediate future at least, both in terms of payment of specialists for day-to-day report writing, for which there must be adequate provision in PPG16 related projects, and with regard to the possibilities of research. Cooper (this volume) notes though that: "The study of material culture in the broad sense is becoming a major research strand within a number of academic departments" (cf. Pearce 2000), but such a process may require further encouragement in an RAE focused academic context. Further, pay rates commanded by some established finds consultants have increased just recently.

Of great concern are the work circumstances of finds

specialists, many of whom have experienced endemic uncertainties in their employment and financial affairs. These are not situations that have passed unnoticed and rates of pay for all free-lance specialists will be comparatively good if related to the Institute of Field Archaeologists (IFA) and other professional guidelines. Training courses and education in finds work have been supported by a range of bodies, not least English Heritage; latterly the Archaeology Training Forum and the Institute of Field Archaeologists have stressed the value of training and structures for career development in archaeology, including work with finds.

There can be no doubt that finds reports have a tremendous role to play in future reporting of sites and surveys, and the move towards integration in reporting will only highlight the value of recovered artefacts for establishing trends and details in the cultural life of sites.

A recurrent message amongst the papers assembled in this volume is that in our investigation of the past through its artefacts it is vital to consider context and site formation processes as these aspects have structured the record and carry in themselves key information about the artefact/s; it will be necessary to re-visit the context of artefacts when writing them up for publication, discussion and synthesis; good site recording, archives and published excavation reports enable this.

Amongst the papers presented here chronology is not a major theme, though it is acknowledged as a vital point of structuring and reference (cf. Cool and Crummy, this volume). Partly, perhaps, this reflects general trends in Roman archaeology, for chronology figures comparatively little in current themes of concern or interest. In large part the background position of chronology in this volume and more widely implies that presently chronology is not viewed as 'problematic' and something in need of investigation. Some recent research, however, suggest that these issues may not be so simple (Jones 1997) and the pendulum of interest may well swing back. Nonetheless, the papers by Martin and Isserlin in this volume emphasize its importance and value in attempts to understanding finds deposition and activity sequences.

The fascination and stir that Roman artefacts often generate amongst the general public in Britain and mainland Europe is readily apparent. Initiatives such as the Portable Antiquities Scheme, educational outreach, heritage and lottery funded projects and the refashioning and redefinition of many museums to become places of tactile experience where artefacts are contextualised and interpreted (such as at the Provinciaal Gallo-Romeins Museum, Tongeren) have developed this interest in the Roman past amongst present day communities. Moreover, such developments have assisted in forming relationships between the public and those concerned with finds at various levels. The further development of this shared curiosity in finds will be advantageous to both sides. By one means or another, the public pay for much work on finds and news of discoveries and dissemination of information to them is both vital and appropriate, and will benefit the archaeological finds 'profession'. Regular communication with the public is now an established aspect of the work of many finds specialists. The growing success of this relationship is an asset and an important justification (together with others) for sustaining research upon the finds of the Roman era. An exciting challenge for the future will be the institution of more studies that engage not only the evidence from Britain but that in other provinces as well (cf. Mattingly 2002). Not that levels of similarity are to be expected between sites and regions in different provinces, rather, greater differences might be recognized than anticipated. Whatever, such work will place finds evidence in a wider perspective which will assist in our attempts to understand the phenomenon of the empire. It is largely through work on finds that the: "patterns of cultural interaction of teeming complexity and endless interest" that, as recognized by James (2003, 183), characterized the empire, may be defined and accounted for.

Bibliography

Aldhouse-Green, M. and Webster, P. (eds) (2002) *Artefacts and Archaeology: Aspects of the Celtic and Roman World*. Cardiff, University of Wales Press.

Allason-Jones, L. (1988) 'Small finds' from turrets on Hadrian's Wall. In J. C. Coulston (ed.) *Military Equipment and the Identity of Roman Soldiers, Proceedings of the Fourth Roman Military Equipment Conference*, British Archaeological Reports (International Series) 394, 197–233. Oxford.

Allason-Jones, L. (2001) Review of Roman 'Small Finds' research. In C. Brooks, R. Daniels and A. Harding (ed.) *Past, Present and Future: The Archaeology of Northern England*, proceedings of a conference held in Durham in 1996, 113–9. Durham.

Atkinson, M. (2002) Special deposits at Heybridge. In R. Hingley and S. H. Willis (eds) *Promoting Roman Finds: Context and Theory. Conference Programme and Abstracts*, 5–6.

Atkinson, M. (forthcoming) *Excavations at Heybridge, Elms Farm, Essex, 1993–5*.

Baker, P. (2004) Roman Medical Instruments: Archaeological Interpretations of their possible 'non-functional' use. *Social History of Medicine*, 17, 3–21.

Barrett, J. C. (1993) Chronologies of remembrance: the interpretation of some Roman inscriptions. *World Archaeology* 25, 236–47.

Barrett, J. C. (1994) *Fragments from Antiquity: An Archaeology of Social Life in Britain 2900–1200 BC*. Oxford, Blackwell.

Barrett, J. C., Freeman, P. W. M., and Woodward, A. (2000) *Cadbury Castle, Somerset: The Later Prehistoric and Early Historic Archaeology*. English Heritage Archaeological Report 20. London, Blackwell.

Booth, P. M. (1991) Inter-site comparisons between pottery assemblages in Roman Warwickshire: ceramic indicators of site status. *Journal of Roman Pottery Studies*, 4, 1–10.

Bowman, A. (1994) *Life and Letters on the Roman Frontier*. London, British Museum.

Bradley, R. (2002) *An Archaeology of Natural Places*. London and New York, Routledge.

Brickstock, R. J., Casey, P. J. and Davies, J. A. (2002) The coins. In P. R. Wilson, *Cataractonium: Roman Catterick and its Hinterland. Excavations and Research, 1958–1997*, CBA Research Report 129, 1–23. York.

Casey, P. J. (1974) The interpretation of Romano-British site finds. In P. J. Casey and R. Reece (eds) *Coins and the Archaeologist*, British Archaeological Reports (British Series) 4, 37–51. Oxford.

Casey, P. J. (1984) *Roman Coinage in Britain*. Princes Risborough, Shire.

Chapman, J. (2000) *Fragmentation in Archaeology*. London, Routledge.

Clarke, D. L. (1972) A provisional model of an Iron Age society and its settlement, in D. L. Clarke (ed.) *Models in Archaeology*, 801–69. London, Methuen.

Clarke, S. (1994) A quantitative analysis of the finds from the Roman fort at Newstead – some preliminary findings. In S. Cottam, D. Dungworth, S. Scott and J. Taylor (eds), *TRAC94: Proceedings of the 4th Theoretical Roman Archaeology Conference, Durham 1994*, 72–82. Oxford, Oxbow.

Clarke, S. (1997) Abandonment, rubbish disposal and 'special deposits' at Newstead. In K. I. Meadows, C. R. Lemke and J. Heron (eds) *TRAC96: Proceedings of the 6th Theoretical Roman Archaeology Conference, Sheffield 1996*, 73–81. Oxford, Oxbow.

Clarke, S. (2000) In search of a different Roman period: the finds assemblage at the Newstead military complex. In G. Fincham, G. Harrison, R. Holland and L. Revell (eds) *TRAC 99: Proceedings of the 9th Annual Theoretical Roman Archaeology Conference, Durham 1999*, 22–9. Oxford, Oxbow.

Clarke, S. and Jones, R. F. J. (1996) The Newstead pits. *Journal of Roman Military Equipment Studies*, 5, 109–24.

Cool, H. E. M. (2004) *The Roman Cemetery at Brougham, Cumbria: Excavations 1966–7*. Britannia Monograph Series, 21, London.

Cool, H.E. M. and Baxter, M. J. (1999) Peeling the onion: an approach to comparing vessel glass assemblages. *Journal of Roman Archaeology*, 12, 72–100.

Cool, H. E. M., Lloyd-Morgan, G. and Hooley, A. D. (1995) *Finds from the Fortress*, The Archaeology of York: the Small Finds, 17/10. York, York Archaeological Trust and the CBA.

Cool, H. E. M. and Philo, C. (eds) (1998) *Roman Castleford, Excavations 1974–85. Volume I: The Small Finds*. Wakefield, West Yorkshire Archaeology Service.

Cooper, N. J. (1996) Searching for the blank generation: consumer choice in Roman and post-Roman Britain. In J. Webster and N. J. Cooper (eds) *Roman Imperialism: post-colonial perspectives*. Leicester Archaeology Monographs 3, 85–98. Leicester.

Cooper, N. J. (2000) Rubbish counts: quantifying portable material culture in Roman Britain. In S. Pearce (ed.) *Researching Material Culture*, Leicester Archaeology Monograph 8, 75–86. Leicester.

Cooper, N. J. (forthcoming) Pottery supply to Roman Cirencester (*Corinium Dobunnorum*): the potential contribution of pottery to the study of Romanization. In M. Tuffreau-Libre (ed.), *La ceramique en Gaule et en Bretagne romaines: commerce, contact et romanisation*. Nord-Ouest Archaeology.

Courtney, P. (1996) In small things forgotten: the Georgian world view, material culture and the consumer revolution. *Rural History*, 7/1, 87–95.

Courtney, P. (1997) Ceramics and the history of consumption: pitfalls and prospects. *Medieval Ceramics*, 21, 95–108.

Creighton, J. D. (1990) The Humber frontier in the first century AD. In S. Ellis and D. R. Crowther (eds) *Humber Perspectives: A Region through the Ages*. Hull, University of Hull.

Croxford, B. (2002) *Ritual activity in the Romano-British Landscape: Beyond the teminos*. Unpublished MA dissertation, University of Durham, Department of Archaeology.

Croxford, B. (2003) Iconoclasm in Roman Britain? *Britannia*, 34, 81–95.

Crummy, N. (1983) *The Roman Small Finds from Excavations in Colchester, 1971–9*. Colchester Archaeological Report 2, Colchester.

Crummy, N. and Eckardt, H. (2004) Regional identities and technologies of the self: Nail-cleaners in Roman Britain. *The Archaeological Journal*, 160, 44–69.

Crummy, P. (1992) *Excavations at Culver Street, the Gilberd School and miscellaneous sites 1971–85, Colchester, Essex*. Colchester Archaeological Report 6, Colchester.

Dannell, G. B. (2002) Law and practice: further thoughts on the organization of the potteries at la Graufesenque. In M. Genin and A. Vernhet (eds) *Céramiques de la Graufesenque*. Archéologie et Histoire Romaine, 7, 211–42.

Deetz, J. (1996). *In Small Things Forgotten: an Archaeology of Early American Life*. New York, Anchor Books Doubleday.

Dennis, G. (1978) 1–7 St Thomas Street, in Southwark and Lambeth Archaeological Excavation Committee, *Southwark Excavations 1972–1974*. London and Middlesex Archaeological Society and Surrey Archaeological Society Joint Publication 1, 291–422. London.

Derks, T. and Roymans, N. (2002) Seal-boxes and the spread of Latin literacy in the Rhine delta, in A. E. Cooley (ed.) *Becoming Roman, Writing Latin? Literacy and Epigraphy in the Roman West*. Journal of Roman Archaeology Supplementary Series 48, Journal of Roman Archaeology, Portsmouth RI, 87–134.

van Driel-Murray, C. (1999) And did those feet in ancient time ... Feet and shoes as a material projection of the self. In P. Baker, C. Forcey, S. Jundi, and R. Witcher (eds) *TRAC98: Proceedings of the 8th Theoretical Roman Archaeology Conference, Leicester 1998*, 131–40. Oxford, Oxbow.

Dungworth, D. (1998) Mystifying Roman nails: clavus annalis, defixiones and minkisi. In C. Forcey, J. Hawthorne and R, Witcher (eds) *TRAC97: Proceedings of the 7th Theoretical Roman Archaeology Conference, Nottingham, 1997*, 148–59. Oxford, Oxbow.

Eckardt, H. (2000) Illuminating Roman Britain. In G. Fincham, G. Harrison, R. Holland and L. Revell (eds) *TRAC99: Proceedings of the 9th Annual Theoretical Roman Archaeology Conference, Durham 1999*, 8–21. Oxford, Oxbow.

Eckardt, H. (2002a) *Illuminating Roman Britain*. Editions Monique Mergoil, Montagnac.

Eckardt, H. (2002b) Paper given to the 'Wither Roman Archaeology' Conference, London, 16th Nov. 2002.

Evans, C. J. (2003) Joined up thinking: Reconstructing the Roman West Midlands from the ceramic evidence, West Midlands Regional Research Framework. www.arch-ant.bham.ac.uk/wmrrfa seminar 3.

Evans, E. (2000) *The Caerleon Canabae: Excavations in the Civil Settlement 1984–90.* Britannia Monograph 16, London.

Evans, J. (1988) All Yorkshire is divided into three parts; social aspects of later Roman pottery distributions in Yorkshire. In J. Price, and P. R. Wilson, with C. S. Briggs, and S. J. Hardman, (eds), *Recent Research in Roman Yorkshire: Studies in honour of Mary Kitson Clark (Mrs Derwas Chitty).* British Archaeological Reports (British Series) 193, 323–37. Oxford.

Evans, J. (1995a) Roman finds assemblages: towards an integrated approach? In P. Rush (ed.) *Theoretical Roman Archaeology: Second Conference Proceedings*, 33–58. Aldershot, Avebury.

Evans, J. (1995b) Function and fine wares in the Roman North. *Journal of Roman Pottery Studies*, 6, 95–118.

Evans, J. (2001) Material approaches to the identification of different Romano-British site types. In S. T. James and M. J. Millett (eds) *Britons and Romans: advancing an archaeological agenda.* CBA Research Report 125, 26–35. CBA, York.

Evans, J. and Millett, M. J. (1992) Residuality revisited. *Oxford Journal of Archaeology*, 11/2, 225–40.

Fairless, K. J. and Coggins, D. (1986) Excavations at the early settlement site of Forcegarth Pasture South, 1974–5. *Durham Archaeological Journal*, 2, 25–40.

Ferris, I. M. (2000) Discussion. In I. M. Ferris, L. Bevan, and R. Cuttler, *The Excavation of a Romano-British Shrine at Orton's Pasture, Rocester, Staffordshire.* British Archaeological Reports (British Series) 314, 72–82. Oxford.

Ferris, I. M. (2002) Paper abstract: A severed head: thinking about the fragment in Roman archaeology and art. In R. Hingley and S. H. Willis (eds) *Promoting Roman Finds: Context and Theory. Conference Programme and Abstracts*, 9–10.

Foley, R. A. (1981) Off-site archaeology: an alternative approach for the short-sited. In I. R. Hodder, G. Issac, and N. Hammond (eds) *Pattern of the Past*, CUP, 157–82. Cambridge.

Freeman, P. W. M. (1993) 'Romanization' and Roman material culture. *Journal of Roman Archaeology*, 6, 438–45.

Fulford, M. G. (2001) Links with the past: persuasive "ritual" behaviour in Roman Britain. *Britannia*, 32, 199–218.

Gardner, A. (2001) *'Military' and 'Civilian' in Late Roman Britain: an Archaeology of Social Identity.* Unpublished PhD thesis Institute of Archaeology, University College, London.

Gardner, A. (2002) Social identity and the duality of structure in late Roman-period Britain. *Journal of Social Archaeology*, 2.3, 323–51.

Goffman, E. (1963) *Behaviour in Public Places.* New York, The Free Press of Glencoe.

Goffman, E. (1978) *The Presentation of Self in Everyday Life.* Middlesex, Penguin.

Going, C. J. (1992) Economic 'long waves' in the Roman period? *Oxford Journal of Archaeology*, 11, 93–117.

Gurney, D. (1999) A Romano-British salt-making site at Shell Bridge, Holbeach St Johns: Excavations by Ernest Greenfield, 1961. In A. Bell, *et al.* Lincolnshire Salterns: Excavations at Helpringham, Holbeach St Johns and Bicker Haven. *East Anglian Archaeology*, Report 89, Heritage Trust of Lincolnshire, 21–69.

Haselgrove, C. C. (1985) Inference from ploughsoil artefact samples. In C. C. Haselgrove, M. J. Millett and I. M. Smith (eds) *Archaeology from the Ploughsoil*, 7–29. Dept of Prehistory and Archaeology, Sheffield.

Hawkes, C. F. C. and Hull, M. R. (1947) *Camulodunum. First Report on the Excavations at Colchester 1930–1939.* Reports of the Research Committee of the Society of Antiquaries of London 14, Oxford.

Hill, J. D. (1995) *Ritual and Rubbish in the Iron Age of Wessex.* British Archaeological Reports (British Series) 242, Oxford.

Hill, J. D. (1997) 'The end of one kind of body and the beginning of another kind of body'? Toilet instruments and 'Romanization' in southern England during the first century AD. In A. Gwilt and C.C. Haselgrove (eds.), *Reconstructing Iron Age Societies,* Oxbow Monograph 71, 96–107. Oxford, Oxbow.

Hill, J. D. (2001) Romanisation, gender and class: recent approaches to identity in Britain and their possible consequences. In S. T. James and M. J. Millett (eds) *Britons and Romans: advancing an archaeological agenda,* CBA Research Report 125, 12–8. York, CBA.

Hingley, R. (1989) *Rural Settlement in Roman Britain.* London, Seaby.

Hingley, R. (1990) Iron Age 'currency bars': the archaeological and social context. *The Archaeological Journal*, 147, 91–117.

Hingley, R. (2005) *Globalization and Roman Culture: unity, diversity and empire.* London, Routledge.

Hingley, R., Moore, H. L., Triscott, J. E. and Wilson, G. (1997) The excavation of two later Iron Age fortified homesteads at Aldclune, Blair Atholl, Pert and Kinross. *Proceedings of the Society of Antiquaries of Scotland*, 127, 407–66.

Hodder, I. R. (ed.) (1978) *The Spatial Organization of Culture.* London, Duckworth.

Hodder, I. R. (1989) Writing archaeology: site reports in context. *Antiquity*, 63, 268–74.

Hoffmann, B. (1995) The quarters of legionary centurions of the principate. *Britannia*, 26, 107–52.

Hoskins, J. (1998) *Biographical Objects: How Things Tell the Stories of Peoples' Lives.* London, Routledge.

Hughes, G. and Woodward, A. (forthcoming). *The Excavation of an Iron Age Settlement at Covert Farm (DIRFT East), Crick, Northamptonshire.*

Hull, M. R. (1958) *Roman Colchester.* Reports of the Research Committee of the Society of Antiquaries of London 20, Oxford.

Hunter, F. (1998) Discussion of the artefact assemblage. In L. Main, Excavation of a timber round-house and broch at the Fairy Knowe, Buchlyvie, Stirlingshire. *Proceedings of the Society of Antiquaries of Scotland,* 128, (293–417), 393–401.

Hunter, F. (2001) Roman and native in Scotland: new approaches. *Journal of Roman Archaeology*, 14, 289–309.

Inman, R., Brown, D. R., Goddard, R. E. and Spratt, D. A. (1985) Roxby Iron Age settlement and the Iron Age in north-east Yorkshire. *Proceedings of the Prehistoric Society* 51, 181–13.

James, S. T. (2003) Roman archaeology: crisis and revolution. *Antiquity*, 77, No. 295, 178–84.

James, S. T. and Millett, M. J. (eds) (2001) *Britons and Romans: advancing an archaeological agenda.* CBA Research Report 125. York, CBA.

Johnson, M. (1999) *Archaeological Theory. An Introduction.* Oxford, Blackwell.

Jones, S. (1997) *The Archaeology of Ethnicity: Constructing Identities in the Past and the Present*. London, Routledge.

Kenyon, K. M. (1948) *Excavations at the Jewry Wall Site, Leicester*. Reports of the Research Committee of the Society of Antiquaries of London 15, Oxford.

Laurence, R. (1999) Theoretical Roman archaeology. *Britannia*, 30, 387–90.

Leach, P. with Evans, C. J. (2001) *Fosse Lane, Shepton Mallet 1990. Excavation of a Romano-British Roadside Settlement in Somerset*. Britannia Monograph 18, London.

van der Linden, E. (forthcoming) *Terra Sigillata at Nijmegen*, doctoral study. Nijmegen, Katholieke Universiteit.

Martin, T. S. (2003) The neglect of Richard Neville, paper presented at TRAC2003, the 13th Theoretical Roman Archaeology Conference. Leicester 2003.

Mattingly, D. J. (2002) Vulgar and weak 'Romanization' or time for a paradigm shift? *Journal of Roman Archaeology*, 15, 536–40.

Meadows, K. I. (1994) You are what you eat: diet, identity and Romanisation. In S. Cottam, D. Dungworth, S. Scott and J. Taylor, (eds) *TRAC94: Proceedings of the 4th Theoretical Roman Archaeology Conference, Durham 1994*, 133–40. Oxford, Oxbow.

Meadows, K. I. (1997) Much ado about nothing: the social context of eating and drinking in early Roman Britain. In C.G. Cumberpatch and P. W. Blinkhorn, (eds) *Not So Much a Pot, More a Way of Life*. Oxbow Monograph 83, 1–35. Oxford, Oxbow.

Millett, M. J. (1979) An approach to the functional interpretation of pottery, in M. J. Millett (ed.) *Pottery and the Archaeologist*. London Institute of Archaeology Occasional Paper 4. London, London Institute of Archaeology.

Millett, M. J. (1980) Aspects of Romano-British pottery in West Sussex. *Sussex Archaeological Collections*, 118, 57–68.

Millett, M. J. (1987) A question of time? Aspects of the future of pottery studies. *Bulletin of the Institute of Archaeology*, 24, 99–108.

Mills, P., Evans, J. and Millett, M. J. (forthcoming) The Roman pottery database, in M. J. Millett and P. Halkon, Excavations at the Iron Age and Roman Settlement at Hayton, East Yorkshire. *Internet Archaeology*.

Mudd, A., Williams, R. J. and Lupton, A. (1999) *Excavations alongside Roman Ermin Street, Gloucestershire and Wiltshire. The Archaeology of the A419/A417 Swindon to Gloucester Road Scheme*. Oxford.

Orton, C. R. (1978) Is pottery a sample? In J. F. Cherry, C. Gamble and S. Shennan, (eds) *Sampling in Contemporary British Archaeology*. BAR British Series 50, 399–402. Oxford.

Orton, C. R. (1982) *Mathematics in Archaeology*. Cambridge, CUP.

Orton, C. R. (1989) An introduction to the quantification of assemblages of pottery. *Journal of Roman Pottery Studies*, 2, 94–7.

Parca, M. (2001) Local languages and native cultures. In J. Bodel (ed.) *Epigraphic Evidence: Ancient History from Inscriptions,* 57–72. London, Routledge.

Pearce, S. (ed.) (2000) *Researching Material Culture*. Leicester Archaeology Monograph 8, Leicester.

Price J. and Cottam, S. (1998) *Romano-British Glass Vessels: a Handbook*. York, CBA.

Reece, R. M. (1983) Discussion. In J. E. Mann and R. Reece, *Roman Coins from Lincoln 1970–1979*, The Archaeology of Lincoln, 6/2, 64–70. London, CBA.

Reece, R. M. (1988) *My Roman Britain*. Cotswold Studies 3, Cirencester.

Reece, R. M. (1993a) Roman sites and their Roman coins. *Antiquity*, 67, 863–9.

Reece, R. M. (1993b) Theory and Roman archaeology. In E. Scott (ed.) *Theoretical Roman Archaeology: First Conference Proceedings*, 29–38. Aldershot, Avebury.

Reece, R. M. (1995) Site-finds in Roman Britain. *Britannia*, 26, 179–206.

Revell, L. (1999) Constructing Romanitas: Roman public architecture and the archaeology of practice. In P. Baker, C. Forcey, S. Jundi, and R. Witcher (eds) *TRAC98: Proceedings of the 8th Theoretical Roman Archaeology Conference, Leicester 1998*, 52–8. Oxford, Oxbow.

Rippengal, R. (1995) *Romanization, Society and Material Culture: an Archaeological Study of the Significance of Romanization in the Context of Roman Britain*. Unpublished PhD Thesis, University of Cambridge.

von Schnurbein, S. (2003) Augustus in *Germania* and his new town at Waldgirmes east of the Rhine. *Journal of Roman Archaeology* 16, 93–108.

Shanks, M. and Tilley, C. (1987) *Social Theory and Archaeology*. Cambridge, Polity Press.

Shanks, M. and Tilley, C. (1992) *Reconstructing Archaeology, Theory and Practice*, 2nd edition. London, Routledge, .

Sharples, N. M. (1991). *Maiden Castle: Excavations and Field Survey 1985–6*. English Heritage Archaeological Report 19. London, Historic Buildings and Monuments Commission for England.

Sharples, N. M. (1998) *Scalloway: A broch, Late Iron Age Settlement, and Medieval Cemetery in Shetland*. Oxbow Monograph 82. Oxford, Oxbow.

Shennan, S. (1997) *Quantifying Archaeology*. Edinburgh, Edinburgh University Press.

Snape, M. E. (1993) *Roman Brooches from North Britain*. British Archaeological Reports (British Series) 235, Oxford.

Snape, M. E. and Bidwell, P. T. (2002) The Roman Fort at Newcastle upon Tyne. *Archaeologia Aeliana*, Fifth Series, 31, Extra volume for 2002.

Steer, K. A. and Keeney, G. S. (1947) Excavations in two homesteads at Crock Cleuch, Roxburghshire. *Proceedings of the Society of Antiquaries of Scotland*, 81, 138–57.

Swift. E. (2000) *Regionality in Dress Accessories in the Late Roman West*. Montagnac, Editions Monique Mergoil.

Swift. E. (2003) *Roman Dress Accessories*. Princes Risborough, Shire.

Taylor, J. (2001) Rural society in Roman Britain. In S. James and M. Millett (eds) *Britons and Romans: advancing an archaeological agenda*. CBA Research Report 125, 46–59. York, CBA.

Tyers, P. A. (1996) *Roman Pottery in Britain*. London, Batsford.

Vanderhoeven, A., Martens, M. and Vynckier, G. (2001) Romanization and settlement in the central part of the Civitas Tungrorum. In S. Altekamp and A. Schäfer (eds) *The Impact on Settlement in the Northwestern and Danube Provinces. Lectures held at the Winckelmann-Institut der Humbolt-Universität zu Berlin in winter 1998/99*. British Archaeological Reports (International Series) 921, 57–90. Oxford.

Wallace, C. R. (1990) Roman pottery studies in Britain 1890–1919. *Journal of Roman Pottery Studies,* 3, 80–7.

Webster, J. (2001) Creolizing the Roman provinces. *American Journal of Archaeology,* 105, 209–25.

Wheeler, R. E. M. (1921) An insula of Roman Colchester. *Transactions of the Essex Archaeological Society,* second series, 16, 7–41.

Willis, S. H. (1994) Roman imports into late Iron Age British societies: towards a critique of existing models. In S. Cottam, D. Dungworth, S. Scott and J. Taylor, (eds) *TRAC94: Proceedings of the 4th Theoretical Roman Archaeology Conference, Durham 1994,* 141–50. Oxford, Oxbow.

Willis, S. H. (1998) Samian pottery in Britain: exploring its distribution and archaeological potential. *The Archaeological Journal,* 155, 82–133.

Willis, S. H. (2003) Nettleton and Rothwell: interim report on excavations and field survey, 2000–2. *Lincolnshire History and Archaeology,* 37, 11–20.

Willis, S. H. (2004) The Study Group for Roman Pottery: Research Framework document for the study of Roman pottery in Britain, 2004. *Journal of Roman Pottery Studies,* 11, 1–21.

Willis, S. H. (2005) *An E-monograph: Samian pottery, a Resource for the Study of Roman Britain and Beyond. The results of the English Heritage funded Samian Project. Internet Archaeology,* 17.

Willis, S. H. (forthcoming a) Samian and society in Roman Britain and beyond. *Britannia.*

Willis, S. H. (forthcoming b) The context of writing and written records in ink: the archaeology of samian inkwells in Britain. *The Archaeological Journal.*

Wilson, P. R. (2002) *Cataractonium: Roman Catterick and its Hinterland. Excavations and Research, 1958–1997.* CBA Research Reports 128 and 129, York, CBA.

Witcher, R. (1998) Roman roads: phenomenological perspectives on roads in the landscape. In C. Forcey, J. Hawthorne and R. Witcher (eds) *TRAC97: Proceedings of the 7th Theoretical Roman Archaeology Conference, Nottingham 1997,* 60–70. Oxford, Oxbow.

Worrall, S. (2007) Detecting the Later Iron Age: a view from the Portable Antiquities Scheme. In C. C. Haselgrove and T. Moore (eds) *The Later Iron Age in Britain and Beyond.* Oxford, Oxbow.

2 Small Objects, Small Questions? Perceptions of Finds Research in the Academic Community

Ellen Swift

Introduction

Debate at various conferences recently has highlighted growing concern that unless more people are attracted into the study of Roman finds there will be a shortage of informed specialists in years to come. The possibility of this problem arising has also been noted in recent surveys on training needs in archaeology (Chitty 1999, 22). Nor is it only a future problem; there are already difficulties, for example, in recruiting experienced finds specialists as part of the portable antiquities scheme. Until we gain a clearer picture of the state of finds research and a better understanding of the variety of possible reasons behind a possible shortage in finds specialists, we are unlikely to be able to progress very far in promoting finds studies. It is illuminating, for example, that most of the discussion to date has centred around a future skills shortage in the identification of objects, rather than the constraints on academic enquiry created by the neglect of finds as a serious research area. This paper examines the current state of finds research in British archaeology and perceptions of this research, and discusses possible reasons for the position which Roman finds research holds in relation to other areas of archaeological research. Given the limited space, I will concentrate on finds research in universities; examining the status of finds researchers in other areas such as unit archaeology deserves a paper of its own, and may be something which can be subsequently addressed.

Documenting Roman finds research

A questionnaire was chosen as the principal method of investigating Roman finds research (Fig. 2.1). It was circulated by e-mail among Roman finds researchers in universities and related organisations, and as a flyer in the newsletter of the Roman Finds Group whose membership comprises a heterogeneous group of unit and freelance specialists, museum staff, university staff and other finds researchers. 48 responses were received. In addition, information was sought from university web sites, from the web site listing theses completed in British universities, and from a survey of publications in the journal *Britannia* over the last twenty years. Results could usefully be compared with a wider survey of careers in archaeology, *Profiling the Profession* (Aitchison 1999). Among the respondents to the questionnaire, finds researchers were divided pretty evenly between universities, museums and freelance or unit posts (Fig. 2.2), a similar pattern in employment to that established across the archaeology profession (Aitchison 1999).

Age

Respondents to the questionnaire were asked to indicate their age range. Assuming that respondents are generally a representative sample of Roman finds researchers as a whole, the results confirm the previously voiced suspicion that finds specialists are an ageing population. The single most frequent age range was that between 41 and 50 years of age, with fairly substantial proportions in the 31–40 and 51–60 age brackets (Fig. 2.3). This contrasts with the general age profile in archaeology as a whole provided by Aitchison, in which the average age is 36, and the peak is in the 30–39 age bracket, with a much steeper decline in proportions of older archaeologists (Fig. 2.4).

Employment in universities

Using *The Guardian* web site listing of university departments offering archaeology (*http:\\education.guardian.co.uk.guides*), 69% included Roman archaeologists. Just under half of departments offering Roman archaeology included some employees who described themselves as Roman finds researchers. Among respondents to the Roman finds questionnaire, only 4 out of 48 Roman finds researchers held full-time university lecturing posts, with a further 5 holding joint posts as university lecturers combined with consultancy, museum directorships or field unit employment. From the information available on university web sites in early June 2002, however, 18 people described themselves as participating in finds research in British Universities. 10 of these people held full time lecturing posts; the remainder were research fellows or associates, or university museum or unit directors with teaching and research as part of their job. Anecdotally it was known that several others included finds work in their research area, but these were not listed as they had apparently chosen not to identify themselves as finds researchers in publicity material.

ROMAN FINDS RESEARCH: SURVEY

*Debate at various conferences recently has touched on an important area of concern- that unless we attract more people into the study of Roman finds we will face a shortage of informed specialists in years to come. I would be very interested to hear your views on careers in finds study and perceptions of finds research in the archaeological community and would be very grateful if you would spare the time to fill in this questionnaire. I will be putting the results together to present at a conference in Durham later this year, **Promoting Roman finds in context and theory**, details available from Dr R Hingley & Dr S Willis:*
richard.hingley@durham.ac.uk/s.h.willis@durham.ac.uk

Please send completed questionnaires to Ellen Swift, SECL, Cornwallis Building, University of Kent at Canterbury, Canterbury, Kent CT2 7NF. E.V.Swift@ukc.ac.uk I would appreciate return by April 31.

Please circle as appropriate   M / F
age   18-25 26-30 31-40 41-50 51-60 61+

What is your specialist area within Roman finds?

Are you .....1) freelance or archaeology unit finds specialist □ 2) museum curator/assistant □
3) museum voluntary/temporary staff □ 4) university lecturer □ 5) post-doctoral researcher
□ 6) postgraduate student □ 7) other □

Why /how did you become interested in the study of Roman finds?

Do you have a postgraduate qualification?
MA / MSc./ M Phil./ Ph.D / other

How has choosing a finds specialism (or it choosing you!) affected your career in archaeology?

How would you assess the importance of finds research to Roman archaeology?

How do you think finds study is perceived 1) in academia 2) in the wider archaeological community?

How do you think we can encourage people to specialise in finds?

Fig. 2.1. Questionnaire on Roman finds research

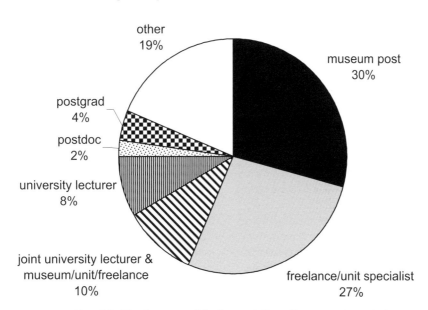

Fig. 2.2. Employment of finds specialists (from questionnaire)

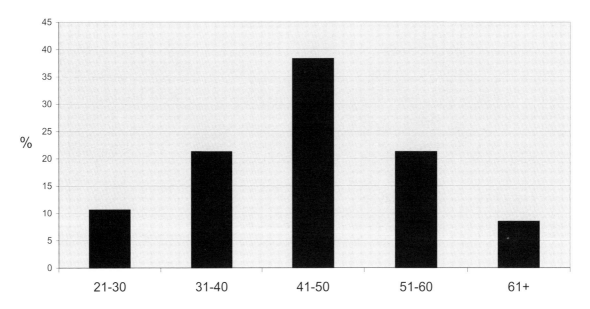

Fig. 2.3. Age range of finds specialists (from questionnaire)

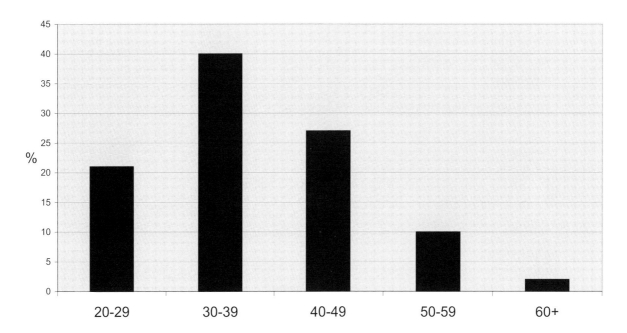

Fig. 2.4. Age range of archaeologists, from data in Aitchison (1999)

Gender profile

11 men (61%) and 7 women (39%) described themselves as finds researchers on university web sites (Figs. 2.5 and 2.6). Of these, 3 women and 7 men held full-time lecturing posts. These proportions can be compared with the overall proportions of men and women in archaeology in British universities (65% and 35% respectively, see Fig. 2.7, compiled from Aitchison 1999); and regarding the proportions of men and women responding to the finds questionnaire (47% men and 53% women, Fig.

2.8). University finds researchers have a similar gender profile to that of academic archaeologists as a whole, despite the impression given by the finds questionnaire that women are more strongly represented in finds research generally than in other areas of archaeology.

Qualifications

The comparatively small numbers of university personnel describing themselves as finds researchers is apparently

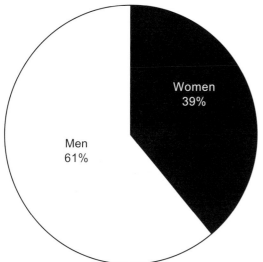

Fig. 2.5. Percentage of women and men in British universities who describe themselves as Roman finds researchers

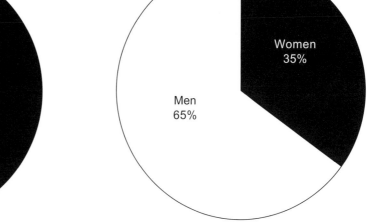

Fig. 2.7. Percentage of female and male archaeologists in British universities, from data in Aitchison (1999)

University/initials		self description	post held
UCL KL	m	numismatics	Lecturer
UCL DR	m	numismatics	Senior Research Fellow/Unit Director
Reading JC	m	use /influence of coinage	Lecturer
Reading JB	f	material culture	Research fellow
Leicester NC	m	Roman pottery & small finds	Finds officer/ tutor
Leicester HE	f	material culture	Lecturer
S'hampton DP	m	pottery, stone	Professor
Durham JP	f	ancient glass & artefacts	Professor
Oxford EH	f	IA/Roman pottery & small finds	research assistant
Oxford PK	m	Hellenistic and Roman pottery	research officer
Oxford ES	m	Roman monetary history	post-doctoral research fellow
Cardiff PG	m	Roman coinage	Lecturer
Cardiff PW	m	Roman period ceramics	Senior Lecturer
Nottingham YS	f	Roman glass	research associate
St Andrews JC	m	Roman military equipment	Lecturer
Newcastle KG	m	Roman ceramics	Senior Lecturer
Newcastle LA	f	artefact studies	Reader, Director of Museums
Kent ES	f	finds	Lecturer

Fig. 2.6. Self-descriptions and job titles of Roman finds researchers in universities

not a result of finds specialists lacking appropriate formal qualifications. 80% of finds researchers who responded to the questionnaire held a postgraduate qualification, with 54% holding a research degree, the vast majority of which were doctorates (Fig. 2.9). Some interesting points also arise from a consultation of the titles and abstracts of theses produced in British universities in the twenty years 1981–2001, available at *http:\\www.theses.com* (excluding M. A., M. Sc., etc., but including M. Litt and M. Phil.). Firstly, a high proportion of Roman finds-based theses, compared to other theses in Roman archaeology in the 1980s and 90s, has seemingly not translated into similar proportions of finds-based researchers in universities. Secondly, there has been a noticeable decline in the number of theses on finds from the late 1990s onwards (Fig. 2.10).

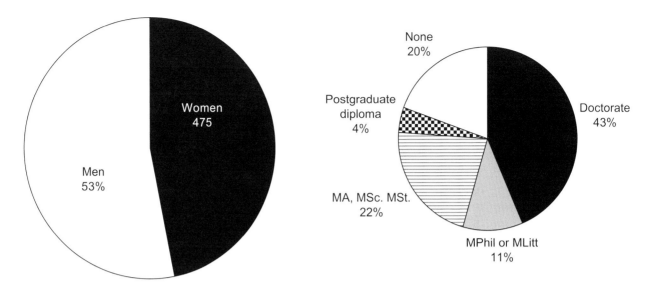

Fig. 2.8. Percentage of female and male finds researchers responding to Roman finds questionnaire

Fig. 2.9. Post-graduate qualifications held by Roman finds specialists (from questionnaire)

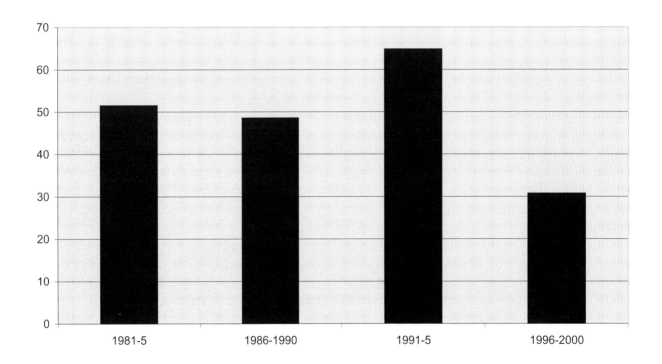

Fig. 2.10. Percentage of Roman M. Phil. and Ph.D. theses on finds topics

Publications

Despite the relatively large number of completed theses on Roman finds research topics in the last 20 years, relatively few articles exclusively concerned with finds appear to be published in journals. Information was collected on the proportion and character of finds-based articles published in Romano-British archaeology's pre-eminent journal, *Britannia*. The journal usually contains about 13 full-length articles (*i.e.*, not including the shorter notes sections). Across a 20–year time span from 1981 to 2001 (*Britannia,* volumes 12–32) publications concentrating on finds were relatively few – usually about 2 or 3 in each volume. Most of these were publications of previously unpublished material rather than broader syntheses and interpretations of finds-based data.

Gender bias within finds research

Within different categories of finds research some notable gender bias can be securely established. It is hardly an over-generalisation to say that men study coins and pottery and women study other categories of finds. Taking self-descriptions from university web sites, with one exception, all men described a specialist area including coins or pottery. (The exception was a man who described his area of study as military equipment, perhaps revealing in itself). By contrast, no women described themselves as studying coins, with the majority either studying a combination of pottery and other material, or other categories such as glass and small finds (Fig. 2.11). This patterning was borne out by the results of the finds questionnaire, which also showed men concentrating on coins and pottery and women studying other categories of finds including dress accessories, leather, vessels, glass and the like, though a significant minority, 8 men and 7 women, did not indicate a particular specialism within finds research (Fig. 2.12).

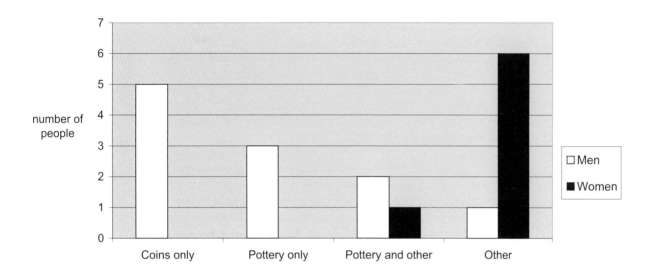

Fig. 2.11. Types of finds research carried out by women and men in British universities

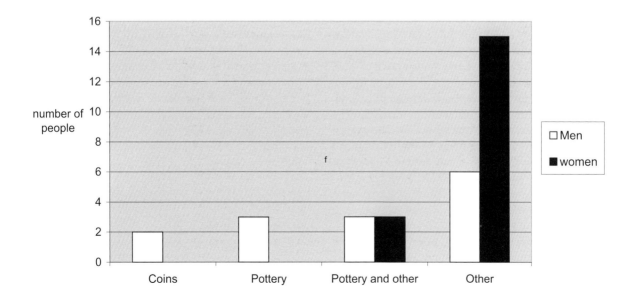

Fig. 2.12. Types of finds research carried out by questionnaire respondents

Perceptions of Roman finds research

As might be expected, respondents (who were all finds specialists) felt that finds research was of central importance in archaeology. It was generally felt to be at best under-valued and at worst completely disregarded by other sectors of the archaeological community. Respondents to the questionnaire were asked how they felt finds research was viewed in the academic community and wider archaeological communities. About two-thirds thought that finds work was viewed in a very negative way among academics; a sample of quotes: 'tedious', 'uninteresting', 'secondary to fieldwork', 'old-fashioned', 'atheoretical', 'time consuming', 'unintellectual', 'uncreative', 'limited', 'trivial', 'inferior', 'unimportant', 'women's work'. The remainder of respondents either had no view, thought finds was regarded neutrally, or thought that there was a positive view. Several respondents drew attention to a recent change in the academic climate in which finds research had begun to be perceived in a more positive way. The conference on Promoting Roman Finds, of which this volume forms the proceedings, is undoubtedly a symptom of this change.

If overwhelmingly negative views of finds research really are widespread, it might be expected that this would hinder career progression among finds researchers. Respondents were asked how, in their view, their choice of finds research had affected their subsequent career. Drawbacks most often cited were lack of career structure, few permanent posts and a high degree of job insecurity, low pay, little time and/or opportunity to carry out and publish independent research (which was in any case time-consuming compared to other research areas), being considered too specialist/limited for university posts or advancement within universities, and little understanding or appreciation of their work by supervisors and managers. Gilchrist (1991, 250) observes that in general the archaeological management structure works to the advantage of excavators and to the disadvantage of finds workers, a point also noted by questionnaire respondents. All of these points suggest that Roman finds research is indeed held to be of low value by the archaeology profession in general.

Advantages in career terms were perceived to be flexibility and autonomy, and that the appropriate experience gained enabled respondents to find interesting and enjoyable jobs in archaeology and succeed in a variety of arenas – particularly in museum work (though it was noted by some that museum work tended to be low-paid). For many, finds work was a useful supplement to or a stop-gap between other forms of employment. Some felt that it was no more insecure than other niches within archaeology, such as that of an excavator habitually employed on short-term contracts. The necessity or opportunity to work freelance was perceived negatively by some and positively by others.

Finds research therefore appears to hold a somewhat marginal position in the general arena of academic archaeology. It is under-represented in terms of publication and studies which go beyond essential publication of new material. Few university posts are held by finds researchers (and it should be noted that this is one of the only areas in archaeology with a defined career path and promotion opportunities). There is a poor career structure for finds researchers outside the universities, despite a large number of highly qualified candidates and despite the quantity of material continually being produced by excavation and survey. Several authors have drawn attention to the mass of data available and the shortage of synthetic approaches to this data (Cooper 2000, 77; Ault and Nevett 1999, 45–6). This probably results from the small numbers of academics working in finds research and the time pressures on other types of finds specialists which often means working unpaid overtime if anything beyond a basic catalogue is to be published.

Given all this, and the consequent paucity of undergraduate courses which introduce students to the study of finds (Allason-Jones pers. comm), it is no wonder that young researchers are not choosing finds as a research area.

Why does Roman finds study (and perhaps finds study in general) have low status academically? Hutson (1998) discusses the constraints on academic discourse and the bias to certain 'acceptable' research topics. This is an inevitable product of the current academic system which produces and maintains hierarchies which become closely related to the prestige of both individuals and groups. He argues that those at the top of the power structure tend to perpetuate trends which have become dominant as this ensures the maintenance of their own prestige. Similarly, some research areas and approaches become unacceptable and tainted with undesirable connotations of lack of prestige. It seems clear that finds research is one of these areas. Many questionnaire respondents cited the current academic climate as being hostile to finds research. This has been viewed as a dichotomy between prestigious fieldwork projects and back-room specialist work, for example, by Blinkhorn and Cumberpatch (1998). Some respondents to the questionnaire (among those within or with exposure to the academic world) felt that the recent academic focus on, and privileging of, theoretical approaches to archaeology had resulted in finds research being marginalised or viewed as second-rate (*e.g.* Catherine Johns pers. comm.)

Archaeological theory and finds research

Artefact analysis has, of course, always entailed a theoretical positioning, more or less apparent, and it could be argued that the association of artefact studies with unfashionable theoretical perspectives has been a significant factor contributing to its present low status. Perhaps the most high-profile research which was heavily reliant on objects, which tried to address broad questions and develop an overarching narrative through the analysis of finds, was Gordon Childe's culture historical approach. This having been discredited, it may have put researchers off subsequent attempts to answer broad rather than specific, context-dependent questions through finds research and led to the view that finds research is really only reliable as a tool subservient to other areas of archaeological enquiry. Cumberpatch and Blinkhorn (1997) draw attention to the widespread perception that finds research is only useful to answer questions of chronology and provenance, or is quite simply descriptive (1997, 5). There are numerous other examples of this view of finds study; most particularly from site reports, but also from journals such as *Britannia*, which over the last 20 years has published few analytical or synthetic articles on finds.

Despite the long persistence of the view that finds research is merely an adjunct to other research areas (which is still fairly widespread, according to questionnaire respondents), finds research still formed a substantial proportion of the theses completed in British universities in the 1980s and 90s (Fig. 2.10). There is even a noticeable increase in completed theses on Roman finds in the early 90s. It could be argued that Roman archaeology was still catching up with trends in archaeological theory which had been initiated some time before, particularly the approaches of processual archaeology, while Roman finds provided datasets conducive to large-scale analysis using statistical and other 'hard science' techniques. Hilary Cool (pers. comm.) points out that in more recent years, the rejection of positivism by the post-processualists also entailed a move away from finds research because of the now unfashionable reliance on hard data. This suggestion is apparently borne out by a seeming decline in finds-based theses from the mid-90s (though this decline may also be connected to the recent retirement of several academics who were prepared to take on Ph. D students specialising in finds; Nina Crummy pers. comm.) A particularly interesting question is why the quantity of finds theses completed in the 1980s and early 90s did not translate into similar quantities of academics with finds specialisms holding posts in the universities. From the responses to the questionnaire, it might be suggested that this is partly because many of these researchers chose other archaeology posts, for example, in museums, which became available to them as a result of their acquisition of finds expertise. From a comparison of an academic's current research areas with the research topic of their thesis, though, it can be suggested that many of those researchers who did start off on finds-related theses (particularly pottery) have in their subsequent university careers moved away from specialist finds research into broader research areas. This may be because a finds-related research area was felt to be restrictive academically and not viewed as conducive to academic advancement. Finds may have been viewed as a useful starting point for an aspiring researcher – one who would make inroads into the backlog of unpublished material from sites and compile

useful catalogues and analyses – but one from which the researcher was encouraged to move on, leaving the catalogues to be used merely as reference works for identification of objects, rather than as the building blocks for further sustained analytical and interpretative publications.

In the very recent past there have been some significant changes in attitudes to material culture studies. The portable antiquities scheme has highlighted the shortage of finds researchers which now appears to be taken seriously. In the universities, and despite the widely touted reluctance of post-processualists to engage with 'real archaeology', Hodder and others have been influential in encouraging a more nuanced approach to the study of material culture and its 'meaning'. Contextual studies have considerable potential and wider interest in the potential of finds in this respect is growing. It could also be argued, though, that addressing broad themes through finds research is also important. It is only in this way that finds study will achieve academic parity with other sub-disciplines such as landscape and site studies. In addition, finds researchers should not feel discouraged from an engagement with empirical work. Other academic disciplines (which have been mired in the whole debate about theory-laden data for much longer than has archaeology), are now re-engaging with the possibilities of data-constrained analysis and 'real facts' (Sarah Cardwell pers. comm.). Similarly, at TRAC 2002 John Barrett observed that what was needed in Roman archaeology was more empirical work. Wylie (1996) has suggested that a reconciliation between empirical and post-processual approaches is possible. She notes that the privileging of theory over observation has led to just as much distortion as the previous positivist view (Wylie 1996, 325). She asserts that, though knowledge is to some extent a construct: 'it is constrained...by conditions that we confront as external realities' (1996, 314). This gives encouragement to finds researchers working from datasets, and it could be argued that an acknowledgement of the viability of empirical approaches is necessary to the long-term future of finds research.

Women's work?

Anecdotally, it is generally acknowledged that women tend to graduate towards finds study, and several respondents to the questionnaire cited the tendency for women to go into finds research as being something which has both constrained women's careers in archaeology and perpetuated the low status accorded to finds work. It is certainly apparent from a comparison of questionnaire results with Aitchison's profile of archaeological jobs (Aitchison 1999) that women are better represented in finds research than in other areas of archaeology. There have been a number of suggestions to account for this, usually split along a nature/culture axis; for example, that women are 'better' at or 'naturally' more interested in finds work, or on the other hand that social conditioning prompts men and women to fall into accustomed gender roles. According to Gero (1988, 35), for example, women tend to do the 'archaeological housework' of finds research and scientific analysis, as opposed to men carrying out broader and more prestigious theory and fieldwork studies. She suggests that men and women both follow clearly defined gender roles; for example, men active, women passive; or men outdoors, women indoors. Men tend to dominate the more élite research areas. They perpetuate the view that these fields of study are more valuable or worthwhile, despite the likelihood that analysis of existing data will actually tell us more about the past than new fieldwork (Gero 1988, 42–3). Similarly, Gilchrist (1991, 250) notes the possibility that women are steered away from fieldwork, or that they feel their choice is constrained to 'support' roles such as finds work and conservation. There may be general expectations about what women should or can do, both on the part of the women themselves and those around them. O'Sullivan (1991, 252) notes a possibly similar tendency with respect to women's choice of publication arena for their research. Women are apparently less likely than men to publish in prestigious journals, for example. Others would argue that women have deliberately carved out a niche for themselves in finds study, according to Sørensen, 'as a survival strategy in a hostile environment' (1998, 43), given the male dominance of 'élite' topics such as theoretical archaeology and fieldwork.

From the profile of finds researchers in Britain constructed from the questionnaire, finds work is certainly an area where women have found a niche; and all of these factors may be contributory. From the data collected, however, it is apparent that many men also work in finds research. At first, this appears to undercut Gero's analysis. When we investigate the different categories of finds that men and women study, however, the dominance of men in established 'élite' research areas is in fact maintained. Especially in the universities, men study coins and pottery to the exclusion of other categories. It has been suggested that men (always dominant in academia) have a tendency

to generally avoid areas related to culture, preferring to concentrate on themes such as political organisation. Cultural (domestic?) studies are viewed as a female sphere and regarded as being essentially of peripheral interest and value (Spencer-Wood 1999, 164). It could be argued, in similar vein, that men have chosen to study coins and pottery because the potential of these categories of finds in tackling broad economic and political questions, of a kind valued by the established hierarchy, is widely recognised. Coins and pottery studies are more 'mainstream' or academically respected. More prosaically, there are larger quantities of these items from sites than other finds, more is known about production and distribution systems, and there has been interest in them as viable subjects of archaeological research for much longer than is the case with other categories of archaeological finds. Comparatively, a greater number of theses are completed in these areas, and a high proportion of university employed finds researchers work on pottery or coins. Shanks and McGuire (1996, 82) suggest the following hierarchies in archaeological research: theorists > specialists, field director > lab assistant, synthesiser > faunal analyst; the following could also be suggested: theoretical archaeology > fieldwork > coins > pottery > small finds (Fig. 2.13).

Women have seemingly either been discouraged from choosing to study coins or pottery or have made their choices with less regard to the general perceived 'value' and profile of particular research topics. Hutson (1998) says that the bias to certain research areas and methodologies is directly driven by the power structures and hierarchies which exist in universities and suggests that choice of research topic is inevitably constrained by wider factors, such as likely reward in terms of career development, Research Assessment Exercise-driven assessment of research, *etc.* It could be argued that women do not view their choices in this way. Acker (1994) cites a study of gender differences in career choices which uncovered a dichotomy in career perception between men and women. Men viewed their career as a planned series of objectives to be achieved, leading to a particular outcome (in academe,

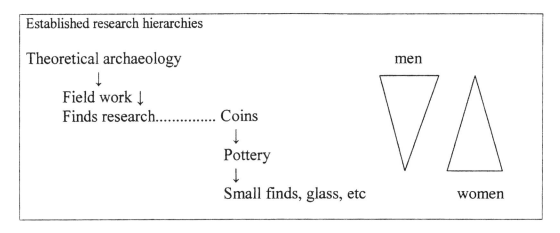

Fig. 2.13. Established research hierarchies in Roman archaeology in Britain

a chair?) while women regarded their career as an arena in which they could show their competence and dedication (Acker 1994, 129). It might be suggested from this that women are perhaps more likely to choose research areas which they are interested in or 'good at' and perhaps less likely to take an instrumental approach focusing on where their research area will get them in their career in the long term. It could also be suggested that women's approach to their lives as a whole, in which their career is only one element among many (many more women than men work part-time, and women still take a larger role in child-care in most relationships, for example) may contribute to the tendency for women to be less constrained than men by power relations within their discipline when they choose their specialist areas. Women may also be reluctant to validate and conform to dominant, masculine hierarchies of research topics and, prompted by feminist deconstructions of academic practice, may have been quick to observe that these hierarchies are in themselves rather arbitrary. (As Carol Van Driel Murray (pers. comm.) puts it: 'specialist research is regarded as limiting in a way house plans are not...')

It is interesting to note that finds studies are more central in other period divisions in archaeology, for example, in Anglo-Saxon archaeology. This is undoubtedly because for many years finds-rich cemeteries were the main source of evidence for this period, and this seems to have led to more find specialists, and hence some women, achieving greater career success in Anglo-Saxon archaeology (Sørensen and Diaz-Andreu 1998, 9). There is also thought to be a more even gender balance in medieval archaeology generally (O'Sullivan 1991, 252). If it is true that men tend to choose their research area with one eye on its prestige value, it might be expected that proportionately more men might undertake finds research in Anglo-Saxon archaeology than they do in Roman archaeology, and it would be interesting to test this out.

Whatever the causes of gender difference in research choices it seems clear that the low status of finds research continues to affect those who choose finds as a research area, whether men or women, and helps to perpetuate women's position on the margins of academic archaeology.

The future of finds research

From the preceding analysis, it can be suggested that the general state of finds research in Roman archaeology is indeed a cause for concern. It appears that fewer and fewer people are choosing a career in finds research, and that finds studies are at the margins of academic archaeology. The principal underlying problem appears to be widespread and negative perceptions of the usefulness and value of finds research.

It can be suggested that these views have been influenced a good deal by the history of the development of the discipline and the changing relationship between finds study and archaeological theory. A rehabilitation of empirical approaches in archaeological research, together with the current trends towards a more in-depth consideration of the 'meaning' of material culture, can only be beneficial to the future of finds research.

It can also be suggested that a complex relationship exists between the existence of academic hierarchies in research fields, and the choice of research area which academics and researchers individually make; there appear to be significant gender differences in such choices. To move forward it is necessary to critically re-evaluate both finds research itself and academic hierarchies which inhibit rather than foster academic enquiry. A consideration of these questions will hopefully provide some impetus for a more widespread change in attitude in the future which will help rather than hinder finds research in achieving its potential and in continuing to make an essential contribution to the archaeology of the Roman period.

Bibliography

Acker, S. (1994) *Gendered Education: sociological reflections on women, teaching and feminism*. Buckingham and Philadelphia, Open University Press.

Aitchison, K. (1999*) Profiling the Profession: a survey of archaeological jobs in the UK*. London, Council for British Archaeology.

Ault, B. and Nevett, L. (1999) Digging houses: archaeologies of Classical Greek and Hellenistic domestic assemblages. In P. Allison (ed.) *The Archaeology of Household Activities and Related Articles*, 43–56. London and New York, Routledge.

Blinkhorn, P. and Cumberpatch, C. (1998) The interpretation of artefacts and the tyranny of the field archaeologist. *Assemblage* 4, http:\\ww.shef.ac.uk/assem/4/4bln_cmb.html. Sheffield, University of Sheffield.

Chitty, G. (1999) Training in professional archaeology: a preliminary review, commissioned by English Heritage on behalf of the archaeology training forum. Council for British archaeology web site, *http:\\www.britarch.ac.uk/training/survey.html* as accessed on 29/05/02.

Cooper, N. (2000) Rubbish counts: quantifying portable material culture. In S Pearce (ed.) *Researching Material Culture*, 75–86. Leicester; School of Archaeological Studies, University of Leicester.

Cumberpatch, C. and Blinkhorn, P. (1997) Not so much a pot more a way of life: recent approaches to artefact studies. *Oxbow Monograph* 83. Oxford, Oxbow.

Gero, J. (1988) Gender bias in archaeology: here, then and now. In S. Rosser (ed.) *Feminism within the Science and Health Care Professions: overcoming resistance*, 33–43. Oxford and New York, Pergamon Press.

Gilchrist, R. (1991) Men and women in archaeology: issues of employment and education. *The Field Archaeologist* 14, 250–51.

Hutson, S. (1998) Strategies for the reproduction of prestige in archaeological discourse. *Assemblage* 4, http:\\ww.shef.ac.uk/assem/4/4hutson.html. Sheffield, University of Sheffield.

O'Sullivan, D. (1991) Mapping women's place in contemporary archaeology. *The Field Archaeologist* 14, 251–3.

Shanks, M. and McGuire, R. (1996) The craft of archaeology. *American Antiquity* 61, 75–88.

Sørensen, M. (1998) Rescue and recovery: on historiographies of female archaeology. In M. Diaz-Andreu & M. Sørensen eds. *Excavating Women: a history of women in European archaeology*, 31–60. London/New York, Routledge.

Sørensen, M. and Diaz-Andreu, M. (eds.) (1998) *Excavating Women: a history of women in European archaeology*, 31–60. London/New York, Routledge.

Spencer-Wood, S. (1999) The world their household:changing meanings of the domestic sphere in the 19th century. In P. Allison (ed.) *The Archaeology of Household Activities and Related Articles*, 162–89. London/New York, Routledge.

Wylie, A. (1996) The constitution of archaeological evidence: gender politics and science. In P. Galison and D. Stump (eds.) *The Disunity of Science*, 311–46. Stanford, Stanford University Press.

3   The Last Chance

Catherine Johns

The last forty years or so have seen an ever-deepening gulf developing in British archaeology between those who initiate and conduct excavation and other forms of fieldwork and those who specialise in the study of so-called 'small finds'. It used to be axiomatic that active research on artefacts was a central feature of the discipline of archaeology, but a specialised knowledge of portable objects has gradually been sidelined and is now evidently perceived in many quarters as a peripheral, and indeed optional, archaeological skill. My main thesis in this short paper is that archaeology cannot advance in a rational, balanced and productive manner without the full re-integration of finds research into our study of past societies.

Background

The historical background is directly relevant to the changing picture of archaeological research. The historiographical approach invariably helps us to understand the current position.

Though many aspects of archaeology, especially the study of the classical world, had long figured in university teaching, the subject as an integrated discipline, including the practical techniques of excavation, was not taught to British undergraduates until after the Second World War. Those who taught it in the 1950s and early 1960s had grown up in a self-taught tradition where fieldwork and excavation, historical and language expertise, and the connoisseurship required of an artefact specialist were all expected of anyone who practised archaeology.

I make no apology for the word *connoisseurship*. It is usually associated with art history and, because it sounds totally unscientific and rather precious, is generally frowned upon within archaeological circles. It is, nevertheless, a convenient term that conveys an intricate combination of intellectual, academic knowledge, research, practical experience, and highly developed visual and tactile memory. Together, these often enable a person to identify and classify an object with a speed and accuracy that can appear mystifying and almost arbitrary to an onlooker. Some are therefore tempted to dismiss connoisseurship as an intuitive 'knack' that is easy and instinctive for those who are born with it and requires no cerebral input. It is nothing of the sort. A degree of innate aptitude is certainly required, but so are rational analytical and deductive processes that precisely parallel those employed

in all other forms of archaeological research. Nina Crummy examines and explains the processes involved in her paper in this volume (p. 60).

Excavators during the early and mid-twentieth century generally assessed, and often wrote up, most of their own finds, so that there was a seamless, integrated approach to the interpretation of a site. Small finds were not immediately set aside to go off to a specialist but were continually evaluated as the work advanced, and they therefore influenced the progress and design of the excavation. There were, indeed, scholars who were known primarily for their expertise in certain aspects of material culture, such as Felix Oswald and T. D. Pryce, the undisputed authorities on samian pottery (Oswald and Pryce 1920), but the director of any excavation was usually quite knowledgeable about all the finds and, by the same token, the 'finds specialists' were generally excavators in their own right. A scholar such as Eric Birley might write a specialist report within a colleague's excavation report (*e.g.* 'The Mortarium Stamps' in Kenyon 1948), but that would not define him as 'just' a finds specialist. While it would be futile to pretend that the published results of this, as we should call it, multi-skilled approach, were necessarily any better than more recent work, they were often a great deal more coherent and plausible (perhaps sometimes dangerously and misleadingly so, in the hands of such supremely self-confident individuals as Mortimer Wheeler).

During the 1950s, then, students were taught that in order to be an archaeologist it was necessary to command a very wide range of scholarly knowledge and practical technique. For the Roman period, this would include the relevant history and language, a working knowledge of all the classes of structure and artefact that might be encountered and the intricacies of such esoteric matters as the Roman Army, as well as the techniques of surveying and digging, and of recording sites and objects by photography and drawing. This remains a noble ideal, but it eventually became impossible for any one individual, however brilliant, to command all the required skills to an equally advanced level. The whole subject of archaeology expanded out of all recognition in the second half of the twentieth century.

There were several aspects of that growth. The development of much more demanding excavation methods was one, in response to theoretical approaches which demanded fuller and more accurately recorded data. Many respected excavators of Roman sites in the mid-twentieth century would, without the slightest twinge of conscience, totally ignore post-Roman finds, and would unhesitatingly discard, unrecorded, material such as animal-bone. Such conduct was increasingly, and quite rightly, regarded as unacceptable. Environmental evidence and the history of a site before and after the principal period which happened to interest the excavator had to be taken into account. These more refined, holistic and meticulous excavating and recording methods produced far more potential information but they changed the role of the site director, who could no longer expect to have a detailed knowledge of every single aspect of the work.

The eagerness to examine all possible aspects of the evidence by all possible means encouraged the increasing involvement of the natural sciences in both fieldwork and finds analysis, a development that brought about major advances in understanding. It also meant that students with liberal arts backgrounds could not hope to master all the necessary skills. The concept of the specialist adviser who was not an archaeologist or historian at all, but whose knowledge and methods could shed light on important aspects of ancient society and the ancient environment, encouraged the concept of detached specialists around the outskirts of archaeology.

At the same time as each excavation was becoming more complicated, with larger quantities of finds and very elaborate systems of recording, there was also an enormous increase in the actual number of excavations, especially urban rescue sites. This branch of work arose initially from the opportunities provided by the clearing and redevelopment of Second World War bomb-sites, and evolved further with the extensive urban building programmes of the 1960s. Such sites are, almost by definition, complex, multi-period deposits rich in both structural remains and small finds. The sheer volume of material coming to light could not be processed without some degree of specialisation.

Furthermore, there was greater depth as well as greater breadth in the discipline. Topics that had been studied for many generations, like Romano-British pottery, turned out to have undreamed-of new possibilities. At the Oxford Roman Pottery conference of 1972 the then senior figures in Romano-British pottery studies quite clearly believed that there was no need for any more research on Romano-British pottery because it had all been 'done'. All that was necessary was to set out what was known in a convenient way for newcomers to study and learn it. This was about the point at which a whole range of new approaches, from thin-section analysis to detailed quantification and the application of statistical methods, made a younger generation of pottery specialists aware of the immense untapped potential in the subject. Rather than seeing the final wrapping-up of that field of study, the early 1970s saw a new beginning. The whole landscape changed, and some specialisms became so demanding in themselves that they left the practitioner little or no time to be a conventional generalist. A degree of diffusion and dispersal in archaeological research thus became unavoidable. We were entering the familiar era of excavation reports that have, not a single name, nor even a modest half-dozen, but as many as fifty contributors' names on the title page (*e.g.* Jackson and Potter 1996).

The nature of finds research and publication

It is one thing to acknowledge that the complexity of our discipline now demands the existence of many separate specialisms within and around it, but it is another matter entirely to put about the notion that certain specialisms should be relegated to a low stratum within an arbitrary hierarchy of academic respectability. The palaeozoologist or the metallurgist is regarded with the respect he or she deserves, as a person with highly developed knowledge, who can contribute something unique and enlightening to archaeological interpretation. How has it come about that the expert on 'small finds' and the skilled museum curator are regarded as peripheral, no more than the humble handmaidens of those who frame the newest archaeological theories and conduct the excavations and other fieldwork designed to validate them?

Work on finds is extremely labour-intensive and the more we learn, the more complex it becomes. Once a person has acquired some degree of expertise, it is easy to become locked into an endless round of writing finds reports for volumes that will be published under the name of the site director, with 'contributions by…' on the title page. There is always plenty of work, albeit ill-paid, for the finds specialist, but there is comparatively little opportunity for him or her to write independent general books or major articles that will raise their profile in the academic world. Books of synthesis and theoretical articles in learned journals still carry far more weight in the eyes of the world than any number of contributions to excavation reports, however detailed and scholarly the latter may be. This is the process whereby the finds specialist is, almost unconsciously, assigned a lower ranking in the archaeological hierarchy than the excavator who initiates and co-ordinates fieldwork.

Many good finds specialists happen to be female (partly owing to a genuine tendency for women to enjoy detailed work more than men, and to be better at it), and it is perhaps not completely paranoid to believe that this circumstance has subtly supported the perception that artefact study is a minor and second-class intuitive talent rather than a hard-won intellectual discipline. This aspect of the subject is more fully addressed by Ellen Swift in this volume (pp. 20, 23, 25–26). Archaeologists who have a particular interest in portable objects also tend to gravitate towards museum work rather than the universities, and museum work outside the national museums was (and still is) very poorly paid. If you are willing to work for low wages, the world thinks you must be stupid. Many who were initially drawn to specialised areas of research on material culture felt that their careers would benefit from renouncing, or at any rate, sidelining, those interests and concentrating on other aspects of archaeological endeavour.

Over the last twenty years or so, the increasing emphasis on theoretical approaches (many of them rather tired hand-me-downs from anthropology and other social studies), and on landscape archaeology and field survey work, has marginalised the role of artefact studies even more, since portable objects feature far less prominently in these areas of work than they do in conventional excavation. Indeed, in some cases they may be totally ignored, just as they can be when using most types of document-based historical methodology. All these approaches have their own importance and validity, of course, but their high profiles as fashionable intellectual positions have helped to keep intensive and sharply focused finds research in its artificially secondary and subordinate position.

Interestingly, these attitudes do not appear to be current on the Continent. Major scholars whose contributions are universally recognised, such as Ernst Künzl and François Baratte, have emerged from the museum sector, and have built their deservedly outstanding reputations on work that has centred on various aspects of material culture. It would appear that connoisseurship and art-historical skills are still respected within provincial Roman archaeology in other countries, not only in Europe but also in the United States.

The Treasure Act (1996) and the Portable Antiquities Scheme

Given the background briefly surveyed above, what of the present and the future? The effects of the new Treasure Act (1996) and the voluntary Portable Antiquities Scheme (PAS) (most conveniently summarised on the website *http://www.finds.org.uk*) have already placed intense new pressures on museums and their staff. This is a situation that has evidently not yet made a major impact on the university sector, but it needs to be scrutinised and taken fully into account by all who teach archaeology. Just as the urban development of the 1960s provided new opportunities and posed new problems for archaeologists, the heritage policies of the 1990s and the present will do likewise.

As the PAS began to function at the end of the 1990s, the British Museum started to run teaching sessions in artefact identification for newly appointed Finds Liaison Officers and for the Society of Museum Archaeologists. With the upsurge in the reporting of amateur finds resulting from the operation of the new Treasure Act and the PAS, it quickly became painfully clear that the younger generation of trained and intelligent archaeologists, with good degrees and a sound understanding of the nature of evidence and theoretical issues, frequently knew less about the dating

of a given Roman fibula type, for example, than the average metal-detectorist equipped with well-worn copies of the works of that diligent and dedicated amateur, the late Richard Hattatt (Hattatt 1982, 1985, 1987 and 1989). This is not a criticism of the intelligence and abilities of either students or teachers. It simply reflects the choices made by both, whereby serious study of objects was accorded a lower academic status than other aspects of archaeological research, was regarded as relatively unimportant and consequently neglected.

The now traditional mutual suspicion between detectorists and archaeologists is due in no small part to the supercilious attitude to small finds that has been adopted by many university archaeologists in the last twenty-five years or so. Detectorists were often unable to acquire the information they sought from local museums because many of those initially, and very unwisely, operated a deliberate policy of ignoring metal-detector finds. Finders who had the courage to approach University archaeology departments were sometimes snubbed and given the impression not only that metal-detecting ought to be classified as a borderline criminal activity, even when carried out on unscheduled land and with the landowner's full permission (*i.e.* legally), but also that small finds were somehow beneath the notice of real archaeologists. This was not helpful and we are still living with the consequences. The loathing felt by some detectorists for the whole profession of archaeology may well be rooted in some long-ago humiliation when they were treated with arrogant contempt by a professional archaeologist who made it very clear that their collection of scruffy little objects was of no significance in the rarefied intellectual pursuit of interpreting the past. That dismissive response on the part of some archaeologists may well have had its roots in their own sketchy knowledge of artefact identification.

A lack of interest in the basic identification of ancient objects on the part of archaeologists is damaging both for the public image of archaeology and for the efforts that are being made to improve the relationship between professional archaeologists and amateur finders, whether users of metal-detectors or not. We all know that there is a great deal more to archaeology than being able to date a sherd or identify a coin quickly, but it is usually through that process that amateur enthusiasts of all ages are first drawn to archaeology. Initially their respect for the professional will be directly related to his or her ability to discourse intelligently on a small find; not necessarily instantly to date and identify it with complete precision, but rather to explain what is being looked for and how the evidence is gathered and evaluated. In short, the professional is expected to take the matter seriously. As novices learn more they will begin to appreciate the wider picture and will start to see how individual objects fit into that picture. The first spark of interest, however, is most unlikely to be ignited through reading or hearing a lively debate on systems theory or processualism and post-processualism; it arises in most cases from contact with ancient objects and the realisation that it is possible to identify many of them and to know when, how and where they were made and used by our ancestors. We should actively seek ways of engaging and retaining the interest and support of the public for archaeology – on a purely practical level, public engagement is vital for funding purposes – and although impressive advances have been made in educating people in the aims, methods and processes of archaeology, their primary interest is still rooted in the individual objects, the personal possessions of people who lived in the past.

The Finds Liaison Officers employed within the PAS have performed brilliantly in this respect and have helped to raise the profile of archaeology amongst the general public in a very positive manner, but a much wider network of people with good artefact skills is still required so that amateur fieldwalking and metal-detector finds may be properly recorded and fully taken into account in general archaeological research.

The importance of re-integration

There are major problems for the future. There is a theoretical or ideological dimension and a practical one, the first being concerned with the scholarly imperative to re-integrate finds research more closely into archaeology and accord it the status it deserves, and the second addressing the practical issues of how that should be done. The second aspect leads to questions about museums and the relationship between them and the universities.

Theoretical issues

It is in the nature of academic research that it should progress unevenly on different fronts; the ebb and flow of fashion is endemic in academia just as it is in other areas of life. When certain research topics become trendy, others become passé and fall out of favour. As the years and decades roll by the emphasis will shift again. It appears that the importance of artefacts actually *is* starting to be recognised again and the conference that gave rise to this publication is one of the indicators of that fact, but the intellectual respectability of connoisseurship must be conceded and there is as yet no sign that this is the case. Archaeologists have long been desperately anxious to be perceived as scientists or, at least, social scientists, and have been terrified of being mistaken for art-historians, apparently envisaged as effete, limp-wristed persons wearing spotted bow-ties.

Showing an interest in small finds seems at present to be held academically reputable only if the artefact research is secondary evidence brought in to support independently-generated theoretical perspectives. Unfortunately, the resulting conclusions will be flawed if the object evidence presented is based on superficial or incomplete knowledge. It is not enough to observe that something about a given

type of object (for example, its function, date or distribution) seems to support an audacious new interpretation of some burning issue of social status or ethnic predilections. It is also necessary to have a sufficiently comprehensive understanding to be perfectly certain that there is nothing about that or another contemporary type of artefact or, indeed, the *absence* of another class of artefact, that might undermine the hypothesis. A reliable and extensive working knowledge of portable objects should therefore be an archaeological *sine qua non*, like knowing the historical framework for historical periods, and should form one of the foundations upon which theoretical speculations are to be constructed. The understanding of artefacts is a *primary* requirement for the intelligent development of theoretical approaches, not a bolt-on optional extra picked up to illustrate a full-blown theory.

Deep and detailed familiarity with the everyday portable objects of a period in itself promotes and inspires lines of research and speculation that would not even arise when the subject is approached from another angle and can thereby cast new light on many aspects of the ancient society concerned. Portable objects, after all, happen to constitute a very large part of our available evidence for the interpretation of past societies. Marginalising them is not likely to improve our understanding. As well as restoring a balance in the general progress of research, more work on artefact studies would make better and fuller use of the full range of evidence.

Practical issues

The best way in which students can effectively be taught to integrate the knowledge of portable artefacts into their archaeology courses is by closer co-operation between university archaeology departments and the larger (national, regional and university) museums. Extensive and representative collections of objects are required and very few university teaching collections, where they exist at all, can provide the necessary range of material. Excavation experience and the study of specific excavation archives, while essential, cannot introduce the chronological and typological variety represented in an extensive and long-established museum collection. The will for close liaison between university teachers in archaeology and museum curators has often been lacking in the past, but appropriate mechanisms can still be developed. However, while a detailed knowledge of artefacts is regarded as some kind of second-class and discretionary skill, it will not happen.

It will also not happen if the present serious threats to museums remain uncontested and are allowed to proceed to their obvious conclusion. For far too long in this country museum archaeologists, precisely because of their primary concern with portable objects, have been seen as not quite real academics. This view is now increasingly being peddled by modish government policies and by theoretical approaches that relegate museums firmly to the leisure and entertainment sector, somewhere between a colourful shopping mall and a useful local crèche facility. The idea that museums might be serious educational resources and centres of higher learning and independent pure research is anathema in some quarters; to many powerful individuals and lobbies such concepts are 'élitist' and therefore must be avoided at all costs.

Add to this the vociferous demands from all quarters, international, national and local, for restitution and decentralisation of museum artefacts and collections and the older, established museums are under a very serious threat indeed. The breaking down of larger collections implicit in the demands of the restitution lobbies, and the loss of expertise that would inevitably follow would mean that a chain of knowledge painstakingly forged over the last two hundred years and more would be broken and that future generations of archaeologists would be deprived of the cumulative expertise of many generations of dedicated scholars. In the matter of artefact studies, the principal repository of data and information, and the major repository of the necessary human skills, namely the larger and older museums, are now in real danger of being seriously undermined as academic institutions by a combination of official government policy and ignorant fashionable opinion that promotes a grotesque trivialisation of the place of museums in society. I have examined this issue more fully elsewhere (Johns 2002), and shall not repeat myself here. Closer co-operation between universities and major museums would be mutually beneficial, on the one hand enriching the teaching of archaeology and on the other perhaps helping to avert the current decline in the position of museums by demonstrating and emphasising their valuable role in higher education.

If it is conceded that artefact research needs to be consciously and deliberately integrated back into the mainstream of archaeological endeavour and accorded its full value as an advanced area of scholarly research, then it should feature much more prominently in university archaeology courses at undergraduate level. It must be recognised for the very complex skill that it is.

There are many ways in which this could be achieved. Museum collections are, and always have been, available for study by all scholars, students and seriously interested laypersons, not only by the curators who care for them. This is their *raison d'être*. Students studying archaeology are usually encouraged to visit the public galleries of museums and are sometimes even accompanied by their teachers on such visits, but far too little use is made of behind-the-scenes sessions in which small groups of undergraduates are shown specific classes of material from the study ('reserve') collections, given the opportunity of examining and handling the objects, and hearing them fully described and explained by the relevant curator.

Museum curators are not generally invited to contribute even an occasional lecture on material culture to courses on British archaeology, yet they are willing and able to do so. This is presumably because any focused study of artefacts is thought to be an optional rather than a core element in the acquisition of archaeological skills. It is also, perhaps, forgotten by some University archaeologists that curators, in addition to researching the material in their collections and publishing the results, are in the business of providing information on a daily basis about those collections and their significance to enquirers representing all levels of interest and knowledge, from primary-school children to scholars of international standing. They are well able to communicate effectively with undergraduates.

While one hopes that there will always be some archaeology students who will choose to write their dissertations and theses on subjects that centre on portable objects, we should be even more concerned about the others, those whose only study of the small, everyday possessions of antiquity takes place during their basic training as undergraduates. All undergraduates who hope to become archaeologists should have to write at least some essays on themes connected with portable objects, should spend time examining them and should be given some formal training and practice in drawing them. Instruction in drawing is important, not only because it is a useful skill, but because it teaches the kind of minute visual examination that needs to become second nature when handling artefacts.

This approach would not mean that every person who has studied archaeology to first-degree level should or could become an expert in all, or even any, of the now highly specialised and complex ranges of knowledge commanded by today's pottery specialists, numismatists, metalwork experts and others. What it does mean is that by acquiring a better general working knowledge of these areas by the time they obtain a first degree, their research choices and eventual career choices will be extended and their ability to communicate and collaborate with specialists in the future will be greatly enhanced. Since we can no longer command all the specialist areas that benefit archaeological research, it becomes ever more vital that we know enough about them to be able to communicate productively and intelligently with our colleagues. Those whose interests and abilities do lead them specifically towards artefact research will, of course, also have a sounder start.

A return to closer liaison between academic curators in the old-established museums and university teachers is desperately needed if more emphasis is to be placed on artefact research but, if the situation is ignored for much longer, the opportunity may be lost. Experienced curators, and even the museum collections themselves, may no longer be available. The future is bleak if attitudes are not changed, and changed quickly. Archaeology will naturally continue to advance on many fronts, though it will be held back increasingly on others as the museum sector withers and dies. At some point in the future, if humankind continues to be interested in its past, a lot of wheels will have to be reinvented. It would be much better if we could avert that necessity at this point by addressing the need to take the study of portable objects more seriously and by making the effort to re-integrate this branch of archaeological learning fully into the discipline as a whole.

Acknowledgements

I am most grateful to the friends and colleagues who have been kind enough to read and comment upon this paper; namely, Don Bailey, Ralph Jackson, Nina Crummy, Richard Hobbs, J. D. Hill and Gill Varndell.

Bibliography

Hattatt, R. (1982) *Ancient and Romano-British Brooches.* Sherborne.

Hattatt, R. (1985) *Iron Age and Roman Brooches.* Oxford.

Hattatt, R. (1987) *Brooches of Antiquity.* Oxford.

Hattatt, R. (1989) *Ancient Brooches and other Artefacts.* Oxford.

Jackson, R. P. J. and Potter, T. W. (1996) *Excavations at Stonea, Cambridgeshire, 1980–85.* London.

Johns, C. (2002) Centralization or dispersal? Archaeological collections in museums. In M. Aldhouse-Green and P. Webster (eds) *Artefacts and Archaeology: aspects of the Celtic and Roman World,* 257–67. Cardiff.

Kenyon, K. M. (1948) *Excavations at the Jewry Wall Site, Leicester.* Oxford.

Oswald, F. and Pryce, T. D. (1920) *An introduction to the study of Terra Sigillata.* London.

4   Promoting the Study of Finds in Roman Britain: Democracy, Integration and Dissemination. Practice and Methodologies for the Future

Nicholas J. Cooper

Introduction

This paper aims to bring current approaches used by the 'finds community' to the attention of archaeologists and others interested in material culture. It develops ideas and themes outlined in an earlier discussion of the potential for the quantified analysis of artefacts to enrich the study of past communities (Cooper 2000a). The intention here is to concentrate initially on exploring ways in which the importance of studying finds can be promoted through education, community archaeology and regional research frameworks, in order to benefit archaeology more generally before looking at the development of approaches more specifically.

Much of what follows is derived from a personal viewpoint, which stems from the fact that, like many others, although I would be considered a 'finds person', my title of 'Finds Officer' within a contracting field unit in a university, hides a rather more varied job description. As Ellen Swift's survey indicates (this volume), the finds community comprises people from a variety of backgrounds, whose 'careers' (always a term to be applied loosely) have often evolved in a very haphazard way; lurching from contract to contract, and picking up 'just-in-case' skills along the way. Fortunately, I have evolved into one of those hybrids who has the opportunity both to study excavated finds on a day to day basis and to teach students about them; be they degree level, postgraduate or lifelong learners. One other hat that I have worn recently has been to co-ordinate the East Midlands Archaeological Research Framework sponsored by English Heritage and supported by the region's local authorities, independent archaeologists and contracting units.

All these experiences have encouraged me to believe that we have much to be positive about in archaeology but that institutional communication barriers often get in the way of efforts to push the whole edifice forward. Conflicting interests abound and we seem to lose sight of what archaeology is about and why we chose it as a career in the first place, rather than getting a job that actually paid us more than the average national wage (Aitchison and Edwards 2003, xii), as any 'professional' would expect. Lest we forget, the simple reason was that we were passionate about working out what happened in the past. The return to this simple pleasure was a sentiment I heard recently in talks given by David Jennings of Oxford Archaeology about Framework Archaeology's Terminal 5 Project at Heathrow. David also stressed the desire to turn our perception of the archaeological resource on its head and think of it as infinite rather than finite. At first such sentiments appear glib or facile even, until their simple truth is confirmed if you talk to any member of the public, who thinks 'how wonderful it must be to be an archaeologist' and would be surprised to hear us complaining. Yet every 'professional' finds conference discussion session (including this one too), after starting out positively, eventually devolves into a demoralising and de-motivating moan about the poor state of the profession. Surely it is possible for us to start doing some of that joined up thinking that everybody talks about these days?

In this vein I would like to explore three interlocking areas in which the study of finds could be promoted: first, the teaching of 'finds' in universities and more broadly within lifelong learning and the profession itself; second, the promotion of 'community archaeology' and third, the pivotal role of regional research frameworks. In all three areas it is essential that a bottom up approach is taken, and the study of finds, for so long marginalised, could take on a central role. Throughout discussions in the development of research frameworks, two fundamental problems continually emerge: there is either not enough primary data or not enough synthesis of the mountain that we already have. Promotion of the three areas above could help to solve these problems. As ever, the solution can only begin with education.

Teaching finds in university, lifelong learning and continual professional development

As Nina Crummy has demonstrated in her paper (this volume), studying finds is really very straightforward and is an easy way to engage students of all ages. Whether you are teaching school children, undergraduates, postgraduates or adults, you are basically starting from the same place and assuring them that they already have the skills they need; their eyes and, in the case of pottery, their fingertips; all the rest is written in books or comes with experience.

Unfortunately, the opportunity for detailed hands-on

study of pottery and small finds is rarely available to undergraduates except sometimes at third year level or as dissertation topics. One reason for this is that often the academic members of staff don't have the necessary experience or interest in artefacts, having bypassed the finds shed earlier in their careers. However, while a good number of departments have contracting field units attached to them, with the necessary expertise only a sherd's throw away, it is apparent that their potential contribution to teaching is not being exploited as fully as it might. I'm not arguing for a return to the learning of brooch typologies 'by rote'; such things can only be learnt by applying them to real material on a daily basis and there is no doubt that students do much more interesting things in their degrees now than twenty years ago. The problem is that so much of their undergraduate experience is synthetic and far removed from primary data. In my experience, there is a good chance that many will have completed a degree without ever consulting an excavation report.

There is a clear need to engage students in artefact study much earlier on in their degrees not only to familiarise them with the use of primary data generally, but also so that they can make informed choices at dissertation, masters and doctoral thesis level about research topics involving such data. There are a number of specific masters courses in Archaeological Practice available, for example at Leicester and Birmingham, which specifically include options in post-excavation analysis of finds. However, unless students have had some initial experience of such work it is unlikely that they will think of applying for such courses and potentially good quality practitioners could be lost to the profession.

The potential for training in finds extends to lifelong learning as well, on both accredited courses such as higher education certificate courses (as at Leicester) and non-accredited courses run by adult education colleges and the WEA (Workers Educational Association), and many students have passed through such courses and taken up degrees, masters courses and even doctorates studying ceramics. Others have used these skills to support their own independent fieldwork, which has direct relevance to the promotion of 'Community Archaeology' and will be explored below. The last important strand is the need for more 'on the job' training opportunities for those already in the profession but who cannot attend full-time campus based MA courses, mainly because of the lack of funding opportunities. Whilst there are now more people in the profession than ever before, there is still very little opportunity for career advancement, the attainment of 'professional' qualifications or the development of specialisms. The development of distance learning MAs and degree courses is already providing one avenue, but these are less suitable for finds training where hands-on experience is required. The creation of the Archaeological Training Forum (ATF) by the Institute of Field Archaeology and the development of NOS (National Occupational Standards) in Archaeology points to the way ahead on this

issue generally (http://www.archaeologists.net/training.html), but the finds sector has its own particular problems, linked to the difficulties of curating knowledge and passing on skills to the next generation.

The structure of local authority archaeology units, which developed during the 1970s and usually had strong links to the respective museum service, formed a solid foundation for the development and curation of specialist knowledge at the county level particularly with regard to pottery, assemblages of which have local and regional character. The disintegration of this structure has caused a discontinuity in skills and loss of knowledge, often held in the heads of specialists who may no longer practise full-time. So, while there are many more organisations (776) practicing archaeology and more actual professional archaeologists (5712) (Aitchison and Edwards 2003, 21), there has been no increase in the number of specialists (and certainly no dramatic increase in the membership of the specialist study groups). Many organisations do not employ finds specialists and subcontract work to a small number of freelancers whilst a relatively small number of the larger contracting units employ several specialists, who may have to familiarise themselves with material from all over the country. The pooling of knowledge in specialist consultancies or large contracting units is no bad thing as long as there is a mechanism for training up replacement staff and passing on that head-bound knowledge. The appointment of the Roman pottery traineeship at the MacDonald Institute at Cambridge in 2003, funded by English-Heritage, could hopefully set a crucial precedent for future initiatives.

Regression analysis is older than punk rock, shock! Something should be done!

The lack of finds teaching in universities is matched by an equally low regard for finds research within academic departments. To gauge the perception of work on Roman finds within the academic world we would do well to remind ourselves that Fulford and Hodder's classic regression analysis of Oxfordshire pottery (1974), now thirty years old, and the distribution of *Sestius* stamped amphorae (Manacorda 1978; Lyding Will 1979), are the only examples of work on pottery that you will find in a first year undergraduate text book such as Renfrew and Bahn's *Archaeology: Theories, Methods and Practice* (2000, 370 and 367 respectively). Elsewhere, we have to be grateful to Martin Millett for bringing the work of other such *alumni* of the finds community as Chris Going (1987) to the attention of second and third year students in his *Romanization of Britain* (1990, 125 and 164). Sadly, other pieces of ground-breaking research, such as Chris's 'Economic Long Waves' paper (1992), appear to have been completely ignored by the academic world.

There is light at the end of the tunnel, however, which the 'finds community' should try to exploit. The study of material culture in the broad sense is becoming a major research strand within a number of academic departments and indeed, the volume in which ideas developed within this present paper initially appeared (Pearce 2000), contributed to the last Research Assessment Exercise (RAE) submission from Leicester, which demonstrates the commitment of that department to this area of research. The study of portable material culture more specifically, *could* and *should* be making a bigger contribution to this area. To a large extent it is our responsibility to get more of our work into the mainstream; this means making the information more digestible for a non-finds audience in order to get it published in the major national and international peer reviewed journals. This will allow our work to get the academic recognition that it merits and access to potential funding for future research. An important start has been made to this process with the research agenda volume *Britons and Romans* (James and Millett 2001), which includes papers on both pottery and small finds (Evans 2001; Allason-Jones 2001). Other important papers on the potential of new approaches have also hit the mainstream and include Steve Willis' work on samian ware (1998; 2005) and Hilary Cool and Mike Baxter's application of correspondence analysis to finds assemblages (1999; 2002). Hopefully the present volume will act as an important foundation statement and flag up the significance of this area of research. It is vitally important that we demonstrate how finds analysis is relevant to exploring the big questions which mainstream archaeology is interested in. Such questions do not come much bigger than assessing the relationship between an indigenous population and its conquerors and whether you prefer to call it Romanization or Creolization (Webster 2001), there is no doubt that finds data are crucial to addressing the issue. The second half of this paper will explore some very simple ways in which the analysis of quantified finds data can reveal patterns relevant to this research question.

The promotion of community archaeology

While there is a clear need to get ourselves noticed in the academic mainstream there is an equally important obligation for us to demystify the subject to the public and to empower them to study *their own* heritage. The role of the public in archaeology is always a subject of debate as exemplified by the mountain of web correspondence relating to *Time Team*'s 'Big Dig' in June 2003. However, we cannot ignore the fact that public interest in archaeology has never been higher than today with programmes like *Time Team* and *Meet the Ancestors* regularly topping three million viewers. This is not simply a media bubble which is about to burst, it taps into a fundamental interest the public has in its past, the same interest that got us into

the profession. We are dismissing an enormous resource which wants to be involved and with simple training and opportunity *could* be. With this in mind we need to take advantage of the fact that 'heritage' issues are also higher on the agenda of public policy than ever before as the government attempts to fulfil its commitment to social inclusion and sustainability. Government-sponsored documents such as *Power of Place* (English Heritage 2000, London, Recommendations 11 and 14) and *The Historic Environment: a Force for our Future* (DCMS 2001, London, 25–31 and 41–2) both demonstrate a commitment to public involvement (though with no specific mention of the idea of 'community archaeology' it might be noted) and the importance of finds and research. In tangible terms this means access to funding through the Heritage Lottery Fund in particular. The most visible sign of this commitment has been the extension of the Portable Antiquities Scheme nationwide. While currently riding the crest of a media wave with a high profile BBC series '*Hidden Treasures*' and an accompanying British Museum exhibition, the scheme is proving a very effective vehicle for bringing the public on side whilst immeasurably enhancing the baseline data resource particularly for metal finds.

Whilst such high profile schemes should be applauded, I would like to focus on the example of the community archaeology scheme in Leicestershire, which has been quietly demonstrating for over 25 years that involving the public in discovering their own heritage can transform our knowledge of a county's archaeology. Far-sightedly, in 1976, one of the few integrated countywide museum services in the country appointed an archaeological survey officer whose brief included the co-ordination of an embryonic Leicestershire Fieldworkers Group, membership of which has since risen from 30 to 400 (Liddle 2004, 9). The Fieldworkers currently comprises twenty-six local groups working at the parish level, with at least one hundred people actively undertaking fieldwalking and other survey, including metal detecting, across the county at weekends. The group is supported by a training handbook (Liddle 1985) and an annual training session in finds identification and survey techniques, with up to 45 new trainees each year taking part. Many members have also undertaken the university's Higher Education Certificate in Archaeology evening course which itself has been running for thirty years. The group even has its own annual awards ceremony and a flourishing branch of the Young Archaeologist Club. The involvement of local communities has been further boosted by the launch of the Leicestershire Archaeological Network in 1995, to which 180 parish councils (representing 67% of the county) have signed up, by appointing an archaeological warden to be the local eyes and ears of the planning process (Liddle 2004, 9). This mobilisation of local resources has been achieved at very little cost and provides a model which could be adopted elsewhere, perhaps in conjunction with the Portable Antiquities Scheme, to harness otherwise disparate local interest groups and direct them toward a common goal.

The rewards, in terms of increased knowledge across the County, have been considerable. Even in the 1970s it would not be an exaggeration to say that Leicestershire did not really have a pre-medieval archaeology to speak of and was still locked in the vision of W.G. Hoskins, who portrayed it as a relict medieval landscape upon which even the Romans had made little impression due to thick forest cover and heavy clays soils (Hoskins 1957, 2). Fieldwork by independent archaeologists has largely been responsible for completely dispelling this myth and very busy prehistoric (Clay 2002), Roman and Anglo-Saxon landscapes (Bourne 1996) have duly revealed themselves. Aside from this fundamental finds and settlement data, members of the group have been responsible for discovering remarkable sites, which are unlikely to have been found otherwise, including a rare Creswellian open site and the largest Iron Age coin hoard ever found in the country (Priest, Clay and Hill 2003). The group has recently celebrated twenty-five years of work and a conference volume, which acts as a very good record of the current state of knowledge for the county as well as a testament to the Group's achievements, is now published (Bowman and Liddle 2004).

The role of regional research frameworks

The only downside of producing so much new data is, of course, that someone has to synthesise the results and feed it into the bigger picture by indulging in some of that forbidden fruit: research. But who has the time and expertise to undertake this vital work? Herein lies the nub of the problem, and where the building of bridges between the various sectors of the archaeological community is the vital prerequisite for rebuilding of a 'research culture'. The English Heritage Survey 'Frameworks for our Past' (Olivier 1996) painted a picture of a fragmented profession: the curators could not make informed decisions about the resource because no one had informed them; the contractors were too busy generating more resource preserved by record which no one could access; the academic world went abroad in search of the research that would be regarded as internationally important by their RAE judges, and the independent sector just felt excluded (Olivier 1996, Sections 4 and 5).

The solution was seen to lie in the formulation of regional research frameworks built from assessments of the resource in the individual counties. The research framework is seen to run in tandem with a management framework to form a universal framework. Each research framework comprises three elements (Olivier 1996).

- *The resource assessment*: an overview of the current state of knowledge
- *The research agenda*: identifying the potential of the

resource, gaps in our knowledge and an unprioritised list of research topics.
- *The research strategy*: a prioritised set of research topics, drawn from the agenda, which are tackled by the implementation of projects, the results of which feedback into the resource and modify the agenda and strategy accordingly.

The Frameworks initiative, facilitated by English Heritage is currently progressing across most parts of the country with documents published by the Eastern Counties (Glazebrook 1997, Brown and Glazebrook 2000), The Greater Thames Estuary (Williams and Brown 1999), London (MoL, 2002), the East Midlands (www.le.ac.uk /archaeology), the West Midlands (www.bham.ac.uk) and Yorkshire (Manby, Moorhouse and Ottaway 2003), and has provided an important forum for archaeologists from all sectors to discuss issues. The production of documents and their effective implementation are, of course, two different things and unless the frameworks are embraced by all sectors then the process will fail. There is no doubt that the curators will embrace the framework for they have been instrumental in supporting the initiative and have been badly in need of an up to date foundation upon which to base decisions about the future of the resource. Similarly, the contractors will realise the full relevance of the data they produce, as curators produce more informed briefs for them to adhere to and they write more imaginative project designs to justify spending money on research at the analysis phase.

The primary value of PPG16 archaeology is that it routinely takes archaeologists into areas that would never have been investigated before (such as the suburbs of our historic towns and the historic cores of our villages) and that interventions, how ever small, provide building blocks for research. The problem is that the potential of this enormous new resource has not been fully appreciated by the academic sector whose role in the effective implementation of the framework is vital. One problem concerns access to the mountain of grey literature (unpublished reports written for developers), which professional field archaeology now generates. Strides are being made to solve this electronically through the Archaeological Data Service and the Archaeological Investigations Project (Darvill and Russell 2002), and whilst these initiatives cannot actually provide us with more time to read the information it at least makes it more digestible. The second and most important problem, however, is that academic departments often do not have a research commitment to their region, even if their interest lies in Britain (Selkirk 2003), as if they refuse to believe that internationally important research can be done on their doorsteps. It would not be possible to change this perception overnight but small steps could be taken quickly; it just requires an awareness that the local researchable resource exists and is accessible. Every regional research framework will contain a wealth of potential research topics towards which undergraduate dissertations and postgraduate theses could contribute, and through these, academics will begin to recognise the potential of the local resource for themselves. From the finds viewpoint the resource not only includes artefacts which are being newly discovered, not least by the Portable Antiquities Scheme and other independent fieldwork, but also the examination and reappraisal of extensive museum collections which are currently under used and often poorly understood.

What is required is the forging of a partnership between the sectors in each region, in order to share expertise and continue the momentum generated by the formulation of the research frameworks. This could take the form of an annual meeting to review the framework, consider how new work is contributing and how existing topics could be fed into university student research or flagged for research funding by contractors, via English Heritage Commissions, for example. A good example of a PhD topic, which demonstrates how the various elements in this discussion can combine, has recently received funding at Leicester. The evolution of the Roman to Saxon settlement pattern and the subsequent nucleation of villages is recognised by the regional research framework as a priority which the East Midlands is well positioned to address (Vince 2001, 34; Lewis 2001, 9). The thesis focuses on comparing and contrasting the process in Leicestershire and Northamptonshire and takes advantage of the large numbers of Roman and Anglo-Saxon pottery scatters recovered by the independent sector, as well through PPG16 archaeology (importantly when undertaken in village cores), the county museum survey team and the university. Significantly, the thesis is being undertaken by a mature student, who was originally a Leicestershire Fieldworker, and who then undertook the certificate, then the degree, followed by an MA.

There is no reason either why members of the independent sector should be deterred from undertaking and publishing research based on their own fieldwork, rather than seeing their data reach the SMR and then go no further. Much of the identification and analysis of field scatters can be demystified by simple training and there is no reason why some of the approaches outlined in the following section, cannot be applied to survey material in order to place them within the wider context. It is largely a matter of confidence and access to guidance, which the independent sector currently lacks (Cooper 2004).

Approaches to quantifying portable material culture in Roman Britain

The second half of this paper aims to review the range of approaches currently being used by artefact specialists within the field of Roman archaeology in Britain. Whilst the study of artefacts has traditionally been oriented towards the chronological interpretation of sites through the development of type-series, the intention here is to highlight the potential of quantified approaches in addressing not only economic issues but also those related to site function, status and the evolution and diversification of material culture. Such approaches have grown out of a realisation that artefacts could and should have a much more important role to play in the interpretation of archaeological sites and more broadly in revealing the complexities of interaction between historically defined groups. The belief that underpins this assertion is that the artefactual (and environmental) remains of a site have the potential to provide a far more sophisticated profile of its inhabitants than can bland interpretative labels such as 'town' or 'villa' based on architectural evidence alone. Individual finds and their contexts represent the smallest units of interaction and if quantifiable, should give us a much higher resolution picture of this process in action. The portable material culture profile of a site should therefore provide an independent way of testing the currently perceived hierarchies of settlement and site status or for example the entrenched dichotomy of 'Roman' and 'native'.

Unfortunately, the tendency has been to expend most effort on the identification and cataloguing of site assemblages rather than their synthesis and therefore an enormous resource, often hidden away in monographs or archives, remains largely untapped (Cool and Baxter 1999, 72). However, a number of factors could help to bring finds centre stage. First, a new post-colonial generation of researchers not content with traditional interpretations could usefully explore this resource to reveal agendas concealed within the data. Second, the need for detailed research designs encourages the integration of finds specialists into the decision making process and provides them with the opportunity to devote post-excavation expenditure on addressing questions related to the economic and social aspects of sites rather than just chronology. Third, improved methods of retrieval and recording such as controlled metal detection has vastly increased sample sizes for small find and coin assemblages for example on East Anglian sites such as Scole (Cooper forthcoming b) and more generally through the Portable Antiquities Scheme. Additionally the application of statistical methods such as correspondence analysis is proving to be a very effective way of comparing the make up of large numbers of site assemblages of glass (Cool and Baxter 1999), small finds (Cool, Lloyd-Morgan and Hooley 1995) and pottery (Tyers 1996, 44) and should be used more routinely (Cool and Baxter 2002).

Theoretical and methodological caveats

The Roman period provides the opportunity to assess the impact of an incoming group upon an indigenous population; a process of interaction traditionally but misleadingly termed 'Romanization'. Its colonialist origin dictates that the term effectively ignores the indigenous contribution to what was in fact a complex two-way process of interaction between two cultures producing a unique hybrid. Whilst the existence of a hybrid Romano-British culture has been acknowledged since Collingwood in the 1930s, it was seen as one which evolved with the mute participation of the Britons, who were required only to be safe in the knowledge that the Roman way was better and that indigenous traditions persisted only through ignorance (Webster 2001, 212).

Like punk rock in the late 1970s, the 'nativist' backlash led by Richard Reece (1980) can now be seen as an essential step in wiping the slate clean and opening the door to the post-colonial generation to challenge what had become a dull orthodoxy. Martin Millett's recasting of the Romanization process was seminal in questioning that assumed passivity and placed the Britons firmly in the driving seat with competitive emulation as the motor of choice. Millett's essay was important not least because he placed quantified archaeological data at the heart of his arguments and this helped lay the foundation for the 'TRAC' generation of the 1990s. A newly improved paradigm of theory-enriched 'Romanization' has since emerged with those previously hidden indigenous ingredients now listed on the side of the packet (see Annual Proceedings of the Theoretical Roman Archaeology Conference TRAC).

However, Jane Webster has been correct in asserting that despite a decade of discussing the flaws of the Romanization model we are only now in a position to replace (or at least supplement) it, with a new framework, namely creolization (Webster 2001, 209). The Romanization model does not totally satisfy because the motor of competitive emulation is a top down, elite-driven mechanism which depends, like Thatcher's Britain of the 1980s did, on the persuasiveness of the promised trickle down effect. It therefore does not take into account that uncalculated proportion of the population who were uninterested, or unable to share, in a slice of that particular cake. A bottom up approach is therefore needed to fill that void and as Webster demonstrates clearly, current research in the Americas into the evolution of creolized cultures, provides a comparative framework which we cannot afford to ignore (Webster 2001).

The late James Deetz defined creolization as 'the interaction of two or more cultures to produce an integrated mix which is different to its antecedents', and in a specific instance, that hybrid culture of both African and English values which emerged in the American South (Deetz 1996, 213–4 quoting Mechal Sobel's book *The World They Made Together*). The term was originally a linguistic one but over the last few decades has extended increasingly to the study of the material culture of African-American populations. Significantly, as he acknowledges, the original edition of Deetz's book *'In Small Things Forgotten'* (1977) did not include a chapter on African-American archaeology, as it was not then a recognised area of research, blossoming as it did in the 1980s. By 1996 it was impossible to ignore the fact that the previously invisible 'other' was now visible. We would do well to recognise our own silent

majority in Roman Britain by heeding Deetz's reminder that 'few people when viewing the memorable scene in (the film) *Deliverance* (starring Burt Reynolds!) realise that the young boy playing *Duelling Banjos* is using an African musical instrument while seated on a porch which owes its origins to West African architectural forms (1996, 213–4). I will return to the potential of creolization as a comparative approach later in the paper.

So how might the quantified study of the portable material culture of Roman Britain help us to better understand this process of interaction? At first glance the transition from the Iron Age to the Roman period appears to signal the almost complete replacement of one material culture by another with wheel-thrown, kiln-fired pottery a ubiquitous element, classical architecture in stone appearing to replace timber forms, and the British bow brooch representing the only survivor that could not be bettered amongst a new array of metal dress accessories. The transplantation of Mediterranean cuisine, fashions and customs to an outpost of the Empire would therefore appear to have been comprehensive and successful 'Romanization' achieved. Before we could accept such a thesis we would need to test aspects of the data and accept certain caveats.

The first is to acknowledge that we are dealing with rubbish and, in the case of coins and many small finds, affordable accidental losses as well as a debatable amount of ritual deposition. The data set is therefore skewed but is essentially (and helpfully) providing a measure of access to replacement items. During the Roman period the sheer volume of rubbish indicates that access was relatively easy (though arguably sporadic) and this is due primarily to the rise in workshop scale production and many other factors related to the growth of the Empire (see Hopkins 1983, ix; Greene 1986, 14; Millett 1991). The data set is further enhanced because of its visibility and the durability of ceramics and stone and so there is a danger of overestimating the Roman impact and underestimating the indigenous contribution, which was often in less durable materials such as wood, handmade ceramics or other organic products such as hides and textiles. The second caveat is to ask why, if *Romanitas* was so entrenched within British society, did its material culture disappear so quickly? The answer partly lies within a number of factors related to the collapse of workshop production and the corresponding skills loss within what had become a consumer society, as well as differences in the nature of the Germanic transition in Britain and on the Continent, but most importantly it lies in our need to appreciate that the Roman World was but one, admittedly significant, influence on a continuously evolving British material culture which adopted and adapted certain aspects and rejected others (Cooper 1996). *Romanitas* did not so much disappear as devolve to each province in which uniquely it was incorporated. As I have argued elsewhere (1996, 86), we mistakenly use the term 'Roman' as an ethnic label for material culture of the Roman period. Many who used these objects may well have wanted to be identified ethnically as Roman whilst others may simply have used the material culture that was available to them. The significance of this distinction is emphasised with reference to a case-study from the Bahamas later in the paper (Wilkie 1999).

To test if this 'Romanization' was complete we would need to establish whether variation existed within the material culture data set across space and time. Once any patterns had been established we would then be in a position to explore the likely factors creating them and their connection with the process of interaction we were trying to identify. In establishing these patterns we hit the first problem; the data set is so large that relatively little headway has been made towards synthesising it. While workers recognise that huge variation exists and suspect that variability in the process of interaction, amongst other factors, is responsible they are still a long way from establishing norms against which new assemblages can be compared. The quantified study of coins has led the way in the creation of such norms through the establishment of the 'British Background' against which future assemblages can be compared (Reece 1995) and significant progress has been made in other finds categories such as samian ware (Marsh 1981; Willis 1998) and vessel glass (Cool and Baxter 1999). However, until this has been undertaken more comprehensively we cannot exploit finds to their full potential.

Approaches to pottery

As the most ubiquitous artefact type and the one least affected by factors of preservation, recycling and retrieval, pottery should present itself as potentially the best index of broad economic and social change within Roman Britain. The two attributes which underpin the classification of the material, vessel form and vessel fabric, provide the major ways of analysing it. While vessel form traditionally provided the classificatory lynchpin through the development of form type series (*e.g.* Gillam's typology of coarse pottery from northern Britain, 1970), increasing interest in addressing economic issues of production and distribution as well as technology during the 1970s, brought the study of fabric to the fore.

Patterns of supply

Figures 4.1 and 4.2 illustrate the changing nature of pottery supply to a single consumer site (the tribal capital at Cirencester, *Corinium Dobunnorum*) during the High and Low Empire periods respectively. Each period is divided into four ceramic phases (CPs) and quantification by fabric is obtained from the best-preserved stratified groups selected from over two decades of excavation in the town during the 1960s and 1970s (Cooper 1998, 324; forthcoming a). The early Roman period or 'High' Empire is typified by close commercial links with the Continent,

particularly involving the large-scale samian tableware producers in southern and central Gaul as well as the importation of other fine wares and foodstuffs contained in amphorae. This remarkably cosmopolitan pattern is, however, largely confined to the period of military occupation (CP1), the fort being tied into an administered, non-economic supply network, which also supplied the Rhine Frontier, before the town and its market was established. Utilitarian kitchen wares used for cooking and storage, are supplied locally from North Wiltshire and Gloucestershire during the High Empire completing a two tier pattern of imported and local supply. However, CP 3 and 4 contain the seeds of change with declining imports and the emergence of non-local British (regional-scale) producers, most importantly Black Burnished ware 1 from Dorset. The later Roman period or 'Low' Empire sees a continued decline in commercial contact with the Continent and a rise in non-local supply from a small number of large, rurally nucleated centres of production with wide distribution networks such as Oxfordshire and the Lower Nene Valley.

The synthesis of supply to Cirencester joins a growing number of quantified studies of pottery from major urban centres such as London (Marsh 1981, Davies, Richardson and Tomber 1994); minor urban centres such as Chelmsford (Going 1987) and Alcester (Evans 1995); rural sites in Milton Keynes (Marney 1989), Warwickshire (Booth 1991) and North Wales (Evans 1998). Each study reflects the same broad pattern of supply to provide a quantified consumer pattern, which echoes what we know of changes in the location of production (Fulford 1977). Indeed, Going has demonstrated how production and supply patterns are probably tied into Empire-wide economic cycles (1992). However, what might comparison of these studies tell us about the degree to which individual consumer sites, representing a range of perceived social status, are tied into both the economic and social network of the Roman World, *i.e.* to what extent was the Roman element within the creolization process apparent?

The urban/rural divide

The threefold division of the assemblage into local (within *c*.15 miles), non-local British and imported supply categories may represent the simplest way of highlighting such trends and enables us to summarise data from a large number of sites on to a ternary diagram. Figure 4.3 summarises data from a range of urban and rural sites across the Roman period. Considering the urban data first, the assemblages tend to cluster either side of the 20% import level line but vary more considerably in terms of their local and non-local supply levels. Where chronological ceramic phase data is available; from Cirencester (Cooper 1998), Leicester (Clark 1999), and London (Davies, Richardson and Tomber 1994), assemblages progress from the top left of the diagram (*e.g.* CP2 and LP1 and 2) towards bottom right (*e.g.* LP6,

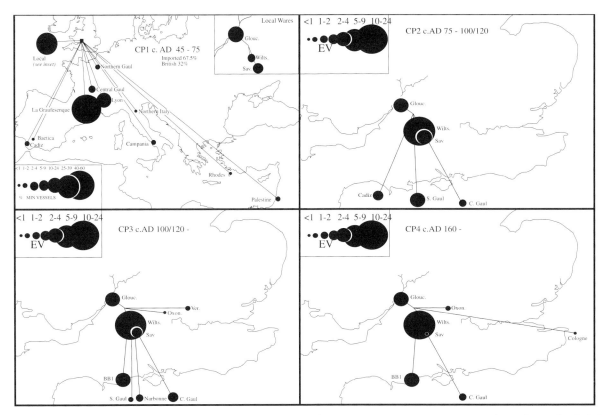

Fig. 4.1. Sources of pottery supplied to Cirencester: the High Empire. (Min = Minimum number of vessels, EVES = Estimated Vessel Equivalents)

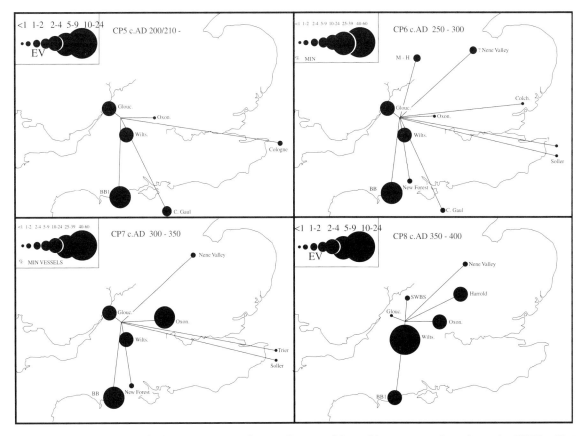

Fig. 4.2. Sources of pottery supplied to Cirencester: the Low Empire. (Min = Minimum number of vessels, EVES = Estimated Vessel Equivalents)

RCP5, CP7 and 8). The early assemblages are typified by a two-tier import and local supply pattern (with military period CP1 representing the extreme), and later assemblages display declining import and local supply levels coupled with an increasing non-local contribution. The pattern outlined earlier for Cirencester is therefore followed by another tribal capital, Leicester and a similar situation is found at other urban sites such as Chelmsford (Going 1987) and Gloucester (Ireland 1983). London as both the mercantile and likely provincial capital during the High Empire however, produces a slightly different picture. Ceramic phases (RCP1–5) span the early Roman period only *c.* AD 50–AD 160 and yet maintain a non-local supply contribution of around 50%, and generally high import levels throughout.

The figures for rural sites comprising farmsteads, villas and small towns, tell a different story. The assemblages cluster along the right hand axis with very low import levels and generally very high local contributions. While the two villa sites show relatively high import levels

compared to the farmsteads and small towns they are not as high as those for urban centres. Trends over time for Milton Keynes (Marney 1989) and Empingham, Rutland (Cooper 2006b, 93) show a general progression in line with urban sites with the earliest assemblages (*e.g.* EP1 and MK1) being entirely local in origin and the later assemblages having a much higher proportion of non-local pottery (*e.g.* MK 15–17 and EP3–5). However, the trend for non-local supply is not as clear-cut as it is on the urban sites, and depends much more perhaps on the status of the site and, in particular, its proximity to the major late Roman regional scale suppliers such as Dorset Black Burnished ware, Oxfordshire and the Lower Nene Valley. The later assemblages from Empingham (EP3–5) illustrate this point well, being almost entirely dominated by the Lower Nene Valley industry which, while being by definition a non-local supplier, is actually only 14 miles distant. Significantly then, the greatest proportion of pottery supplied to rural sites throughout time is therefore seen to be of *local* origin.

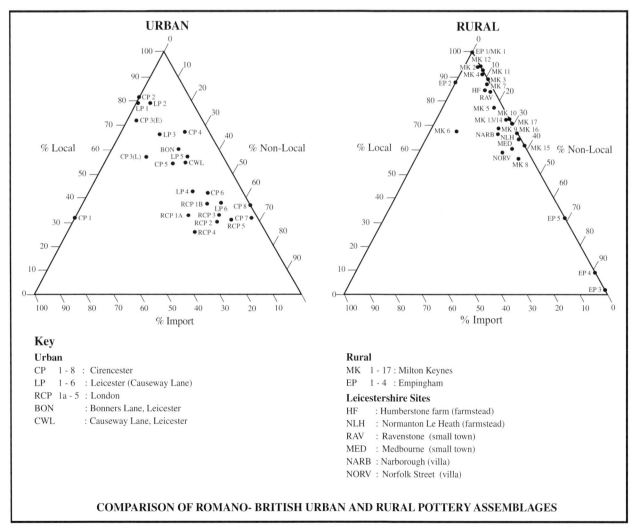

COMPARISON OF ROMANO- BRITISH URBAN AND RURAL POTTERY ASSEMBLAGES

Fig. 4.3. Ternary diagrams comparing composition of urban and rural Romano-British pottery assemblages

The analysis of pottery and glass assemblages by vessel form can help to investigate these urban and rural trends more fully. Steven Willis' work on creating a nation-wide database of samian tableware has finally begun to unlock the potential of a resource previously only valued as an instrument for dating sites. The fact that it is so well dated means that the changing nature of assemblages from a range of different sites can be charted year by year (Willis 1998). This provides expected patterns against which each new assemblage can be compared. Jeremy Evans (1993 and 2001) has analysed the proportion of vessel types from a large number of pottery assemblages detecting differences between perceived site types and changes over time. Comparing the relative proportions of jars (used primarily for cooking) and dishes and bowls (used for serving and eating food), indicates that a greater proportion of urban assemblages are made up of the latter, whilst jars are more common on rural sites with figures for villas lying between (Evans 2001, 27, figs. 5 and 6). Similarly if we look at the range of vessel forms found within typical urban (compiled from Clark 1999) and rural (Cooper unpublished) assemblages from Leicester-shire (Fig. 4.4) distinct differences are apparent. In the urban assemblage the range of forms (other than jars) is wider and their proportionate contribution is greater than in rural assemblages, where jars forms contribute 88%. Of interest though is the fact that mortaria make up the same proportion in each (3%).

The comparison of vessel glass assemblages has also detected distinct differences in vessel use between urban and rural sites, and considering trends over time, the disappearance of closed vessels such as jugs and flagons in the later Roman period echoes that for pottery where the assemblage as a whole returns to a jar based repertoire not dissimilar to both the prehistoric one from which it sprang and the early Anglo-Saxon one which was soon to replace it in areas which didn't otherwise become aceramic (Cooper 1996, 91).

Access or desire: exploring Reasons for the divide

Having established that distinct urban and rural patterns of pottery supply exist and that certain trends are detect-able over time it is necessary to explore what factors might be responsible. At the provincial level, the trends detectable over time have been used to support broad models of economic change developed by Fulford (1977 and 1984), whereby evidence of pottery is used to demonstrate Britain's economic dependence on the Continent during the High Empire, giving way to greater self-sufficiency in the Low Empire. Subsequently, Millett has used the same early and late division to provide the basis for his model of the decentralisation of economic activity away from the major urban centres in the later Roman period which linked the changing location of pottery production to the changing

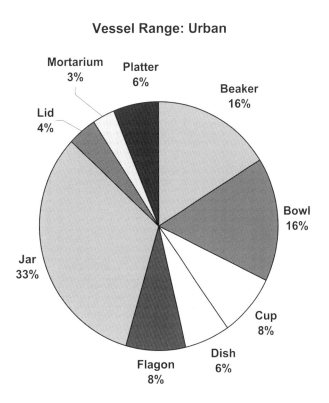
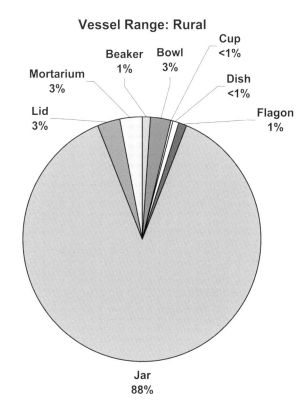

Fig.4.4a. Typical Range of Romano-British vessel types from Leicester: Causeway Lane (data from Clark 1999, Table 15, Phase 3 early-mid 2nd century)

Fig.4.4b. Typical range of Romano-British vessel forms from rural Leicestershire (data from excavations along the Wing to Whatborough pipeline, Cooper 1996, unpublished)

economic and social roles of civitas (tribal) capitals and small towns (Millett 1990, 148, Table 6.3).

Both these models provide very useful foundations but it is clear from the rural pattern of pottery supply that the heavy dependence on imported fine and specialist wares (and presumably the organic products forming the bulk of the cargo), seen as fundamental to the High Empire picture painted by Fulford (1984), is really only of relevance to urban centres and, in particular, London during the High Empire where the figures might be assumed to reflect the pulling power of its market and the correspondingly cosmopolitan tastes and aspirations of (at least some of) its population. If pottery can be taken as an index of trade in other goods then it would appear in contrast, that rural folk obtained most of their needs, and probably discharged their social obligations, locally.

The inference from the analysis of vessel forms is that the inhabitants of rural sites used table wares less and continued to use pottery mainly for cooking in the same way as they had during later prehistory. The trend echoes that established for supply mechanisms (Fig. 4.3), with local potteries producing mainly jar forms. However, the fact that most of the vessel repertoire available to urban sites does get to rural areas, if in much smaller quantities, illustrates that rural dwellers did have an interest in incorporating new vessel forms into their daily lives, even if the uses to which they were put may arguably have been different from their urban or continental counterparts. To what extent then is the pattern a reflection of difference in social practice between urban and rural communities, or simply a question of availability and access? Monaghan (1997, 854) has portrayed the supply of pottery as one typified by perpetual shortage and this might go some way to explaining the observed differences, whereby marketing mechanisms simply did not take certain wares into rural localities. Acceptance of this straightforward explanation however, denies the possibility that there is actually a more interesting story to tell, and it is an acceptance underpinned by two fundamental assumptions which have never really been questioned until recently.

The first assumption is that the indigenous people's only desire was to emulate their Roman conquerors and the second is that much of the population were actually free to do so. To question the first assumption, a hungry post-colonial generation of researchers, seeking those hidden agendas, has begun a more comprehensive comparison of finds assemblages to include animal bone, plant material and coins, in order to tackle the thorny questions of cuisine (Meadows 1994; Hawthorne 1998; Hawkes 2002) and the degree to which different populations were necessarily involved in a monetary or 'free market' economy (Gerrard 2002; Taylor 2001, 56).

Lessons from America: the potential of creole approaches

The second assumption, concerning the identification of slave or servile populations in Roman Britain through material remains, though intimately linked with the first, is only now being addressed head on (Webster forthcoming) and there are clearly useful parallels to be drawn with slavery in the Americas between the sixteenth and nineteenth centuries. It is important to distinguish at this point between the earlier slave owning (or slave using) societies of the north-eastern states of America (Massachusetts, Maryland and Virginia) where slaves often lived within households, and the later development of plantation slavery in the southern states (Virginia, the Carolinas and Georgia) where, after 1700, slaves increasingly lived in separate, purpose-built quarters (Webster forthcoming). In the former case, slaves can be very difficult, though not impossible, to identify materially (Yentsch 1994) but in the latter, the excavation and analysis of documented slave quarter assemblages has revealed distinct differences between them and those of their masters (Deetz 1996, 232). The distinction is not always as straight forward as the example cited by Deetz might indicate and other case studies show an atypical occurrence of high status ceramics in slave quarters, perhaps due to the hoarding or concealment of broken sherds as an act of resistance or the acquisition of certain vessels as status symbols (Courtney 1997, 101).

As Jane Webster's paper demonstrates, there is a similar potential in reassessing the significance of the often meagre finds assemblages from sites where the presence of slaves in Roman Britain has previously been inferred such as at Chalk in Kent characterised by small numbers of sherds a high proportion of which bear incised crosses or *grafittos* (Johnson 1972). In doing so we have to cast aside our urge to apply modern concepts of economy and fashion to explain the occurrence of particular wares and instead focus on how an unfree sector of the population might have used the material things available to them (Webster forthcoming).

An equally poorly understood sector of the population of Roman Britain are the *coloni*, the later Roman agricultural labour force of tenants tied to the land through hereditary service in an essentially feudal manner (Millett 1990, 203; Salway 1981, 546). Might it be possible for us to identify this population archaeologically? Did they have a distinctive material culture? Presumably they lived in those 'basic' rural sites which fill the spaces between the villas but were they free enough to buy their own pots or were these supplied by the estate owners? Such a scenario would, of course, be impossible to prove, but acknowledging that such a population existed might encourage us to look for patterns in the data. With this in mind, another case-study from the America illustrates our need to look at assemblages with fresh eyes.

It is generally recognised now that during the late seventeenth to early nineteenth centuries, African-American slaves in Virginia and South Carolina produced and used a distinctive handmade pottery known as Colono ware with a vessel repertoire comprising small and large round based cooking pots and shallow bowls with copies of some European forms such as pipkins also occurring (Deetz 1996, 236–44, fig.15). Analysis of associated food remains comprising a wide variety of wild game (hunted by the slaves themselves) and the well-documented starchy rations dished out by slave owners has encouraged the assertion that the slaves were continuing to follow foodways with a strongly African element and that the vessel repertoire with its use of bowls rather than plates was suited to the eating of the 'Creole' style dishes such as gumbo, with the large pot used to prepare the rice and the small one used for the sauce containing meat or fish. By 1820 the use of Colono ware declines, but what replaces it in slave quarters are bowls in the bog-standard pearlware from Staffordshire known as annular ware which was now cheap enough to import and which Deetz argues was probably issued to slaves alongside their rations (1996, 234). Hence we find a European object being used to continue an African-based 'Creole' cuisine. In this respect, what significance might there be in the ubiquitous vessel combination of cooking pot, bead and flanged bowl and plain rimmed 'dog' dish which becomes the bread and butter of many Romano-British pottery producers including Black Burnished ware (Holbrook and Bidwell 1991) and the widely distributed later products of the Lower Nene valley (Howe, Perrin and Mackreth 1980) and the Harrold shell-tempered industry (Brown 1994). Were these cheap enough to be given out as rations to estate workers and what might they indicate about the continuation of specific 'foodways'?

A further case study from the slave quarters of Clifton Plantation in the Bahamas illustrates again, that whilst the 'vocabulary' (origin) of the material dialogue may be European, the 'grammar' (the way in which the objects are selected and used) is African (Wilkie 1999; 2001). As Wilkie states, due to the unusual policy of their owner (slave reformer William Wylly), the slaves of this estate (a mixture of African born and first generation Creoles) were encouraged to sell their own produce and were thus able to buy their own pottery at market. Their consumer choices, though dictated by the European origin of the ceramics, illustrate a selection based on decoration, colour and motifs which differs from the ceramics used in the planter's house. The slave cabin assemblages showed a preference for hand-painted ceramics using motifs such as chevrons, bands and dots coloured in browns, oranges, yellows and greens and commonly found both in West African cloth design and body adornment. In one instance an English potter had inadvertently painted a motif on the interior of the vessel base similar to the Bakongo cosmogram (circle quartered by a cross, surrounded by four dots representing the seasons), which had seemingly

been selected because of this. When found on slave-produced pottery in the New World, this symbol denotes vessels used for preparing *nkisi* (sacred medicine) (Wilkie 1999, 274).

The presence of slaves or servile groups in Roman Britain is not going to be easy to demonstrate but as Webster (forthcoming) has powerfully argued their assumed archaeological invisibility is exactly the problem which held back their study in the Americas for so long. The emergence of an archaeology of Roman slavery is something to which the finds community can make a unique contribution both through the study of ceramics and small finds.

Approaches to small finds

As a category, small finds are less easily defined in terms of form and function than pottery and the data are therefore perhaps less easy to analyse. The category includes all material, other than bulk finds such as pottery and tile, and usually includes all metal finds other than coins, as well items of worked bone, glass (other than vessels), stone, and ceramic. An enormous data set of published and archive information exists, but as with pottery little headway has been made in synthesising it to see if any patterns exist within the profiles produced by individual sites.

However, a major step forward was made in 1983 with the publication of the small finds from excavations in Roman Colchester (Crummy 1983). For the first time a very comprehensive catalogue was arranged in terms of the functional category to which an object belonged rather than the material from which it was made and the volume continues to be one of the standard works of reference on the subject. At once a more intimate connection could be made between the objects and the people who used them; the categories ranging from items of personal adornment or dress such as jewellery, household utensils, objects used in craft activities such as weaving or metal working, through to military equipment, recreational items and objects associated with religious beliefs such as votive figurines.

Functional profiles

At face value it would appear that small finds could potentially provide a direct reflection of the activities undertaken by the inhabitants of a site and that all we needed to do was count how many we had by functional category and make comparisons. While this has acted as an obvious way ahead and has been used in a number of reports (Ellison 1987; Wilmott 1991; Viner 1998; Cooper 1999), it will be clear from the following examples that the equation between the amount of finds and the amount of activity represented is not straight forward. However, this should not deter us from pursuing the possibility that patterns exist.

Excavations at Causeway Lane in Leicester in 1991 (Connor and Buckley 1999), one of the largest ever undertaken in the city, produced over 6000 objects classified as small finds, two-thirds of which were iron nails. Of the remaining 2000 finds, 362 were complete enough to be categorised by function. Table 4.1 below illustrates the breakdown of the assemblage into functional categories alongside similar analyses for three other currently unpublished sites in Roman Leicester; The Shires, Blue Boar Lane and Great Holme St (Cooper 1999, 242), and a selection of published analyses compiled by Ellison (1987) and Viner (1998). Figures from Scole are unpublished (Cooper forthcoming b). Sites include the *Colonia* of Colchester, the tribal capitals of Cirencester and Dorchester, and a series of rural small towns as well as the villa at Gatcombe.

While minor inconsistencies, in the way that certain finds are classified between reports and during the compilation process, have distorted the figures slightly, the overall pattern is clear. Irrespective of sample size, which varies from 66 to 2082 finds, or the perceived function and status of the site, the profiles are remarkably similar and follow a common pattern. With the exception of Scole (due to the fact that the household figures are inflated), personal objects are by far the most common, varying from 36% to 73% but usually contributing at least 50–60% of the assemblage. In addition, the rest of the assemblage is consistently provided by objects from the next three categories, covering textiles, household and recreational activities (giving an overall total of 95% at Causeway Lane), with the other categories often being poorly represented. Of the other categories which show variation, tools (usually knives) and fittings such as locks are often not specific enough functionally and in the former case are very much affected by the preservation conditions for iron. Rural sites do not show an increase in agricultural items even though this must have represented the dominant economic activity and even military sites do not produce profiles which are markedly different. It appears that the dominant rubbish producing activity

Table 4.1. The proportion of Roman small finds from urban and rural sites by functional category

Site	*Pers*	*Text*	*Hou*	*Rec*	*Writ*	*Agri*	*Tool*	*Fitt*	*Reli*	*Craft*	*Samp*
CWayLane	73	4	7	12	1	1	1	–	<1	1	362
The Shires	54	6	15	11	1	1	10	–	1	–	165
GHStreet	63	8	4	13	–	1	1	6	2	–	269
BBLane	39	7	16	8	–	–	3	27	–	–	87
Colchester	65	4	4	20	<1	–	4	3	NC	NC	1241
Cirencester	56	3	8	6	4	1	4	18	NC	NC	2082
Dorch Lib	62	6	14	3	5	–	8	3	NC	NC	66
Dorch Grey	58	6	5	22	2	–	4	3	NC	NC	418
Poundbury	58	4	10	2	2	1	24	–	NC	NC	110
Ilchest town	66	17	1	1	1	1	7	5	NC	NC	76
Ilchest sub	57	8	5	5	6	2	13	4	NC	NC	143
Kingscote	67	5	4	7	5	1	7	3	NC	NC	518
Catsgore	46	8	14	14	4	<1	11	3	NC	NC	182
Gatcombe	53	9	15	4	<1	<1	14	4	NC	NC	125
Scole*	36	2	42*	1	7	2	6	–	2	2	591

Abbreviations: The functional categories have been slightly simplified from Crummy (1983) as follows.
Pers = 1: Personal Adornment or Dress and 2: Toilet, Surgical or Pharmaceutical Instruments
Text = 3: Objects Used in the Manufacture or Working of Textiles
Hous = 4: Household Utensils and Furniture
Rec = 5: Objects Used for Recreational Purposes
Writ = 6: Objects employed in weighing and measuring and 7: Written communication.
Agri = 8: Objects Associated with Transport and 12: Objects associated with agriculture
Tools= 10: Tools and weapons
Fitt = 11: Miscellaneous Fasteners and Fittings
Reli = 14: Objects Associated with Religious Beliefs and Practices
Craft = 15–17: Objects Associated with metal working, bone working or pottery manufacture
Samp = Sample: number of small finds in the assemblage that could be categorised
NC = Not calculated but usually less than 1%
* = Household figure for Scole also includes vessel glass.

is consistent at all sites and is residential in nature rather than agricultural, commercial, industrial or military for example. There are clearly taphonomic factors (both behavioural and related to preservation), which are dominating the formation of assemblages and masking what must have been a more varied set of activities. A consideration of some of the most commonly occurring finds will highlight some of the major factors.

The overwhelming predominance of dress accessories and, in particular, brooches and hairpins, is not only a reflection of their common usage but also the ease with which they are lost (if not deliberately deposited in burials or votively). As with other small items such as coins, the time you spend searching for them depends on their intrinsic value and because replacement accessories were presumably easily available, those losses escaped recycling or transference to the next generation and thus entered the archaeological record. By counting the numbers of such items in an assemblage we could in fact be measuring how wide the gaps were between the floorboards of local residences or how muddy the roads were! A quick scan of the objects belonging to the other commonly occurring categories reveals that again they are predominantly small, easily lost or broken, and easily replaced; pairs of tweezers, bone sewing needles, or counters for board games. However, another functional category, written communications, whose constituents, *styli* and seal-boxes for securing documents, also fit those criteria are relatively unusual finds, and could perhaps be used as a sensitive indicator of the presence of literacy within a population. For example Causeway Lane, lying in an architecturally poor district of Roman Leicester produced no objects belonging to this category whilst the small town site of Scole produced seven which together with evidence for commercial activities such as weights and measures produced an

unusually high figure of seven percent for this category. Other categories such as craft activities will include specific tools which will be carefully curated or recycled and so more rarely enter the archaeological record. Even low occurrences of such items (for example wool combs at Great Holme Street) could therefore be more significant than we realise. Additionally, the waste products; such as lumps of iron slag or fragments of bone-working waste are difficult to quantify in meaningful terms and this has not been undertaken in the compilation of data above.

Criticisms are easy to level at such analysis but dwelling on them detracts from what we are actually after which is the identification of broad trends in the data rather than exact quantified comparison. The examination of functional categories at least gives us an expected pattern to use as a baseline from which divergence can be acknowledged and investigated. It should also alert us to the need to be more selective in our choice of assemblages and more imaginative in our approaches. For example the prevalence of dress items should be seen as an asset rather than a hindrance and research could usefully be focused upon the many questions of fashion and ethnicity that they raise. One possible direction (Cool in press) is to look at the occurrence of specific but unusual finds types such as spoons and calibrate their presence against common ones such as brooches or hairpins which you would expect to find on all site types.

Considering whole assemblage figures, it is almost certain that our data set is too coarse and that we are expecting to detect specific activities from a relatively small assemblage (*c*.200 finds) covering perhaps four hundred years of occupation, and deriving from rubbish disposal across a wide townscape perhaps. Large open area excavations with shallow stratigraphy such as that at Scole have, however, allowed the spatial distribution of activity to be mapped across a settlement when the assemblage is divided into discrete areas (Cooper forthcoming b). As with pottery, it would be preferable to be able to look at small finds at the level of individual contexts so that we are capturing a small snapshot in space and time and occasionally this is possible. For example, correspondence analysis has been used to demonstrate similarities and differences between assemblages from the Roman legionary fortresses at York and Caerleon, in an attempt to determine the functions of the buildings to which they relate (Cool, Lloyd-Morgan, and Hooley 1995, 1626).

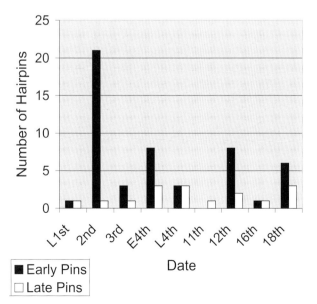

Fig. 4.5. The stratigraphic distribution of Roman bone hairpins from Causeway Lane, Leicester

Stratigraphic profiles

The stratigraphic distribution of a small finds assemblage as a whole may help to gauge the scale of activity on a site over time, particularly on deeply stratified urban sites. At Causeway Lane, the period AD 120–200 represents the time of maximum small find deposition yielding 27% of the assemblage and corresponding to the period of accelerating activity (and therefore rubbish disposal) in the town generally signalled by the major public building projects. By AD 200, 41% of the phased assemblage has been deposited with only a further 22% being deposited in the succeeding 200 years to the end of the Roman period. Whilst other factors such as the disturbance of later Roman layers could be taken to explain what otherwise might be taken as a decline in activity, the trend is also reflected in the distribution of a single datable artefact type such as the Roman bone hair pin (Fig. 4.5) which, unlike brooches, appear to be used commonly throughout the Roman period judging from the evidence from Colchester (Crummy 1983, 19–25).

Considering Causeway Lane, the assemblage contains a much higher proportion of early types dated up to 200, than later types dated to the third and fourth century. The deposition pattern follows that for the finds assemblage as a whole with 22 (43%) of the 51 phased early pins having been deposited by AD 200 and 72 % of all phased pins having been deposited by the end of the Roman period (early types outnumbering late types by 36:9). In post Roman levels early types still outnumber late types by 15:7 with redeposition occurring during a period of medieval robbing of Roman stone buildings (Cooper 1999, 242). This picture is repeated in other large Leicester assemblages such as the extra-mural site at Great Holme St (Boothroyd 1994), and The Shires (Cooper forthcoming c), and this is in marked contrast to the assemblage from Colchester which shows such a marked prevalence of later Roman types. Such evidence can be added to that of pottery and structures to suggest a later Roman decline or change in the nature of residential activity in the town. Recent work by Hilary Cool has also revealed the potential of small finds at the end of the Roman period, when the traditional sources of dating evidence, coins and pottery cease to be of use. By isolating contexts dating to the later fourth century and clearly into the fifth century it is possible to identify the emergence of a distinctive new suite of dress accessories and other finds, quietly evolving irrespective of the apparently significant political date of AD 410 (Cool 2000).

Access and wealth profiles

Another approach that might yield useful comparative information is to consider the relative use of different materials in the manufacture of a common artefact type like the hairpin. Judgements of relative values are of course subjective but it is likely that the use of bone (occasionally stained to imitate copper) represented the cheap alternative to the use of metal, which involved high temperature technology. Jet, which becomes more fashionable in the later Roman period, represents a material to which access was more limited with supplies coming from the North Sea coast around Whitby. Looking at the ratios of the use of these three materials might help to create a profile of relative wealth or access amongst a population.

Table 4.2 compares figures from Leicester sites with those from Colchester and Scole. To judge from Causeway Lane and Great Holme St a typical ratio for Leicester appears to have been about 1:10, but at Colchester (Crummy 1983) it was nearer 1:7 and if jet is considered it brings this down to nearly 1:5, which may suggest greater access to more expensive materials. The reverse ratio of 2:1 at Scole on the other hand is almost certainly due the use of controlled metal detection and possibly the poor preservation of bone artefacts due to soil conditions, although the existence of regional variation in style choices is recognised (Cool 1990)

Conclusion

This paper has been deliberately broad ranging in content and hopefully has hit as many buttons as possible. Its aim has been to remind the finds community of the significance of the skills it possesses whilst alerting the wider audience to the potential for using finds data to address important research questions. However, unless the discipline as a whole starts to do some joined up thinking, with the regional research frameworks acting as the pivot, then nothing will change. The targeting of relatively small amounts of money to set up community archaeology programmes for example or to encourage undergraduate departments to pay for external teaching by artefact specialists, would mobilise a largely untapped resource and improve the quality of students entering the profession. Improved and sustained communication between different sectors of the discipline, but vitally incorporating the academics, using the research frameworks as a conduit, would engender a research commit-

Table 4.2. Roman hairpins in different materials from different sites

Site	CuA	Bone	Jet	Total
Leicester Causeway Lane	10	105	–	115
Leicester Great Holme St	10	101	–	111
Colchester	49	342	15	406
Scole	30	15	–	45

ment at the regional level and make a research strategy something which is actually implemented rather than something that sits on a shelf.

If Roman archaeology is currently marginalised (James 2003, 179) and artefact study in Britain is held in poor regard (above) then by inference, the study of Roman artefacts must be almost invisible! As with Roman archaeology generally, this does not have to be the case, but we need to promote the relevance of finds at every level from school upwards. In particular the study of finds needs to be made more relevant to the study of people's everyday lives and there is a strong argument for aligning more closely with historical archaeology (James 2003, 182), particularly in America, where the study of portable material culture is held in much higher regard and taken much more seriously as a research tool (Courtney 1996 and 1997). The quality of the dataset is not in question and new approaches are being developed, but it is up to us to improve its profile and thus attract the necessary funding for research. The following quote, which closes the late James Deetz's *In Small Things Forgotten: An Archaeology of Early American Life* (1996, 259–60), seems an appropriate rallying call to end with here too.

'It is terribly important that the "small things forgotten" be remembered. For in the seemingly little and insignificant things that accumulate to create a lifetime, the essence of our existence is captured. We must remember these bits and pieces, and we must use them in new and imaginative ways so that a different appreciation for what life is today, and was in the past, can be achieved. The written document has its proper and important place, but there is also a time when we should set aside our perusal of diaries, court records, and inventories, and listen to another voice. Don't read what we have written; look at what we have done.'

Acknowledgements

I am very grateful to Jane Webster for allowing me to refer to her, frankly, ground breaking paper prior to publication and for discussing these issues over a number of years. Steve Willis suggested changes to an earlier draft, as well as a more profound title than the original. Thanks are due to the referees for their comments and suggestions and I hope I have strengthened the paper accordingly. I was pleased by the positive response the paper received at the conference and the final text has benefited from discussions with Hilary Cool, Paul Courtney, Nina Crummy, Hella Eckardt and Jeremy Taylor.

Bibliography

Aitchison, K. and Edwards R. (2003) Archaeology Labour Market Intelligence: Profiling the Profession 2002/3 http://www.archaeologists.net/docs/profile/LMI_report_010403.pdf
Allason-Jones, L. (2001) Material culture and identity. In James and Millett (eds), 19–25.
Booth, P. (1991) Inter-Site Comparisons Between Pottery Assemblages in Roman Warwickshire: Indicators of Site Status. *Journal of Roman Pottery Studies*, 4, 1–1
Boothroyd, N. (1994) *Small Finds from two extramural sites of Roman and Medieval Leicester: Great Holme St and the Austin Friars*. Unpublished MA in Post-excavation skills dissertation, University of Leicester Library.
Bourne, J. (ed.) (1996) *Anglo-Saxon Landscapes in the East Midlands*. Leicester, Leicestershire Museums, Art Galleries and Records Service.
Bowman, P. and Liddle, P. (2004) *Leicestershire Landscapes*. Leicestershire Museum Archaeological Fieldwork Group Monograph no. 1. Leicester.
Brown, A. E. (1994) A Romano-British Shell-gritted Pottery and tile manufacturing site at Harrold, Beds. *Bedfordshire Archaeological Journal*, 21, 19–107.
Brown, N. R. and Glazebrook, J. (eds) (2000) *Research and Archaeology: a Framework for the Eastern Counties 2. Research Agenda and Strategy*. East Anglian Archaeology Occasional Paper no. 8.
Clark, R. (1999) The Roman Pottery. In Connor and Buckley, 95–164.
Clay, P. N. (2002) *The Prehistory of the East Midlands Claylands*. Leicester Archaeology Monograph 9. Leicester, University of Leicester, School of Archaeology and Ancient History.
Connor, A. and Buckley, R. J. (1999) *Roman and Medieval Occupation in Causeway Lane, Leicester.* Leicester Archaeology Monograph 5. Leicester, University of Leicester, School of Archaeology and Ancient History.
Cool, H. E. M. (1990) Roman Metal Hair Pins from Southern Britain. *The Archaeological Journal* 147, 148–82.
Cool, H. E. M. (2000) The Parts Left Over: Material Culture into the Fifth Century. In T. Wilmott and P. Wilson (eds), *The Late Roman Transition in the North*. Oxford, British Archaeological Report British Series 299, 47–65.
Cool, H. E. M. (in press) Some notes on spoons and mortaria. In B. Croxford, H. Eckardt, J. Meade and J. Weekes (eds) *TRAC: Proceedings of the Thirteenth Theoretical Roman Archaeology Conference, Leicester 2003,* Oxford, Oxbow Books.
Cool, H. E. M. and Baxter, M. J. (1999) Peeling the Onion: an Approach to Comparing Vessel Glass Assemblages. *Journal of Roman Archaeology* 12, 72–100.
Cool, H. E. M. and Baxter, M. J. (2002) Exploring Romano-British Finds Assemblages. *Oxford Journal of Archaeology* 21 (4), 365–80.
Cool, H. E. M, Lloyd-Morgan, G. and Hooley, A. D. (1995) *Finds from the Fortress*. The Archaeology of York: The Small Finds 17/10. York, York Archaeological Trust.
Cooper, N. J. (1996) Searching for the Blank Generation: Consumer Choice in Roman and Post-Roman Britain. In Webster and Cooper (eds), 85–98.
Cooper, N. J. (1998) The Supply of Pottery to Roman Cirencester. In N. Holbrook (ed.) *Cirencester: the Roman Town Defences, Public Buildings and Shops*, Cirencester Excavations 5, 324–350. Cirencester, Cotswold Archaeological Trust.
Cooper, N. J. (1999) The Small Finds. In Connor and Buckley (1999), 239–282.
Cooper, N. J. (2000a) Rubbish Counts. In Pearce (2000), 75–86.
Cooper, N. J. (2000b) The Roman Pottery. In N. J. Cooper, *The Archaeology of Rutland Water. Excavations at Empingham*

in the Gwash Valley, Rutland, 1967–73 and 1990. Leicester Archaeology Monograph 6. Leicester, University of Leicester, School of Archaeology and Ancient History.

Cooper, N. J. (2004) Pottery, landscape and trade: what are the sherds telling us? In Bowman and Liddle (eds), 81–94.

Cooper, N. J. (forthcoming a) Pottery Supply to Roman Cirencester (*Corinium Dobunnorum*): the potential contribution of pottery to the study of Romanization. In M. Tuffreau-Libre (ed.), *La ceramique en Gaule et en Bretagne romaines: commerce, contact et romanisation*, Nord-Ouest Archaeologie.

Cooper, N. J. (forthcoming b) The Portable Material Culture of Roman Scole. In T. Ashwin, *Excavations at Roman Scole 1993.* East Anglian Archaeology.

Cooper, N. J. (forthcoming c) The Roman and Medieval Small Finds. In R. J. Buckley, and J. Lucas, *Roman and Medieval Excavations at Little Lane and St Peter's Lane (The Shires), Leicester.*

Courtney, P. (1996) In Small Things Forgotten: the Georgian World View, Material Culture and the Consumer Revolution. *Rural History* 7(1), 87–95.

Courtney, P. (1997) Ceramics and the History of Consumption: Pitfalls and Prospects. *Medieval Ceramics* 21, 95–108

Crummy, N. (1983) *The Roman Small Finds from Excavations in Colchester 1971–9.* Colchester, Colchester Archaeological Report 2.

Darvill, T. and Russell, B. (2002) *Archaeology after PPG16: archaeological investigation in England 1990–1999.* Bournemouth, University of Bournemouth School of Conservation Sciences Research Report 10.

Davies, B., Richardson, B. and Tomber, R. (1994) *A Dated Corpus of Early Roman Pottery from the City of London.* The Archaeology of Roman London Volume 5, CBA Research Report 98. York, Council for British Archaeology.

Deetz, J. (1996) *In Small Things Forgotten: an Archaeology of Early American Life* 2nd edn. New York, Anchor Books Doubleday.

Ellison, A. B. (1987) Discussion: the finds. In Green, C.J.S., *Excavations at Poundbury, Dorchester, Dorset, 1966–1972, volume 1: the Settlements.* Dorchester, Dorset Natural History and Archaeology Soc. Mon. 7, 138–41.

Evans, J. (1993) Pottery function and finewares in the Roman North. *Journal of Roman Pottery Studies* 6, 95–118. Oxford, Oxbow Books.

Evans, J. (1995) Discussion of the Pottery in the Context of Roman Alcester. In S. Cracknell and C. Mahany, (eds.) *Roman Alcester: Southern Extramural Area 1964–66 Excavations Pt.2 Finds and Discussion.* CBA Research Report 97, 144–49. York, Council for British Archaeology.

Evans, J. (1998) The Roman Pottery. In D. Longley, N. Johnstone and J. Evans, Excavations on Two Farms of the Romano-British Period at Bryn Eryr and Bush Farm, Gwynedd. *Britannia* 29, 185–217.

Evans, J. (2001) Material Approaches to the Identification of Different Romano-British Site Types. In James and Millett (eds), 26–35.

Fulford, M. G. (1977) The Location of Romano-British Pottery Kilns: Institutional Trade and the Market. In J. Dore and K. T. Greene, *Roman Pottery Studies in Britain and Beyond.* Oxford, British Archaeological Reports, Supplementary No. 30, 301–16.

Fulford, M. G. (1984) Demonstrating Britannia's Economic Dependence in the First and Second Centuries. In T. F. C. Blagg and A. C. King (eds), *Military and Civilian in Roman Britain.* Oxford, British Archaeological Reports, British No. 136, 129–139.

Fulford, M. G. and Hodder, I. (1974) A regression analysis of some late Roman pottery: a case study. *Oxoniensia* 39, 26–33.

Gerrard, J. (2002) Pots for cash? A critique of the role of the 'free market' in the Late Roman Economy. In M. Carruthers, C. van Driel-Murray, A. Gardner, J. Lucas, L. Revell and E. Swift (eds.) *Proceedings of the Eleventh Annual Theoretical Roman Archaeology Conference 2001*, 13–23. Oxford, Oxbow Books.

Gillam, J. P. (1970) *Types of Roman Coarse Pottery in Northern Britain.* Newcastle-upon-Tyne, Oriel Press.

Glazebrook, J. (ed) (1997) *Research and Archaeology: a Framework for the Eastern Counties 1. Resource Assessment*, East Anglian Archaeology Occasional Paper no. 8.

Going, C. J. (1987) *The Mansio and Other Sites in the South-Eastern Sector of Caesaromagus: The Roman Pottery.* London, Council for British Archaeology, CBA Research Report 62.

Going, C. J. (1992) Economic Long Waves in the Roman Period: A Reconaissance of the Ceramic Evidence. *Oxford Journal of Archaeology*, 11, 93–117.

Greene, K. T. (1986) *The Archaeology of the Roman Economy*, London. Batsford.

Hawkes, G. (2002) Wolves' nipples and otters' noses? Rural foodways in Roman Britain. In M. Carruthers, C. van Driel-Murray, A. Gardner, J. Lucas, L. Revell and E. Swift (eds.) *TRAC2001: Proceedings of the Eleventh Annual Theoretical Roman Archaeology Conference 2001*, 45–50. Oxford, Oxbow Books.

Hawthorne, J. W. J. (1998) Pottery and Paradigms in the Early Western Empire. In C. Forcey, J. W. J. Hawthorne and R. Witcher (eds.) *TRAC 97: Proceedings of the Seventh Theoretical Roman Archaeology Conference 1997, 160–172.* Oxford, Oxbow Books.

Holbrook, N. and Bidwell, P. T. (1991) *Roman Finds from Exeter.* Exeter Archaeological Report 4, Exeter.

Hopkins, K. (1983) Introduction. In P. Garnsey, K. Hopkins and C.R. Whittaker (eds) *Trade in the Ancient Economy*, ix–xxv. London, Chatto and Windus.

Hoskins, W. G. (1957) *Leicestershire: an Illustrated Essay on the History of the Landscape.* London, Hodder and Stoughton.

Howe, M. D., Perrin, R. J. and Mackreth, D. F. (1980) *Roman Pottery from the Nene Valley: a Guide.* Peterborough, City Museum Occasional Paper 2.

Ireland, C. (1983) The Roman Pottery. In C. M. Heighway *The East and North Gates of Gloucester.* Western Archaeological Trust Monograph 4, 96–124.

James, S. (2003) Roman Archaeology: Crisis and Revolution. *Antiquity* 77, 178–84.

James, S. and Millett M. (eds) (2001), *Britons and Romans: advancing an archaeological agenda.* York, Council for British Archaeology, Research Report 125.

Johnson, D. E. (1972) A Roman Building at Chalk, near Gravesend. *Britannia* 3, 112–148.

Lewis, C. (2001) An Archaeological Resource Assessment and Research Agenda for the medieval period in the East Midlands http://www.le.ac.uk/ar/pdf_files/emidmed.pdf

Liddle, P. (1985) *Community Archaeology: a Fieldworker's*

Handbook of Organisation and Techniques. Leicestershire Museums Publication 61. Leicester, Leicestershire Museums, Art Galleries and Records Service.

Liddle, P. (2004) 'Community Archaeology in Leicestershire 1976–2001' in Bowman and Liddle (eds.), 8–9.

Lyding Will, E. (1979) The Sestius Amphoras: a reappraisal. *Journal of Field Archaeology* 6, 339–50.

Manacorda, D. (1978) The Ager Cosanus and the Production of the amphorae of Sestius: new evidence and reassessment. *Journal of Roman Studies* 68, 122–31.

Manby, T. G. Moorhouse, S. and Ottaway, P. (eds) (2003) *The Archaeology of Yorkshire: An Assessment at the Beginning of the Twenty-first Century*. Yorkshire Archaeological Society Occasional Paper 3. 393–97

Marney, P.T. (1989) *Roman and Belgic Pottery from Excavations in Milton Keynes 1972–82*. Buckinghamshire Archaeological Society Monograph no.2, Aylesbury.

Marsh, G. (1981) London's Samian Supply and its Relationship to the Development of the Gallic Samian Industry. In A.C. Anderson, and A.S. Anderson (eds.) *Roman Pottery Research in Britain and North-West Europe* pt. (i), 173–238 Oxford, British Archaeological Reports Supplementary Series 123.

Meadows, K. (1994) You are What You Eat: Diet, Identity and Romanisation. In S. Cottam, D. Dungworth, S. Scott, and J. Taylor (eds.), *TRAC 94 Proceedings of the Fourth Annual Theoretical Roman Archaeology Conference, Durham 1994*, 133–140. Oxford, Oxbow Books.

Millett, M. (1990) *The Romanization of Britain: an Essay in Archaeological Interpretation*. Cambridge, Cambridge University Press.

Millett, M. (1991) Pottery: Population or Supply Patterns? The Ager Tarraconensis Approach. In G. Barker and J. Lloyd (eds.) *Roman Landscapes: Archaeological Survey in the Mediterranean Region*, 189–26, London, British School at Rome.

Monaghan, J. (1997) *Roman Pottery from York*, Archaeology of York The Pottery 16/8. York, York Archaeological Trust.

Museum of London (2002) *A Research Framework for London Archaeology*. London, Museum of London.

Olivier, A. (1996) *Frameworks for our past: A Review of Research Frameworks, Strategies and Perceptions*. London, English Heritage.

Pearce, S., (ed.) (2000) *Researching Material Culture*. Leicester Archaeology Monograph 8. Leicester, University of Leicester, School of Archaeology and Ancient History.

Priest, V., Clay, P. N. and Hill, J. D. (2003) Iron Age Gold from Leicestershire. *Current Archaeology* 188, 358–62.

Reece, R. (1980) Town and Country: the end of Roman Britain *World Archaeology* 12.1, 77–91.

Reece, R. (1995) Site-finds in Roman Britain. *Britannia* 26, 179–206

Renfrew, C. and Bahn, P. (2000) *Archaeology: Theories,*

Methods and Practice (Second Edition.). London, Thames and Hudson.

Salway, P. 1981 *The Oxford History of England: Roman Britain*. Oxford, Clarendon Press.

Selkirk, A. (2003) Are your research frameworks really necessary? An open letter to English Heritage from Andrew Selkirk. In Manby, Moorhouse and Ottaway (eds), 393–97.

Taylor, J. (2001) Rural Society in Roman Britain. In S. James and M. Millett (eds), 46–59.

Tyers, P. A. (1996) *Roman Pottery in Britain*. London, Batsford.

Vince, A. (2001) An Archaeological Resource Assessment and Research Agenda for the Early and Middle Anglo-Saxon period in the East Midlands http://www.le.ac.uk/ar/pdf_files/emidas.pdf

Viner, L. (1998) The Finds Evidence. In N. Holbrook (ed.) *Cirencester: the Roman Town Defences, Public Buildings and Shops*. Cirencester Excavations 5, 294–323 Cotswold Archaeological Trust.

Webster, J. (2001) Creolizing the Roman Provinces. *American Journal of Archaeology* 105, 209–25.

Webster, J. (2005) Archaeologies of slavery and servitude: bringing 'New World' perspectives to Roman Britain. *Journal of Roman Archaeology*, 18, 161–79

Webster, J. and Cooper, N. J. (eds) (1996) *Roman Imperialism: post-colonial perspectives*. Leicester, Leicester Archaeology Monograph 3, University of Leicester School of Archaeology and Ancient History.

Wilkie, L. A. (1999) Evidence of African Continuities in the material culture of Clifton Plantation, Bahamas. In J. B. Haviser (ed.) *African Sites Archaeology in the Caribbean*. Princeton, Marcus Weiner.

Wilkie, L. A. (2001) Methodist Intentions and African Sensibilities: the victory of African consumerism over planter paternalism at a Bahamian plantation. In P. Farnsworth (ed.) *Island Lives: Historical Archaeologies of the Caribbean*, 272–300, University of Alabama Press, Tuscaloosa.

Williams, J. H. and Brown, N. (eds) (1999). *An Archaeological Research Framework for the Greater Thames Estuary*. Chelmsford, Essex County Council.

Willis, S. H. (1998) Samian Pottery in Britain: Exploring its Distribution and Archaeological Potential. *Arch. Journal* 155, 82–133.

Willis, S. H. (2005) *An E-monograph: Samian Pottery, a Resource for the Study of Roman Britain and Beyond. The results of the English Heritage funded Samian Project. Internet Archaeology*, 17.

Wilmott, T. (1991) *Excavations in the Middle Walbrook Valley, 1927–1960*. London and Middlesex Archaeological Society Special Paper no.13.

Yentsch, A. E. (1994) *A Chesapeake Family and their Slaves: a study in Historical Archaeology*. Cambridge, Cambridge University Press.

Method and Theory

5   Telling Stories About Brougham, or the Importance of the Specialist Report

H. E. M. Cool

In many respects the Roman world was very different from what had gone before and what was to come after it. One of the most obvious differences, especially noticeable in a peripheral area such as Roman Britain, is the sheer wealth of material culture that often appears to have been made, used and discarded with almost reckless abandon. This is a resource of almost infinite potential. Not only does it normally provide the detailed time frame for any individual site, it clothes the bare skeleton of structural narratives, placing the people who lived at the sites in their social contexts. Within Romano-British archaeology, it has been traditional for this material to be studied by a community of specialists who act as the gatekeepers to what are seen as areas of arcane knowledge. The specialist reports they produce are the primary data on which our pictures of the past are founded. After all, a fragment of pottery only becomes useful after someone has identified what sort of pot it would have come from, when that pot would have been used, where it might have been made, *etc*. Generally within our discipline these reports are an under-used resource. This paper explores why this should be, suggests a way forward for overcoming the problem and finally considers why a better appreciation of specialist work is fundamental for the future health of the discipline.

How best to publish the results of archaeological excavations has been a matter of anxious debate ever since the rescue boom of the 1960s and 1970s showed the volume of material that could be expected from large urban excavations, and how expensive consequent publication was. One of the areas that was felt to be expendable was the specialist report. Solutions ranged from banishing them to the archive and producing a synthetic overview, to reproducing them on microfiche. Neither was felt to be particularly successful by either the specialist communities or the excavators (see, for example, McWhirr 1986, 14), but it is easy to see why they were tried. Traditionally, specialist reports have been seen as appendices. A glance at many excavation reports makes this explicit. Sometimes they are explicitly referred to as such (*e.g.* Barker *et al.* 1997), and sometimes they are just placed where one might expect appendices, *i.e.* after the site narrative and the wider discussion of the site within its social and chronological setting, and before the index (*e.g.* Neal *et al.* 1990). This position within the text, reminiscent of an afterthought, has frequently been matched by a lack of

integration of the information they contain into the sections devoted to the wider discussion of the site. Equally, the use of the term 'specialist report' places them slightly to one side of archaeological endeavour. One does indeed need specialist knowledge to produce a report on samian stamps, intaglios or fish bones. Equally, however, one needs specialist knowledge to excavate a site and produce a coherent site narrative, yet the people who do the latter are not, to my knowledge, commonly referred to as stratigraphic specialists.

These are not merely matters of semantics; but reflect a deeper malaise where the work of the stratigraphic specialists was perceived, and perhaps still is, as the 'real' archaeology with the other contributions seen, whether explicitly admitted or not, as optional extras once the dating evidence has been extracted. An additional problem has been that as excavation reports have traditionally been drawn together by the stratigraphic specialist, and as the stratigraphy has been given primacy, the interactions between the different strands of data that have been emphasised have tended to be vertical rather than horizontal. It is the interaction between the stratigraphy and single aspects of the finds data that is mainly considered; the use of pottery to provide spot-dates and thus a chronological framework for the site is a classic example of this. The interactions between all the different strands of the data where the stratigraphy may take a subsidiary role are less often emphasised. To a certain extent, this is not surprising as far too many specialist reports are written with a specialist audience in mind, and others outside of that circle may struggle to extract useful information from them. Though a specialist would be failing in their duty if their reports did not contain the type of high level information that their fellows will need to carry the study forward, it should not be forgotten that one of the main aims of a report should be to convey clearly to a non-specialist what that material is saying about that particular site.

Changes in attitudes can start to be seen as a result of the more thoughtful planning and management of large archaeological projects that has developed since the publication of MAP2 (Andrews 1991). The pendulum has also swung back to much fuller print publication following the realisation that the specialist reports are: 'a resource to be used, questioned, reinterpreted, hopefully many times and over many years' (Wilson 2002, xviii).

Increasingly there are also attempts to provide overviews to make explicit what the specialist reports can contribute to the understanding of a site. This is especially noticeable within the domain of small finds where specialist knowledge is perhaps most fragmented (see for example Viner 1998, 309–12; Cooper 1999, 239–46; Cool 2002). There remains, however, the problem of how to integrate all strands of information in a site report so that, while providing all the data for future re-analysis, it also provides a coherent narrative of the site.

One way of solving this problem is to take the view that any archaeological excavation that is considered worthy of publication has a story to tell, and that the report should be structured so as to tell that story. This involves planning from the beginning, so that the eventual publication is the outcome of a project design that is firmly based in what the best theoretical and practical models for the type of site are. This doesn't mean that the story is pre-ordained at the outset, for it will emerge through the interactions of the data, the models and the team members. It does mean, however, that everyone working on the project must realise that their contribution is not a self-contained whole, but part of a larger organic process. To illustrate this approach, the analysis of a site that I and others have recently worked on will be considered.

The site is at Brougham in Cumbria which, in Roman terms, lies where the road over the Pennines via Stainmore meets the main western north–south road. Very little is known about the site. The fort has seen very little excavation (Higham and Jones 1991, 20, 39), and most information comes from epigraphic evidence. The presence of a cult centre dedicated to Balatucadrus, for example, might be suspected from the number of dedications to him found over the years (RIB I, nos. 772–7); and a cemetery is also indicated by chance finds of tombstones (RIB I nos. 784–8). In 1966 and 1967 rescue excavations were carried out by the then Ministry of Public Buildings and Works in advance of, but mainly at the same time as, major road improvements. These uncovered a large cremation cemetery dating to the third century on a hilltop outside the fort and *vicus*. This remains the largest cemetery ever to have been excavated outside of a military site in the north. Various attempts had been made to analyse and publish the material over the years, but without success because the stratigraphic records were poor. In some cases it has to be suspected that the original records had been lost; in others it was likely that, due to the extremely difficult circumstances of excavation, detailed records had never been made. What did survive in large quantities were all the finds, consisting of cremated human and animal bone, vessels of pottery, glass and metal, items of jewellery, *etc.* The records of the associations of these were relatively good, consisting of both formal registers, information written on the bags, and annotations on the grave plans, where they existed.

When we were approached early in 2000 by English Heritage to re-assess the archive with a view to analysis and publication, it became apparent that any analysis would have to be designed around what would normally be the specialist reports, and that only with full integration would there be any hope of making progress. Given that the site was a cemetery the obvious story to attempt to tell was that of the funerals that had taken place in it. To do this it was immediately apparent that it would be helpful to look beyond what was the normal frame of reference for writing up a Romano-British cemetery, and to consider how the insights gained by colleagues working in different geographical areas and periods could help us. As it was a cremation cemetery, for example, advances made in the understanding of cremation processes derived originally from the study of Bronze Age and Anglo-Saxon cemeteries (see, for example, McKinley 1997; 2000) were particularly helpful. They suggested that in a cemetery one might expect to find a range of features with cremated remains and not just formal urned burials. This agreed with the observation made a quarter of a century or so previously by Todd, to the effect that German archaeologists working on Roman cemeteries recognised a far wider range of cremation-related deposits than those working in Roman Britain did (Todd 1977, 39). This was a state of affairs which, judged by Philpott's survey, had continued to be the case until relatively recently (Philpott 1991, 8). One of our models at the outset, therefore, was that though the urned cremation burials formed the most obvious funerary-related deposit it was likely that there were other types, such as re-deposited pyre debris deposits, which would also provide evidence about the funerals.

This was of great help in solving one of the problems that had beset previous attempts to publish the cemetery. The excavators were of the opinion that approximately 40% of the deposits had been robbed. Though there was drawn evidence in three or four cases of secondary pits within the grave removing something, on the whole robbed graves appeared to be characterised by not having whole groups of vessels like the urned cremation burials, but rather having a muddled fill of sherds, fragments, *etc.* These deposits seemed likely to be good candidates for being pyre debris rather than formal urned burials that had been robbed. As already noted, the intellectual climate in Britain when this site was dug, and when earlier attempts had been made to study it, would not have made the recognition of such deposits likely. Suspecting this was the case was one thing; proving it was more difficult in the absence of any systematic recording of charcoal or fuel ash in the original records, as it is this material that would normally be used to identify such deposits. Instead, the presence or absence of pyre goods (melted beads, burnt bone veneers, melted copper alloy pieces) were used and were found to be more common in the proposed pyre debris deposits. A Chi Square test was carried out, and it showed that the distribution pattern was statistically significant. This interaction between the data contained in three separate small finds reports therefore provided the evidence on which the deposit types could be defined (urned cremation burial, unurned formal cremation burial, re-deposited pyre debris, *etc*). It is a good example of how finds can be used to provide information about a variety of processes, here depositional, other than the mere dating role they are often relegated to.

When planning the analysis of all the material it was also obvious that, as we were trying to explore funerals, what we were looking at was how the living behaved and what their attitudes were to the dead. Such behaviour is culturally conditioned, and it was felt important to examine what the patterns in the data could tell us about this, rather than relying on models of what 'Roman' burials ought to be. The people at Brougham were burying their dead in the third century almost on the very edge of the Empire; and it has to be suspected that their funerals would be different to the ones which often feature in such works as Toynbee's *Death and Burial in the Roman World* with its emphasis on an earlier period and the Mediterranean.

Much ethnographic and archaeological literature suggests that different treatments are accorded to people depending on their age and sex (see, for example, Parker Pearson 1999). To explore this it was obvious that the osteological examination of the human bone was central, and would have remained so even if we had had a better stratigraphic record. In the human bone report, Jacqueline McKinley was able to identify 17 different age states, many of which overlapped. In order to explore whether people of different ages and sexes were being treated differently, it was necessary in the first instance to simplify this to acquire samples that could be meaningfully compared. The 17 age categories were thus reduced to four: infant (5 years or younger), immature (5–18), adult (over 18) and uncertain. The adults could be divided into three (male, female and uncertain) and there was also a category of double burials where two individuals had been buried together. Once this framework was in place it was possible to examine the distribution of the different pyre and grave goods both by age and sex, and through time. The graves had been furnished with large numbers of Black Burnished I jars and these provided an invaluable dating tool as the dated typology of these in the third century is well established (Bidwell 1985, 174; Holbrook and Bidwell 1991, 95). It was possible to divide many of the deposits between three phases within the overall timespan which stretched from AD 200/20 to AD 300/310.

The results surpassed all expectations. It was possible to demonstrate a major difference between the way the younger people (infants/immature) and the adults were treated at all stages of the funeral process; from the preparation of the body and its transfer to the pyre, to the goods that were burned on the pyre with the individual, and finally to the grave goods that were thought appropriate to place with the individual in the formal deposition. The adults, for example, appeared to have been taken to their pyres on richly decorated biers and burned with many pyre goods, both objects and animals. One of the most important findings was that amongst this community much of the wealth expended at the funeral literally went up in smoke. There was clearly an emphasis on public consumption visible in the funeral procession and on the pyre, as opposed to the private consumption in the privacy of the grave. Young people were not associated with the remains of the biers or the same range of pyre goods. It was at this point that the date at which these excavations were undertaken was most problematic. In the 1960s there was no routine wet-sieving of the remains as there would have been more recently. We have no way of discovering whether the pyre goods would have included fruit and other organic remains, as has been found more recently in other cremated deposits (see for example Giorgi 2000). The pyres of the children currently look bare, but they might have been covered with fruit and flowers, and showered with perfumes. All we can say is that children and adults were definitely treated differently. There were strong suggestions that different pyre goods were also appropriate for adult males and females. There is a tendency, for example, for large metal buckets only to be found with females.

The age and sex differences continued with the formal deposition of the remains as urned cremation burials. Glass drinking vessels, for example, were only ever placed with adult males, while samian Drag form 33 cups were appropriate for young children. Items that would have been antiques by the time they were deposited in the grave were repeatedly deposited with the oldest members of the community. There are even intriguing hints that some people may have adopted a different gender role to that of their biological sex. One adult male, in a particularly elaborate and unusual double cist, had both the beads that are an undoubted female attribute at Brougham as well as glass drinking cups that are a male one. Interestingly, amongst his grave goods were beads from a segmented jet bracelet of the same type as worn by a young man at Catterick who, had he dressed in life as he was dressed in death, would undoubtedly have been regarded as a transvestite (Cool 2002, 41).

As well as being able to describe the different sorts of funerals that were appropriate to different types of people, it also became apparent that the community showed many signs of not being Romano-British, however that may be defined. Rather they gave every appearance of having come from the Danubian provinces, perhaps in the area of Pannonia or even from the *barbaricum* beyond the frontiers. Such a link was suggested by many different strands of the specialist reports such as epigraphic evidence and the repeated recovery of finds that are otherwise only found in that area. The suggestion that this community was in someway alien was also supported by such factors as the decision to suddenly start burying the dead in this new cemetery, their habit of burning horses on the pyre, and their unusual choices of pottery vessels for items to deposit with the dead.

The patterns of behaviour in the cemetery sketched here are only a small subset of those noted during the analysis, and full details are provided in the full publication (Cool 2004). It is worth asking, though, whether the approach of deliberately structuring the report as a story from the outset had any advantages. It seems likely that the intrusive element of the Brougham community would have been noticed during the analysis, no matter what questions had been asked. I feel, however, that it is highly unlikely that the detailed and complex picture of how the dead were treated would have emerged if we had not been attempting to tell the story of the funerals. That required us to question each element and find. We needed to know the answers to questions such as 'where in the ritual would this have been used', 'who would it have been used for' and 'why might it have been used'? Some of the age/sex associations were very strong, others were weaker because of the variable quality of the recording; but once the overall pattern of behaviour had been established then this evidence could be re-examined. The charcoal, for example, had only been collected randomly, and therefore could not be subjected to the formal statistical analysis that many other categories of data were examined by. Hints had emerged that sweet-smelling species might have been selected for the pyres of particular categories of people. Little could be made of this observation on its own but, set against the evidence of many other types of finds, it fell into the pattern of funeral rites strongly influenced by the age and sex of the deceased.

Paradoxically, the weakness of the structural narrative was one of the strengths of this analysis as we were forced to look at horizontal interactions between all the specialist reports, rather than the vertical interaction between the stratigraphic evidence and each individual report, as normally happens. We were also fortunate to be dealing with a remarkably rich data-set from a cemetery in use for a relatively short length of time. Clearly, a well-excavated urban multi-period site would be a much more complex proposition, but the principle will remain the same. The site will have a story, and a much more textured and detailed version of it will be extracted if there are explicit attempts to try to tell it by looking at all the interactions between the different classes of evidence.

Some will argue that it is difficult enough to bring a basic excavation report to publication and that telling stories is for others to do with the data that is provided. Some specialists could reasonably point out that they are so overwhelmed with work that they do not have the time to write the reports on their own material, let alone consider the rest of the finds and how they might interact. I would argue that these are understandable but impoverished attitudes. Presumably we are archaeologists because we are interested in the past, and that past has to be more than a tidy collection of catalogues and context descriptions. If those of us who generate the primary data are not prepared to explore it, then who will? Where better to investigate and understand a site than in the report

which publishes it? New stories will be told of a site as techniques improve and different theoretical positions emerge, but that should not prevent us from doing the best we can with the data now.

For the future of the discipline, it is also important that we show how important good specialist knowledge is and what can be done with it, and that will only happen if excavation reports become somewhat more interesting than many of them currently are. Roman archaeology in Britain sits on a demographic time-bomb. The age profile of the majority of the specialist community is heavily skewed towards older individuals. The younger scholars who might eventually take the places of the established individuals are few and far between, and certainly insufficient to replace them. The specialist communities have been aware of this for some time (see, for example, Fulford and Huddleston 1991, 48) and concern is now spreading more widely (Hill 2001, 18). There are a variety of reasons for this shortage, including the lack of exposure to finds work at student level and the lack of a career structure that would encourage people to enter the field. I would also suggest that it arises because specialist work is perceived as rather dry and rather boring, certainly not the stuff that engages regularly with the themes and interests that are displayed each year in conferences such as those devoted to Theoretical Roman Archaeology. I have spent a quarter of a century doing specialist work and in my experience that perception is entirely wrong. We have to do all in our power to dispel it and encourage a new generation to develop specialist skills. Otherwise we shall reach a point where there is no more Roman archaeology. The stratigraphic specialists may continue to dig to their heart's content, but all they will find will be holes in the ground filled with bits of pottery and bone, and those will be mute. There will be no-one to tell them what the fragments are and what they mean. They will be left alone without the equal partners necessary if new Roman pasts are going to continue to be created in the future.

Acknowledgements

The Brougham analysis took place by courtesy of a splendid and helpful team of which I was only one part (glass and small finds). In alphabetical order, the specialists who dealt with the bulk of the material were Julie Bond (animal bone), Brenda Dickinson (samian), Jeremy Evans (pottery), Andrew Fitzpatrick (inscribed and sculpted stones), Stephen Greep (worked bone), Brian Hartley (samian), Jacqueline McKinley (human bone and cremation rituals), Quita Mould (small finds), Hedley Pengelly (samian) and Fay Worley (animal bones). Other contributors were Lindsay Allason-Jones, Justine Bayley, Mike Baxter, Sarnia Butcher, Gill Campbell, David Dungworth, Martin Henig, Jacqui Watson, Tony Wilmott and the late Frank Jenkins. To all of these, my thanks. English Heritage funded the work and have allowed me to consider it here in advance of full publication; my thanks to them and especially to Sarah Jennings, the EH monitor for the project who was unfailing in her support.

Abbreviations

RIB I Collingwood, R.G. and Wright, R.P. (1965) *Roman Inscriptions of Britain, 1. Inscriptions on Stone.* Oxford, Oxford University Press.

Bibliography

Andrews, G. (1991) *Management of Archaeological Projects.* London, English Heritage.

Barker, P., White, R., Pretty, K., Bird, H. and Corbishley, M. (1997) *The Baths Basilica Wroxeter: Excavations 1966–90.* English Heritage Archaeological Report 8, London, English Heritage.

Bidwell, P. T. (1985) *The Roman Fort of Vindolanda at Chesterholm Northumberland*, Historic Buildings and Monuments Commission Archaeological Report 1. London.

Cool, H. E. M. (2002) An overview of the small finds from Catterick. In P.R. Wilson,*Cataractonium: Roman Catterick and its hinterland. Excavations and Research, 1958–1997. Part II*, 24–43. Council for British Archaeology Research Report 129. York.

Cool, H. E. M. (2004) *The Roman Cemetery at Brougham, Cumbria: Excavations 1966–7.* Britannia Monograph Series, 21, London, Society for the Promotion of Roman Studies.

Cooper, N. J. (1999) The small finds. In A. Connor and R. Buckley, *Roman and Medieval Occupation in Causeway Lane, Leicester*, 239–82. Leicester Archaeology Monograph 5. Leicester, School of Archaeological Studies.

Fulford, M. G. and Huddleston, K. (1991) *The Current State of Romano-British Pottery Studies: a review for English Heritage.* English Heritage Occasional Paper 1. London, English Heritage.

Giorgi, J. (2000) The plant remains – a summary. In A. Mackinder *A Romano-British Cemetery on Watling Street*, 65–6. Museum of London Archaeology Service, Archaeology Studies Series 4. London.

Higham, N. J. and Jones G. D. B. (1985) *The Carvetii.* Stroud, Alan Sutton Publishing Limited.

Hill, J. D. (2001) Romanisation, gender and class: recent approaches to identity in Britain and their possible consequences. In S. James and M. Millett (eds) *Britons and Romans: advancing an archaeological agenda,* 12–8. Council for British Archaeology Research Report 125. York.

Holbrook, N., and Bidwell, P. T. (1991) *Roman Finds from Exeter*, Exeter Archaeological Report 4. Exeter.

McKinley, J. I. (1997) Bronze Age 'Barrows' and the funerary rites and rituals of cremation. *Proceedings of the Prehistoric Society* 63, 129–45.

McKinley, J. I. (2000). Pheonix rising: aspects of cremation in Roman Britain. In J. Pearce, M. Millett, and M. Struck (eds.) *Burial, Society and Context in the Roman World*, 38–44. Oxford, Oxbow Books.

McWhirr, A. (1986) *Houses in Roman Cirencester.* Cirencester Excavations III. Cirencester.

Neal, D. S., Wardle, A. and Hunn, J. (1990) *Excavation of the Iron Age, Roman and Medieval Settlement at Gorhambury, St. Albans.* English Heritage Archaeological Report 14. London, English Heritage.

Parker Pearson, M. (1999) *The Archaeology of Death and Burial.* Stroud, Sutton Publishing Limited.

Philpott, R. (1991) *Burial Practices in Roman Britain. A survey of grave treatment and furnishing AD43–410.* British Archaeological Reports (British Series) 219. Oxford.

Todd, M. (1977) Germanic burials in the Roman Iron Age. In R. Reece (ed.). *Burial in the Roman World*, 39–43. Council for British Archaeology Research Report 22. London.

Toynbee, J. M. C. (1971) *Death and Burial in the Roman World.* Baltimore and London. Johns Hopkins University Press (1996 reprint).

Viner, L. (1998) The finds evidence. In N. Holbrook (ed.) *Cirencester: The Roman Town Defences, Public Buildings and Shops,* 294–323. Cirencester Excavations V. Cirencester.

Wilson, P. R. (2002) *Cataractonium: Roman Catterick and its hinterland. Excavations and Research, 1958–1997. Part I*, Council for British Archaeology Research Report 128. York.

6 Six Honest Serving Men: a Basic Methodology for the Study of Small Finds

Nina Crummy

I keep six honest serving-men
(They taught me all I knew);
Their names are What and Why and When
And How and Where and Who.

Rudyard Kipling, *The Elephant's Child*

Introduction

This paper is based on work done sporadically over many years with primary school children, sixth form college students, local societies and continuing education students in Colchester, London and Reading. It is more specifically developed from sessions with undergraduate students working on the University of Reading's training excavation at Silchester.

Work with primary school children suggests that they are all perfectly capable of engaging in an *intrinsic* study of an individual object (and this is true even, and in some cases particularly, of those with learning or social difficulties) and many are also capable of *extrinsic* studies, looking beyond the object to its relationship with others of its kind, to the context from which it derives, to other objects within that context, to directly related contexts, to its socio-economic implications, *etc.* Obviously their perceptions are simple, but they are also acute. There is, therefore, no reason why the same should not apply to undergraduates and post-graduates.

At the same time, small finds are a rich and diverse artefact group, particularly in the major 'consumerist' periods (Roman, medieval and post-medieval). Each large excavation will turn up objects not found in the standard works of reference and even well-known types of objects may still be either under-researched or ripe for updating. On the one hand, then, we have a large artefact base available for either basic or further research, on the other a body of intelligent and capable people. Therefore, the current paucity of small finds (as opposed to pottery and coin) research undertaken in British universities is, I hope, a passing phase.

The following methodological guide, applicable to small finds of all periods, is quite deliberately both simple and simply presented, aimed at the beginner, not the expert. It falls into two parts. The first is a question-led guide for those with either no previous knowledge, or very little, and has been devised for the study of a single object. The second part is pattern-led and covers the study of groups of like objects and of whole assemblages. It is not intensively developed here, but a few references are given to related articles or to examples of best practice. Obviously, the two approaches interlink, each providing data for the other.

Though this guide aims to be positive and encouraging, it also includes a great many cautionary notes, the first of which is appropriate here: *there is no substitute for experience*. Identifying an object is not simply an intellectual question-and-answer session, but an appeal to the senses, sight and touch in particular. The would-be small finds specialist must not only look at a great many objects in display cases and images in books but also *handle* a large amount of material before s/he will be able to say of an unidentified object 'It *feels* Roman'. Such a statement is largely instinctive, based upon the colour and texture of an object, how it was made and decorated, its weight, its shape, *etc.* The *feel* for objects can only be learned through experience.

Question-led study

The study of an object is essentially a three-stage process which is achieved by asking and answering a series of questions. The three stages are 1) identification, 2) description, and 3) discussion. There is no reason to regard failure to identify an object at stage 1 as a reason to stop at that point. Stages 2 and 3 may resolve the problem, or at least limit the possibilities.

The basic questions which allow stages 2 and 3 to proceed are ten in number and are not just developed from Kipling's 'six honest serving men', but also from that old standby of the police detective, *cui bono*, 'who benefits', which can, in some cases, be surprisingly applicable.

The ten questions are:

1. What is it?
2. How was it made?
3. Is it similar to or different from others of its general type?
4. Why was it made? (= What was it used for? = How was it used?)
5. Who made it?
6. Who for?
7. When was it made, and for how long was it in use?
8. Where was it made?
9. Who benefited from its manufacture?
10. Where was it found?

Many of these questions are not appropriate in all circumstances, particularly where there are commercial considerations, and time cannot be spent researching each object in depth. Similarly, where a provincial or international study has already been done of that type of object there is no need to rehearse all the available evidence when a simple statement and reference will do.

Many of the questions interlink, many will be unanswerable without some research, others will be unanswerable without intensive research and some will remain unanswerable. It is not compulsory to find an answer, and it is always better not to guess or to try to persuade oneself against all reason that the mystery object in the hand is precisely the same as the identified object in the book, despite the fact that the two differ in dimension, style and technical detail. No-one can possibly know everything about everything, and there is no shame in admitting defeat. Every assemblage always contains one or two (or more) mystery objects and the positive aspect of this is that there is always something new to learn. There is, however, an answer to question 1 for any object, even if it is just 'object', and there is an answer to question 10 for any object, even if it is just 'unprovenanced' or 'unstratified'.

Question 10 is not placed last here because it is the least important. It is, on the other hand, one of the most important questions that can be asked in archaeology and the one that facilitates the exchange of information between the site director and the small finds specialist. It can provide two-way dating evidence, interpretations of land or building use, and evidence of social and economic activity. In the setting of a burial it can supply the age, the gender, the status, and even the occupation of the deceased. It is the catalyst for turning antiquarianism into archaeology.

Answers to the ten questions may be developed by a series of observations and/or further questions. Some examples are given below, but are by no means comprehensive. A few cautionary notes are also included.

1. What is it?

This question enables the production of a 'catalogue entry' with the following minimum information: material, simple name, further description, size. For example:

material	bone
simple name	strip
further description	broken at each end, edges damaged, rectangular in section
dimensions	length, width, thickness (mm)

In some cases this can be more highly developed:

material	copper-alloy (analysis will permit closer identification, *e.g.* brass, bronze)
simple name	brooch
complex name	one-piece bow brooch
type name	Nauheim derivative, and/or a typology number
subtype	with single curve wire bow
further description	pin missing, three transverse nicks halfway down bow
dimensions	length (mm)

Beware calling an object gold simply because it is yellow and shiny. It may be copper-alloy that has been buried in waterlogged soil.

Terminology is important. Consider how much more information is immediately available if finger-ring, harness-ring, curtain-ring, strap-junction ring, *etc.* are used rather than ring. The indices of large and detailed catalogues are invaluable guides to accurate identification and correct use of terms (*e.g.* Manning 1985). Many organisations using databases to manage artefact collections or records (*e.g.* museums, Scheduled Monument Records, field units) will already have a key-word list for objects, either based upon that developed by the Museums Documentation Association or devised in-house. The list of the Portable Antiquities Scheme, for example, is online at *www.finds.org.uk*. None of these lists is perfect. Most are not all-embracing, and not all the people using them are experts at identification; some objects will therefore be 'misfiled'. It is always best to play safe and offer a general term rather than a specific one that may not be accurate.

Be aware of differences of usage between cultures. A long pin in one culture may be a dress pin, but in another a hairpin. The function of some objects is a matter for debate, *e.g.* Anglo-Saxon modified pig fibulae, some of which are pierced, some not, have been variously described in the past as awls, pins or needles, but current research suggests that they are weaving tools.

Similarly, be aware that some things do not change their shape through time (see question 7).

2. How was it made?

This question is the basis of a more detailed 'catalogue entry', but requires rather more expertise to answer. While use of the correct technical term is best, a description of observed features such as colour, markings, *etc.*, will often be perfectly adequate. Dr Michael Faraday's report, written in 1835, on a copper-alloy lamp from one of the Bartlow Hills (Fig. 6.1) is a good example of what may be deduced by sight and touch alone:

The bronze leaf which rises from the handle must have struck you as being not merely very ornamental but also as a shade to the eyes, a protection to the hand when the lamp was carried, and a counterpoise by its weight to the projection of the lamp at the place of the wick; the lamp would in fact be very unsteady without it.

Later in his report, Faraday, analysing the contents of a glass vessel, takes dedication to scientific observation to limits that it would be unwise to emulate today, but which show that using one's sight and touch alone may not be enough: *"It had a pale brown colour; was very sweet to*

Fig. 6.1. The lamp from 'The Great Hill' at Bartlow.

the taste (with a degree of roughness on the tongue); and had a faint vinous or apple-like smell" (Faraday 1836, 309).

Useful technical terms to be aware of include:

cast	lathe-turned
wrought (= forged)	carved
rolled	polished
filed	pierced
engraved	painted
incised	plated
inlaid	repaired
enamelled	adapted
nielloed	unfinished
sawn	

There are many more. Sources of technical terms for the Roman period are (among many others): Hodges 1964; Wild 1970; Strong & Brown 1976; Bateson 1981; Hattatt 1987; McWhirr 1982; White 1984/1986; MacGregor 1985; Manning 1985; Allason-Jones 1996; Johns 1996. *Archaeometallurgy* in the English Heritage Centre for Archaeology's Guidelines series (2001) covers all periods, is clearly written and well illustrated, and includes a section on 'Where to get help'.

It might also be appropriate at this stage to consider why a particular technique was used. For example, was the object decorated with cells of enamel to produce a zoomorphic appearance? Was a handle carved into a particular form to provide a firm grip?

3. Similar or different?

This question requires that an image of the object and its verbal description are compared to images/descriptions of others. Differences should be carefully noted and their relevance considered.

If it is different, how? Is it in terms of material, the method of manufacture, the suggested date range or the provenance? Is it the only copper-alloy example when all others are iron? Is it the only cast example when all others are wrought? Is it the only small example when all others are large? Is it the only one from northern Britain when all others are from the south?

If it is different, why might that be? Is it small, cast, and copper-alloy because it is a votive model of a large wrought iron object?

4. Why was it made?
(= What was it used for? = How was it used?)

This question asks for consideration of the function of the object. This is often implicit in the name *e.g.* finger-ring, axe, sword, *etc.*

A simple identification of function is not always enough, however, and in some cases it may be appropriate to explore further.

Further questions might be similar to the following four examples. *a.* Did it fulfil this function successfully? Does a buckle, for example, actually work as a buckle, or is it for display only? *b.* Are there signs of wear through use and are these in any way distinctive? Does a shoe sole, for example, display the wear found with normal walking or that caused by pigeon-toed walking? *c.* Is it unused yet broken? For example, bone mounts might split when the last attachment hole is drilled. *d.* Has it been adapted for reuse as a different type of object? For example, has a hairpin been turned into a fish-hook?

Be aware that the identification and function of many objects in the Roman period, or indeed in any other, is not an absolute given. The objects currently identified as wax spatulae have, in the past, been identified as razors (Boon 1991, 30–32; Feugère 1995). No discredit attaches to Boon for putting forward a theory that has now been superseded. Size can matter in terms of an object's function: *e.g.* small shears were used for personal grooming, medium-sized ones for shearing sheep or cutting cloth, and large ones again for cutting cloth (Manning 1985, 34).

Be aware also of some odd conventions. Spindlewhorls are usually shown upside down (though see Woodland 1990), as are Roman brooches, which are always drawn with the head up, though they were worn with the foot up. There is, however, some advantage to showing brooches head up, as they then appear as viewed by the wearer.

Moving away from the practical towards the theoretical, a suitable question at this stage might be: is it a symbol of status, authority, or belief? This can be further explored under questions 6 and 9.

5. Who made it?

Is it a thing of beauty made by a master craftsman? Is it a standard item made by a competent artisan? Does it look rather less competently made and, therefore, could it be home-made? Is it worse than that? (I make no apologies for the use of the word 'craftsman', which I regard not as gender-specific but as representing a standard to be aspired to by any person, male or female.)

The majority of items will, of course, belong to the second question and require no comment. To place an object in any of the other categories requires sound knowledge of the comparative material.

6. Who was it for?

This question raises issues of distribution, marketing, identity, *etc.* The following possible areas for investigation might be worth considering: age, gender, status, civilian, military, local, regional, national, international. Care should be taken not to over-interpret from inadequate data, not to decide on the answer before the data is gathered and examined and also to try not to allow one's own identity and prejudices to colour any answer.

Cemeteries are a rich source of answers to this question, as Hilary Cool's paper in this volume shows. However, do not be lured into assuming that what is true in one cemetery

is true for all. Burial practices can and do vary from one grave to another, from one area of a cemetery to another, from one cemetery within a settlement to another, as well as from one settlement to another, and from one country to another.

7. When was it made?

This question, that of the date of the artefact, can be answered in the general, the specific, or the very specific, drawing upon previous published work and, perhaps, one's own observations. The answer should be examined in the light of the example currently considered.

A general answer might be 'Roman', a specific one 'first-century' and a very specific one AD 60–80. If the object is from an excavation then the answer should be checked against the stratigraphic information. Anomalies should be flagged up and either the date for the object/ type refined (perhaps this is the earliest stratified example) or the site director alerted that perhaps the phasing needs checking.

Be aware that many things, iron tools in particular, did not change through time. Without an archaeological context to provide a date, shears of the Late Iron Age cannot be distinguished from those of the Roman period, and it is well-nigh impossible to separate out residual Roman nails from medieval ones in a fourteenth-century pit group.

Please note that if an object occurs much later than its usual date range there may be no cause for alarm or excitement, it may simply be residual in a secondary context (*e.g.* disturbed by pit-digging and then redeposited). There are several other ways in which an object can be shifted between strata, forwards and backwards in time, though they occur far less frequently than is often supposed. Animal disturbance can cause objects to move through the ground, though animal holes will usually be picked up by experienced diggers. Frost and wind action can cause the sides of excavated features to 'leak' objects out of the section and so be trowelled up and accidentally allocated to an inappropriate period. This is matched by 'digger's boot syndrome', when a small object may be carried in mud on a boot from one part of the site (or even the site hut) into a feature. Another danger is the deliberate and irresponsible salting of an excavation with unrelated material. This can have far-reaching consequences if not detected. Similarly irresponsible and misleading are false claims of provenance to mask illegal activities (*e.g.* Hull & Hawkes 1987, 187–9; Stead 1998).

Watch out for objects that have been reused or valued in some way in a later period. There are many instances of Roman and earlier objects in Anglo-Saxon graves or on Anglo-Saxon settlement sites, some of which are examples of deliberate selection and curation, others of reuse in precisely the same way as intended during the period of origin (White 1988; West 1985, 25, 31, 34, fig 82, 5, fig 118, 5, fig 129, 7). Palaeolithic and later stone tools and Bronze Age tools also sometimes occur in contexts of the Iron Age or Roman period, which shows that they were considered to have had religious significance (*e.g.* Turner and Wymer 1987).

8. *Where was it made?*

There are seven basic answers: *a.* not known; *b.* locally; *c.* in a particular place; *d.* in a particular region; *e.* somewhere in Britain; *f.* in mainland Europe (place, region, country?); *g.* on another continent (place, region, country?). In some cases it may be possible to add more detailed information, such as: Was it the product of a single workshop, or a type produced in more than one workshop?

When studying a single object, this question can usually only be answered if the type has already been researched and the research published. If the item is clearly 'home-made' (see question 5), however, then the answer must be 'locally'.

Distribution maps are very useful tools for locating manufacturing centres. They should, however, be treated with caution, as has clearly been shown by Evison for the early Anglo-Saxon period (1981), because a great many factors, let alone the accident of recovery, can affect their accuracy. Accidents of loss affect what reaches the ground in the first place, and accidents of survival affect what remains intact to be removed from the ground. An object made of a costly material is less likely to have passed into the archaeological record through casual loss, as items with a real (economic) value are less likely to be thrown away if broken and will be searched for if dropped. Some materials survive better in some soils than others and some require very specific burial conditions to survive at all (*e.g.* wood and textile need anaerobic conditions). The means whereby objects become buried can also be a factor. Artefacts are often better preserved in inhumation graves than cremations because grave goods were sometimes burned on the pyre with the deceased rather than placed in the grave intact.

The techniques available to assist identification are another factor. In recent decades the use of X-radiography has improved the identification of iron objects considerably and it is noticeable that many more iron styli and iron brooches are now being recovered, fragments of which would often have been confused with nails in the past. Selection for publication also affects what percolates through to the public domain and, if time and funding permit, it is always wisest to go back to the site archive to make sure that all examples of an object from a particular excavation are included in the distribution data, particularly when dealing with the early literature. This is less of a problem with very recent small finds reports as either a full catalogue might be published whether all the objects are illustrated or not, or some sort of quantification may be included, or at the very least a note to the effect that 'six other examples' were found apart from the one illustrated.

Finally, the quality of the library available to researchers can also affect data retrieval, especially in these days of stringent budget cuts.

As a final word of caution, if research is undertaken to look at a type of object from a tightly-defined region, especially one based on modern political boundaries, care should be taken to check if the object type occurs outside it. If this task is not undertaken, it is possible to miss completely a manufacturing centre just on the other side of the county or country boundary.

9. *Who benefited from its manufacture?*

In any exchange, it may be presumed that both the seller and the purchaser benefit. However, was the seller a middleman or the maker? If it is a signed workshop product, was the owner of the workshop also the maker, or did he employ artisans/slaves?

Did the state benefit in any way? Was there any tax to pay? Or is the object the product of an imperial-owned manufacturing process (*e.g.* lead pigs).

Is it a votive offering? In other words, did the purchaser then donate it to the gods in the hope of benefiting from divine assistance?

Occasionally someone is intended to lose by the manufacture and use of an artefact. A shackle, for example, can scarcely be said to benefit the wearer, while a curse tablet placed in a temple has several implied types of 'benefit', but a distinctly malign intent. As a piece of sheet lead the tablet has been bought and paid for; a professional scribe may have been paid in a separate transaction to write the curse upon it; separate to both these transactions, a gift may have been made to the temple when the curse was placed there; the person placing it in the temple hoped to benefit from the assistance of the particular deity named within it; but, most important of all, the curse will call for someone to suffer, preferably horribly (*e.g.* Tomlin 1988, especially 230–1).

10. *Where was it found?*

Even if question 1 is the only one that has been answered so far, there is always an answer to question 10, even if it is only 'unprovenanced' or a site code plus 'unstratified'.

If better information than this is available, then the questions that follow on are: In what context? Is it a primary context? Were others found in the same context or other (similar?) contexts on this site and on other sites? Can any conclusions be drawn?

A single awl, for example, in a primary context on an excavation (*e.g.* a floor) is good evidence for leather-working in that room, but the same awl in a secondary context (dumped soil) or unstratified (including metal-detected) is only evidence for leather-working in the area. Several awls in the same or similar contexts reinforce these pictures. Several awls, a cobbler's last, lots of hobnails, leather offcuts, and both finished and unfinished shoes in closely associated contexts (*e.g.* floors and pits) are unequivocal evidence of a shoemaker's workshop.

Context thus leads on to the pattern-led study of an object or of a group of similar and/or related objects.

Pattern-led study

This type of study may be defined as turning the focus of attention away from the object onto the site or away from the individual object onto its type as a whole, with provenance being an important factor.

Examining several examples of a type of object for unifying patterns should produce information that will help to answer a question-led study and should ideally include sections on: material, function, typology, manufacture, marketing, date, distribution, site type and context type. (Artefacts acquired by antiquarian collectors or found by metal dectorists or by fieldwalking rather than by excavation will at best only have a provenance that may allow the site type to be identified, but will not have a context. This is true not only of metal-detected finds, but also of many of the accessions in a museum collection). Good examples of typological studies become standard works of reference for small finds specialists (*e.g.* Cool 1990, which deals with Roman metal hairpins from southern Britain; Allason-Jones 1989 on Roman earrings; or Hagen 1937, Lawson 1976 and Allason-Jones 1996 on Roman jet/shale objects). Some typologies are embedded within the small finds reports from a particular site or group of sites (*e.g.* Clarke 1979, 301–14; Crummy 1983). Such site- or place-specific typologies are unlikely to be, and were never intended to be, applicable to the country as a whole, though they may be useful starting points in searching for parallels.

Nicholas Cooper's paper in this volume deals with how a small finds assemblage, or a specific type of small find from a number of sites, can help to interpret the peak periods of activity on a site, and the type of activity. He rightly points out that in the Roman period (and not only then) dress accessories tend to dominate any assemblage. This means that the 'background noise' is, in fact, the loudest thing on the site. Screening out dress accessories might be useful or, alternatively, concentrating on dress accessories alone, as Cooper has done with bone hairpins. Sometimes, though, the dress accessories are excellent evidence for the use and date of a site. On Nornour, Isles of Scilly, brooches accounted for 80 per cent of the small finds assemblage because they were the principal votive deposit at a shrine. Other forms of dress accessory accounted for at least a further 6 per cent.

Cooper uses the functional divisions defined in Crummy 1983 for the large assemblage of Colchester small finds, but it should be noted that these were designed for a town with military origins and subsequent domestic occupation and are not always appropriate for other assemblages. Moreover, Hella Eckardt's paper, also in this volume, shows the value of treating lighting equipment as a single functional group. Rather than adhere rigidly to the Colchester categories, it can be better to let the assemblage under examination dictate the divisions. Thus, if there is a lot of evidence for leather-working or salt-production, create functional categories to cover them. Just as small finds are themselves diverse, approaches for dealing with them usefully must also be diverse.

Table 6.1. Tabulation of a hypothetical small finds assemblage by functional category and phase

Category	Phase 1	Phase 2	Phase 3	Phase 4	Phase 5	Phase 6
dress accessories	10	25	2	10	4	40
toilet instruments	–	10	–	2	1	–
textile working tools	–	–	–	1	–	–
household utensils	5	5	–	3	1	–
lighting equipment	5	10	–	1	1	–
writing equipment	–	2	–	–	–	–
recreation	15	2	–	3	1	–
tools	–	–	12	2	–	–
knives	1	2	–	1	1	–
military equipment	20	–	–	–	–	–
religion	1	1	–	1	1	–
bone-working	–	–	–	–	–	200

Finding the pattern

As extrinsic studies are informed by patterns in data, then computer software can play a vital part. With some assemblages only a simple table may be needed, but large and complex assemblages call for more sophisticated sorting of the data (Cool and Baxter 2002). Assuming that anyone dealing with a complex assemblage will be in no need of a basic methodology, what follows here is deliberately kept simple.

Certain fields are always essential in a pattern-led study. The minimum used should ideally be:

1. the object's unique reference number (small find, registered find, accession)
2. site context number
3. feature number, where applicable
4. context/feature type (pit, ditch, posthole, dump, demolition debris)
5. site phase
6. object type
7. material
8. functional group

Even though sorting may only be intended on phase and function, the inclusion of the other fields permits easy reference back to both the catalogue and the detailed site data. Sorting on phase and function should display clusters of objects and/or changes in object use over time, and also any particular style of deposition such as a concentration of copper-alloy objects in pits as opposed to mixed materials in ditches.

Table 6.1, in which the data are shown as real numbers and there is no residual material clouding the picture, presents a very simplified (and over-imaginative) picture of the use of a site as reflected in the small finds assemblage. It could never be this easy in real life.

Table 6.1 demonstrates the following story of the site through time:

Phase 1 has high numbers of dress accessories (all brooches), military equipment (none cavalry), and recreational equipment (counters, dice). It has moderate amounts of household utensils and picture lamps, but only 'background noise' of personal tools (knives) and religious objects (one phallic amulet). This shows early Roman military occupation, perhaps a barrack block, where infantry soldiers cooked and ate their food, played games, and carelessly lost their brooches and fittings from their arms and armour.

Phase 2 has an even higher number of dress accessories (a few brooches, but mainly beads, earrings and hairpins), lots of toilet instruments and lamps, a fair number of household items, board game counters, two styli, *etc.* The high number of dress accessories suggests a strong female presence, many lamps imply considerable activity after sunset and the board game counters imply that there was time for leisure pursuits. Has the barrack block been converted into a brothel? The styli suggest literacy. Perhaps the brothel keeper kept a careful record of transactions?

Phase 3 is a complete change. There are only two dress accessories (both buckles), several chisels and gouges, a saw, a plane, a drill-bit and an axe. This is a carpenter's workshop. The absence of brooches may show that they have gone out of fashion, or that they are female accessories and so will not be found in a male environment.

Phase 4 is a real mixed bag. The dress accessories include armlets for the first time. There are no brooches, so their absence in Phase 3 did show a change in fashion. The two tools are a pruning hook and a rake prong. Dress accessories predominate, as usual. No other functional group is particularly large, though many are represented by one or two items. This is a family house.

Phase 5 is much the same, but there are fewer finds. This may mean a decline in the level of activity for some reason. Perhaps the house was abandoned and later demolished.

Phase 6 shows another complete change. There are 200 pieces of bone-working waste, all smashed splinters and offcuts, and lots of bone hairpins of fourth-century form, none complete and few well-finished. All the objects have been dumped in a deliberately back-filled ditch, along with a lot of smashed-up animal bone. This is debris from bone-working, but the context suggests it was not created on the site but in another part of the settlement.

Of course, a real site assemblage will never be as simple as the one invented above and its more obvious aspects will already have been spotted on excavation. With most assemblages it is a question of trying to tease out the information from a lot of background noise. This may be done by including other fields, such as object date as well as site phase, building and room number, *etc.* Breaking down the object type may also be useful. In an inter-site study site type should be added (villa, small town, town, military, *etc.*) The fields selected will be dictated by the size and type of site and assemblage, and will in turn dictate the type of analysis and how the results are presented.

Conclusion

Ellen Swift's paper in this volume points to a recent decline in the (already low) number of small finds theses undertaken over the last few years. I suspect that this may be due to the retirement of W. H. Manning from the University of Cardiff and of Richard Reece from the Institute of Archaeology in London, both of whom have supervised small finds theses over their years in post. Cardiff, indeed, is the *alma mater* of many small finds specialists.

The loss of Professor Manning and Dr Reece as supervisors, however, need not be the death-knell of small finds research in universities. The basic methodology presented above shows that studying small finds (or learning how to study them) is a matter of first answering certain questions and then looking for and interpreting any patterns in a dataset. First understand the material, then listen to what it says. There is an enormous bibliography of previous work both in Britain and on the Continent, and advice can always be sought through specialist small finds groups such as the Roman Finds

Group, the Quern Study Group, the Archaeological Leather Group and Instrumentum, a European working party covering Iron Age and Roman crafts. *Instrumentum* has produced a useful bibliography of publications since 1994 dealing with Iron Age and Roman small finds, divided by function and/or material (Feugère 2001). Members of these organisations are often professional (field) archaeologists and museum curators and have the practical expertise in a wide range of excavated material that some university staff may lack.

So, given access to a decent archaeological library, an object or set of objects to work with, some telephone numbers and e-mail addresses plus some basic common sense, what is stopping you?

Acknowledgements

I am grateful to Catherine Johns, Hella Eckardt, and Nicholas Cooper for their comments on the original draft.

References

Allason-Jones, L. (1989) *Ear-rings in Roman Britain*, British Archaeological Report 201 (British Series). Oxford, British Archaeological Reports.

Allason-Jones, L. (1996) *Roman Jet in the Yorkshire Museum*. York, Yorkshire Museum.

Bateson, J. D. (1981) *Enamel Working in Iron Age, Roman and Sub-Roman Britain*, British Archaeological Report 93 (British Series). Oxford, British Archaeological Reports.

Boon, G. (1991) *Tonsor humanus*: razor and toilet knife in antiquity. *Britannia* 22, 21–32.

Clarke, G. (1979) *The Roman Cemetery at Lankhills*, Winchester Studies 3.ii. Oxford, Clarendon Press.

Cool, H. E. M. (1990) Roman metal hair pins from southern Britain. *The Archaeological Journal* 147, 148–82.

Cool, H. E. M. and Baxter, M. J. (2002) Exploring Romano-British finds assemblages. *Oxford Journal of Archaeology* 21.4, 365–80.

Crummy, N. (1983) *The Roman Small Finds from Excavations in Colchester 1971–79*. Colchester, Colchester Archaeological Trust.

Evison, V. I. (1981) Distribution maps and England in the first two phases. In V. I. Evison (ed). *Angles, Saxons, and Jutes: essays presented to J. N. L. Myres*. Oxford, Clarendon Press.

Faraday, M. (1836) Report on objects from the 'Great Hill' at Bartlow. In J. Gage, Discovery of Roman sepulchral relics at Bartlow, in Essex. *Archaeologia* 26, 300–17.

Feugère, M. (1995) Les spatules à cire à manche figuré. In W. Czysz, C.-M. Hüssen, H.-P. Kuhnen, C. S. Sommer, and G. Weber (eds), *Provinzialrömische Forschungen. Festschrift für Günter Ulbert zum 65 Geburtstag*, 321–38. Espelkamp, Verlag Marie Leidorf.

Feugère, M. et coll. 2001. *Bibliographie Instrumentum, 1994-2001*, Montagnac, Editions Monique Mergoil.

Hagen, W. (1937) Kaiserzeitliche Gagatarbeiten aus dem rheinischen Germanien. *Bonner Jahrbucher* 142, 77–144.

Hattatt, R. (1987) *Brooches of Antiquity*. Oxford, Oxbow Books.

Hodges, H. (1964) *Artefacts: an introduction to early materials and technology*. London, John Baker.

Hull, M. R. and Hawkes, C. F. C. (1987) *Corpus of Ancient Brooches in Britain: pre-Roman bow brooches*, British Archaeological Report 168 (British Series). Oxford, British Archaeological Reports.

Johns, C. (1996) *The Jewellery of Roman Britain*. London, University College London.

Lawson, A. J. (1976) Shale and jet objects from Silchester. *Archaeologia* 105, 241–75.

MacGregor, A. (1985) *Bone, Antler, Ivory, and Horn. The technology of skeletal materials since the Roman period*. Beckenham, Croom Helm

Manning, W. H. (1985) *Catalogue of the Romano-British Iron Tools, Fittings and Weapons in the British Museum*. London, British Museum Press.

McWhirr, A. (1982) *Roman Crafts and Industries*. Princes Risborough, Shire Books.

Stead, I. M. (1998) *The Salisbury Hoard*. Stroud, Tempus Publishing.

Strong, D. and Brown, D., (eds) (1976) *Roman Crafts*. London, Duckworth.

Tomlin, R. S. O. (1988) The curse tablets. In B. Cunliffe (ed.), *The Temple of Sulis Minerva at Bath 2: the finds from the sacred spring*. Oxford University Committee for Archaeology Monograph 16. Oxford, Oxford University Committee for Archaeology.

Turner, R. and Wymer, J. (1987) An assemblage of palaeolithic hand-axes from the Roman religious complex at Ivy Chimneys, Witham, Essex. *Antiquaries Journal* 67.1, 43–60.

West, S. (1985) West Stow, The Anglo-Saxon village. *East Anglian Archaeology* Report 24. Ipswich, East Anglian Archaeology.

White, K. D. (1984/1986) *Greek and Roman Technology*. London, Thames and Hudson.

White, R. (1988) *Roman and Celtic Objects from Anglo-Saxon Graves*, British Archaeological Report 191 (British Series). Oxford, British Archaeological Reports.

Wild, J. P. (1970) *Textile Manufacture in the Northern Roman Provinces*. Cambridge, Cambridge University Press.

Woodland, M. (1990) Spindle-whorls. In M. Biddle, *Object and Economy in Medieval Winchester*, Winchester Studies 7.ii. Oxford, Clarendon Press.

7 Developing Methodology for Inter-Provincial Comparison of Pottery Assemblages

Robin P. Symonds and Ian Haynes

Introduction

Pottery studies represent a vital element of all archaeological projects that tackle the Roman period, yet across the lands that once constituted the empire they are approached in widely differing ways. While diversity in approach will always be necessary to some degree and can indeed help advance promising new methodologies, the authors of this paper wish to concentrate on the extent to which harmonisation is achievable. Understanding the Roman Empire requires developing and employing systems of analysis that can identify both local patterns and empire-wide ones. In discussing, for example, evolving provincial and regional identities, it is important to be able to assess the extent to which material culture was used in similar ways within some zones and in distinctly different ones in others. Similarly, if we want to assess, for example, the extent to which life in one type of site in one province resembled that in an ostensibly similar site in another, we need to have broadly comparable information with which to work. In short, comparative studies require a certain amount of agreement on recording procedures for wide-scale comparison to take place. While this basic point may apply to most categories of archaeological material, it is particularly pertinent to pottery. Here the sheer volume of data involved may make it extremely difficult for scholars undertaking synthetic research to reclassify artefacts for comparison with other assemblages after work using a specific methodology has been completed by the site team.

Though in this paper we confine ourselves to a discussion of ceramics, we are both very aware of the importance of more holistic approaches, such as the comparisons of mixed assemblages. Our focus on pottery here is not in any sense a rejection of such strategies, but is based rather on the belief that there are certain themes in ceramic studies that require special attention.

Readers of this paper will also be aware that its thrust is focused on post-excavation. We are anxious to stress, however, that the most fruitful results will emerge only when data processing is understood to be integrated with data capture. If we want to move beyond a focus on distinctive wares or rudimentary quantification to more complex analyses, such as use patterns, such an integrated vision is essential. It is also important to emphasise that pottery studies may not be divorced from the complex and still poorly understood processes of site formation (cf.

Martin, this volume). As we will note, only through the adoption of certain field recording techniques can such phenomena as residuality be better understood.

In this paper we outline two case studies that we believe illustrate steps towards building methodologies for inter-provincial comparative studies, and the different forms that such steps may take, but we begin with a survey of the extent to which current methods vary across the area once occupied by the Roman Empire.

The range and diversity of Roman pottery methodology

In Britain the Museum of London, and in particular the Department of Urban Archaeology (DUA) in the 1970s and 80s, was a driving force in the development of methodologies for recording, analysing and reporting on pottery assemblages. The baton has been passed on through the successor organisations, the Museum of London Archaeology Service (MoLAS) and now the Museum of London Specialist Services (MoLSS). Nevertheless, the foundations were laid in the DUA with the development of the fabric reference collection in Polstore cabinets and the encoding of fabric, form and decoration types, along with other significant details. In a direct evolution from that development there is now also a national fabric reference collection for Britain which was conceived with a similar philosophy and with close links to the London collections. The national collection has an associated publication (Tomber and Dore 1998), while two major London publications show how the London fabric system can be applied to the study of large assemblages (Davies *et al* 1994; Symonds and Tomber 1991).

There can be little doubt that the methods developed at London in the 1970s and 80s (cf. Marsh and Tyers 1978) had a considerable importance in the evolution of pottery recording and reporting throughout Britain. That evolution led in two main directions, which ever since have been at the heart of a great deal of stress suffered by British pottery researchers working in a commercial environment. The first development was fabric analysis, which provided a means of learning a mass of new information about ancient economic and social systems by identifying the origins of thousands of hitherto unidentifiable small sherds of pottery. It could be shown not only that products like wine, olive oil, fish sauce and alum were transported across wide areas of the Roman Empire, but also that a city like London received a considerable variety of coarse pottery types throughout the Roman period from production centres located hundreds of kilometres away, as well as from those in the city itself and its surrounding area.

The second development was the encoding of fabric, form and decoration types, which, coupled with the advent of computers and other technology, led to the quantification of pottery assemblages. Quantification is all about trying to represent the vast numbers of pottery sherds which get excavated, in particular on urban sites, and which form an important part of the archaeological record but cannot be represented by illustrations or described in detail.

One of the important but under-debated issues concerning quantification is the diversity that exists in current practice. There are currently perhaps five or six different methods of quantification in common use, four or five of which are used in Britain, while another is used in the rest of Europe. There are certainly advantages in using more than one method for the same body of material, but there are undoubtedly also some disadvantages in using too many methods at once. Yet whereas in France there was a recent attempt to bring together researchers in order to achieve broad agreement on quantification (with the results published in Arcelin and Tuffreau-Libre 1998), this has not happened in Britain or elsewhere in Europe.

Before we discuss the individual methods of quantification, it is important to recognise that quantification can be used at various levels of recording. In Britain nowadays there is normally a phase of initial identification and dating of pottery from recent excavations, known in London as 'spot-dating', which forms an essential contribution to the assessment of pottery from each excavation prior to analysis and eventual publication. During a post-assessment phase of analysis, in which contexts may be brought together in stratigraphically-defined subgroups, groups or phases, it may be appropriate to use more detailed quantification methods than would normally be used during the spot-dating phase. In London it is now considered to be of critical importance that all pottery should be spot-dated to a basic standard and that it should include quantification by sherd-count, particularly in view of the fact that in many instances it derives from small excavations. The assessment may remain the only complete record of what was found for the foreseeable future.

Another aspect of spot-dating that is fundamental to quantification is the ordering of the basic elements of pottery sherds or vessels in the recording process. Recording in Britain normally assumes that every sherd of pottery from a stratified context will be recorded, and therefore fabrics must be recorded first, before forms and decorations, because the fabric is the only aspect that must always be present. *Fabrics* represent production, *i.e.* clay + tempering + surface treatment + firing, and they must be specific to a place. *Forms* represent shapes which may

be unique to a production centre but which may also have relations with other fabrics, whether fabric types that are made at the same production centre (*e.g.* 'reduced' or oxidised productions), or at workshops in the same region or far away (*e.g.* sigillata from Gaul influencing locally-made sigillata as well as, occasionally, coarse wares). *Decorations* can also be independent from fabrics and forms. All of these aspects may evolve chronologically in an independent way and it is therefore useful to have a coding system that records each of these aspects separately.

Quantification methods in current use in Britain

This subject has arguably been discussed by pottery researchers in Britain more than anywhere else. The first summaries of quantification methods currently in use were published by Young (1980, 5–6) and Blake and Davey (1983, 24), and a somewhat more recent survey was published by Fulford and Huddlestone (1991, 44–5). Blake and Davey list six "measures of quantity in common use" including four methods discussed below plus 'total volume of fabric' ("which can be measured as the volume of a fluid displaced from a measuring cylinder by the sherds") and 'total surface area of sherds' (*ibid.*, 24). The use of EVEs was first described by Orton (1975), and broader discussions of the merits of various methods can be found in Millett (1979), Orton (1993), Orton, Tyers and Vince (1993, 166–181) and Tyers (1996, 204–5). A comparison of three methods used at Colchester (number of examples, weight and EVEs) was published by Symonds (1990; cf. Symonds and Wade 1999), while a further comparison of three methods used at London (rows, sherd count and weight) has been published in two papers by Symonds and Rauxloh (Rauxloh and Symonds 1999; Symonds and Rauxloh 2003).

Sherd count

Although this is arguably the easiest and most widely-used method, it is not universal in Britain since some modern reports have used only weight and estimated vessel equivalents (EVEs). At Museum of London Specialist Services all sherds are now counted at the spot-dating phase and the method is considered essential at all levels. Sherd count is biased by the relative fragility or robustness of vessels, which may be influenced by the nature of the fabric and firing temperature and conditions and by the shape and size of the vessel and the thickness of the walls. Some experimental work (Rauxloh and Symonds forthcoming) has shown, however, that sherd-count is more or less as reliable as any other method of pottery quantification commonly in use.

Weight

Use of weight is far from universal in Britain but does tend to be used for particular ceramic categories, notably amphorae and ceramic building materials. At Museum of London Specialist Services all pottery has been weighed at the spot-dating phase since 1999 and the measure was previously used for 'full quantification' of selected assemblages. Weight has the obvious disadvantage of being very biased by vessel types: amphorae are usually heavy and eggshell wares are light. But weight can be employed for comparisons of specific types within assemblages, and in amphora studies weight can be useful because some painted inscriptions refer to the empty and full weights of the vessels (Peacock and Williams 1986, 13–14).

Estimated vessel equivalents (EVEs)

First described in print in 1975 (Orton 1975), this method is widely thought (in Britain) to be the most statistically valid means of counting vessels. It has never been universally accepted, however, perhaps because it is thought to be a slow method for recording large assemblages and perhaps also because the numbers generated are abstract rather than real quantities. At Museum of London Specialist Services EVEs are nowadays recorded only for specific pottery assemblages where analysis using EVEs may be useful.

Rows (or records)

This method is used in London at Museum of London Specialist Services. It was developed as a way of including data from spot-dating before 1995 (when sherd count was introduced for all pottery). The present MoLSS/MoLAS Oracle database is constructed in such a way that the key fields for each context are fabric, form and decoration, and in data-entry the computer will not accept two records which have the same fabric-form-decoration combination. Each row therefore represents the sum total of sherds of a unique fabric-form-decoration combination of data. In post-1995 data rows can be compared with sherds as a method of analysing the data, but for pre-1995 data rows are all that is available.

Estimated numbers of vessels (ENVs)

This method (not to be confused with EVEs) is also used in London at Museum of London Specialist Services. It was primarily used by post-Roman pottery specialists from the early 1990s, and it is meant to be a general measure of the number of vessels represented within a single record (see rows, above). EVAs are therefore an assessment of vessel numbers based on all the sherds of a specific type. Although it cannot always be precise when applied to large assemblages, and the adding together of ENVs is potentially invalid statistically, it

does provide a basic idea of the numbers of vessels present which is often useful in post-spot-dating analysis.

Importantly, sherd counts, weights, EVEs and rows from different archaeological contexts or from separately-recorded parts of the same context can be added together to create grouped totals, whether or not sherds of individual vessels may join together. It is more problematic to add together ENVs and in practice this is rarely done.

Quantification methods in current use in Europe

Sherd count

See above.

Minimum numbers of individuals (French: *nombre minimum d'individus* or *NMIs*)

In fact, NMIs are mainly used in France and in franco-phone countries such as Belgium, Switzerland and, to a lesser extent, in other western countries such as Spain, Flemish Belgium and Holland. This was the only method under serious discussion at a round table held at the European Archaeology Centre at Mont Beuvray, Glux-en-Glenne, in April 1998. The papers were subsequently published in a volume (Arcelin and Tuffreau-Libre 1998) that shows both the positive results of years of reflection on the problem of quantification of archaeological ceramics in France, and the negative results of the failure of continental ceramics researchers to observe and understand the debate in Britain during the same period. That failure was mutual, which is why there are very few pottery reports which contain statistics which can be compared with sites across the Channel. NMIs nowadays have the great advantage of being used by a large number of researchers. They have the disadvantage, however, of requiring re-calculation when assemblages are combined by sub-grouping or grouping contexts into periods or phases. If one joins together pottery from several adjacent archaeological entities, one cannot simply add together the NMIs of each entity, but rather one should spread out the vessels and see if their numbers have increased or not. This fundamental problem is not addressed in the Mont Beuvray publication – perhaps in part because in many cases French researchers are fortunate to have facilities that include large amounts of table-space for spreading out assemblages, which is seldom the case in Britain.

Another aspect of NMIs is that unlike most of the British methods they do not oblige or inherently encourage the researcher to identify and quantify every sherd of pottery present in a stratified context. This in turn means that fabric is not necessarily always seen as the first aspect of a ceramic sherd or vessel, and recording systems can develop which concentrate mainly on forms, with fabrics treated as a secondary element. Comparison between fabric-based and form-based recording systems can be extremely difficult.

As one travels eastwards in Europe, pottery quantification seems to largely disappear, except when the pottery comes from excavations conducted by westerners. What is significant about this fact, and it is something which British pottery specialists may generally prefer to ignore, is that a remarkable amount of information about the pottery from a site can be transmitted in a report without any form of quantification at all. Twenty-five years of quantification in Britain have not necessarily blinded us to the unquantified interests of pottery, but they have tended to make us assume that quantification is essential, whereas in reality it is merely useful, or even, one ought to say, potentially useful, since so much of the time we gather the numbers generated by quantification but we do relatively little with them. Or, perhaps, we try to analyse the numbers generated but are eventually defeated by the problems of interpretation which are the natural result of having too many methods of quantification to choose from. Or we manage to generate some interesting results from our data, but we find that the editors of publications do not like to see pottery reports full of graphs and tables. Thus the results end up in an electronic archival data mountain not dissimilar to the discarded amphorae of the Monte Testaccio in Rome.

Recording methods for comparative study

Given the diversity that exists in current practice, it is important to consider the feasibility of introducing methodology that allows for comparative study across modern and ancient frontiers. To explore this theme, the authors offer two case studies. Ian Haynes was not involved in the first project, which was designed to examine port sites, but both authors were instrumental in the development of the second, part of a study focussed on the sites of the lower Danube.

The Caesar Project

The Caesar Project was launched in late 1996 by Mercedes Urteaga, head of the Arkeolan, an archaeological unit based at Irún, near San Sebastian in the Basque Country. From its conception the project was designed as an international endeavour that brought Arkeolan together with the regional archaeology service for Aquitaine, based at Bordeaux, and the Museum of London Archaeology Service, MoLAS. There were two main objectives, one being to try to look at ways of harmonising the methodology of pottery recording between the three units, and the second being to then compare the pottery between the units, focussing particularly on their respective Roman port sites at Irún, Bordeaux and London.

The development of methodology at Irún proved to be the most straightforward part of this study. Ms Urteaga had visited and worked for a short period with the DUA in London in the mid-1980s, and she had been recording her stratigraphy using Museum of London methods ever since – even using photocopied DUA site labels and finds cards – and now that she was ready to study pottery from Irún she wanted advice on how to go about it, and a system.

Establishing a new system from scratch at Irún at first seemed like a fairly daunting task. The range of fabrics present at the Calle Santiago site, however, was almost unbelievably similar to the normal range of pottery found in London between the mid-first and mid-second centuries AD. It was simply a case of defining the series of fine and coarse, 'reduced' and oxidised fabrics, and of giving them appropriate names.

Since there was no pre-existing recording system for Roman pottery, it was necessary to establish a fabric reference collection for Irún following the same principles as the system in London, along with a form and decoration coding system. The most surprising aspect of this project was the degree to which the two systems overlapped. Although no Romano-British wares have been found at Irún, and relatively few of the large variety of imported wares found at London are also found at Irún, there is an abundance of similarities between the two sites in terms of the types of pottery present – each type of coarse pottery found at Irún has a counterpart in London – and in the forms within the types. Two-thirds of the form codes used to describe pottery found at Irún are used to describe the same types at London. New form codes have been required at Irún almost exclusively for *sigillata hispanica* types and for the locally- (or regionally-) produced very coarse pottery ('Golfo de Bizkaia ware') which as a type is clearly paralleled in Britain by black-burnished ware, even if the forms are somewhat different. Apart from these two exceptions, roughly 95% of the ordinary pottery in use at London and Irún in the first and second centuries AD was made in directly comparable forms.

As a consequence of this overall compatibility in the pottery, the development of a recording system for Roman pottery from Irún based on the principles of the MoLAS system proved a comparatively simple task. The pottery from Calle Santiago was examined used a x20 binocular microscope; fabrics were identified and described, samples were selected for the fabric reference collection (*cerámoteca*), forms and decorations were encoded using the MoLAS system where possible or with new codes where appropriate, and recording was computerised using a standalone version of the MoLAS Oracle system. It is hoped that this is the foundation of a system which will continue to be appropriate for the recording of Roman pottery from all future sites in Irún and its surrounding area, and that it will continue to be expanded and adapted for use by local and regional archaeologists.

What was perhaps the most interesting part of the work provoked by the Caesar Project was the much more complicated effort to try to involve the pottery specialists at Bordeaux, both to compare the pottery at Bordeaux with that at London and Irún, and to try to adapt the methodology which was then in use at Bordeaux in order to make the comparisons. In truth the comparisons are yet to be made in real depth, because the main port site at Bordeaux is still being excavated, and the team were obliged to use pottery from a rather different kind of site. But a larger difficulty was posed by the fact that the recording of Roman pottery at Bordeaux, and in France generally, follows a slightly different philosophy than most British recording systems. There are two main differences: firstly, there is an attitude to fabric recording which does not always record the fabric as the first key aspect (and which is not microscope-oriented); and secondly, the names and definitions of forms are noticeably more variable and less clear than in the current London system. Table 7.1 is an attempt to show a correspondence between the London and Bordeaux form series.

Whereas the London form system is essentially based on the system established by Marsh and Tyers in their 1978 type series for Southwark – 1 for flagons, 2 for jars, 3 for beakers, 4 for bowls, 5 for dishes, 6 for cups, plus, since 1995, 7 for mortaria, 8 for amphorae and 9 for miscellaneous forms – the Aquitaine system is based on the 1979 volume by Jacques and Marie-Hélène Santrot (Santrot and Santrot 1979). The arrows on this chart show the corresponding forms but, wherever there is a dashed line, the correspondence is not really one to one. For example, vessels that in Britain would simply be called flagons could be classified as pichets, cruches

(flagons) with one handle, or flagons with two handles in Aquitaine. In the same way, what we call jars or beakers may all be classified there as closed vessels without handles. Happily, the Aquitaine system does not include the two enigmatic jar/bowl/dish names often used elsewhere in France, 'jattes' and 'écuelles' – on several occasions French researchers use diametrically opposed definitions of these form names.

In comparing and harmonising the London system with others, it must be said that what the London system gains in logic it may sometimes lose in efficiency (cf. Symonds 1998). Identifying fabrics through a binocular microscope is unquestionably time-consuming and, although our form system is generally well-organised, it is much better for the early Roman period (*c*. AD 50 to 160/200) than it is for later Roman pottery. In London there is perhaps a more definite break in pottery styles between the early and later Roman periods than in some other parts of Britain, but it is unfortunate that the form system fails to recognise the continuity which is obvious in imported wares from less affected parts of the country.

It is not yet clear what long-term influence the use of a London-style system at Irún will have on other pottery recording in neighbouring regions. There is no Roman pottery research group for Spain as a whole, perhaps because the country is so regionalised. As a result, some Spanish researchers regularly attend the meetings of the

Table 7.1. A comparison of form types used at London and Bordeaux

London					Aquitaine		
No.	Form type	No. of types	Type		No.	Type	No. de types
1	flagons	31	cruches		1	couvercles	30
2	jars	53	pots		2	assiettes	40
3	beakers	29	gobelets		3	vases tripodes	26
4	bowls	57	bols		4	gril	1
5	dishes	35	assiettes		5	patères	2
6	cups	26	coupes		6	coupes	82
7	mortaria	31	mortiers		7	mortiers	29
8	amphorae	96	amphores		8	coupes à pied/calices	7
9A	lids	1	couvercles		9	vases fermés sans anse	110
9B	amphora seals	1	bouchons d'amphore		10	bouchons d'amphore	11
9C	tazze	1	tazze		11	filtres tripode	1
9D	seria/dolia	1	seria/dolia		12	tirelires	4
9E	triple vases	1	vases triples		13	pichets	28
9F	tettinae	1	biberons		14	gourdes-tonnelets	1
9G	Castor boxes	1	boîtes à Castor		15	cruches à anse unique	68
9GB	Castor box base	1	pieds de boîte à Castor		16	biberons	1
9GL	Castor box lid	1	lèvres de boîte à Castor		17	vases ovale à deux anses	1
9H	strainer	1	filtres (1)		18	cruches à deux anses	38
9J	paterae	1	patères		19	oenochoés	28
9K	cheese press	1	pressoire à fromage		20	amphorettes	4
9LA	lamp	1	lampes		21	supports d'enfournement	2
9LB	lampholder	1	support à lampes				**514**
9M	colander	1	filtres (2)				
9N	unguentaria	1	unguentaria				
9NP	unguentaria/ amphora stoppers	1	unguentaria/ bouchons d'amphores				
9P	counters	1	jetons				
9RT13	inkwells	1	encriers				
9S	amphora stoppers	1	bouchons d'amphores				
9T	crucibles	1	creusets				
9U	buckets	1	seaux				
		382					

French national group, the SFECAG (Société Française de l'Étude de la Céramique Antique en Gaule), and the European group, RCRF (Rei Cretariae Romanae Fautores). Quantification was discussed at SFECAG back in the early 1990s (*cf.*, for example, Symonds 1990 and 1991), but since the Mont Beuvray meeting and subsequent publication (described above) neither group has broached the subject.

Communication and exchange on the Roman Lower Danube

The grant of an AHRB exchange award provided an opportunity for Symonds and Haynes to pool their knowledge of archaeological ceramics and recording systems from the Roman Lower Danube. Prior to the exchange, Haynes' experience of the region was restricted to Transylvania in Romania while Symonds' was limited to work undertaken in Serbia.

During the four months of the award, Haynes and Symonds undertook to develop teaching and research links between Birkbeck College, University of London and the Museum of London Specialist Services. They also conducted a survey of ceramic collections and recording methodologies from the area of the Roman Lower Danube, established a system of computerised fabric and form codes for use within part of the region and worked on a recording system that would allow inter-site comparisons. The following section looks at this latter element in the particular context of one of the sites studied within the communication and exchange programme. The site, which lies within *colonia* Aurelia Apulensis (Alba Iulia, Romania) has been the focus of work by the Apulum Project team since 1998. The pottery recording methodology for Apulum was developed from 1998 onwards by Fiona Seeley, Manuel Fiedler, Constanze Höpken and Robin Symonds.

The importance of proper recording of ceramic evidence, vital at all Roman period sites, was especially significant to the Apulum Project, because the excavation element involved the excavation of both distinctive cult ceramics and major pottery production areas. Not only was accuracy vital, so too was a system efficient enough to process very large quantities of material. So far the total number of sherds excavated at the site exceeds 600,000. To give the reader some sense of scale, the largest site in the MoLAS / MoLSS Oracle database is the recently-excavated City site at Gresham Street (GSM97), which at the time of writing has reached a total of just over 70,000 sherds. The area excavated by the Apulum Project is no more than about half the size of the Gresham Street site. When combined with the evidence for production, the implication of this extraordinary quantity is clear: a very substantial percentage of the Apulum sherds comes from vessels which were in some way flawed and which were therefore produced at the site and broken before they could be transported away from the site or used in any way. Wasters

can be difficult to identify, especially if they are sherds from vessels that were flawed in a fairly minor way, or merely somewhat under- or over-fired. There are many examples of the efforts that were expended to ensure quality control at pottery workshops of the Roman period – the production at Apulum was no exception.

With so much material to record at Apulum, the Project Team needed a system that could process and document a large number of finds quickly and in a way that would allow for comparison with other sites, as one of the Project's directors (Haynes) was particularly interested in recovering data from Apulum that would allow more detailed comparison with similar sites elsewhere. Yet despite the array of talented fieldworkers who had worked at Apulum prior to the beginning of the Project no agreed type series existed for the region and there had been no systematic attempt to undertake pottery fabric analysis.

In 1998 and 1999 the Project began by adopting the Museum of London's system of single context planning on site and by trying to impose a London-style recording system, establishing a fabric reference collection and a form type series. But where this concept really came apart, despite the heroic efforts of ceramic specialists from the Museum of London, was in the work on the fabric collection.

The reason that the wholesale importation of the London model proved problematic is to be found in the different circumstances associated with occupation sites at Londinium and a production site at Apulum. In London, despite the fact that production sites are known within the city, including the important site at Northgate House excavated in 2000 (Seeley and Drummond-Murray in prep.), occupation sites reveal competing pottery types in the same styles from a variety of sources both nearby and at some distance. In the first and second centuries pottery from Verulamium (25 km distant), Highgate (10 km), North Kent (about 40 km), and Alice Holt in Surrey (more than 50 km) is found within the city in substantial quantities. In the third and fourth centuries the distances become even greater, with pottery coming from Oxfordshire, the Nene Valley and Much Hadham. As a result, we are simply obliged to look at the fabrics of most of the pottery used in London through a microscope if we want to know where it comes from, because identifying the forms is not enough.

At Apulum, the picture becomes completely different when one realises that most of the variations in fabrics do not represent different production sources, but rather the variability that can be seen in the fabrics of unsuccessful vessels from one single source. That is one problem. Another practical problem was the sheer volume of pottery that needed to be processed and identified, by a small team working for only a few weeks each season. Looking at sherds through a microscope is not a rapid process, even when one knows it will be rewarding in terms of results. If we had tried to continue with it, we could only have touched a tiny percentage of the pottery from the site. The most convincing evidence for pottery production at the site, the sheer numbers of sherds, would have remained hidden in a bland statement to the effect that we had been unable to process more than a nominal percentage of the material present.

Table 7.2 represents the recording sheet currently used in London; this allows for the possibility of full quantification, if necessary.

Table 7.3 represents the recording sheet recently adopted by the pottery team for the Apulum Project (see acknowledgements below). We are now recording only numbers of sherds according to the most basic of criteria, with the aim of identifying specific assemblages within the material which will merit full quantification in the final analysis of the material. Among such assemblages already quantified or currently in the process of quantification are major deposits that appear to represent dumps of the main early production on the site. Interestingly these deposits almost exclusively contain coarse grey wares, while those related to the latest production found *in situ* in one of the kilns on the site consist almost entirely of buff oxidised wares. It is becoming clear to us that the proportion of 'reduced' to oxidised wares is of some significance at sites throughout the lower Danube region, and the quantification of these assemblages is an important first step towards being able to analyse this phenomenon.

The final report on the pottery from the site needs to be mainly concerned with presenting the vessel types made at the site (along with any significant vessel types which we think may not have been made locally). It should also identify any possible evolution or development in those products from the earliest layers to the latest. The concurrent study of the so-called 'cult pottery' from the site, mainly the study of various vessel forms associated with ritual activities such as snake vessels and tazze, will be complementary to the study of the production on the site. At the end of the study we aim to have reached an understanding of how the nearby cult activities may have interacted with the pottery production.

Recommendations

Experience of different approaches to the quantification of pottery suggests to us that several important aspects of the way the ceramic record is formed are frequently overlooked. Building secure recording systems that will sustain inter-site and inter-provincial comparisons requires that researchers remain alert to certain basic points.

Current knowledge of site formation processes in the Roman world remains limited. Yet we can assert with some confidence that most pottery was cheap for most pottery users and that, once broken, vessels were worth

Table 7.2. The Museum of London Specialist Services recording sheet

Museum of London Specialist Services									Pottery Spotdating Sheet				
Site Code:					Comments:				Recommendations:				
Context:		**Period:**							☐ Illustrate/Comment on selected vessels:				
Date range:		**Size:**							☐ Quantify/Illustrate as group: Box ct:				
		Name: Comp:							☐ Other work:				
		Date:			☐ Residual		☐ Intrusive						
Fabric	**Form**	**Dec**	**Sh**	**Smp**	**ENV**	**State**	**I/D/R**	**Comments**		**ED**	**LD**	**RimD**	**EVE**	**Wt.**

still less to their owners. Though there are cases of structured deposition, of grave good assemblages and ritualised disposal of cult vessels, for the most part there is little evidence to suggest that there were particular rules that governed the disposal of discarded vessels. So when we generate percentages of pottery in assemblages of casually discarded waste, we are by definition quantifying something that may be representative of the moment when it was deposited, or which on the other hand might be wholly unrepresentative. It is also often by no means certain how representative the excavated part of a site may be of the remaining unexcavated area.

When relating pottery quantification to site interpretation, we find that different reports can reflect differing levels of awareness of the significance of residuality. Indeed, it is notable that in some languages used in pottery recording no convenient translation of the term exists. Most archaeologists are aware of the significance of the phenomenon in practice, but its scale and significance are not always grasped. In London, for example, the percentage of first-, second- and third-century pottery in fourth-century contexts can often exceed 90%, and there is often simply no way of knowing how long the residual vessels had remained in circulation before their eventual breakage and entry into the archaeological record.

Though there have been attempts to estimate the average life span of domestic pottery, it is also important to note that some relatively ordinary vessels had extraordinarily long lives. For example, in burial 326 at the eastern cemetery of Roman London, the excavators found a small, delicate Cologne ware beaker dated *c.* AD 100 to 140 beside a black-burnished ware type 1 everted-rimmed jar dated *c.* AD 250 to 400 (Symonds 2000). The beaker thus seems likely to have been at least 110 years old when it was deposited in the burial. It might even have remained in use for as much as 200 years, from the early second century until the late third or fourth. The possibility remains that it was an heirloom, but although it is small and fragile this beaker is apparently nothing special as Cologne ware beakers go. It is undecorated, and the surfaces are pretty worn, and there were some far more complex vessels coming into Roman London from Cologne and Trier and other sources throughout its probable lifetime. Sometimes, of course, we do see evidence for deliberate attempts to extend the longevity of pottery. There is plenty of evidence for repairs to samian ware, for example, but the beaker in this case never underwent such treatment.

We also feel that it is vital to remain alert to the miscellany of processes that can lead to the widespread dispersal of fragments from individual vessels. This is, of course, a theme that may be better illuminated by some types of site recording methods than others. The process of dispersal can be affected by an array of post-depositional factors such as ploughing, but also by ancient cultural activity. Examples of the latter include partial

clearance of broken vessels in sweeping a surface or what one might call a 'baseball (or cricket) practice theory' of Roman pottery. This provides an answer to a question that is frequently asked in any pottery-processing environment: 'Well, those sherds come from a nice vessel, but where is the rest of it?' An answer is simply that in antiquity pottery was cheap and if a pot got slightly damaged in everyday use it must have been great fun to set a broken pot on a suitable podium, and either practice one's aim by throwing stones or other objects at it, or else to hit it as hard as one could with a bat or stick, just for the pleasure of watching the sherds fly off in many directions.

One must therefore conclude that neither the proven longevity of some vessels nor the obviously brief lives of others can tell us much about the value of pottery vessels to their owners. It is possible that vessel types broke in an 'average' sort of way, but there is never any way of knowing if any given vessel had an 'average' sort of life or, perhaps, a totally extraordinary one. While further research may shed more light on general, regional and local rules of pottery discard, it is clear that our ignorance of the mechanics of these processes needs to be borne in mind when offering statistically-based comparisons of sites.

Finally, we wish to reaffirm an important principle in the use of statistics. It is very seldom useful to generate percentages when the total number of items quantified is less than 100. This might seem obvious, but it happens all the time. It is also important always to show the total number of items from which a table of percentages has been generated. Without a total number of items, the value of percentages may be doubted. When these two rules are not obeyed, there can be considerable danger in drawing comparisons between sites on the basis of percentage figures.

Conclusion

The future for Roman archaeology is bright and exciting, but its potential will be severely limited if there is not a more determined attempt to record data in a form that facilitates more refined inter-site comparison. This is, of course, as much a problem within many provinces as it is across provincial boundaries. We are very conscious that the quest for total homogeneity in recording would probably prove detrimental to good practice, but remain optimistic that a higher level of consensus may be achieved.

Though our comments and approach clearly reflect our enthusiasm for the London model, we do not believe that this model can, or indeed should, always be exported wholesale to projects elsewhere. Rather, we hope that by making explicit some widely held, yet seldom published, concerns with recording, and by offering real-life case studies that show how we have tried to address them, we will encourage others seeking new insights into the unity and diversity of the Roman empire.

Table 7.3. The Apulum recording sheet

Category	Numbers of sherds per bag											Total
Reduced ware												
Oxidised ware												
Oxidised ware with white slip												
Obvious wasters												
Sigillata												
Other fine ware												
Amphorae												
Mortaria												
Dolia												
Tazze												
Other special types												
Notes SN = snake pot FD = fish dish P = patera G = glazed												
Initials												
Date												

Animal bone		Stone	
Human bone		Iron nails	
Glass			
CBM			
Kiln furniture			

SF no.	Small find description

Drawing numbers:										

Context notes: **Initials:**

Acknowledgements

The authors gratefully acknowledge the AHRB Exchange Award and a grant from the Roman Society which have made it possible to undertake collaborative research into this theme.

The authors acknowledge with gratitude the generous assistance of many colleagues during the exchange award for the Roman Lower Danube project. Alexandru Diaconescu and Alfred Schaefer, Ian Haynes' co-directors at Apulum, and Manuel Fiedler, Constanze Hopken and Fiona Seeley for their work on the recording methodology.

The recording sheet currently used in London was developed from earlier versions by all of the various Roman, medieval and post-medieval specialists working at the Museum of London Specialist Services in 1995, including Roy Stephenson, Lyn Blackmore, Jaqui Pearce, Richenda Goffin, Roberta Tomber, Louise Rayner, Fiona Seeley and Robin Symonds. The recording system now used at San Sebastian and Irún was developed at the invitation of the director of Arkeolan, Mercedes Urteaga, and the president of Arkeolan, Jaime Rodriguez Salis, with the collaboration of Maria del Mar López Colom and Pía Alkain.

The recording sheet recently adopted by the pottery

team for the Apulum Project was developed at a meeting
of the project's pottery specialists, Constanze Höpken,
Manuel Fiedler and Robin Symonds, kindly hosted by
Friederike Hammer, in the early spring of 2001. The
recording sheet was based on earlier forms developed at
various sites in Germany and Greece, most specifically
the form developed by Antje Düerkop for excavations at
Köln-Alteburg in 1998. The method was first implemented
in the summer of 2001 by Mariana Egri and Marco Neri,
under the supervision of Constanze Höpken, and it has
continued to be implemented since then by Mariana Egri
under the supervision of Robin Symonds.

Bibliography

Arcelin, P. and Tuffreau-Libre, M. (1998) La Quantification
des Céramiques: conditions et protocol. *Collection Bibracte,
2. Actes de la table ronde du Centre archéologique européen
du Mont Beuvray (Glux-en-Glenne, 7–9 avril 1998).*

Blake, H. and Davey, P. (eds) (1983) *Guidelines for the
Processing and Publication of Medieval Pottery from
Excavations.* Directorate of Ancient Monuments and Historic
Buildings, Occasional Paper 5.

Davies, B., Richardson, B. and Tomber, R. S. (1994) *A Dated
Corpus of Early Roman Pottery from the City of London.*
The Archaeology of Roman London, Volume 5. Council for
British Archaeology Research Report 98.

Fulford, M. G. and Huddlestone, K. (1991) *The Current State
of Romano-British Pottery Studies.* English Heritage, Occasional Paper no. 1.

Marsh, G. and Tyers, P. A., (1978) The Roman pottery from
Southwark. In J. Bird, A. H. Graham, H. Sheldon and P.
Townend (eds) *Southwark Excavations 1972–4.* Southwark
and Lambeth Archaeology Excavation Committee, Joint
Publication 1, London and Middlesex Archaeology Society
/ Surrey Archaeology Society, 533–86.

Millett, M. (1979) How much pottery? In M. Millett (ed.)
Pottery and the Archaeologist. Institute of Archaeology,
University of London, Occasional Paper 4, 77–80.

Orton, C. R. (1975) Quantitative pottery studies: some progress,
problems and prospects. *Science and Archaeology* 16, 30–
5.

Orton, C. R. (1993) How many pots make five? – an historical
review of pottery quantification. *Archaeometry* 35, 169–
84.

Orton, C. R., Tyers, P. A. and Vince, A. (1993) *Pottery in
Archaeology.* Cambridge Manuals in Archaeology,
Cambridge, Cambridge University Press.

Peacock, D. P. S. and Williams, D. F. (1986) *Amphorae and
the Roman Economy: an introductory guide.* London,
Longman.

Rauxloh, P. and Symonds, R. P. (1999) The effect of computerisa-
tion on pottery recording, computer applications in archaeology. In L. Dingwall, S. Exon, V. Gaffney, S. Laflin, and M.
Van Leusen (eds.) *Archaeology in the Age of the Internet
CAA97, Computer Applications and Quantitative Methods*

in Archaeology. BAR International Series 750. Oxford,
Archaeopress.

Rauxloh, P. and Symonds, R. P., (forthcoming).

Santrot, M.-H. and Santrot, J. (1979) *Céramiques Communes
Gallo-Romaines d'Aquitaine.* Paris, CNRS.

Seeley, F. and Drummond-Murray, J. (2005) *Roman Pottery
Production in the Walbrook Valley. Excavations at 20–28
Moorgate, City of London, 1998–2000.* MoLAS Monograph
25. London, Museum of London Archaeological Service.

Symonds, R. P. (1990) La quantification des céramiques de
l'époque romaine à Colchester et à Londres. *Société Française de l'Etude de la Céramique Antique en Gaule, Actes
du Congrès de Mathay-Mandeure,* 135–47.

Symonds, R. P. (1991) Datation et résidualité: où sont les
limites de la certitude? *Société Française de l'Etude de la
Céramique Antique en Gaule, Actes du Congrès de Cognac,
1991,* 137–51.

Symonds, R. P. (1998) Quelques aperçus sur le port romain de
Londres provoqués par les travaux du Projet César. *Société
Française de l' Etude de la Céramique Antique en Gaule,
Actes du Congrès d'Istres, 1998,* 339–48.

Symonds, R. P. (2000) Pottery. In B. Barber and D. Bowsher
*The Eastern Cemetery of Roman London: excavations 1983–
90.* Museum of London Archaeology Service Monograph 4.

Symonds, R. P. and Rauxloh, P. (2003) A ceramic case-study
comparing the data contained in the spot-date files and
quantified data from selected contexts at the study area. In
Cowan, C, *Urban Development in North-West Southwark,
Excavations 1974–90.* Museum of London Archaeology
Service Monograph 16, 135–9.

Symonds, R. P. and Tomber, R. S. (1991) Late Roman London:
an assessment of the ceramic evidence from the City of
London. *London and Middlesex Archaeological Society
Transactions* 42, 59–99.

Symonds, R. P. and Wade, S. M. (1999) *The Roman Pottery
from Excavations at Colchester, 1971–1985.* Colchester
Archaeological Report no. 10. Colchester, Colchester
Archaeological Trust.

Tomber, R. and Dore , J. (1998) *The National Roman Fabric
Reference Collection: a handbook.* London.

Tyers, P. A. (1996) *Roman Pottery in Britain.* London, Batsford.

Urteaga, M. M. (ed). (1998a) *CAESAR: Proyecto de valorización
de las cerámicas arqueológicas en el eje atlántico europeo.*
Unpublished, Report to the European Commission.

Urteaga, M. M. (1998b) La contribución de ARKEOLAN: Calle
Satiago de Irún. In M. M. Urteaga (1998a), 81–100.

Urteaga, M. M. and Lopez Colom, M. (2000) Aperçu des
principaux groupes de production mis en évidence lors des
fouilles du port d'Irún. *Société Française de l'Etude de la
Céramique Antique en Gaule, Actes du Congrès de Libourne,*
129–44.

Urteaga, M. M. (ed.) (forthcoming) *El Proyecto Caesar* (final
report). Irún.

Young, C. J. (ed.) (1980) *Guidelines for the Processing and
Publication of Roman Pottery from Excavations.* Directorate
of Ancient Monuments and Historic Buildings, Occasional
Paper 4.

8   Mine's Bigger Than Yours: Comparing Values of Late Roman Hoards

Richard Hobbs

Introduction

This paper is the result of ongoing search on *c*. 1800 deposits of late Roman hoards (Hobbs 1997b). The main criterion for qualification to the database of these deposits was that they must contain a precious metal element, *i.e.* gold or silver, but the type of object was not relevant. The database thus included deposits containing silver plate, gold and silver coinage (from late Roman gold solidi to base silver third-century 'radiates'), *Hacksilber*, gold and silver jewellery and bullion (for instance ingots). Single finds considered to be site finds accidentally lost were excluded. The geographical range was also wide, covering both the eastern and western provinces of the Roman Empire as well as areas beyond the frontiers which produced Roman or Byzantine material. The chronological limits were the beginning of the reign of Septimius Severus in AD 193, and the end of the reign of Justinian II in AD 711. This research was the first instance when such a broad range of different assemblages of precious metal objects had been brought together for comparison.

The principal objective of this research was to identify broad patterns in the deposition of precious metals over this wide spatial and chronological span. Having described these broad patterns, attempts were then made to establish both the factors which influenced the ownership of these objects and the subsequent reasons underpinning burial and non-retrieval. In order to do this, the individual contents of different finds were largely ignored, with the emphasis placed rather on the amount of precious metals contained within each find and the geographically and chronologically distinct groups of finds which emerged.

Within this paper it is not possible to examine all the conclusions reached nor to describe all the patterns observed. Instead, I have focused on the issue of 'value' of these different precious metal finds, on what is meant by that term and on examining ways in which this concept can be explored when some of these deposits are compared.

The 'value' of precious metal deposits

The 'value' of any objects owned by people in the past is enormously difficult to assess. Fundamentally, this is because the link between the original owner and the objects has been broken. Once basic cataloguing and descriptive work has been completed, those studying these finds should attempt to understand the type of relationship which the owners had with their objects. The other difficulty which needs to be overcome was raised a number of years ago in a paper which criticised, in particular, past approaches to the study and interpretation of late Roman British precious metal finds (Millett 1994). One of Millett's criticisms was that there was a tendency to impose modern value judgements on finds of 'treasure' – another loaded term – rather than considering that the original owners of these objects would have had their own, and potentially different, ways of valuing their precious metal possessions. Millett, however, did not distinguish between values placed on the objects during their lifetime and the values placed on them which led to a decision being made to bury the objects. For reasons which will become clear, these are very important distinctions to make. The Mildenhall treasure will be used as an example of these value judgements.

The Mildenhall treasure is one of the most magnificent sets of silver tableware ever discovered (Painter 1977). The find contained 34 pieces of silver consisting of two large plates, a fluted bowl, two smaller platters, six flanged dishes, a covered dish, two small flat platters, five ladles with detached handles (one of which is missing) and eight spoons with pear-shaped bowls. The pieces fall into distinct stylistic groups, and were probably made between the mid third and the late fourth century AD. Although there is still some controversy over its discovery and the way it eventually entered the public domain (Hobbs 1997a; Ashbee 1997), let us assume for the sake of argument that it is accepted as a British find owned by someone resident in the province. This provides us with the following stages during the life of the assemblage where value judgements had been made by the original owners. These judgements are equally applicable to other precious metal assemblages.

Value judgements and the 'birth' of the Mildenhall treasure

There are a number of ways in which the assemblage could have been acquired. The vessels could have been purchased from a craftsman or workshop in a simple financial transaction, for instance, the handing over of gold coins. Alternatively, the pieces could have been commissioned specifically, perhaps with the original raw materials handed over to a craftsman and instructions given with regard to the thematic content of the decoration. In both such circumstances the value of the pieces in financial terms would have related not just to the purity and weight of the precious metal in the vessels but to the 'cut' which the craftsman or workshop would take. This would depend upon the skill of the work, the time taken to produce the pieces and the reputation of the designer. It has been suggested that the 'mark up' on the Great Dish may have been as high as 50% over and above the value of the precious metal, although references in literary sources on this matter are contradictory and range between 10% and 50% (Cameron 1992; Painter 1993).

Another possible means of acquisition would not have required any direct financial transaction with the maker/s of the pieces at all by the eventual owners (who I am assuming are the same as those who buried the hoard). Instead, the pieces could have been received as gifts from other individuals in order to bestow favour (bearing in mind that they themselves would have borne any financial costs, as outlined above). Gift exchange was undoubtedly an important mechanism for the distribution of precious metals in the later Empire by the transitory Imperial Court, with the high quality of silver plate, at between 96–8% pure, used as one argument in favour of this (Painter 1988).

Another alternative gift exchange mechanism might have been inheritance. Given that at least one of the pieces in the find was more than 50 years old when buried, the idea of the silver being passed down to the next generation is perfectly feasible. This also raises the additional dimension of added value through antiquity, in the same way that antiques owned in modern times have increased in value (both sentimental and financial) because of their rarity and quality of production.

Another type of more personal relationship which must be considered is inter-marriage; it may well be the case that some or all of the pieces related to a betrothal which was seen as mutually beneficial to both sides. This has been alluded to in a recent publication in one of a series of imaginary vignettes (Henig 2002, 121–4).

Whichever way the Mildenhall assemblage was acquired, and it could well have been a combination of the above methods, there are two types of judgement which need to be considered when we try to attach a 'value' to the find. The first is a financial value which would be, in somewhat vulgar terms, the price which the pieces would fetch if sold, which could have been received as gold bullion but might have come in other forms such as land or property. I have already suggested that this would relate to the precious metal content of the find in terms of weight and the mark up which related to the aesthetic quality of the pieces.

The other value judgement made by the owners was sentimental value. This is more or less impossible to quantify as it depends upon the relationship which the owners had with the pieces. A suggested scenario has

been that the pieces were received as gifts. In such circumstances the sentimental value would relate to the strength of emotion associated with the family member, peer or patron making the gift.

We must also bear in mind with all such assemblages that, although we might think they are of huge significance, this was not necessarily the view of the original owners. If the family or individual already owned huge amounts of wealth tied up in land or property, the treasure may have seemed fairly irrelevant, constituting only a minor part of their overall inventory of personal belongings. In the case of the Mildenhall treasure, the problems presented by this lack of context become very clear, as we do not even have a nearby villa estate or dwelling from which we can categorically say the silver originally belonged (although the remains of a hypocaust were discovered near to the supposed findspot in the 1930s (Salway *et al.* 1970, 237).

Value judgements during the 'life' of the Mildenhall treasure

Once in ownership, value judgements again had to be made about how the service was treated. The first decision would have been where to put it. Although we do not know exactly where the pieces were produced, there is more evidence for production in a Mediterranean workshop than in Britain itself (Painter 1977, 14–17). So at some point the silver had to be brought to the province. If this was carried out by the owners themselves, assuming it was not an acquisition through trade, then why did they decide it should come to Britain? Obviously, if that was where they lived then this is clear; but if they had more than one estate, it becomes an important question. Did their other estate have another set of silver? Or even a set of even higher quality vessels perhaps made of gold which have not come down to us? In practical terms there are transport costs involved in getting the set to East Anglia, again assuming that it was located near to where it was eventually buried, which is something else which we cannot be sure of.

Assuming the pieces were then kept in a private residence rather than belonging to members of the late Roman civil service, then value judgements had to be made about how it was stored and used in the household. Was it permanently displayed for all to see who came into the house? Was it only brought out on special occasions? If so, was it actually used to serve food? Or was it stored away out of site as a source of bullion for emergencies, whatever they might be?

On the last point, it is interesting to note that a silver plate hoard recovered from the House of the Menander at Pompeii had almost certainly been stored from at least the time of the earthquake of AD 62 until the destruction of the city seventeen years later (Painter 2001). Although this is probably more likely to be related to the fact that the owner was having his house substantially remodelled at the time of the eruption, which suggests that he wanted to keep it out of site of prying eyes, it is nonetheless possible that it was only used as a store of wealth and not for opulent display and dining. So we have to accept that the Mildenhall treasure might also have been locked away somewhere prior to burial, rather than playing a central role in the activities of the household.

Alternatively, let us suggest that the treasure was used in a functional manner in the home. To modern eyes, the beauty of the figurative work on the vessels means it is often viewed, as are most silver plate vessels of the Roman period, as being purely for display as pieces of art. The vessels and utensils could, however, have been used as part of a dining service. Unfortunately, the cleaning of the silver during the four or so years in which it was kept concealed by one of the original finders means that it is no longer possible to ascertain if it was ever used to dine from, but this does not mean that we should not consider that as an option.

Literary references to the use of silver plate in the home for dining are not extensive, although silver is certainly shown in pictorial representations to be 'in use'. An example of the latter comes from the *Vergilius Romanus* in the Vatican Museums, a fourth-century manuscript which some believe may have originated in Britain. In this example, diners are shown reclining on a late Roman *stibadium*, the curved couch preferred at this period, and a silver vessel is shown with a fish on it (reproduced in Henig 2002, fig. 50).

The main literary source for the use of silver for dining in the Roman period is Petronius' satire *The Satyricon*, the most relevant section being the Cena Trimalchionis, which is generally accepted as dating to Neronian times. There are a number of references to silver being used at the dining table (Table 8.1); are they at all instructive on the issue of how silver was valued in a domestic setting and social attitudes towards its use?

All these quotations are interesting for different reasons. They collectively tell us that vessels and utensils were used for eating from or at least serving from, although Petronius' protagonist Encolpius does not tell us if the vessels were plain or decorated. The first quote also tells us quite clearly that Trimalchio sets out to

impress his guests, using his vessels for ostentatious display – why else have a visible inscription of the weight of the vessel and his own name on the rim? This might also suggest that the bullion value of silver was seen as perhaps outweighing the artistic value of any decoration or of the additional value which might be associated with the manufacturing technique. In reality, surviving silverware shows that weight inscriptions were not placed visibly on rims but were usually hidden underneath the vessels, a practice which remained consistent throughout the Empire. The Mildenhall treasure itself has what are almost certainly weight inscriptions on three of the pieces (Painter 1977, cats. 5, 9, 10). In addition, names do appear on vessels, but once again these are hidden underneath and are usually interpreted as being names of craftsmen rather than owners (although some exceptions to this are described below). Within the Mildenhall treasure itself the name 'Eutherios' appears in Greek on the back of the two Bacchic platters (Painter 1977, cats. 2–3) and this may be a reference to the maker.

The second reference is clearly an example of exaggeration befitting of satire. Once again the idea of spoons weighing half a pound is presented as Trimalchio's vulgar way of showing off his wealth. The average weight of each spoon in the silver treasure from the house of the Menander, broadly contemporaneous with the time when Petronius was writing, is about 42.5 g. This probably means that spoons were made in a group of 12 from 1.2 lbs. of Roman silver (Martin 1984, 92–3).

The third reference would seem even less plausible, given the exaggeration evident in the previous quote, but nonetheless shows us that we cannot assume that silver vessels were treated with reverence. The final reference to Trimalchio's wealth is once again something which we cannot take as being in any way reflective of the potential wealth of a freedman – it may have been based upon the author's own experiences, or may be exaggerated once again – but it does tell us that silver was probably just a small part of the inventory of a wealthy family's possessions.

In the case of the Mildenhall treasure it is clear from the nature of the pieces that they were mainly designed

Table 8.1. References to the use of silver plate in Petronius' The Satyricon *(taken from J. P. Sullivan's translation, first published 1965, Penguin)*

Sat. 31.	'Over the ass were two pieces of plate, with Trimalchio's name and the weight of the silver inscribed on the rims.'
Sat. 33.	'We took up our spoons (weighing at least half a pound each)....'
Sat. 34.	'..... in the confusion one of the side-dishes happened to fall and a slave picked it up from the floor. Trimalchio notices this, had the boy's ears boxed and told him to throw it down again. A cleaner came in with a broom and began to sweep up the silver plate along with the rest of the rubbish.'
Sat. 37.	(in reference to Trimalchio himself): 'The old boy himself now, he's got estates it'd take a kite to fly over – he's worth millions and millions. There's more silver plate lying in his porter's cubbyhole than any other man owns together.'

for serving food from as part of communal eating rather than as individual serving dishes. The exceptions to this are the flanged bowls which could conceivably have been meant for individuals with place settings, and of course the spoons and ladles which could have been used personally throughout the course of a meal or to serve portions of food to individuals around the table. The most obvious absence from the assemblage is that of drinking vessels (despite the fact that when reversed the two small platters [Painter 1977, cats. 13, 14] look like shallow goblets). This does not mean that the owners had nothing to drink out of but that they probably had drinking vessels made from other materials, perhaps glass. The conical beakers, dated to the early fifth century, in the nearby Burgh Castle hoard (Harden 1983) might have been the type of vessel used (although as a Saxon Shore fort Burgh Castle is a rather different find context).

In summary, during the life of the Mildenhall treasure a number of value judgements would have been made. If it was used as a store of wealth and usually kept hidden from view, this tells us that its value was mainly seen as bullion. Alternatively, it might have been brought out only on certain occasions, perhaps to impress visiting guests, and even used to serve food, with the figurative decoration providing talking points for the diners (when not obscured by foodstuffs). Or it may have been always on open display for all family members and visitors to see at all times, allowing the full splendour of its craftsmanship and iconography to be viewed and discussed; and never used for dining purposes.

The way in which the silver was re-used after its discovery in 1942 is surprisingly relevant to our interpretations of possible use by its original owners. Sidney Ford, one of the finders of the treasure, spent a number of months cleaning the silver in his agricultural workshop, but after this the treasure effectively became multi-functional. Some unpublished notes by Sydney Ford, the grandson of Sydney Ford senior, reveal the following:

> *When it was all cleaned it was arranged on the two sideboards in the front sitting room for all to see but not to touch...every visitor who came to the house was shown it. The Big Dish (sic) was one of the pieces that was used. My mother remembers that it was her job to arrange apples, oranges, pears and nuts, in a pyramid shape, for the table decoration at Christmas. It was the only time it was ever used. The only other piece which was used was one of the spoons which Grandfather kept in the cutlery drawer in the kitchen. He used it every day for his breakfast and dinner.*

Value judgements and the 'death' of the Mildenhall treasure

The burial of the Mildenhall treasure again required a value judgement to be made. The deliberate burial of all precious metal objects in the past represents a change in the relationship between the owner and their objects. However, the objects were used during their lifetime, be they for open display, actual functional use for dining or concealed storage

as a source of bullion; burial meant that a decision was made to change that relationship and abandon the possessions. Reasons for burial have exercised the minds of archaeologists for many years and usually fall into two schools of thought: burial for safekeeping, and burial for votive reasons. If we think of it as an exercise in safekeeping, there are a number of ways by which this might have occurred. With a combined weight of 85 Roman pounds, the silver might have been seen as being too heavy to transport around. Does this mean that the owner needed to move quickly, taking only the essentials of survival with him or her or them? What is certain is that the owner did not want anyone else to get their hands on the silver, almost certainly because of its bullion value but also because perhaps being caught with it would have betrayed a social status which was seen as being a liability in itself. Or it might have been buried for tax avoidance purposes – maybe a directive had been issued that all precious metals were to be handed over to boost the imperial coffers. Far less likely, but not impossible, was that the silver was buried for safekeeping after theft; a hoard of robber's loot, which is more commonly forwarded as an argument to explain hacksilver hoards, as the act of dividing silver into smaller pieces has been taken to imply the division of spoils between thieves (Curle 1922, 108), but has also been suggested as a possible explanation for hoards containing complete pieces, for instance the Water Newton silver (Painter 1999).

Votive reasons tend not to be forwarded to explain the burial of such material at this date but should not be dismissed out of hand. Maybe Mildenhall was buried as an offering to the gods. Perhaps some catastrophic event had occurred, such as the death of more than one family member in quick succession and an attempt was being made at appeasement of the gods. In such instances a value judgement was obviously being made; the silver was viewed as being of suitable size to meet the requirements of the ritual act. It is somewhat odd to think that such explanations are rarely forwarded by Roman specialists to account for late Roman precious metal hoards but are invariably the accepted ways of explaining precious metal deposits of the late Iron Age such as the recent jewellery set from Winchester (Hill *et al.* 2004). The burial of pewter hoards from Britain, broadly contemporary with Mildenhall and sharing strong similarities with silver vessel forms, have in contrast been persuasively argued as being almost entirely ritual in nature (Poulton and Scott 1993).

One very interesting aspect of the burial of the Mildenhall assemblage relates to the portability issue. Many of the vessels in the assemblage, particularly the Great Dish and the niello platter, would have been heavy and cumbersome to transport (Painter 1977, cats. 1, 4). But the question must be asked, why not at least take the spoons, which were eminently portable and easily concealed? This is all the more curious given the fact that two of the spoons have personal names on them, which must have had some pertinence to the owners, if we come back to the theme of a sentimental value (*ibid.* cats. 7, 8). (Unlike scratched graffiti underneath vessels, referred to earlier as probably examples of craftsmen's names, these are deliberately visible incised inscriptions). The fact that these spoons were buried with the rest of the assemblage might suggest that there was a desire to keep the assemblage together (even though, of course, we do not know if it was complete). This might in turn suggest that there was an intention to come back and retrieve the material at a later date. Burial and abandonment and the reasons behind them thus present a whole different set of value judgements.

Portable wealth and value judgements

A few miles away from Mildenhall, the village of Hoxne produced another large assemblage of late Roman gold and silver in 1992 (Bland and Johns 1993). The interesting thing about this assemblage is that it consists entirely of small, portable items – in stark contrast to the majority of pieces in the Mildenhall treasure. Admittedly, the owners had so many of these small portable precious objects that as a whole they would have been extremely difficult to carry around if mobility became an issue. Within this find, it is also interesting to note that one object, the tigress handle, had been deliberately detached from a larger vessel (probably an amphora similar to that known from the Sevso hoard (Mango and Bennett 1994), turning it into portable wealth. The fact is, however, that despite the portability of the objects in the Hoxne hoard, they were still buried as a complete group and this act was undoubtedly carried out with great care. The excavation of the find by the Suffolk Archaeological Unit revealed good evidence for the use of textile and organic wrapping and support for the objects, at least two inner caskets with small padlocks and a large wooden outer box with iron fittings. In this instance, again, the intention to return and recover these objects is a persuasive argument to underpin the burial, as so much time was invested in ensuring the objects' survival in the ground.

Another way of creating portable wealth at this period, hinted at by the detachment of the tigress handle for a larger vessel in the Hoxne hoard, was the creation of *Hacksilber*, where larger pieces of silver are chopped into smaller more manageable chunks. The best example of a British *Hacksilber* hoard comes from Traprain Law (Curle 1922). The process of chopping up silver in this manner must tell us a great deal about the ways in which values of these silver objects were perceived. Iconography and workmanship were being completely disregarded in favour of pure bullion value of easily transportable size. In addition, the function was also disregarded – obviously, hacking a silver amphora to pieces rendered it useless for pouring wine. I would also suggest that the clipping of siliqua coinage (Burnett 1984), which is a curiously British practice, is all part of the same process of attempting to expand the availability of portable wealth in the form of silver. Clipped coins would not have fooled

anyone but they still had a weight of precious metal which gave them an intrinsic worth. The clippings were probably melted down and recast into contemporary copies, a large number of which were present in the Hoxne hoard (Guest forthcoming).

The creation of portable wealth, either from the point of manufacture or by reshaping an existing object, thus involves another set of value judgements. When this occurs, it implies that the ability to move this wealth around easily is of primary importance, with the bullion value of the object more important than other factors such as artistic merit or craftsmanship.

Comparing the intrinsic values of precious metal hoards

Leading on from this idea that portability and bullion value were of primary importance in the way in which precious metal objects were perceived in the late Roman period, the second part of this paper looks at a method for assessing bullion value. No attempt is made to factor in other value judgements such as sentimental value, as these types of value are entirely subjective and only pertinent to the original owners.

Assessing the value of different precious metal assemblages is important because it might provide some kind of index of the status of the original owners. This can only be achieved by comparison between different assemblages, as it is not possible to assess individual finds without knowing if they conform to the norm or differ from it. This is not dissimilar to work on coins from Roman sites, where a 'normal' coinage profile is established in order that each assemblage can be placed against it (*e.g.* Reece 1995). As for the original owners of these finds, they could be both private individuals, such as someone burying a coin hoard of loose change, to whole families who owned a number of estates and had silverware and gold jewellery as one element of their household inventory. Alternatively, precious metals could be owned by groups of individuals who had pooled their resources for what they perceived as the common good, with the silver in the hands of the early Christian church providing one example. So the material evidence might be one way of comparing the social status of the private individual with the family estate and the early church community. This in turn might tell us something about how attitudes to the ownership of precious metals changed over time, if we see, for instance, a drift of precious metal materials out of the hands of private individuals into communal ownership.

In addition, comparing assemblages of precious metals can also be conducted as regional and chronologically distinct groups; for instance, comparing precious metal deposits from third-century Iberia with those of fourth-century Britain. This can be used to understand wider economic changes and leads to interesting questions about why some areas seem to produce far more precious metal assemblages than others.

Before any comparisons between assemblages can be made, some methodological problems have to be overcome. As we have seen, I believe the only objective way of comparing assemblages is to look purely at the bullion value contained within them. This will provide an indication of their 'intrinsic value'. Making these calculations is problematic, however, for two reasons. The first is that silver coinage in particular was often debased, which means that simply calculating the weight of a particular find will not provide the precious metal content or intrinsic value for that deposit. In these instances, an assessment has to be made based upon 'known' metallurgical compositions of different coinage issues (cf. Walker 1978) which, though now known to be inaccurate, is the only overall survey available. Fortunately, this is only a problem for deposits containing third century coins, as the later siliqua coinage is of high silver purity. The gold coinage remains consistently high in quality throughout the period covered by this study, as does silver plate and, as would be expected, raw bullion in the form of ingots.

The second problem is how to compare gold and silver. How does a hoard of silver plate, for example, compare with a hoard of gold coins in terms of their relative intrinsic value? This problem has to be resolved by providing each assemblage with a common value, termed its 'Equivalent Gold Weight' which allows comparisons to be made.

Calculating Equivalent Gold Weight (EGW)

Literary sources provide some means of assessing the relationship between gold and silver in the Roman world. Table 8.2 summarises a range of literary sources which allude to this relationship. The first reference, in Dio's *Roman History*, has long been accepted as providing a relationship between the Augustan aureus and denarius at 1:25 (Sutherland 1984, 3). By looking at the mean weights of the aureus and denarius in the early Empire this provides a correlation in weight terms of 1 gram of gold to 11.8 grams of silver.

For the solidus and siliqua coinage system of the late Empire the relationship has largely hinged upon two passages in the Theodosian Code. The first passage implies a ratio of four solidi to a pound of silver, the second a slightly higher figure of five solidi. This represents a ratio of between 1:14.4 and 1:18 between gold and silver. Other literary sources, such as Diocletian's *Price Edicts* and a number of Egyptian papyri also provide additional indications of the relationship between the two metals.

For sake of argument, a median value of 1:15 was chosen to allow a calculation to be made. Calculating EGW is not an exact science, but the point of the exercise is to allow deposits with different metallic components and a range of object types to be compared. Some of the results of this work and how these might be interpreted are provided below. More discussion is provided elsewhere (Hobbs 1997b).

The largest gold and silver deposits across the Empire: regional differences

Table 8.3 sets deposits with an EGW of more than 250 g against the total number recorded from different parts of the Roman Empire, its successor states, and areas outside the frontiers which produce precious metals of Roman imperial origin. Africa tops the group, but produces a relatively low number of finds overall. Similar results are provided by Macedonia and Oriens, where around half the deposits appear to be above average in size. Comparative data from provinces where large numbers of finds have been recorded, for example, Britain and Gaul, have less than 10% of finds with an EGW of more than 250 g. Why might this be the case? On first inspection, it might be seen as an indication that individuals or groups of individuals in the Roman parts of Africa and the East were able to amass greater quantities of precious metals than in some other parts of the Empire. In turn, this might suggest that there are different economic processes in place which mean that precious metals are circulating in very different ways. In the other parts of the Empire, the suggestion might be made that precious metals are more evenly spread around the population, with large assemblages of material rarely ending up in private hands. This would have obvious

Table 8.2. Relative values of gold to silver from literary sources

Approx date	Source	Ratio
27 BC – AD 14	NH33.3; Dio LV12	1: 11.8
AD 41 – 54	NH33.3; Dio LV12	1: 11.7
AD 301	Diocletian's Edict	1: 12.75 – 1: 15.93
AD 301	Diocletian's Edict	1: 17.1 – 1: 17.8
AD 307	P. Oxy 1653	1: 14.94
AD 312	Papyrus de Theadelphie 33	1: 15.08
AD 324	C Th 13.3.2	1: 14.4
AD 422	C Th 8.1.27	1: 18

Table 8.3. Equivalent Gold Weights (EGW) arranged in descending order of % of total finds by region

Region	EGW >250g	Total no. recorded	% of total
Africa	11	22	50
Macedonia	2	4	50
Oriens	9	19	47.4
Scotland and Ireland	2	5	40
Iberia	7	44	15.9
Gaul	35	453	7.7
Eastern Eurasia	10	129	7.7
Illyricum	8	127	6.3
Scandinavia	4	76	5.3
Thrace/ Dacia	9	211	4.3
Britannia	13	335	3.9
Russia	1	27	3.7

The modern countries corresponding with the regions described are: Africa – Tunisia, Algeria, Morocco; Macedonia – Greece, islands of the western Aegean; Oriens – Syria, parts of s. Turkey, Jordan, Israel, Cyprus; Iberia – Spain, Portugal, the Balearics; Gaul – France, Belgium, Luxembourg, Germany and Netherlands w. of the Rhine, Channel Islands; Eastern Eurasia – Yugoslavia n. of the Danube, Romania, Moldava, Ukraine, Belarus, Lithuania, Latvia, Estonia; Illyricum – e. Austria, Croatia, Slovenia, Bosina & Hercegovina, Hungary w. of the Danube; Britannia – England, Wales; Scandinavia – Sweden, Denmark, Norway; Thrace/ Dacia – Bulgaria, Yugoslavia s. of the Danube, Macedonia, n. Albania, Turkey w. of the Bosporus.

implications for our understanding of the organisation of societies in different parts of the Roman world and the mechanisms which underpin precious metal circulation.

Unfortunately, when you look closely at the data from the provinces which appear to produce a higher proportion of large finds, it becomes clear that many of the accounts of the discoveries were exaggerated. Most of the deposits were found at the turn of the 19th century and the size of the finds are usually based on estimates of numbers which are often much higher than was probable in reality. At least four of the North African deposits fall into this category, an example being a hoard of gold solidi from Carthage with an estimated 200 pieces (Mosser 1935, 17) which is likely to be an exaggeration and there is now no means of verification. Having said that, Africa has produced sizeable gold coin deposits; for example, 119 solidi from Ain Meddah (Morrison 1987, 335) which might be considered as above average. The data-set from the region is, however, probably a little too small to be able to be sure that something different was happening here than in other parts of the Roman world.

Where there are larger data-sets, for example, in Gaul and Thrace/Dacia, hoards with an EGW of more than 250 g are low in number; in these cases 7.7% and 4.3% of the total number recorded respectively. This again might suggest that these parts of the Empire were operating differently to the southern and eastern regions. At this stage, because of the problems with the data from North Africa and the East, this should not be over emphasised, but the point of the exercise is to provide a background against which new finds can be set. By looking at such a large dataset, anomalous deposits, in this case ones which are larger than average, become

clear, and these individual finds can then be scrutinised to try to understand why they differ from the norm.

The largest gold and silver deposits across the Empire: differences in composition

Another approach to this type of analysis is set out in Table 8.4. In this instance, deposits with an EGW of more than 1kg are compared, each consisting of finds chosen because they have different internal components. Topping the list is a hoard from Paris (Rue Clovis), found in 1867 (Blanchet 1900, no. 327), a find of a reported 1,200 aurei running up to the early third century AD. If this account has not been exaggerated, which as we have seen is the problem with many of the African finds, this would equate to over 8 kg of gold. This is followed by Kumluca (Boyd and Mango 1993) with over 7 kg EGW of silver church plate of the 7th century AD. Next in scale come gold ingots and solidi of the fourth and fifth centuries from Crasna, Romania, followed by assemblages of fourth- and fifth-century plate and jewellery deposits from Hoxne, Sevso and Beaurains. At the bottom of the list are relatively modest finds in comparison to those at the top, comprising plate finds from Mildenhall, hacksilver from Traprain Law and a large coin hoard from Cunetio.

What does this type of comparison tell us? Firstly, large assemblages of gold and silver were able to be amassed over the whole period subject to study here. In fact, the largest two finds are at both ends of the chronological timespan, the early third century AD and 7th century AD respectively. So it does not seem that there is any major difference in the ability of individuals or groups

Table 8.4. Equivalent Gold Weights of finds with a range of compositions. AV = gold, AR = silver

Location	Reference	Broad content/ date	EGW (g)
Paris (Rue Clovis), France	Blanchet 1900, no. 327	2nd c. AD AV aurei	8521
Kumluca, Turkey	Boyd & Mango 1993	7th c. AD AR church plate	7138
Crasna, Romania	Mommsen 1888	4th c. AD stamped AV ingots	6431
Szikancs, Hungary	Duncan 1993, 26	5th c. AD AV solidi	6404
Hoxne, England	Bland & Johns 1993	4th c. AD AV/AR jewellery, coins, plate	5214
'Sevso', unprovenanced	Mango & Bennett 1994	5th c. AD AR domestic plate	4567
Beaurains, France	Bastien & Metzger 1977	early 4th c. AD AV/AR coins & jewellery	2831
Mildenhall, England	Painter 1977	3rd/ 4th c. AD domestic plate	1735
Cunetio, England	Besly & Bland 1983	3rd c. AD radiates	1481
Traprain Law, Scotland	Curle 1922	4th / early 5th c. AD hacksilver	1454

to amass large assemblages of precious metals at the height of the Roman Empire or in the early days of Byzantium. Taking this one step further, it could be argued that the Paris deposit represents the wealth of one private individual, whilst the Kumluca find is clearly that of an early Christian church community. Does this suggest that attitudes towards the ownership of precious metals had changed over five centuries? We probably cannot take things that far. Kumluca is, nonetheless, the only find which seemingly belonged to a group of individuals, whilst all the other finds are usually interpreted as belonging to one individual or a family group (although earlier church plate – and therefore communal ownership – does, arguably, exist: Water Newton being a case in point (Painter 1999)).

Cunetio deserves a special mention because it is such an unusual find (Besly and Bland 1983). It consists of about 55,000 coins, found in 1978 near the village of Mildenhall in Wiltshire. All the coins were contained in a large storage vessel so we may be fairly sure that all the pieces were recovered. Calculating the EGW of this find was a major undertaking, because of the difficulty in assessing the amount of silver in a hoard which contains coinage of such inconsistent quality. Nevertheless, despite the huge number of pieces, it can be seen that it is not one of the largest finds in the group. It is not that much smaller, however, than the Mildenhall (Suffolk) treasure in terms of size. So what might this say about the relative status of the owners of Mildenhall and Cunetio? That they were of similar social standing, because they seemingly possessed similar quantities of silver, even if it was tied up in very different forms? If so, why did the owner of Cunetio not possess silver plate, a far more attractive medium of wealth storage than base silver radiate coins? Silver plate is certainly available in the third century, but is mainly found in three areas of modern France, one of the anomalies of late Roman silver plate distribution (Hobbs 1997b).

None of this comparative work provides any clear-cut answers. Indeed, it raises more questions *than* answers. Nevertheless, I would argue that these comparisons between different assemblages are a vital way of beginning to address issues such as ownership and value, and we should not be constrained by traditional approaches which tend to be material, geographic, or chronologically specific.

Conclusions

In this paper I have put forward some ideas regarding the issue of value in relation to late Roman precious metal hoards. Although this subject is fraught with difficulty, it is potentially of great importance and needs to be addressed in novel ways. As part of this process it is hoped that the proposed method for comparing the bullion value of precious metal finds, by providing each with an index termed Equivalent Gold Weight, will prove to be a useful tool for comparison.

Acknowledgements

Many thanks are due to Ralph Jackson, J. D. Hill and Richard Reece for their comments on earlier drafts of this paper.

Bibliography

Classical sources
C. Th.   Codex Theodosius
Dio   Dio, Roman History (Loeb Classical Library, 1917)
NH   Pliny, Natural Histories
P. Oxy.   The Oxyrhynchus Papyri (ed. P. Grenfell and A.S. Hunt, London, 1898–1996).

Ashbee, P. (1997) Mildenhall: memories of mystery and misgivings. *Antiquity* 71, 271, 74–6.
Bastien, P. and Metzger, C. (1977) *LeTrésor de Beaurains*. Paris.
Besly, E. M. and Bland, R. F. (1983) *The Cunetio Treasure: Roman coinage of the third century A.D.* London, British Museum Press.
Blanchet, A. (1900) *Les Trésors Monnaies Romaines et les Invasions Germaniques de la Gaule*. Paris.
Bland, R. F. and Johns, C. M. (1993) *The Hoxne Treasure. An illustrated introduction*. London, British Museum Press.
Boyd, S. and Mango, M. (eds.) (1993) *Ecclesiastical Silver Plate in 6th century Byzantium*. Washington.

Burnett, A. M. (1984) Clipped siliquae and the end of Roman Britain. *Britannia* 15, 163–8.

Cameron, A. (1992) Observations on the distribution and ownership of late Roman silver plate. *Journal of Roman Archaeology* 5, 178–85.

Curle, A. O. (1922) *The Treasure of Traprain.* Edinburgh.

Duncan, G. L. (1993*) Coin Circulation in the Danubian and Balkan Provinces of the Roman Empire AD 294–578.* London, Royal Numismatic Society.

Guest, P. S. W. (forthcoming) *The Late Roman Gold and Silver Coins from the Hoxne Treasure.* London, British Museum Press.

Harden, D. B. (1983) The glass hoard. In S. Johnson, Burgh Castle, Excavations by Charles Green, 1958–61*, 81–8. East Anglia Archaeology* 20.

Henig, M. (2002) *The Heirs of King Verica. Culture and politics in Roman Britain.* Tempus.

Hill, J. D., Spence A. J., La Neice S. and Worrell, S. (2004) The Winchester Hoard: a find of unique Iron Age gold jewellery from Southern England, *The Antiquaries Journal* 84, 1–22.

Hobbs, R. (1997a) The Mildenhall treasure: Roald Dahl's ultimate tale of the unexpected? *Antiquity* 71, 271, 63–73.

Hobbs, R. (1997b*) Late Roman Precious Metal Deposits, AD 200–700: changes of time and space.* Unpublished thesis, University of London.

Mango, M. M. and Bennett, A. (1994) The Sevso treasure: Part 1. *Journal of Roman Archaeology Supplementary Series* 12, 1. Ann Arbor.

Martin, M. (1984) Esslöffel. In H. Cahn and A. Kaufmann-Heinimann (eds) *Der spätrömische Silberschatz von Kaiseraugst,* 56–96. Derendingen.

Millett, M. (1994) Treasure: interpreting Roman hoards. *TRAC 94, Proceedings of the Fourth Annual Theoretical Archaeology Conference Durham 1994,* 99–106. Oxford, Oxbow Books.

Mommsen, T. (1888) Goldbarren aus Sirmium. *Zeitschrift fur Numismatik* 16, 351–8.

Morrison, C. (1987) La circulation de la monnaie d'or en Afrique à l'époque vandale: bilan des trouvailles locales. In H. Huvelin, M. Christol and G. Gautier (eds) *Mélanges de numismatique offerts à Pierre Bastien.* Wettern, 325–44.

Mosser, S. (1935) A bibliography of Byzantine coin hoards. *American Numismatic Society Notes and Monographs* 67. New York.

Painter, K. S. (1977) *The Mildenhall Treasure. Roman silver from East Anglia.* London, British Museum Press.

Painter, K. S. (1988) Roman silver hoards: ownership and status. In F. Baratte (ed.) *Argenterie Romaine et Byzantine. Actes de la Table Ronde,* 97–112. Paris.

Painter, K. S. (1993) Late Roman silver plate: a reply to Alan Cameron. *Journal of Roman Archaeology* 6, 109–15.

Painter, K. S. (1999) The Water Newton Silver: votive or liturgical? *Journal of the British Archaeological Association* 152, 1–23.

Painter, K .S. (2001) *The Insula of the House of the Menander at Pompeii. Volume IV: the silver treasure.* Oxford.

Poulton, R. and Scott, E. (1993) The hoarding, deposition and use of pewter in Roman Britain. In E. Scott (ed.) *Theoretical Roman Archaeology Conference: First Conference Proceedings,* 115–32. Aldershot, Worldwide Archaeological Series 4.

Reece, R. M. (1995) Site finds in Roman Britain. *Britannia* 26, 179–206.

Salway, P., Hallam, S. J., and l'Anson Browmwich, J. (1970) *The Fenland in Roman Times.* Royal Geographical Society Research Series 5, London.

Sutherland, C. H. V. (1984) *The Roman Imperial Coinage 1, revised edition, 31 BC AD 69.* London, Spink & Son.

Walker, D. R. (1978) *The Metrology of the Roman Silver Coinage.* British Archaeological Reports, Supplemetary Series 40. Oxford.

9   Techniques for Exploring Context, Deposition and Chronology

T. S. Martin

Though frequent mention has been made by antiquaries of large holes filled with black mould and débris, on various ancient sites, they have usually been indiscriminately termed rubbish pits; but I am not aware that ... any steps have been taken to elucidate the penetralia of these mysterious repositories.

Richard Cornwallis Neville, *Fourth Lord Braybrooke* (1855, 109)

Introduction

Context and deposition have attracted the attention of archaeologists studying Roman Britain since the mid-19th century. Even though the features excavated on Romano-British sites can no longer be viewed as 'mysterious repositories', little attempt has been made towards analysing them in depth. This lies in contrast to the work undertaken for the Iron Age by Hill (1995). This paper explores the ways that investigation of pottery deposition can provide important insights into the character and dating of Romano-British rural settlements. In doing so, it emphasises the need for a considerable degree of objectivity in the way dating and phasing is approached. It has three inter-related aims. Firstly, to explore the prospect that recurring depositional and chronological patterns can be recognised through the study of pottery deposition; secondly, to see how these patterns can be used as dating and phasing tools; and thirdly, to present a framework that will allow Romano-British rural sites to be evaluated through their artefacts, especially pottery. The identification and analysis of structured deposition within features is outside the scope of this paper, although a search for patterning in the way pottery is deposited on sites is an essential prerequisite for such a study.

In this paper, questions relating to context, deposition and chronology are seen as being inter-linked. Consequently, the aims outlined above are investigated through answering the following four questions:

1. which feature category or categories produce the most pottery?
2. within each feature category, what type of context or contexts (i.e. primary, secondary, top fill, etc) produces the most pottery?
3. are there any discernible chronological variations in the way pottery is deposited?
4. what can spot-dates tell us about site chronology in general?

The answers to these questions form the main lines of inquiry throughout this paper. Pottery has been used, not only because it is closely datable, but also because it is by far the most common portable artefact type, in terms of numbers of items and weight, recovered from Romano-British rural sites in Essex (the case study area). Furthermore, as Cooper (2000, 77 and also this volume) has pointed out, pottery is the artefact type that is least affected by factors of preservation, recycling and retrieval. By comparison, other closely datable portable artefact types are virtually absent, so it is rarely, if at all possible to use these in the same way as pottery. Consequently, pottery as an indicator of depositional and chronological trends is vitally important. It is hoped that the methods described below will go some way to revitalising chronologically-orientated approaches to the analysis of pottery by demonstrating new research possibilities, particularly where the study of artefacts might assist in general site interpretation. It is also hoped that this paper will be of interest to finds specialists and site directors alike, but above all thought provoking.

The data-set

Context, deposition and chronology are examined using the data principally from two sites in Essex: Bulls Lodge Dairy, Boreham and Great Holts Farm, Boreham. The site at Bulls Lodge is a possible *'principia'* (Lavender 1993) or rural shrine (Wallace 1995) dating to the 3rd century with some earlier unrelated activity. The site at Great Holts Farm is a 4th century villa complex with traces of an earlier field system in the surrounding landscape (Germany 2003). Both of these sites are to the north of Chelmsford and are located approximately 1.1km apart (Figs. 9.1–9.3). They thus provide the opportunity to examine the development of the Romano-British landscape in a relatively confined area. These sites have been subjected to extensive archaeological investigation, which has resulted in substantial stratified pottery assemblages being recovered. Bulls Lodge Dairy produced 8,504 sherds weighing 72.3kg, while Great Holts Farm produced 13,471 sherds weighing 195kg. Great Holts Farm will be examined in more detail because it produced the largest assemblage and has been more intensely studied. Other sites will be mentioned in passing, but these have produced much smaller amounts of pottery and smaller areas have been excavated. More detailed presentation and consideration of the data from Great Holts Farm and Bulls Lodge Dairy is to be found in the full pottery report (Martin 2003a).

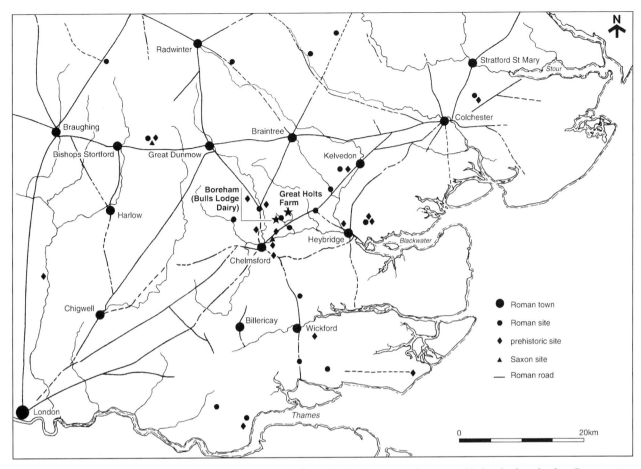

Fig. 9.1. Location map showing Bulls Lodge Dairy and Great Holts Farm in relation to Chelmsford and other Roman sites in Essex (after Germany 2003)

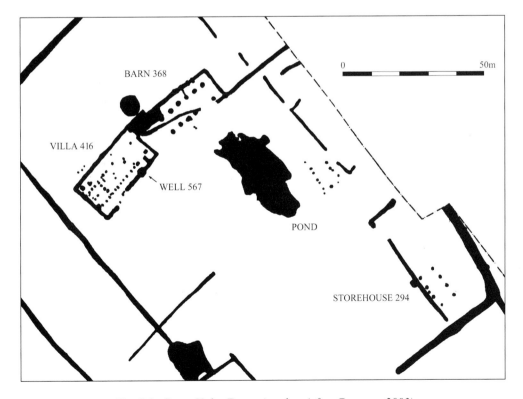

Fig. 9.2. Great Holts Farm site plan (after Germany 2003)

Fig. 9.3. Bulls Lodge Dairy site plan (after Lavender 1993)

The five key methodologies

The questions posed in the introduction all relate to specific aspects of the analysis of context, deposition and chronology. To answer them five key methodologies have been adopted. These are:

1. the Chelmsford typology – as a means of classifying and comparing pottery assemblages;
2. the dating of groups based on the *latest* identifiable sherds in a context;
3. the use of stratigraphic relationships to refine dating;
4. quantification (sherd count and weight) – to compare assemblage sizes and as a guide to the reliability of context dates;
5. the Chelmsford ceramic time-sequence – as a way of comparing the chronology of site A with site B.

How each of these methodologies relates to the questions posed in the introduction is summarised in Table 9.1.

The Chelmsford typology (Going 1987, 3–54), which allows pottery to be quantified and analysed by both form and fabric, has formed the main point of reference for the study of Roman pottery in Essex since the late 1980s.

It has been successfully applied to a number of excavated assemblages within the immediate hinterland of Chelmsford (*e.g.* Great Holts Farm and Bulls Lodge Dairy), as well as material from more distant sites (*e.g.* Great Dunmow). Indeed large quantities of pottery, from various sites, have now been published using the Chelmsford typology; in consequence the kind of dataset that could form the basis of a thorough regional study, such as that produced for Kent (Pollard 1988), is now available. Indeed, if the use of the Chelmsford typology was to be suddenly abandoned it would probably set the realisation of this back at least two decades!

When assigning a date to a context based on the pottery recovered from it the specialist must be fully aware of the presence of pottery that may be either residual or intrusive. In some cases both intrusive and residual material may be present. Having said this, the dating of groups based on the *latest* identifiable sherds in a context is a standard practice in Romano-British pottery studies and has been adopted for the sites covered in this paper. The presence of intrusive material may be identified because it may be much later than the rest of the pottery in a context and clearly out of place when stratigraphy is also taken into account. Often this material will comprise very small sherds that could have and probably did, arrive in their final resting place through worm or animal activity. The presence of residual pottery may be identified as it is often in poor condition and exhibits high levels of abrasion. It will also be quite clearly much earlier than the bulk of the pottery in the context. No context can be dated on the presence of residual pottery. Residuality and the possibility of sherds being intrusive have all been taken into account when assigning dates for contexts on the sites examined here. Where residual and or intrusive sherds have been recognised, these have been rejected as dating evidence; otherwise dating is based on the latest pottery present.

The use of stratigraphic relationships to refine dating is also helpful, especially where the dating evidence comprises groups that are small or largely undiagnostic (as is often the case with rural sites). One of the most important aspects of this study concerns how pottery data can be viewed in relation to stratigraphy. The need to examine artefact and stratigraphic data in tandem and not in isolation is something that I have been convinced of for some time. For any study of context, deposition and chronology this is essential. Even so, it is important to emphasise the fact that a high degree of objectivity is called for. Interpretation of site data must be kept to the barest minimum if the results of this exercise are to be of any value. Before it is possible to examine depositional issues in detail, it is essential that the types of stratigraphic relationships encountered on rural sites are appreciated.

Five basic relationships may be identified:

1. Single fill features cutting natural
2. Single-fill features cutting or cut by another single-fill feature

3. Multi-fill features cutting natural
4. Multi-fill features cutting or cut by single-fill features
5. Multi-fill feature cutting or cut by another multi-fill feature

Where possible, the existence of these relationships have all been taken into account when providing dates for contexts that contain pottery that is not especially diagnostic of any particular ceramic phase. More often than not, the only stratigraphic relationships encountered on rural sites are those that are confined to a series of fills within a cut. This is discussed in more detail below.

To emphasise the value of stratigraphic relationships for dating purposes where they exist, an example may be provided from Old House, Church Langley, Harlow. Here a late 3rd to mid-4th century ditch (F6) produced mainly undiagnostic pottery in its top fill. However, what was present would not have been out of place in a 2nd century context. On the other hand, the lower fill gave a much clearer indication of the feature's date in the form of several late 3rd to mid-4th century vessels, suggesting that the pottery in the top fill is entirely residual (Martin 2000, 53). This example illustrates the usefulness of stratigraphic relationships where a securely dated context is sealed by one that is poorly-dated.

The quantification of pottery by sherd count and weight is used to compare assemblage sizes and as a guide to the reliability of context dates. While it is outside the scope of this paper to delve into the relative merits of each method of quantification commonly in use in pottery studies (cf. Evans 1991; Pollard 1990), something needs to be said about why pottery is quantified and which methods can be applied to specific aims. During the spot-dating of the Great Holts Farm assemblage, the decision was taken to record all pottery using sherd count and

Table 9.1. The four main questions regarding context formation processes in terms of pottery deposition and site chronology, and the methodology adopted to investigate them

Question	Methodology
(1) Which feature categories generally produce the most pottery?	Quantification (sherd count and weight) – to compare assemblage sizes and as a guide to the reliability of context dates
(2) Within each feature category, which type of context or contexts (i.e. primary secondary, top fill, etc) generally produces the most pottery?	Quantification (sherd count and weight) – to compare assemblage sizes and as a guide to the reliability of context dates
(3) Are there any discernible chronological variations in the way pottery is deposited?	The Chelmsford typology – as a means of classifying and comparing pottery assemblages; dating of pottery based on the latest identifiable sherds in a context; use of stratigraphic relationships to refine dating
(4) What can spot-dates tell us about site chronology in general?	Quantification (sherd count and weight) – to compare assemblage sizes and as a guide to the reliability of context dates; the Chelmsford typology – as a means of classifying and comparing pottery assemblages; the Chelmsford ceramic time-sequence – as a way of comparing the chronology of site A with site B

weight by fabric, while only selected groups were analysed using EVEs. Sherd count and weight were used to look at questions relating context, deposition and chronology, while EVEs was used to examine economic issues and study vessel form and use.

The question of quantification is a fundamental one, even more so as it constitutes one of the key methodologies for the study of context, deposition and chronology. It is used here to provide a measure of how much pottery is present in each feature category, fill type and ceramic phase. However, presently there does seem to be a lot of quantification being published for the sake of it, without any obvious appreciation of what it is that is going to be achieved by doing so. I would like to pass several comments on this here. Firstly, I believe that it is only worth publishing quantified data if the amounts being studied are going to represent something that is going to be statistically meaningful. This raises the question of how much pottery is needed before quantification is valid. Much depends on why the pottery is being quantified in the first place. The main use of quantification is to provide data concerning economic issues and function/social status. There is a suggestion that there are minimum thresholds below which the validity of the results seems to be questionable and that these vary according to the measure used. Going (1993, 68, but see also Cooper this volume) has briefly summarised some of the current thinking on the matter and has concluded that figures obtained from groups below five EVEs should be treated with caution. Consequently, only large groups should be selected for quantification, as has been the practice in Essex since the 1980s, if it is economic issues that are being addressed. However, the quantification of much smaller groups may also provide useful information, especially where questions regarding economic or function/social status are not the primary objective, as I demonstrate below.

Secondly, any quantified data that is published must be tied down to a narrow date-band. I do not see the point of publishing figures for period/phase assemblages that are given date ranges in excess of 100 years, that is date ranges that exceed two of the Chelmsford ceramic phases if the aim is to provide data about economic issues. Over the past decade I have developed a deep mistrust of data derived from composite groups and period/phase assemblages, especially where economic issues are the main concern. I have come to the belief that it is always more instructive to study single deposits of large accumulations of pottery that can be placed within a narrow date-range. This is to a large extent down to my experience of dealing with 'latest' Roman pottery in Essex (Martin in prep. a). In Essex, groups of this period are characterised by the presence of a range of fabrics that are first introduced from *c*. AD 360. Are groups that contain large amounts of Late shell-tempered ware and Oxfordshire red colour-coat, and small amounts of Fine and Sandy grey wares really the same date as those that contain large amounts of Fine and Sandy grey wares and small amounts of Late shell-tempered ware and Oxfordshire red colour-coat? I think not. But if you work with composite groups and period/phase assemblages these differences simply disappear. Yet it is these differences that we need to be identifying and analysing, as they will also be able to offer much data concerning the chronology of pottery supply as well as having the potential to extend overall chronology into the 5th century (Martin in prep. a). The identification of 5th century groups will thus enable context and deposition to be studied in that period as well, something that at present cannot be attempted.

Another problem with period/phase assemblages is that they will inevitably amalgamate groups that have been deposited in a structured manner and those that have not. The effect of this is that the figures may be skewed towards certain types of pottery, such as fine wares. While complete assemblages relating to individual ceramic phases have been used below, these have not been used to glean information about economic and function/social status on the sites analysed below.

The Chelmsford ceramic time-sequence (Table 9.2) forms the basis behind which the chronology of Site A with Site B may be compared. It provides a framework of 8 ceramic phases commencing *c*. AD 60 and ending at the beginning of the 5th century. These ceramic phases offer relatively narrow date bands, which enables inter- and intra-site chronologies to be compared and contrasted. The Chelmsford ceramic time-sequence thus forms the backbone of the study of chronology at Great Holts Farm and Bulls Lodge Dairy.

Table 9.2. The Chelmsford ceramic time-sequence (after Going 1987)

Chelmsford Ceramic Phase	Calendar Years (*c*. AD)
Pre-1	Before 60
1	60–80
2	80–120/25
3	120/25–160/70
4	160/70–200/10
5	200/10–250/60
6	260/75–300/10
7	300/10–360/70
8	360/70–400+

Which feature category or categories produce the most pottery?

This question forms the starting point. It enables the main depositional trends to be identified regardless of any chronological differentiation (Figs. 9.4–9.5). To stress the close relationship between context, deposition and chronology, it will allow the feature types that produce the most pottery dating evidence and those that do not, to be pinpointed. Having answered this important preliminary question it will then be possible to examine more detailed issues relating to context, deposition and chronology.

The following feature categories were identified at Great Holts Farm and are used to compare basic depositional patterning with other sites:

1. Linear (ditches and gullies)
2. Pits
3. Structural (*e.g.* post-holes with in situ packing)
4. Demolition (*e.g.* robber trenches)
5. Funerary (*e.g.* cremations)
6. Water channels (wells, ponds, drains etc)
7. Miscellaneous (*e.g.* hollows and unclassified cuts)

The first two categories represent specific feature categories. Linear features are important manifestations of landscape management but may comprise features as diverse as short lengths of shallow gullies, wide ditches, or deep field boundaries. Arguably ditches are of secondary importance acting simply as quarries for the construction of banks. Pits tend to comprise typically small and generally shallow circular or oval features. These seldom cut each other on rural sites. Structural, demolition and funerary features all represent specific events. Structural deposits represent the construction of a building, while demolition deposits represent the destruction of a building. The need to differentiate between these categories is fundamental to the understanding of structural evidence. Funerary contexts are associated with the ritual disposal of the dead. Water channels form a distinct group in themselves. These have been grouped together because of the potential they have to include ritual or 'structured' deposition in their fills. The final category comprises all the other feature types, that are often difficult to categorise, not included in the previous six groupings, some of which may include very severely truncated pits.

One important aspect that should not be overlooked, however, is the volume of earth excavated in relation to feature category. While no attempt has been made to calculate the volume of earth excavated from each feature category and relate this to the amount of pottery recovered, it is recognised that this would be of considerable interest. It is, however, obvious that post-holes, because of their general small size, are expected to contain less earth and thus are less likely to produce large amounts of pottery.

For linear features, because they are often prominent landscape features, the opposite is often the case.

At Great Holts Farm, linear features produced the majority of the site's pottery and therefore the best dating evidence. Demolition horizons also produced substantial quantities of pottery, while pits and structural contexts contained very little (Fig. 9.4). This general absence of pottery from pit fills may be partly due to the relatively small number of pits on the site. However, 51% of pit fills did contain pottery compared with 49% of linear features (Fig. 9.5). This may suggest that a different type of rubbish was being deposited in pits compared to the linear features. The pottery from pits appears to be extremely fragmented and thus less diagnostic for dating purposes whereas the material from linear features appears to be more complete and thus provides better dating evidence. This may suggest that primary rubbish deposits are more likely to be recovered from the fills of linear features. Moreover, 72% of demolition contexts contained pottery suggesting that a large amount of ceramic rubbish may have been simply left lying around. The incidence of pottery within the fills of each feature category at Great Holts Farm suggests that statistically at least, structural deposits are the least likely to produce pottery. Furthermore, although linear features produce the most pottery, this material is concentrated within a relatively small number of contexts, while pit fills are just as likely to contain some pottery as linear features. Lastly, demolition contexts are the most likely to contain some pottery.

As at Great Holts Farm, the bulk of the pottery excavated at Bulls Lodge Dairy came from linear features (68% by weight). However, unlike at Great Holts Farm, a much higher proportion of the pottery was recovered from pits (22% compared with 3%). Indeed pits seem to be much more widespread at Bulls Lodge Dairy than at Great Holts Farm. Another contrasting depositional trend at Bulls Lodge Dairy is the somewhat minor significance of demolition horizons, although structural deposits are more important in terms of pottery deposition that at Great Holts Farm. However, compared with Great Holts Farm, the range of feature categories represented at Bulls Lodge is much narrower with an absence, for example, of evidence

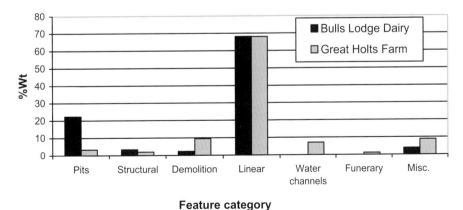

Fig. 9.4. The pattern of pottery deposition at Great Holts Farm and Bulls Lodge Dairy by context type

for wells, ponds and cremations. This suggests that a much narrower range of activities took place at Bulls Lodge Dairy compared with Great Holts Farm that can be recovered archaeologically. On the other hand a much wider area has been investigated at Great Holts Farm.

Analysis of the main characteristics of pottery deposition at these two sites suggests the presence of a number of common trends. Firstly, the amount of pottery recovered from pits is variable, but generally small, while structural deposits will generally produce the least pottery. Secondly, linear features, the most commonly encountered feature category on Romano-British rural sites, will produce the largest amount, usually in excess of 60% of all pottery. The main implications for dating site phases on rural sites using the data from Bulls Lodge Dairy and Great Holts Farm are that linear features are more likely to be closely dated using pottery, while other feature categories are less likely to be closely dated. This data also shows that linear features offer the most research potential, simply because they are more likely to be closely dated. This potential will be analysed in more detail below (Fig. 9.5).

The dominance of linear features as receptacles of pottery deposition is seen on other Romano-British rural sites in Essex even where smaller assemblages have been excavated. Figures from Hill Farm, Tendring, 74.5% (Martin in prep. b), Ship Lane, Averley, 64.9% (Martin 2003b, 139), Brook-House Road, Great Tey, 62.2% (Martin forthcoming) demonstrate this. The figures from Great Holts Farm and Bulls Lodge Dairy also compare well with the amounts recovered from Spong Hill in Norfolk. Here only 11% of the sites' pottery came from non-linear features (Gurney 1995, table 9). Indeed, the need to understand ditch systems on rural sites has been emphasised by Chadwick (1999) in relation to the north-east midlands and has called for a radical review of how these features are approached during excavation. This point is further emphasised by the data from Great Holts Farm and other Romano-British rural sites in Essex.

Within each feature category, what type of context or contexts produces the most pottery?

It is now time to relate the pattern of pottery deposition as outlined above to actual site stratigraphy. This section examines stratigraphic relationships within features. In doing so it investigates what type of context within each feature category produces the best dating evidence. Since analysis has shown that linear features are especially prone to pottery deposition and that they are also more likely to contain more than one fill, this particular category of feature will receive detailed attention here. To allow the pattern of pottery deposition within them to be analysed, each fill is allocated to one of four context categories:

1. Single fills
2. Primary and top (2 fills)
3. Primary, secondary and top (3 fills)
4. Primary, secondary, intermediate and top (4 or more fills)

These context categories may be defined in the following terms. A single fill: no stratigraphy recognised within the cut; primary fill: the earliest context stratigraphically where there is more than one fill; secondary fill: the context sealed beneath either the top fill or by an intermediate fill and sealing the primary fill; intermediate fills: a context or contexts sealing the secondary and primary fills, but sealed by the top fill; top fill: the latest surviving episode of infilling. Essentially, pottery recovered from the primary fills will represent material that has been deposited closest in time to when the feature was cut, while pottery recovered from the top fill will be material that was deposited furthest in time from when the feature was cut.

The pattern of pottery deposition within linear features has only been analysed in detail for Great Holts Farm (Fig. 9.6). This shows that top fills are the most prone to

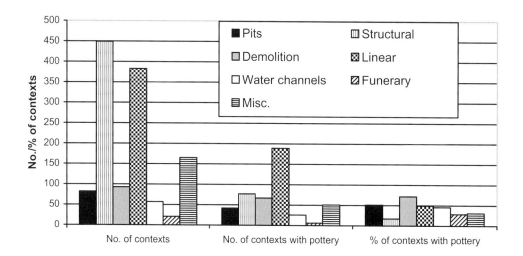

Fig. 9.5. Analysis of depositional trends by feature category at Great Holts Farm

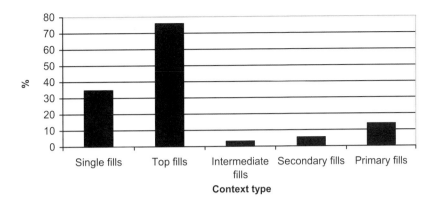

Fig. 9.6. Pottery recovered from contexts within linear features at Great Holts Farm: the relative frequency of pottery by context type.

pottery deposition having produced 75.9% of all pottery recovered from linear features. This means that the most pottery is being deposited in them when the ditch is being allowed to silt up and any sequence of cleaning has ceased. It also suggests something of a termination in the life or usefulness of the ditch itself. This point is further emphasised by the fact that single fill features produced the next largest amount of pottery (34.7%). However, single fill linear features should not automatically be seen as features that were simply left to silt up directly after their excavation without ever being cleaned out. It is possible that these features underwent prolonged periods of dredging and that their uniform fills are a product of the last episode of fill accumulation. This interpretation has been used for Roman field systems in the immediate hinterland of Chelmsford (Isserlin 1998, 56). Primary fills produced the next largest amount of pottery (13.8%), which suggests that linear features may have been prone to small amounts of pottery deposition immediately after they were cut. The smallest amounts of pottery were recovered from the secondary fills (5.4%) and the intermediate fills (3.2%). This suggests that these features went through periods when almost no pottery was deposited in them, prior to the final deluge.

Are there any discernible chronological variations in the way pottery is deposited?

To a large extent the answer to this question is going to be site-specific, given that each site will have its own unique history. The aim is to see how the main depositional trends identified above may be analysed from a chronological perspective and to use this as a phasing tool. The example data provided is principally from Great Holts Farm and is interrogated to identify the following:

1. the chief period or periods of pottery deposition regardless of feature category or context type
2. the main period or periods of ditch cutting
3. the most important period or periods of ditch infilling
4. the dating of the structural evidence

5. the dating of the evidence for the demolition of the structures

Using the spot-dating evidence, the amount of pottery recovered from contexts assigned to each ceramic phase is measured by weight (kg) and sherd count (Figs. 9.7 and 9.8). The earliest surviving contexts are not especially securely dated, but contain pottery that is broadly characteristic of Ceramic phase 2/3. However, the amount of material being deposited at this time is negligible (1.4kg). A slight increase in the amount of pottery being deposited in contexts that are certainly of Ceramic phase 3 is discernible, although the quantities involved are again not large (3.8kg). The amount of pottery present in contexts assigned to Ceramic phase 3/4 again increases, this time to 15kg. There is then a sharp rise in the quantity of pottery recovered from contexts dated to Ceramic phase 4 (34kg). This is dramatic upsurge and suggests that this period was one of great importance regarding context formation. From Ceramic phases 4/5 to 5 the amount of pottery being deposited goes into dramatic decline. Ceramic phase 5 is barely represented producing only 0.8kg of pottery. Contexts dating to Ceramic phase 6 see the beginning of a protracted up-turn in the amount of pottery (3.5kg) being deposited on the site. This trend continues through into Ceramic phase 7 and right to the end of the Roman period. Ceramic phase 7 contexts produced the second largest amount of pottery (35kg), while Ceramic phase 8 contexts produced the largest amount of pottery (64.5kg) from any period. This then is the main period of pottery deposition and context formation on the site. It is notable that these trends are also discernible if sherd count is used to measure the amount of pottery present in each ceramic phase (Fig. 9.8). The main difference is that Ceramic phase 4 is more important in terms sherd count than Ceramic phase 7. Ceramic phase 5 is again barely represented, while Ceramic phase 8 remains the most important single period whichever measure is used.

Detailed examination of the pattern of pottery deposition within linear features also provides useful information about site chronology at Great Holts Farm (Fig. 9.9). The earliest pottery recovered from any of the primary fills of

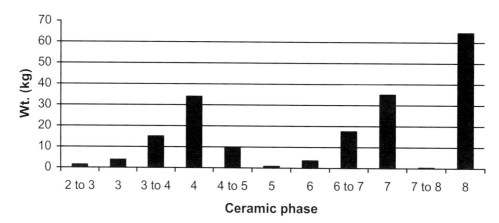

Fig. 9.7. The pattern of pottery deposition measured by the total weight of pottery assigned to each Ceramic phase at Great Holts Farm

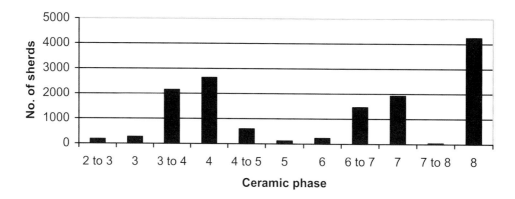

Fig. 9.8. The pattern of pottery deposition measured by the number of sherds assigned to each Ceramic phase at Great Holts Farm

linear features falls within Ceramic phase 4. However, this is not the earliest material to be recovered from linear features. A small amount of pottery (1.3kg) amounting to 1% of the total from linear features, was recovered from top fills and single fill features belonging to Ceramic Phase 2/3. This suggests that the earliest linear features are of this broad period or slightly earlier, given that this indicates evidence for ditch silting/infilling at this time. The amount of pottery recovered from contexts dating to Ceramic phase 3 (3.2kg) represents 2.4% of all pottery from linear features. By Ceramic phase 4 the amount of pottery being deposited in linear features rises dramatically to 34kg. This figure represents 25.3% of all pottery recovered from linear features. Although the bulk of this material came from top fills and single fill features, the amount of pottery recovered from primary, secondary and intermediate fills constitutes the second largest from these context types. This period is important because it is the first period of significant pottery deposition within linear features at Great Holts Farm and shows that it was one where ditch cutting and infilling were both significant episodes.

Pottery dating to Ceramic phases 5 and 6 accounts for only 9% of all material from linear features. This material

comes from top fills and single fill features. Ceramic phase 7 sees a rapid proliferation in the amount of pottery being deposited in linear features, although the quantities do not reach the same level as seen in Ceramic phase 4. The pottery again mainly comes from the top fills of features suggesting another period of ditch silting. By the time we reach Ceramic phase 8, we see massive quantities of pottery being deposited within linear features. This is the main period of pottery deposition at Great Holts Farm. While the bulk of it is once more from top fills and single fill features, a significant proportion was recovered from primary fills. This suggests that Ceramic phase 8 was a major period of context formation represented by large-scale ditch cutting and an even more profound period of ditch silting. When this process finally came to an end is difficult to determine from the ceramic evidence alone.

The need to differentiate clearly between construction and demolition deposits has already been touched on above. It is important that contexts of these categories are analysed separately and the evidence for any such episodes discussed in detail. The evidence from Great Holts Farm may be briefly summarised as follows. The earliest structural deposits are not securely dated but seem to belong to either Ceramic phase 6 or 7. Dating is based on very small

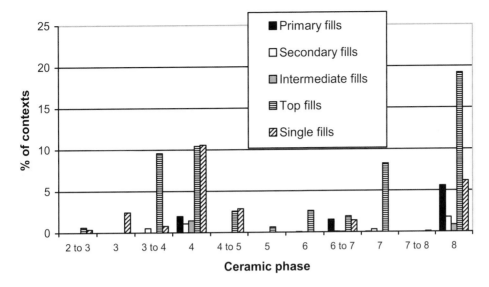

Fig. 9.9. *The pattern of pottery deposition within linear features at Great Holts Farm shown chronologically*

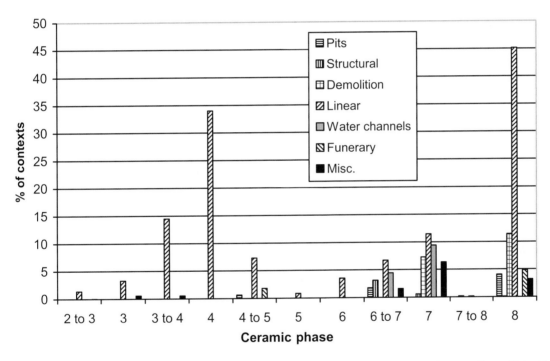

Fig. 9.10. *The pattern of pottery deposition showing feature categories by Ceramic phase at Great Holts Farm*

amounts of pottery (3kg). While there is evidence for later structural deposits, the amount of pottery associated with them is miniscule. The latest, however, belong to Ceramic phase 8. The dating of demolition deposits is, fortunately less problematic. Contexts dating to Ceramic phase 7 comprise the earliest evidence for demolition activity. These contexts produced 7.2kg of pottery. However, the bulk of the demolition deposits are datable to Ceramic phase 8. These contexts produced 11.4kg of pottery.

One last point concerning the pattern of pottery deposition at Great Holts Farm is worth making. Prior to Ceramic phase 7, virtually all of the pottery recovered from Great Holts Farm came from linear features. Al-

though Ceramic phase 4 produced the third largest amount, it was all recovered from linear features. It is only in Ceramic phases 7 and 8 that all seven feature categories are represented containing datable pottery.

The depositional data from Bulls Lodge Dairy, when analysed from a chronological perspective, suggests a very different site history compared with Great Holts Farm (Fig. 9.11). Here the earliest fills within linear features are pre-Ceramic phase 1. There is also a small amount of contemporary structural evidence. The earliest evidence for pits belongs to Ceramic phase 1/2; the dating though is not all that secure. In marked contrast to Great Holts Farm Ceramic phase 4 is poorly represented in terms of pottery deposition, with only a small amount of pottery being deposited in pits. Another contrast with Great Holts Farm sees Ceramic phases 5, 5/6 and 6 producing the most significant quantities of pottery. Deposition of pottery in linear features is specially important in this period. This trend also continues into Ceramic phase 6/7, although at this time pits provide the most important source of pottery data. This is once again in marked contrast with the situation at Great Holts Farm where there is so little material in pits. The only activity certainly taking place in Ceramic phase 7 appears to be the demolition of the main structure. There is nothing from the site that can be dated to Ceramic phase 8.

What can spot-dates tell us about site chronology in general?

Having identified a number of depositional and chronological trends, it is now appropriate to consider their interpretation and compare the data from the two sites in more detail. The aim is not to provide detailed analysis of individual features and structures as this information is covered by the site report (Germany 2003) and more detailed analysis of the pottery in the accompanying specialist report (Martin 2003a). At Great Holts Farm, although some pottery pre-dating Ceramic phase 2 was identified, the amount is minimal and none could be related to contemporary feature-fills. The earliest features are a small number of ditches that were being in-filled at the end of Ceramic phase 2 or in Ceramic phase 3. This is the

earliest evidence for a field system on the site, even if we are in effect dealing with disuse horizons. Although it is possible that the main villa complex (Fig. 9.2) was constructed in Ceramic phase 6, the volume of pottery datable to Ceramic phases 7 and 8 indicates a probable 4th century date. Continued modification of the field system throughout Ceramic phases 7 and 8 is indicated by the persistent deposition of substantial amounts of pottery in ditch fills. Whether this represents boundaries going out of use or simply the dumping of refuse in convenient hollows is another matter.

As noted above, Ceramic phase 8 provides more pottery than any other period at Great Holts Farm. A minor construction or reconstruction horizon is identifiable in relation to the main villa building, suggesting that the building was being maintained into Ceramic phase 8. The next important episode is a major demolition horizon that embraced the main aisled villa building, the bath-house and the remnant of the other aisled building at the back of the bath-house (Fig. 9.2). That this was a major event is shown by its all-embracing, even systematic, nature. After this there is no datable evidence for structures of any kind on the site. A strong case can be made for a radical change in site function, represented by a reversion to field systems unassociated with domestic occupation. Whatever happened, it resulted in the cessation of large-scale pottery deposition on the site.

The reasons for Ceramic phase 8 deposits being especially prone to pottery deposition are unclear; in some instances this may be site-specific. However, this occurrence does seem to fit into a trend seen elsewhere in

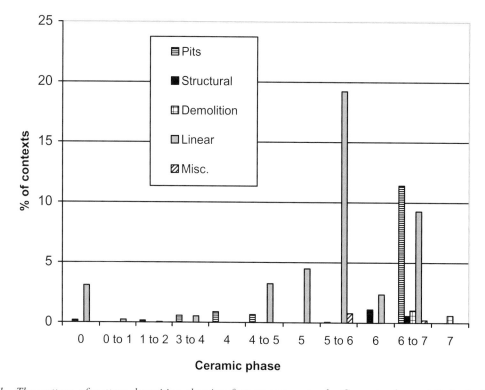

Fig. 9.11. The pattern of pottery deposition showing feature categories by Ceramic phase at Bulls Lodge Dairy

Britain, especially on some urban sites. At, for example, Lincoln (Darling 1977, 3), the presence of a large deposit of rubbish in a roadside ditch dating to the late 4th century, closely associated with a late refurbishing of the defences, was seen to be consistent with the low standard of public hygiene that prevailed in most Roman towns of this period. Reece (1992, 139) has discussed the situation in some detail. He suggests quite logically that rubbish only builds up where households, neighbourhoods or urban units are failing in organisation. He also emphasises the point that drains need to be kept free in order to work, a roadside ditch needs to be regularly emptied in order for it to take storm water, and a building needs to have a well-swept floor if it is to be of maximum use. This is also clearly true of rural sites like the Great Holts Farm villa complex at the end of the 4th century, where significant amounts of rubbish were apparently accumulating in this period. Here field ditches were allowed to fill with domestic rubbish and significantly, buildings systematically demolished and the foundations thoroughly robbed. Whether in a rural or an urban context, the presence of large accumulations of pottery can thus be linked to the final stage of the settlement sequence. At Great Holts Farm, they are associated with the ending of the settlement and presumably its abandonment, but on urban sites they are linked with the final stage of occupation.

As has already been noted, Bulls Lodge Dairy had a very different site history. Firstly, the pottery dating evidence suggests a much longer chronology. There is even some evidence for Iron Age and pre-Flavian activity in the form of ditches and also very tentative evidence for a structure in this period. The digging of pits is first attested at the end of the 2nd or at the beginning of the 3rd century at Great Holts Farm, but at Bulls Lodge Dairy this type of activity commenced in the Flavian period. However, as only small quantities of pottery were recovered from the 'early' Great Holts Farm pits, it is possible that these could be later in date. Although linear features are present in all periods from the early 2nd century onwards at Great Holts Farm, at Bulls Lodge

Table 9.3. Comparison of site chronologies between Great Holts Farm and Bulls Lodge Dairy

Ceramic phase	Period	Bulls Lodge Dairy	Great Holts Farm
0	Late Iron Age to pre-Flavian	Field system; ?structure	No activity
1/2	Late 1st to early 2nd cent.	?Field system; ?pits	No activity
2/3 to 5	Mid-2nd to mid-3rd cent.	Field system; some pits	Field system; some pits.
6	Late 3rd cent.	Field system; probable construction of building A	Field system; earliest possible construction date of main villa building 416; some pits.
7	Early 4th cent.	?Further construction work on building A; demolition of building A	Field system; likely construction date of main villa building 416; in-filling of well 567; construction of bath house 414 & annex 786; likely construction date of buildings 368 & 417; some cremations; some pits.
7	Mid-4th cent.	No activity	Field system; demolition of buildings 417, 294 & annex 786; partial demolition of building 368; silting up of ponds (disuse of bath house); some cremations; some pits.
7/8	Later 4th cent. (*c.* 360/370)	No activity	Field system; refurbishment of main villa building 416; some cremations; some pits.
8	Late 4th cent. (*c.* 370 to 400)	No activity	Field system and disuse; systematic demolition of main villa building 416, bath house 414 & remainder of building 368; robbing of drains; in-filling of cistern 415; some pits.
8+	Early 5th cent. and ?later	No activity	? Final disuse of field system, clearly no domestic occupation.

Dairy they seem to fall within two very broad date bands. The first period covers the Late Iron Age to the mid-2nd century, while the second falls within a 3rd to early 4th century date bracket. In terms of the amount of pottery being deposited the difference between these periods is striking. The first period is associated with smaller amounts of pottery deposition, while the second forms the main period of pottery deposition. The later 2nd century hiatus in ditch digging/infilling at Bulls Lodge Dairy contrasts sharply to what occurred at Great Holts Farm. This also suggests that this second period was one of considerable change – marked by the infilling of ditches – in contrast to what was occurring at Great Holts Farm at this time. While the 3rd century seems to have seen something of a hiatus at Great Holts Farm, this was clearly not the case at Bulls Lodge Dairy. What seems to have occurred at this time is that the landscape was levelled prior to the construction of the masonry building (Fig. 9.3). Although there is evidence for early structures at Bulls Lodge Dairy, like Great Holts Farm the main period of structural activity is in the late Roman period.

Conclusions

In this paper I have presented a number of techniques that I have developed as a means of investigating context, deposition and chronology using data from Romano-British rural sites in Essex. The aims were to explore the prospect that persistent depositional and chronological patterns are recognisable through studying pottery deposition, to see how these patterns can be used as dating and phasing tools, and to present a framework that allows Romano-British rural sites to be evaluated through their artefacts, especially pottery. These aims have been met by answering four basic questions that sought to: identify which feature category or categories produced the most pottery, and, within each feature category, the type of context or contexts that produces the most pottery, in order to see if there are any discernible chronological variations in the way pottery is deposited within features, and to show what spot-dates can tell us about site chronology generally.

The techniques employed above have demonstrated that certain feature categories were indeed more prone to pottery deposition than others, with linear features being especially important. Consequently, it is this feature category that offers the greatest prospect for identifying and analysing chronological variation. It has been shown that top and single fill features produce the most pottery, while smaller, though still substantial quantities come from primary fills, but with relatively little coming from contexts that may lie stratigraphically between primary and top fills. It has also been possible to identify significant chronological variation as well, with some feature categories being prone to pottery deposition in certain periods and not others. This has also been shown to be the case when context types are similarly examined. An important phasing tool has thus been recognised in that

the analysis of pottery deposition can be used to establish, for example, the main period or periods of ditch cutting and infilling.

It has also been possible to use pottery spot-dates to present a wider picture of site chronology. The analysis of pottery deposition has afforded major insights into site character by spotting the main chronological trends, in that the range of feature types present on a site reflect the range and type or types of activities taking place there in any given period or periods. Once the basic pattern of deposition has been recognised the ceramic chronology of the site can then be related back to other aspects of the site evidence by defining what the principal archaeological events are, and how they fit into a chronological scheme based on the pottery dating evidence. In a nutshell, analysis of pottery deposition can provide a means of looking at site chronology objectively with minimal interpretation of site data. Taken from this perspective, pottery is of vital importance to the understanding of Roman sites especially when stratigraphy and artefacts are examined in an integrated manner and not separately, as is all too often the case.

Acknowledgements

I would like to thank my former colleagues at Essex County Council, Mark Germany for providing the site information and Frances van Keulen for reproducing the site plans electronically and also Colin Wallace for discussing a number of issues with me relating to quantification and dating. I would also like to acknowledge English Heritage who provided the funding for the research on which this paper is based.

Bibliography

Chadwick, A. (1999) Digging ditches, but missing riches? Ways into the Iron Age and Romano-British cropmark landscapes of the north midlands. In B. Bevan (ed.), *Northern Exposure: Interpretative Devolution and the Iron Ages in Britain,* 149–71. Leicester Archaeology Monograph, 4, Leicester.

Cooper, N. J. (2000) Rubbish counts: Quantifying portable material culture in Roman Britain. In S. Pearce (ed.) *Researching Material Culture*, 75–86. Leicester Archaeology Monograph 8, Leicester.

Darling, M. J. (1977) *A Group of Late Roman Pottery from Lincoln: The Archaeology of Lincoln 16/1.* Lincoln.

Evans, J. (1991) Not more pot, *Journal of Roman Pottery Studies*, 4, 69–75.

Germany, M. (2003) Excavations at Great Holts Farm, Boreham, Essex, 1992–1994. *East Anglian Archaeology*, No. 105.

Going, C. J. (1987) *The Mansio and Other Sites in the South-Eastern Sector of Caesaromagus: the Roman pottery.* Council for British Archaeology, Research Report 62, London, Chelmsford Archaeological Trust and the Council for British Archaeology.

Going, C. J. (1993) The Roman Pottery. In W. J. Rodwell and K. A. Rodwell *Rivenhall: Investigations of a Villa, Church and Village 1950–1977. Volume 2, Specialist Studies and*

Index to Volumes 1 and 2. Council for British Archaeology, Research Report 80, 64–70, Council for British Archaeology.

Gurney, D. (1995) The Roman pottery. In R. Rickett The Anglo-Saxon cemetery at Spong Hill, North Elmham, Part VII: The Iron Age and Roman and Early Saxon Settlements. *East Anglian Archaeology,* 73, 94–126.

Hill, J. D. (1995) *Ritual and Rubbish in the Iron Age of Wessex: a study on the formation of a specific archaeological record.* British Archaeological Reports, British Series, 242, Oxford.

Isserlin, R. M. J. (1998) William Stukeley's *Caesaromagus,* its basis in fiction and fact, in J. Bird (ed.), *Form and Fabric: Studies in Rome's Material Past in Honour of BR Hartley,* 51–8. Oxford, Oxbow Books.

Lavender, N. J. (1993) A *'principia'* at Boreham, near Chelmsford, Essex: excavations 1990. *Essex Archaeology and History,* 24, (third series), 1–21.

Martin, T. S. (2000) The Late Iron Age and Roman pottery. In S. Foreman, 'Old House Site'. In M. Medlycott, Prehistoric, Roman and post-medieval material from Harlow: investigations at Church Langley 1989–1994. *Essex Archaeology and History,* 31, (third series), 50–9.

Martin, T. S. (2003a) Roman pottery. In M. Germany, Excavations at Great Holts Farm, Boreham, Essex, 1992–1994. *East Anglian Archaeology,* 105, 96–155.

Martin, T. S. (2003b) The Late Iron Age and Roman pottery. In S. Foreman and D. Maynard, A Late Iron Age and Romano-British farmstead at Ship Lane, Aveley. Excavations on the line of the A13 Wennington to Mar Dyke road improvement, 1994–5. *Essex Archaeology and History,* 33, (third series) 138–47.

Martin, T. S. (forthcoming) The Roman Pottery. In S. I. Gibson and P. T. Allen, A Roman and Medieval Site at Brookhouse Farm, Great Tay, and archaeological recording along the Cressing-Great Horkesley Pipeline. *Essex Archaeology and History.*

Martin, T. S. (in prep. a) Latest Roman Essex: Chronology and pottery supply and use *c.* AD 350–450.

Martin, T. S. (in prep. b) The Roman Pottery from Hill Farm, Tendring, a publication draft in Essex CCFAU Archive.

Neville, R. C. (1855) Notices of certain shafts, containing remains of the Roman period, discovered at the Roman Station at Chesterford, Essex. *The Archaeological Journal,* 12, 109–25.

Pollard, R. J. (1988) *The Roman Pottery of Kent,* Monograph Series of the Kent Archaeological Society, 5. Maidstone, Kent Archaeological Society.

Pollard, R. J. (1990) Quantification: towards a standard practice. *Journal of Roman Pottery Studies,* 3, 75–9.

Reece, R. (1992). The end of the city in Roman Britain. In J. Rich (ed.) *The City in Late Antiquity,* 136–44. London, Routledge.

Wallace, C. R. (1995) A rural shrine at Boreham? A re-interpretation. *Essex Archaeology and History,* 26, (third series), 264–9.

10   Experiments in the Analysis of Finds Deposition at Shiptonthorpe: a Retrospect

Martin Millett

Introduction

Having just completed work on a report on the excavations undertaken on a Romano-British roadside settlement at Shiptonthorpe, East Yorkshire, between 1985 and 1991 (Millett in press) it is timely to review the finds research which was central to that project. In this paper I do not want to look in detail at the results of that work, but rather to look at some of the broad conclusions and consider whether all the additional effort was worthwhile. It will, of course, be for readers of the excavation report to consider whether our work has produced interesting and useful results but these reflections may be of value to other excavators who might wish to try to advance archaeological interpretation through similar means.

Work on the Romano-British site at Shiptonthorpe was undertaken as part of a collaborative research project with the East Riding Archaeological Society initiated by Peter Halkon and Martin Millett in 1983 (Figs. 10.1 and 10.2). The first stage of work concentrated on examining the industrial and rural settlement sites in the area around Holme-on-Spalding Moor (Halkon and Millett 1999).

The second focused on the substantial settlement beside the Roman road from Brough on Humber to York at the point where it crossed the Fox Beck at Shiptonthorpe (SE 852422). Most recently, a third stage of the work has been examining the Iron Age and Roman landscape evolution in the vicinity of the Flavian fort at Hayton (Halkon *et al.* 2000).

Fieldwork at Shiptonthorpe

The research at Shiptonthorpe sought to investigate a Roman roadside settlement that was first brought to attention through metal-detecting. The primary research aims included characterizing the site, assessing its preservation, obtaining evidence to aid in the dating of the Holme-on-Spalding Moor pottery production, and examining the relationship between the site and its rural hinterland. In addition, the excavations were designed from the outset to provide new information about how patterns of artefact deposition might be studied. In particular, I was interested in measuring variations in

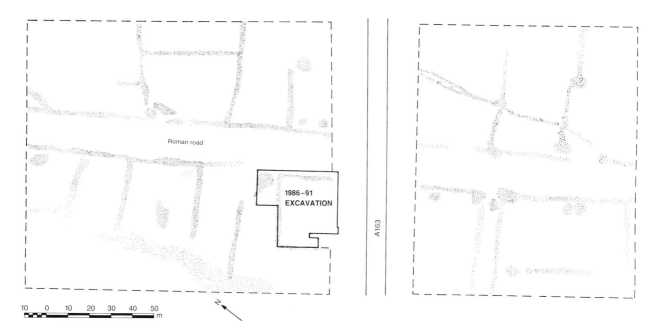

Fig. 10.1. The Roman settlement at Shiptonthorpe, East Yorkshire. Plot of features detected by geophysical survey, showing the main area of excavation

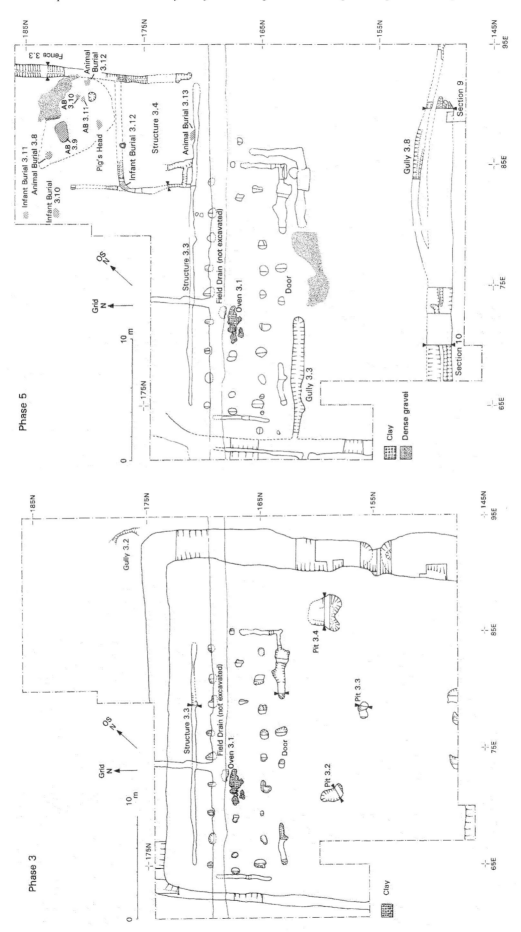

Fig. 10.2. Detail of the Roman settlement at Shiptonthorpe, East Yorkshire with simplified phases shown

the quantities of artefacts in circulation in past societies in the context of debates about the interpretation of surface artefact assemblages (cf. Millett 1985; 1991). These discussions had illustrated the importance of learning more about spatial and chronological patterns in the deposition of artefacts on excavated sites. We therefore set out on a long-term data gathering exercise at the beginning of the excavations. It was recognized that collecting the data to explore these issues would require work on a series of sites and would be a long term process. Subsequently, comparative material has been gathered during excavations at Redcliff (Creighton and Willis 1989; Crowther *et al.* 1990) and Burnby Lane, Hayton (Halkon *et al.* 2000) both in East Yorkshire, as well as at Nettleton, Lincolnshire (Willis with Dungworth 1999; Willis 2001; 2003) and we are beginning to be able to judge the benefits of the approach.

Data gathering involved two complementary procedures. First, in order to examine patterns of artefact deposition, it was necessary not only to quantify the finds recovered but also to obtain estimates of the volume of earth excavated. Whilst finds quantification is now routine, the measurement of excavated volumes is a rarity. In our excavations this was achieved simply through recording a tally of numbers of buckets or barrows of soil removed from each context and converting them to volume measurements on the assumption that a bucket contained $0.015m^3$ of soil and a barrow was equivalent to four buckets or $0.06m^3$. The obvious problems of variations in soil compaction and inaccuracies in estimation were outweighed by its ease of operation on site but we must recognise that the results provide only approximate volume estimates. Second, to facilitate the study of the distribution of artefacts normally recorded as 'small finds' it was felt necessary to metal-detect the soil from each excavated context. To enable the artefacts recovered by metal-detector to be related to their original find-spot, each context was given its own separate and labelled spoil heap. The metal-detected finds assemblages can thus be compared with those recovered from hand excavation.

It should be noted that, as this was a research excavation which used student trainees and other volunteer labour, we were in the fortunate position of being able to excavate the site with a considerable intensity and without undue time pressure. Thus, in contrast to many rescue excavations, we were able to remove substantial volumes of enclosure ditch fills as well as examining all identified minor features, including all those initially interpreted as post-holes.

Finally, we found that in order to interpret the results of our work it was useful to classify the types of deposits excavated into general categories. After considerable debate the following deposit types were used:

A	ploughsoil	**1**	modern
		2	medieval
B	surface deposit	**1**	clearance layer
		2	stratified .1 general/unknown
			.2 within building
			.3 outside building
		3	gravel/rubble surface
C	bank	**1**	general
D	ditch	**1**	cut
		2	primary fill
		3	secondary fills
		4	sinkage in top
		5	general
E	gully	**1**	cut
		2	primary fill
		3	secondary fills
		4	sinkage in top
		5	general
F	pit	**1**	cut
		2	primary fill
		3	secondary fills
		4	sinkage in top
		5	general
G	post-hole	**1**	cut
		2	general
H	beam-slot	**1**	cut
		2	general
I	scoop	**1**	general
J	burials	**1**	cut
		2	general interment

Clearly there will be some variation in the categories needed to classify deposits on different sites – and indeed in the way that they are applied by different analysts – but it may prove useful for any future work if there is some degree of compatibility.

Discussion

These methods required both additional on-site procedures and also extra time and effort in both excavation and post-excavation analysis. It is difficult to estimate the additional time required but I feel confident that the Shiptonthorpe experiments were very worthwhile, although they do perhaps raise some worrying broad issues about the quality of excavated information on which we generally rely. Details of the large amount of data collected in the work undertaken at Shiptonthorpe cannot be presented here but I would like to summarize some of the general patterns noted and assess their implications. Although our work examined the finds holistically, here I shall confine my comments to four separate themes.

1. Excavation strategies

Paying detailed attention to small features on the site and our ability to excavate multiple samples of the enclosure ditches produced an excavation plan that is perhaps rather more complex than is generally seen. More important, it provided two sets of information that may otherwise have been missed. First, the multiple ditch sections revealed spatial differences within the patterning of artefact distributions (see below). This shows clearly that a section or a small number of sections across a ditch targeting a particular sample fraction (often 5%) cannot be expected to provide a 'representative sample' of the whole, as is often assumed. This is not to say that all sites should be totally excavated, but it does emphasize that the kinds of patterns of 'structured deposition' observed on Iron Age sites (Hill 1995) are also present on Roman settlements but that they may be missed if we do not take care in framing appropriate excavation strategies.

Second, when we excavated minor features initially identified as post-holes many turned out to have other functions. In particular, a proportion of this type of feature contained infant burials, the study of which has made a considerable contribution to our understanding of the settlement. It seems very probable that excavation strategies which do not involve systematically seeking and excavating such small earth-cut features will result in the loss of this type of evidence. At both Shiptonthorpe and Hayton study of these human infant burials showed that almost all those found within the settlement had died at around the time of birth (Langston in Millett in press). In other words, burial within the settlement represents a particular rite that was appropriate for those who died at this particular stage. Analysis of the distribution of these burials at Shiptonthorpe showed some very clear patterning in relation to the principal excavated house. Apart from one burial beneath the hearth, the majority were associated with the walls around the eastern end of the building, suggesting the special significance of this part of the house. This is reminiscent of the types of patterning found in some Iron Age houses (*e.g.* Hodgson *et al.* 2001, 147–51). Although details of its meaning are unclear, the pattern may arguably relate to the engendering of space within the home (Millett in press Chapter 15). Whatever the particular interpretation, this evidence well illustrates the value of attention to what appear to be very minor features.

2. Excavated volumes

The collection of information on densities of finds per cubic metre of excavated soil enabled us to examine patterning within the deposition of the more common categories of finds, both through time and according to context type. Despite continued assertions to the contrary (*e.g.* Bintliff and Sbonias 2000), these data confirm beyond any doubt that there were significant variations in the density of deposition of finds like pottery and bone across this site. These differences resulted from a variety of causes which can only be understood through an examination of context. The implications of these depositional variations for the interpretation of assemblages recovered from surface surveys should be self-evident.

The patterning is most easily assessed for the more common artefact types (pottery sherds, bone fragments, coins and iron nails). A variety of patterns emerged from these data, clearly demonstrating that there was considerable variation in deposition. The patterns can be related to site or feature use and rubbish deposition as well as to chronological changes in the frequency of certain object types. Thus the patterns of coin deposition resonate with the changes in coin loss that have long been noted (since Reece 1972). Similarly, patterns of bone density in part reflect the different taphonomic factors which effect surface middens and pit or ditch deposits. In this sense, although the results are not surprising, they do contribute to a general understanding of the nature of finds deposition on the site.

Other patterns are less easy to understand and arguably reveal patterns of behaviour that would otherwise have remained unnoticed. Two examples illustrate this. First, it is perhaps surprising that densities of coins are generally rather low in the major earthfast features (like pits and ditches) and also in those deposits which most likely result from surface middening. This is partly because the larger ditch fills generally date to the period before coin loss became common. Even allowing for these chronological factors, however, there were generally more coins than expected in post-hole and gully fills. This may be because they were associated with inhabited buildings, but the reasons are not obvious and it would be interesting to know whether the pattern is repeated elsewhere. Second, a comparison of deposition between the different excavated sections through the enclosure ditch that surrounded the principal excavated building shows some clear patterns of differential deposition. The stretch of ditch beside the Roman road at the front of the enclosure had consistently lower densities of finds than occurred elsewhere. This indicates that rubbish disposal was organized to keep this frontage relatively clean. There was greater variation in the densities of finds around the other sides of the enclosure but, if we take a high density of bone as indicating fresh rubbish disposal rather than the burial of old midden material, we can suggest that rubbish was being dumped on the flanks of the enclosure, both behind the house and also as far away from it as possible across the enclosure. These patterns show that the organization of rubbish disposal in this enclosure ditch was rather more carefully structured than appeared at the time of excavation.

3. Metal-detected finds

The results show that 46% of all the metal finds from the site were found as a result of metal-detecting. As there is no reason to believe that those digging at Shiptonthorpe were any less careful than those excavating elsewhere, the inescapable conclusion must be that the excavation of any metal-rich site without the use of metal-detectors is no longer a defensible strategy.

The proportions of different types of artefact found by metal-detector rather than by hand excavation do vary. Thus the proportions of coins and lead found by detector were higher than average whilst those of other copper alloy objects and iron were lower. This is largely a result of their differential visibility, a combination of shape, size and colour. Lead objects, in particular, tend to be missed in hand excavation because of the generally amorphous form of the objects and their colour which resembles stone. The low recovery of coins is also probably also a result of visibility, since the majority were fourth century issues of small size and many came from surface deposits that were often excavated with picks and shovels, not trowels. By contrast, other copper alloy artefacts tended to have more distinctive shapes and were more commonly found in hand-excavation also because of the visibility of their corrosion products. Similarly, the rust surrounding iron objects in the soil makes them comparatively easy to see during excavation, especially as they tend to be relatively large.

Whilst the recovery of additional objects has increased our knowledge of the material in use on the site and we have discovered some intrinsically interesting objects, the proportions of different materials present have not been greatly altered by the work. Only the proportion of coins has been significantly increased, so it might be doubted whether the work has had any radical impact on the interpretation of the site. Nevertheless, we can be much more confident in assessing the presence and absence of particular artefacts when the spoil has been systematically screened by metal-detector.

4. Topsoil and surface deposits

One of the clearest patterns to emerge from both the volumetric analyses and also a study of the distribution of those small finds excavated by hand is that many artefacts were originally deposited in surface middens within the settlement. Some of this midden material was subsequently redeposited in other features but there is considerable evidence that vestiges of others survived in the topsoil despite recent ploughing. This confirms the evidence for surface middens presented by Crowther (1983) on the basis on his meticulous comparison of surface and excavated pottery finds at Maxey. At Shiptonthorpe their locations are revealed in the distributions of small finds which were found by hand excavation and three-dimensionally recorded on site. Their distribution showed clear zonation within the enclosure and revealed the existence of clean areas in front of the principal building and beside the Roman road on the main access to the building. Emphasis thus seems to have been placed on maintaining a clean frontage (of both enclosure and building). This contrasts with the presence of surface middens within the enclosure away from the principal building and also the dumping in parts of the enclosure ditch as previously noted.

It is salutary to note what a high proportion of finds derive from these surface deposits rather than earthfast features. This reinforces my belief that excavations which remove surface deposits by machine, even when they have been ploughed, are losing substantial amounts of significant information (cf. Haselgrove *et al.* 1985). Obtaining a better understanding, of the processes of middening is clearly important if we are to make progress in the interpretation of both settlement sites and individual types of finds.

Conclusions

I hope this brief paper gives some insights into the value of this type of work. It reinforces my view that the understanding of the past can only move ahead if we combine the new types of good finds analysis recently seen (*e.g.* Cool and Baxter 2002) with more systematic techniques of excavation. Nevertheless, it is already clear that the type of 'structured' deposition of rubbish identified in Iron Age contexts (cf. Hill 1995) can be identified on Romano-British sites despite the sometimes daunting quantities of finds present. However, we need to address two issues. First, both spatial patterns and differences in assemblage composition are likely to be obscured if we cannot learn to distinguish material that was first deposited in middens before being dumped elsewhere. There are good grounds for believing that weathering and decay altered the content of these deposits before they were finally buried, so establishing the 'signatures' that define such deposits must be a high priority in integrated finds research. Second, some of the trends noted in this chapter will only be susceptible to critical scrutiny once comparable information is available from a wide variety of other sites. I acknowledge that the process of gathering these data is easier on sites like Shiptonthorpe than those with more complex stratigraphy, but this should not deter us from encouraging people to collect the information. Finally, I am left with some concern that the standard techniques of excavation and artefact recovery may not now be sufficient to provide us with the quality of data that we need to address some of the issues which are now of interest. I hope that this paper may stimulate debate on this matter.

Acknowledgements

The Shiptonthorpe excavations were funded by a wide range of bodies who are acknowledged fully in the excavation report but without whose generosity these data would never have been gathered. Those working on the site put up with the additional burden of recording without too much protest and we gratefully thank them for this. The ideas summarized here developed as a result of discussions with various members of the team. I am especially grateful to Jeremy Taylor for his input and to Ed Eastaugh who did much of the initial data processing.

Bibliography

Bintliff, J. L. and Sbonias, K. (2000) Demographic and ceramic analysis in regional survey. In R. Francovich and H. Patterson (eds) *Extracting meaning from ploughsoil assemblages,* 244–58. Oxford, Oxbow.

Cool, H. E. M. and Baxter, M. J. (2002) Exploring Romano-British finds assemblages. *Oxford Journal of Archaeology* 21, 365–80.

Creighton, J. D. and Willis, S. H. (1989) Excavation and survey at Redcliff, Welton, North Humberside 1988. *Universities of Durham and Newcastle upon Tyne Archaeological Reports 12, for 1988,* 40–4.

Crowther, D. R. (1983) Old land surfaces and modern ploughsoil: implications of recent work at Maxey, Cambs. *Scottish Archaeological Review* 2/1, 31–44.

Crowther, D. R., Willis, S. H. and Creighton, J. D. (1990) The topography and archaeology of Redcliff. In S. Ellis and D. R. Crowther (eds) *Humber Perspectives: a region through the ages,* 172–81. Hull, Hull University Press.

Halkon, P. and Millett, M. (eds) (1999) *Rural Settlement and Industry: studies in the Iron Age and Roman archaeology of lowland East Yorkshire.* Yorkshire Archaeological Report no. 4. Leeds.

Halkon, P., Millett, M., Eastaugh, E., Taylor, J. and Freeman, P. (2000) *The landscape Archaeology of Hayton.* Hull; Faculty of Arts, University of Hull.

Haselgrove, C. C., Millett, M. and Smith, I. M. (eds) (1985) *Archaeology from the Ploughsoil.* Sheffield, Department of Prehistory and Archaeology.

Hill, J. D. (1995) *Ritual and Rubbish in the Iron Age of Wessex.* British Archaeological Reports British Series 242. Oxford.

Hodgson, N., Stobbs, G. C., and Van der Veen, M. (2001) An Iron Age settlement and remains of earlier prehistoric date beneath South Shields Roman fort, Tyne and Wear. *Archaeological Journal* 158, 62–160.

Millett, M. (1985) Field survey calibration: a contribution. In C. C. Haselgrove, M. Millett and I. M. Smith (eds.) *Archaeology from the Ploughsoil.* Sheffield, 31–7.

Millett, M. (1991) Pottery: population or supply pattern? The Ager Tarraconensis approach. In G. Barker and J. Lloyd (eds) *Roman Landscapes: archaeological survey in the Mediterranean region,* 18–26. London, British School at Rome.

Millett, M. (ed.) (in press) *Shiptonthorpe, East Yorkshire: archaeological studies of a Romano-British roadside settlement.* Yorkshire Archaeological Report no. 6. Leeds.

Reece, R. M. (1972) A short survey of the Roman coins found on fourteen sites in Britain. *Britannia* 3, 269–76.

Willis, S. H. with Dungworth, D. (1999) *Excavation and Fieldwork at Mount Pleasant, Nettleton, Lincolnshire, 1998: Interim Report.* Lincolnshire County Council and the University of Durham.

Willis, S. H. (2001) Excavation and fieldwork at Mount Pleasant, Nettleton, Lincolnshire, 1999 & 2000. *Universities of Durham and Newcastle-upon Tyne Archaeological Reports, 23 for 1999/2000,* 73–93.

Willis, S. H. (2003) Excavation and fieldwork at Nettleton and Rothwell 2000–2. *Lincolnshire History and Archaeology,* 37.

11 Creolising the Body in Early Roman Britain

Gillian Carr

Introduction

Physical appearance is one of the most important ways in which people construct, express and negotiate their social identities. Identities such as age, gender and status, and others which are more situational and contextual, can all be expressed through appearance in many ways, such as by the manipulation of aspects of clothing, hairstyle, cosmetics, bodily grooming and jewellery. This paper will discuss the increase in the number of toilet instruments in Essex and Hertfordshire in the late first century AD. In contrast to both Hill (1997), who interpreted them as evidence for Romanisation, and Crummy (2001, 3), who suggests that their increase after the conquest may indicate that they were being made by native metalworkers exploiting the large Roman market, I will explore the idea here that, although toilet instruments existed (albeit extremely rarely) during the early and middle Iron Ages (Hill 1997, 98), and appeared in greater number in the later Iron Age, their increase in ownership and use in the Roman period in this region of the south-east could have been more to do with creating and expressing other identities, such as those relating to region, gender, class, age and sub-group. Since the instruments used in this identity creation were Roman, but the identities being expressed were not always necessarily so, it is possible that some toilet instruments could be seen as 'creole' artefacts (cf. Webster 2001). As these instruments were also used by Romans their possible use by people who wanted to express a non-Roman identity poses an interesting question for archaeologists. Rather than seeing *all* 'unusual' instruments in a region as outliers of other typologies I will ask whether variations in styles, especially away from the main Roman centres, indicate a 'creole' nature. By wearing toilet instruments on chatelaines, which hung from the belt and were clearly visible to all, were people making deliberately ambiguous statements about their identity?

Toilet instruments in the early Roman period

Currently seen as an index of 'Romanisation' because of their use throughout the empire (apart from nail cleaners, which would appear to be a British phenomenon; Crummy 2001, 2), sets of toilet instruments usually consist of a nail cleaner, ear scoop and tweezers, which hung together from a *châtelaine*. This is thought to have been attached to the body by means of a belt. Toilet instruments are extremely rare until the late Iron Age (examples of this date include the probe and pair of tweezers from Gussage All Saints in Dorset (Wainwright 1979, fig. 87, 3075 and 3004 respectively), which date to the first century BC/AD; the nail cleaner from the late first century BC grave at Welwyn Garden City (Stead 1967); and the toilet set from grave 112 at Mill Hill, Deal, Kent (Parfitt 1995, fig. 48, 1)). In Essex and Hertfordshire the number of toilet instruments recovered begins to increase rapidly after the conquest, with a peak in the later first century / early second century AD (Carr 2001; forthcoming). However, this dating is slightly problematic and makes direct use of what Jones calls the 'homogeneity principle' (1997, 151 n.2), which assumes that all sites in the region used the same patterns of development (as, in this case, Colchester and Chelmsford, the two sites which produced overlapping typologies, set out by Crummy (1983) and Drury (1988) respectively), with no allowance made for the possibility that such instruments could have been used in the articulation of identities, which would lead to heterogeneity in typology (due to heterogeneity in identities). In fact, heterogeneity is certainly seen throughout the region, as will be discussed later in this paper.

Although de la Bédoyère (1989) believes that the usefulness of toilet instruments is open to question because of their small size, it must be pointed out that they do not differ much in size to contemporary versions. He also suggests that they functioned as a symbol of female adulthood. There is nothing about these artefacts which suggests they were used by females alone, other than the fact that they are used more frequently, but not, it should be noted, solely, by women in our society. Hence for de la Bédoyère to dismiss them in this manner is to neglect much potential information about Romano-British customs and manners.

The fact that these three items were commonly carried on the person raises not only interesting questions about the growing importance of bodily grooming within society in Britain in the early Roman period, but also what was acceptable in public. While we look on with distaste when people clean out their ears or extract dirt from under their nails in public in our society this may have been in contrast to attitudes of the early Roman period in Britain. If we assume that people increasingly carried these instruments around with them in the early Roman period this raises questions about the privacy of certain acts of personal grooming. We can conjecture that it was not considered 'bad taste' to perform such acts publicly. It is possible that it may even have been considered desirable to be seen using these instruments in public (or at least, to be seen carrying them) as the use of these instruments became increasingly popular towards the end of the first century AD, and may even have carried prestige.

The data from Essex and Hertfordshire

A total of 406 toilet instruments were found on the 37 sites examined in Essex and Hertfordshire during my research (see Appendix). While there is no typology for tweezers or ear-scoops, due both to their lack of substantial variation in design and any correlation between design and time, a regional typology *does* exist for nail-cleaners in this geographical area, based on the toilet instruments found at Chelmsford and Colchester; both sites have yielded fairly large numbers of these items. It should also be mentioned here that Crummy has since introduced other regional typologies (see Crummy 2001). Crummy (1983) categorised nail cleaners into types 1 to 4, as seen below, based on the nail cleaners found at Colchester alone. Although these form the vast majority of nail cleaners

found in Essex and Hertfordshire, they are certainly not the only ones. Drury divided the nail cleaners from Chelmsford into types A, B, C and D (1988, fig. 64.42–45), where type B is the same as Crummy type 2a and type D is the same as Crummy type 4. Types A and C are 'new', and are illustrated below in Fig. 11.2 (nos. 1 & 2).

A total of 138 (34%) of all toilet instruments studied were nail cleaners, and given that they sometimes occur in sets with the other instruments in this region, and that they make up approximately one-third of all instruments, it was assumed that their number would also speak for the relative numbers of ear scoops and tweezers with time. (42 out of 375 items, or 9%, were found in a set; interestingly, 5% of instruments in Hertfordshire were in sets whereas this condition accounted for 16.5% of all instruments in Essex).

As mentioned above, heterogeneity was evident throughout the settlement record of Hertfordshire and Essex. Of the 133 nail cleaners that could be studied, 24 (18%) did not fit into the typology and looked somewhat crude and 'home made', or just simply 'unusual' for the region (although some of this latter group may have fitted into other regional typologies).

Apart from the low frequency of types there is no

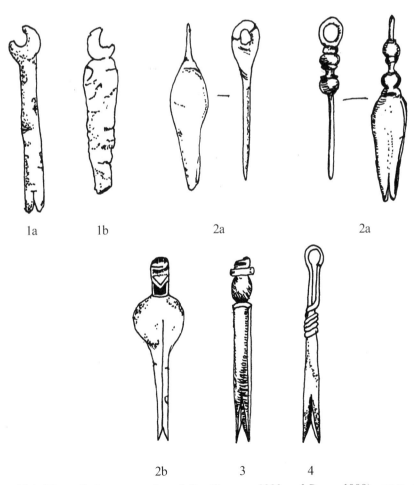

1a   1b   2a   2a

2b   3   4

Fig. 11.1. The nail cleaner typology (after Crummy 1983 and Drury 1988), not to scale

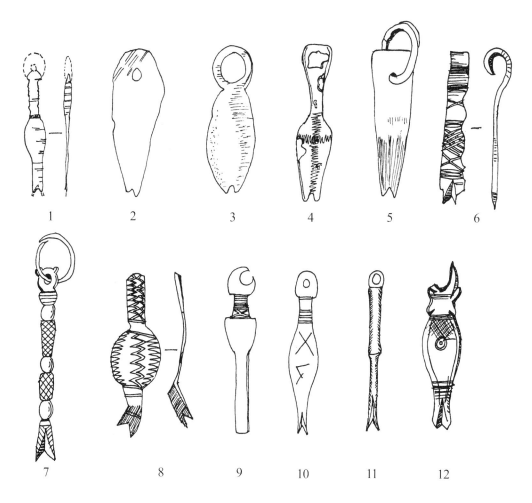

Fig. 11.2. Other types of nail cleaners (not to scale)

reason, however, why the typology could not have been constructed using these 'unusual types', classifying them as 'usual', and some of those at Colchester or Chelmsford as 'unusual'. There is nothing inherently special about varieties from these two sites. The 'unusual' types are seen, for example, in the rich Welwyn Garden City grave (Stead 1967, fig. 15, illustrated above in Fig. 11.2, no. 3; although Crummy (2001, 3) sees this nail cleaner as a template from which some of the later forms develop), and in one-off examples of crude 'home-made' versions, such as those seen at Station Road in Puckeridge (Partridge 1979, fig. 7.3, illustrated above in Fig. 11.2, no. 4), Gadebridge Park (Neal 1974, fig. 62.191, illustrated above in Fig. 11.2, no. 5), and Hill Farm, Gestingthorpe (Draper 1985, fig.12.76, illustrated in Fig. 11.2, no. 6). Further, there are some well-made but very unusual nail cleaners at sites such as Kelvedon (Rodwell 1988, fig. 48.45, 51 & 52, illustrated in Fig. 11.2, no. 7–9), where three out of the four nail cleaners were 'unusual' types. Similarly, types at Gadebridge Park (Neal 1974, fig. 62. 184 and 190; Fig. 11.2, 10–11) were also 'unusual', the former having parallels with Fishbourne (Cunliffe 1971, fig.42, 67–71) and Hill Farm (Draper 1985, fig. 12.77, illustrated in fig. 6.3, no.12). As

mentioned above, it is possible that the more 'unusual' types may fit into other regional typologies.

Other variations in the toilet instrument set as a whole were also seen at the cemetery at Stansted, where the instruments making up two toilet sets comprised a *ligula* (SF347c; Hilary Major pers. comm.) rather than an ear-scoop. A toilet set was also found with a nail file attached in Balkerne Lane, Colchester (Crummy 1983, SF 194/2106), which was also the location of a tooth pick (SF 1939/372). A small knife for attachment to a toilet set was found at Hill Farm, Gestingthorpe (Draper 1985, fig. 12.75). Although some of these 'variations' in the toilet set might actually reflect an originally four-element set, the highest number of elements found on a *châtelaine* in this region was three. Thus, given that 24 out of 133, or 18%, of all nail cleaners able to be studied did not fit into the main typology for the region, and given that there was also a small number (*i.e.* 5 out of 375, or just over 1%) of instruments which did not 'conform' to the 'traditional' toilet instrument range, it appears that heterogeneity was present, but in small numbers, it being more 'normal' to have an unusual type of a 'mainstream' instrument rather than an entirely different toilet instrument.

Nail cleaner chronology

We know that toilet instruments increase in number in the recovered archaeological corpus after the conquest. Precisely when and, more importantly, why this was so is a matter of interest. Did they increase at the same time and rate – *and for the same reasons* – as other instruments of grooming, identity expression and appearance manipulation? Roman-style hairpins first appear in the archaeological record at *c.* AD 50, according to Crummy's typology from Colchester (1979; 1992). The rapid increase of brooches (Hill's 'fibula event horizon') has been dated to the first centuries BC / AD (Hill 1995).

Using the nail cleaner chronology for the region suggested by Crummy (1983) and Drury (1988), I examined how their number varied with time (Table 1, below).

The table shows that the number of toilet instruments (or at least the number of nail-cleaners, assuming that they are representative of numbers of ear-scoops and tweezers because the three types are usually, but not always, considered to have occurred as a set) increases dramatically during the mid-late first century AD and into the second century. This appears to show that detailed modification of the body by personal grooming did not achieve widespread concern at the very outset of the Roman period. Perhaps whatever identities people were concerned with displaying through the use of brooches in the later Iron Age and hairpins in the early Roman period in Essex and Hertfordshire differed from those which required toilet instruments. Although there is a general increase in most recovered artefact categories at this time, the fact that the increase comes later for some than others might strengthen the idea that the expression or creation of different identities was involved.

It is interesting to note that the number of toilet instruments also decreases after the early second century in this region. While this could be a factor of the date of the sites I examined, it could also imply that grooming came into favour during a period when identities were in flux, to construct certain new or alternative identities from the mid-to-late first century. By the mid-to-late second century, they were no longer necessary to maintain outmoded perceptions of gender, status, class (etc). These identities may have then have been created or recognised by other means, such as through clothing.

Contexts of deposition

In many sites in Essex and Hertfordshire patterns in practices of deposition are difficult to identify because of the twin problems of variation in, and ambiguity of, context. A lack of standardisation and clarity in nomenclature of features (or 'non-features') hamper analysis (cf. Carr 2000, 121; forthcoming). How far these mask real patterning remains to be seen, but it was possible to tease a few conclusions from the data, despite the fact that 25 out of the 37 sites examined had five or fewer instruments. This latter tendency could simply reflect the relative dates of (early) sites and the later *floruit* of toilet instruments.

It would appear that temples were considered a 'proper' context of deposition in Essex: Harlow temple yielded 33 and Holbrooks 12 toilet instruments: a total of twelve percent of all toilet instruments from the research area as a whole.

When examining toilet instruments from a funerary context, on the other hand, we must bear in mind that the rich cremation graves in Essex and Hertfordshire date, for the most part, from the mid-first century BC to the mid first century AD, and so do not coincide with the *floruit* of toilet instruments. That is to say they date to a time when toilet instruments are relatively rare in this region. Of the eleven 'rich' graves I examined (see Appendix), only one (and possibly two) yielded any toilet instruments: the Welwyn Garden City grave, which dated from 50–10 BC (Stead 1967), had one nail cleaner, as

Table 11.1. Variation in number of nail cleaners with time

Type of Nail Cleaner	Date	Number
Welwyn Garden City type	c. 50 – 10 BC	1
Drury type A	c. AD 60/5 – 90	2
Crummy type 1b	Mid-late 1st C.	8
Crummy type 1a	Mid-late 1st C. to 2nd C.	18
Crummy type 2a / Drury type B	Mid-late 1st C. to 2nd C.	63
Drury type C	c. AD 150	1
Crummy type 2b	2nd and 3rd C.	6
Crummy type 3	Mid-late 3rd C.	4
Crummy type 4 / Drury type D	Late 3rd – 4th C.	13
Crummy's miscellaneous types	Not Known	24

Table 11.2. Contexts of deposition of toilet instruments from Baldock

Context type	Number and percentage
Pit	18 (= 36%)
Quarry	13 (= 26%)
Ditch	4 (= 8%)
Well	4 (= 8%)
Hollow	2 (= 4%)
Gully	1 (= 2%)
Unstratified	7 (= 14%)

mentioned and illustrated above. This was an early type and was not paralleled by any in Crummy's nail cleaner typology (Crummy 1983). A possible tweezer-like iron object also came from the Hertford Heath burial (Hüssen 1983). We should also consider the fact that, as many grave goods were often burnt on the pyre, the process of cremation may have rendered any toilet instrument into an unrecognisable molten lump. These two factors alone may render obsolete any discussion of the display of toilet instruments at funerals to show the deceased as 'one who groomed'. Perhaps the obviously-groomed appearance of the corpse was enough. Yet, given that a period of 'lying in state' has been proposed for the deceased of several 'rich' graves, so that the mourners could assemble, the funeral feast could be prepared, and the pyre could be built, it is possible that the corpse was often in a state of putrefaction by the time of the funeral, perhaps precluding or diverting attention away from a groomed appearance.

Moving on to consider funerary contexts outside the 'rich cremation' category, that is, the cemeteries of the region, the King Harry Lane cemetery (Stead and Rigby 1989), which dates from AD 1–60, coincided chronologically with several of the rich burials. Was being known as a 'person who groomed' important to these people of lower status? If the toilet instruments they used were for creating certain important personal identities such as class, gender and age, then the answer may have been yes. Four tweezers, two ear scoops, one nail cleaner and one toilet set comprising a nail cleaner and an unidentifiable broken instrument on an iron suspension frame were found. These were spread among just 5 graves (numbers 203, 242, 86, 122 and 422 – three of which date to phase 3, *c.* AD 40–60) out of a total of 472, or just over 1% of all graves. The King Harry Lane cemetery, however, was still a little early for the *floruit* of toilet instruments; from the King Harry Lane settlement (Stead and Rigby 1989), which dated from *c.* AD 70–250, 11 tweezers, 2 ear-scoops and 8 nail cleaners were found.

As regards other cemeteries, the one at Skeleton Green (Partridge 1981) was used from *c.* AD 90–300 plus. Of 59 graves, none had toilet instruments, although a pair

of tweezers were residual in grave 48 and a nail cleaner was found in the cemetery ditch. At Stansted, out of 43 cremations, only two were found with toilet instruments and both of these were complete sets. One grave was pre-Flavian and the other dated to the later first century AD. At Baldock (Stead and Rigby 1986), where the cemetery was used throughout the Roman period, no toilet instruments were found in any graves.

Although not present in huge numbers (19 instruments out of 375, or just over 5% of the total from the study area), the presence of toilet instruments in graves would suggest that the funerary context was one of the 'proper' places of deposition of these artefacts. It is also possible that more were present with cremated bodies but were melted beyond recognition during the cremation process.

As will be seen from the data, it is settlement sites that have yielded a high proportion of examples of these instruments. Attention to site type and context are potentially revealing. As recorded above, few sites with sufficient toilet instruments to make analysis worthwhile had specific, unambiguous contexts of deposition. Of the twelve instruments from the Ermine Street site (Potter and Trow 1988), a part of the wider Braughing-Puckeridge complex, for example, one was found in a ditch, three in a 'silty layer', two were 'unstratified', two were in a 'gravel layer', one in a 'poorly sealed deposit', one in a 'general hillwash layer', one in a 'shallow feature', and one in an 'intrusive feature'. These contexts are by no means unparalleled among the other sites.

Baldock, however, one of the few sites with clear contexts of deposition, and a place full of unequivocally 'strange' depositional contexts (Hingley and Willis pers. com.) had 50 toilet instruments (12% of the total in Essex and Hertfordshire), and was possibly a place of their manufacture. The results are shown above. As can be seen, the most frequent context of deposition was the pit, with these items perhaps deposited as part of Hill's 'Pit Ritual Tradition' (1995).

At Gorhambury (Neal *et al.* 1990), a site with 32 toilet instruments, ten were found divided between two ditches (31%), one in a well (3%), two in a post-hole (6%), two in a building (6%), twelve were unstratified (37.5%) and the rest in random 'non-feature' contexts. At the King Harry Lane settlement, where 21 toilet instruments were found, five were found in a pit (24%), one in a ditch (5%), two in a quarry (9.5%), six in an occupation layer of some sort (29%), one in a post-hole (5%) and the rest in 'non-feature' contexts. Colchester, which had the largest record of toilet instruments (97 individual components plus seven toilet sets) also had one of the largest number of different feature types (or 'non-features'): around 28 in total. The largest number in any one feature type, however, was twelve, all found in a pit. Almost as many were found in a 'dump' (11) although it is not clear what this definition actually meant.

Such seemingly random distribution of toilet instruments might indicate that they were as commonly lost as

Table 11.3. List of sites with more than five toilet instruments

Site name	Site date (all circa)	Site type	Number of toilet instruments
Baldock	Mid-1st century BC – 4th century AD	'Small town'	50
Chelmsford	Bronze Age to 4th century AD	'Small town', fort, *mansio*, and religious complex	17
Colchester	AD 44 – 400+	*Colonia*	94 + 5 sets
Ermine Street site, Braughing-Puckeridge complex	Late 1st century BC – 4th century AD	LIA / Romano-British settlement	12 + 1 set
Gadebridge Park	AD 75 – late 4th / early 5th century	Villa	12 + 1 set
Gorhambury	AD 20 – 350	Villa	32
Great Chesterford	1st to 4th century AD	Fort / 'Small town', and religious complex	8
Harlow	1st century BC – later 4th century	Temple	33
Holbrooks	LPRIA – end of 4th century AD	Temple	12
Kelvedon	Later Iron Age – end of Roman period	'Small town'	8
King Harry Lane cemetery	AD 1 – 60	Cemetery	7 + 1 set
King Harry Lane settlement	AD 70 – 250	Settlement	21
Verulamium	AD 49 – 470	*Municipium*	25

they were deliberately deposited in any favoured feature. Where contexts are more clear, however, pits and ditches do appear to be among the favoured locations of deposition, though this must be evaluated in light of the fact that these are amongst the most frequent context categories at sites of this period (cf. Martin this volume). This can be seen in terms of a continuity of deposition in accordance with Iron Age site-specific rules noted by Hill (*e.g.* 1993; 1994; 1995), although Hill now believes that deposits in pits and ditches in the Roman period did not reflect the same ritual actions as were being carried out in the Iron Age; ritual can, of course, be a creative act, subject to change in its details through time.

The *type* of site on which toilet instruments are found is also of interest. As observed above, 25 out of 37 sites had five or fewer instruments. The table of the twelve sites with more than five instruments is listed below:

First, we must take into account the fact that the smaller excavations would, on the whole, have found less material than the larger excavations. Second, while we can observe that some 'Roman' sites, such the villas of Gorhambury and Gadebridge, had many toilet instruments (relatively speaking), there is no compelling reason why the ownership of a villa should in itself imply any fundamental adoption of 'Roman' ways (Percival 1987, 542), however we may define such concepts. This also helps us to understand the relatively small number of toilet instru-

ments found at the *municipium* of *Verulamium*, if the same principles apply to those who lived in 'Roman' towns. However, we should also consider the possibility that toilet instruments were not inextricably linked only with a 'Roman' identity in the minds of the native Britons. As mentioned above, other identities such as gender, class, age and status may have been created using these instruments – and these may not have been the 'Roman' cultural expressions of these identities, a point to which I shall return.

Current interpretations

How are we to understand toilet instruments? Why did their numbers increase towards the end of the first century AD – did the meaning or use of these instruments change through time? Should we see them as a 'native' or a 'Roman' instrument, or both? It is questionable whether such dichotomies are useful at this period, several generations after the conquest, a time when native society was becoming a more complex and heterogeneous mix – a fusion of cultures. The late first century AD was, however, only 50–60 years after the Claudian invasion; the very eldest in society may have been alive or even fought during the invasion. This was still early enough for people to retain an awareness or concept of 'them' and 'us', indigenous and incomer, although these concepts would have been becoming blurred in urban centres, and may not have mattered to the younger generation. The issue of one's origins may have been of more importance to some than others.

Recent work has challenged old interpretations of these artefacts. Hill has argued that toilet instruments were being used by Iron Age people who were 'actively seeking to alter and distinguish the ways in which they presented themselves in their encounters with others, a concern which seems to have become far more common after the conquest' (1997, 101). He believes that these people were adopting new life-styles as alternatives to existing dominant discourses and power structures; they were forming themselves into a new and distinct class, perhaps a new social élite. With Hill, I argued that these changes were not necessarily the same phenomena as 'Romanization', but were more about a new and increasing concern by certain people with the care, maintenance and presentation of their bodies. This may be seen as a concern that started with costume and clothes (signalled by the increase in brooches), later increased to include hairstyles (signalled by the later adoption of hairpins) and that seemed to reach its height of concern in the late first century AD, signalled by the increase in toilet instruments at this time (Carr 2001).

I would suggest that it is not necessary to invoke Hill's Marxian models of class conflict to understand the way these instruments were used. In 2001 I argued that toilet instruments were incorporated into existing spheres of use and meaning for indigenous practices as part of a pre-existing, pre-Roman trajectory (Carr 2001, 116), based not only on the continuity of use of an artefact type (albeit pre-existing in extremely small numbers), but also on the continuity of use of Iron Age depositional contexts, such as the pit and ditch, for such instruments at some sites, such as Baldock. In the next section I would like to put forward an alternative interpretation.

New interpretations: creolisation and its justification

There is another line of interpretation which I would like to explore: Webster's theory of 'creolisation' (2001), which explores ambiguity and hybridity of material culture within a society where power inequalities exist. Others have also applied models of creolisation to archaeology: African-American creole artefacts have been discussed in Deetz (1977, 213–4); other creolised material culture has also been discussed by Hawkes (1999), who considered the creolisation of food, and this author, who discussed the creolisation and 'pidginisation' of medicine and healing (Carr 2003). Both case studies are set in Roman Britain.

Webster applies linguistic terminology to archaeology, specifically discussing 'creole' languages, which are seen as a hybrid fusion or blend of two different languages. Such languages are often seen in colonial situations, where the language blend will often have a dominant and non-dominant partnership, reflecting the social politics of domination in colonialism. Webster applies the model of 'creolisation' to explain and better understand the processes involved in what has been called 'Romanisation'. Creolisation allows us to think about and hear the native 'voice' in Romanisation, because, for the non-élite Britons, emulation of the élites or striving to 'become Roman' is no longer thought to have been their aim. Roman Britain is increasingly recognised as having consisted of a fusion of distinct cultures in an unequal power relationship – a 'creole' Romano-British culture. Such a creole culture produced creole artefacts – artefacts which borrowed something from each culture, or had the appearance of something from one culture, but were used according to the rules of the other culture. Thus, creole artefacts are often ambiguous in appearance; they also often reflect the unequal power relationship present in that society.

'Creolisation' as a concept for exploring new ways of understanding the processes of Romanisation is already receiving criticism. The popular perception is that creolisation is a historically-specific process linked to the Caribbean, and it is thus inappropriate to apply it to Roman Britain. This, however, is to misunderstand the academic use of the term. 'Creolisation' as a concept has different meanings in different contexts, including both the popular and the academic. The term 'creole', for example, is used in Latin America and the Caribbean to refer to locally born descendants of European families, while in parts of the United States, the term refers to descendants of specifically French families (Seymour-Smith 1986, 57). Though it may be acknowledged that creolisation is often perceived to be associated with historically-specific processes in the Caribbean, creole languages are, in fact, found all over the world (over 200 creoles and pidgins were noted by Hancock (1969) in a survey made 35 years ago), from Haitian and Belizean creole to Swahili (possibly a creole made up of Bantu languages and Arabic). My point here is to illustrate that the term 'creole' has a wide and generalised use, and is not just a historically-specific process. Creole languages are not *necessarily*, but often are, associated within the social context of European political and economic expansion (Jourdan 1991, 191), that is, the colonial context and slavery. I would argue, however, that the fact that creolisation is usually associated with the colonial context is part of its strength as a theory. It is a good tool with which to think and, with its associated concepts of ambiguity, political dominance and subjugation, it allows a more nuanced and informed study of the Roman period than the near-synonymous terms of 'hybridisation' or 'syncretism' (Webster 2001).

I would thus argue that toilet instruments had the potential to be creole artefacts. They resemble Roman artefacts, but may have been used by native Britons according to their own cultural rules, or to create and express their own (counter)cultural categories of identity.

As we have seen, ambiguity is often an important feature of creole artefacts. People were using these instruments to construct and also to symbolise and negotiate their identities. I am not suggesting that every toilet instrument in Roman Britain was a creole artefact and used in an ambiguous way, simply that some toilet instruments had that potential. It is possible that the more 'unusual', 'crude' or 'home-made' instruments discussed above, which were often very different (and deliberately so) to the more 'mainstream' designs found in the Roman colony at Colchester (where 108 out of 375, or 29% of all instruments were found), were the instruments which were more likely to be creole artefacts. Those found at the colony were perhaps more likely to be used by veterans and their families, namely by Roman citizens who were thus more likely to want to express Roman identities. There would have been those who would not want to own or use artefacts identical to those used by people with the powerful military upper hand. The very *difference* of the non-mainstream designs, which signalled their use in creating non-mainstream, non-Roman, non-military, localised, new identities (or rather, new counter-cultural identities), while still being a Roman-inspired artefact type, is what made these instruments creole artefacts.

Conclusion

In this paper I have outlined the chronology, typology and contexts of toilet instruments in Essex and Hertfordshire. I have shown that, while the majority appear to 'conform' to the standard range and typology of instruments which have been found in Colchester and Chelmsford, around 18% did not. These types often had a rougher or more 'home-made' appearance. As emphasised by Jones (1997, 151, note 2), a certain amount of heterogeneity (and not total homogeneity) in the archaeological record is to be expected, as artefacts were used in the articulation of identities – perhaps the alternative, counter-cultural identities in this case were in the minority.

I have also discussed the favoured contexts of deposition of toilet instruments, which included temples, graves and also, at some sites, pits and ditches, perhaps a continuation of an Iron Age practice originally recognised by Hill (e.g. 1995). I have also discussed why, while such instruments may look 'Roman' to us, and while we may associate them with Roman-style practices, it is possible that native Britons did not share these same associations, nor use them as part of the creation of a Roman-style identity, grooming themselves in accordance with any perceived Roman or military-cultural norms. Instead, *some* toilet instruments may have been used, alongside other aspects of costume and dress, to help create creolised Romano-British counter-cultural identities, which perhaps borrowed from or owed more to indigenous concepts of gender, class, and other aspects of identity.

People who used 'alternative' toilet instruments may well have been aware of the ambiguous signals they were generating by carrying toilet instruments. Such deliberate ambiguity is part of the nature of creole artefacts, which are often a resistant adaptation to 'becoming Roman' (Webster 2001, 218). Creole artefacts are often counter-cultural symbols of identity and status, and some of those who used these instruments may have enjoyed playing on the different meanings that these instruments had in different contexts.

We are realising increasingly that many 'indisputably Roman' artefacts were not necessarily 'Roman' at all or, at least, not necessarily used by 'Romans' or élite Britons as part of an aspiration towards a 'Roman' identity or lifestyle, however it may have been defined. Rather, we are learning that the context within which artefacts were used can tell us much more about their meaning. As far as 'Romanising' or 'creolising' the body is concerned, other instruments which, until now, we have associated with Roman identity may also have had other non-Roman meanings in other contexts. Elsewhere (Carr 2001), I have noted that, like toilet instruments, a proportion of Roman hairpins outside Colchester do not conform to the accepted Colchester-based typology; rather, as with toilet instruments, many local designs can be seen, perhaps reflecting local (Romano-British creole) identities. I have suggested that those hairpins may also have been used to create non-Roman (or even pre-Roman) hairstyles. As Hawkes (2002, 48) points out, the difficulties of British women trying to recreate complex Roman hairstyles from coins (their main source of such information) should not be underestimated. Owing to the fact that we have no information about pre-Roman hairstyles we do not know whether hairpins – and perhaps other artefacts related to identity and appearance – may also have been used as part of a 'creolisation of the body' in early Roman Britain.

Addendum

The data and interpretations in this paper formed the basis of chapter 5 of my forthcoming BAR volume (Carr forthcoming). In this chapter, I further develop the ideas suggested here and produce alternative narratives, exploring the role of toilet instruments in helping to create and distinguish class identities in the early Roman period.

Acknowledgements

I would like to thank Mark Atkinson and Philip Crummy for allowing me access to the data from Elms Farm, Heybridge, and Stanway, Colchester, respectively, in advance of publication. The late Richard Bartlett of Harlow Museum allowed me access to the unpublished material from Holbrooks and Harlow temples.

My thanks are owed to the members of the audience at the Roman Finds conference, the editors, and the anonymous referee, who all made many helpful suggestions about this paper.

Appendix: List of Sites examined during the Research

Ardleigh (Brown 1999)
Baldock (Stead and Rigby 1986)
Boxmoor Villa (Neal 1974–6)
Braintree (Drury 1976; Havis 1993)
Camulodunum (Hawkes and Hull 1947)
Chelmsford (Drury 1988; Wickenden 1992; Isserlin and Wickenden forthcoming)
Chignall Villa (Clarke 1988)
Colchester (Crummy 1983; 1992)
Dicket Mead Villa (Rook 1983–6)
Elms Farm, Heybridge (Atkinson forthcoming)
Folly Lane (Niblett 1999)
Gadebridge Park (Neal 1974)
Gorhambury (Neal *et al.* 1990)
Great Chesterford (Draper 1986)
Great Dunmow (Wickenden 1988)
Harlow temple (France and Gobel 1985)
Hemel Hempstead (Neal 1974–6)
Hertford Heath (Hüssen 1983)
Hill Farm, Gestingthorpe (Draper 1985)
Holbrooks Temple (unpublished)
Ivy Chimneys, Witham (Turner 1999)
Kelvedon (Rodwell 1988)
King Harry Lane (Stead and Rigby 1989)
Lexden (Laver 1927; Foster 1986)
Little Oakley (Barford 2002)
Mount Bures (Smith 1852)
Northchurch Villa (Neal 1974–6)
Park Street Villa (O'Neil 1945; Saunders 1961)
Puckeridge-Braughing (Potter and Trow 1988)
St Albans (Wheeler and Wheeler 1936; Frere 1972; 1983; 1984)
Sheepen (Niblett 1985)
Skeleton Green (Partridge 1981)
Stansted (Havis and Brooks 2004)
Stanway (unpublished)
Welwyn A (Smith 1912)
Welwyn B (Smith 1912)
Welwyn Garden City (Stead 1967)

Bibliography

Atkinson, M. (forthcoming) Excavations at Heybridge, Elms Farm, Essex, 1993–5.
Barford, P.M. (2002) Excavations at Little Oakley, Essex, 1951–78: Roman Villa and Saxon Settlement, *East Anglian Archaeology*, No. 98. Essex County Council.
Brown, N. (1999) The Archaeology of Ardleigh, Essex: excavations 1955–1980, *East Anglian Archaeology*, No. 90. Chelmsford, Essex County Council.
de la Bédoyère, G. (1989) *The Finds of Roman Britain*. London, B.T. Batsford.
Carr, G. (2001) 'Romanisation' and the Body. In G. Davies, A. Gardner and K. Lockyear (eds.), *TRAC 2000: Proceedings of the Tenth Annual Theoretical Roman Archaeology Conference, London 2000*, 112–124. Oxford, Oxbow Books.
Carr, G. (2003) Creolisation, pidginisation and the interpretation of unique artefacts in early Roman Britain. In G.

Carr, E. Swift and J. Weekes (eds.) *TRAC 2002: the twelfth proceedings of the Theoretical Roman Archaeology Conference, Canterbury 2002*, 113–125. Oxford, Oxbow Books.
Carr, G. (forthcoming) *Hybrid Bodies and Creolised Identities. Changing identities in the later Iron Age and early Roman period in Essex and Hertfordshire*, Oxford, British Archaeological Reports, British Series.
Clarke, C. P. (1988) Excavations south of Chignall Roman Villa, Essex, 1977–81, *East Anglian Archaeology*, No. 83, Essex County Council.
Crummy, N. (1979) A chronology of Romano-British bone pins. *Britannia* 10, 157–163.
Crummy, N. (1983) *Colchester Archaeological Report 2: the Roman Small Finds from Excavations in Colchester 1971–9*. Colchester, Colchester Archaeological Trust.
Crummy P. (1992) *Colchester Archaeological Report 6: Excavations at Culver Street, the Gilberd School, and other sites in Colchester 1971–85*. Colchester, Colchester Archaeological Trust.
Crummy, N. (1992) The Hairpins. In P. Crummy (ed.), *Colchester Archaeological Report 6: Excavations at Culver Street, the Gilberd School, and other sites in Colchester 1971–85*. Colchester, Colchester Archaeological Trust.
Crummy, N. (2001) Nail cleaners: regionality at the clean edge of Empire. *Lucerna* 22, 2–6.
Cunliffe, B. (1971) *Excavations at Fishbourne 1961–1969*. Reports of the Research Committee of the Society of Antiquaries of London, No. 27.
Deetz, J. (1977) *In Small Things Forgotten: an archaeology of early American life*. New York, Anchor Books.
Draper, J. (1985) Excavations at Hill Farm, Gestingthorpe, Essex. Essex County Council, *East Anglian Archaeology* 25.
Draper, J. (1986) Excavations at Great Chesterford, *Proceedings of the Cambridge Antiquarian Society* 75, 3–41.
Drury, P. J. (1976) Braintree: Excavations and Research, 1971–76, *Essex Archaeology and History* 8, 1–143
Drury, P. J. (1988) *The Mansio and Other Sites in the South-Eastern Sector of Caesaromagus*. Chelmsford Archaeological Trust 3.1, CBA Research Report 66, Chelmsford Archaeological Trust and the CBA.
Foster, J. (1986) *The Lexden Tumulus: A Reappraisal*, Oxford, British Archaeological Reports British Series 156.
France, N. E. and Gobel, B. M. (1985) *The Romano-British Temple at Harlow, Essex*, Gloucester, West Essex Archaeological Group.
Frere, S. S. (1972) *Verulamium Excavations Volume I*, Reports of the Research Committee of the Society of Antiquaries of London, No. 28, Oxford, The Society of Antiquaries.
Frere S. S. (1983) *Verulamium Excavations Volume II*, Reports of the Research Committee of the Society of Antiquaries of London, No. 41, London, The Society of Antiquaries.
Frere, S. S. (1984) *Verulamium Excavations Volume III*, Oxford University Committee for Archaeology Monograph No. 1, Oxford, Oxford University Committee for Archaeology.
Hancock, I. A. (1969) A map and list of pidgin and creole languages. In D. Hymes (ed.) *The Pidginization and Creolization of Languages*, 509–23. Cambridge, Cambridge University Press.
Havis, R. (1993) Roman Braintree: excavations 1984–90, *Essex Archaeology and History* 24, 22–68.
Havis, R. and Brooks, H. (2004) Excavations at Stansted Airport,

1986–91, Volume 1: Prehistoric and Romano-British, *East Anglian Archaeology*, No. 107, Essex County Council.

Hawkes, C. F. C. and Hull, M. R. (1947) *Camulodunum*, Reports of the Research Committee of the Society of Antiquaries of London, No. 14, Oxford, The Society of Antiquaries.

Hawkes, G. (1999) Beyond Romanisation: the creolisation of food. A framework for the study of faunal remains from Roman sites. *Papers from the Institute of Archaeology* 10, 89–95.

Hawkes, G. (2002) Wolves' nipples and otters' noses? Rural foodways in Roman Britain. In M. Carruthers, C. van Driel-Murray, A. Gardner, J. Lucas, L. Revell, and E. Swift (eds), *TRAC 2001: Proceedings of the Eleventh Annual Theoretical Roman Archaeology Conference, Glasgow 2001*, 45–50. Oxford, Oxbow Books.

Hill, J. D. (1993) Can we recognise a different European past? A contrastive archaeology of later prehistoric settlements in Southern England. *Journal of European Archaeology* 1, 57–76.

Hill, J. D. (1994) Why we should not take the data from Iron Age settlements for granted: recent studies of intra-settlement patterning. In A. P. Fitzpatrick and E. L. Morris (eds) *The Iron Age in Wessex: recent work*, 4–8. Salisbury, Trust for Wessex Archaeology on behalf of the Association Française D'Etude de l'Age du Fer.

Hill, J. D. (1995) *Ritual and Rubbish in the Iron Age of Wessex: a study on the formation of a specific archaeological record.* British Archaeological Reports (British Series) 242. Oxford.

Hill, J. D. (1997) 'The end of one kind of body and the beginning of another kind of body'? Toilet instruments and 'Romanization' in southern England during the first century AD. In A. Gwilt and C. Haselgrove (eds), *Reconstructing Iron Age Societies*, 96–107. Oxford, Oxbow Monograph 71.

Hüssen, C.-M. (1983) *A rich late La Tène burial at Hertford Heath, Hertfordshire*. London, British Museum Publications.

Isserlin, R. and Wickenden, N. P. (forthcoming) *The Street Frontage and Other Sites in the Northern Sector of Caesaromagus*.

Jones, S. (1997) *The Archaeology of Ethnicity: Constructing identities in the past and the present.* London and New York, Routledge.

Jourdan, C. (1991) Pidgins and creoles: the blurring of categories. *Annual Review of Anthropology*, 20, 187–209.

Laver, P. (1927) The excavation of a tumulus at Lexden, Colchester, *Archaeologia* lxxvi, 241–54.

Neal, D. S. (1974) *The Excavation of the Roman Villa in Gadebridge Park, Hemel Hempstead 1963–8.* Reports of the Research Committee of the Society of Antiquaries of London, No. 31.

Neal, D. S. (1974–76) Northchurch, Boxmoor and Hemel Hempstead Station: the excavation of three Roman buildings in the Bulbourne Valley, *Hertfordshire Archaeology* 4, 1–125.

Neal, D. S., Wardle, A. and Hunn, J. (1990) *Excavation of the Iron Age, Roman and Mediaeval Settlement at Gorhambury, St Albans*. Historic Buildings and Monuments Commission for England, English Heritage Report 14.

Niblett, R. (1985) *Sheepen: an early Roman industrial site at Camulodunum*, CBA Research Report 57. CBA.

Niblett, R. (1999) *The Excavation of a Ceremonial Site at Folly Lane, Verulamium*, Britannia Monograph Series No. 14, Society for the Promotion of Roman Studies.

O'Neil, H. E. (1945) The Roman villa at Park Street, near St Albans, Hertfordshire: report on the excavations 1943–45, *The Archaeological Journal* 102, 21–110.

Parfitt, K. (1995) *Iron Age Burials from Mill Hill, Deal.* London, British Museum Press.

Partridge, C. (1981) *Skeleton Green, a late Iron Age and Romano-British site*. Britannia Monograph Series No. 2. London, Society for the Promotion of Roman Studies.

Percival, J. (1987) The villa in Italy and the provinces. In J. S. Watcher (ed.), *The Roman World 2*, 527–551. London, Routledge and Kegan Paul.

Potter, T. W. and Trow, S. D. (1988) Puckeridge-Braughing, Hertfordshire. The Ermine Street Excavations 1971–72, *Hertfordshire Archaeology* 10.

Rodwell, K. (1988) *The Prehistoric and Roman settlement at Kelvedon, Essex.* CBA Research Report 63, London.

Rook, T. (1983–86) The Roman villa at Dicket Mead, Lockleys, Welwyn, *Hertfordshire Archaeology* 9, 79–175.

Saunders, A. D. (1961) Excavations at Park Street 1954–57, *The Archaeological Journal* 118, 100–35.

Seymour-Smith, C. (1986) *Macmillan Dictionary of Anthropology*. London, The Macmillan Press Ltd.

Smith, C. R. (1852) *Collectanea Antiqua* vol. 2.

Smith, R. A. (1912) On late Celtic antiquities discovered at Welwyn, Herts., *Archaeologia* lxiii, 1.

Stead, I. M. (1967) A La Tène III burial at Welwyn Garden City, *Archaeologia* 101, 1–62.

Stead, I. M. and Rigby, V. (1986) *Baldock: the excavation of a Roman and pre-Roman Settlement, 1968–72.* Britannia Monograph Series No. 7. London, Society for the Promotion of Roman Studies.

Stead, I. M. and Rigby, V. (1989) *Verulamium: The King Harry Lane Site.* English Heritage Archaeological Report No. 12, London, English Heritage.

Turner, R. (1999) Excavations of an Iron Age Settlement and Roman Religious Complex at Ivy Chimneys, Witham, Essex 1978–83, *East Anglian Archaeology*, No. 88, Essex County Council.

Wainwright, G. J. (1979) *Gussage All Saints: an Iron Age Settlement in Dorset*. Department of the Environment Archaeology Report No. 10.

Webster, J. (2001) Creolizing the Roman Provinces. *American Journal of Archaeology* 105, 209–25.

Wheeler, R. E. M. and Wheeler, T. V. (1936) *Verulamium: a Belgic and two Roman cities*, Reports of the Research Committee of the Society of Antiquaries of London, No. 11. London, The Society of Antiquaries.

Wickenden, N. P. (1988) Excavations at Great Dunmow, Essex: a Romano-British Small Town in the Trinovantian Civitas, Chelmsford Archaeological Trust Report 7, *East Anglian Archaeology*, No. 41, Chelmsford Archaeological Trust.

Wickenden, N. P. (1992) *The Temple and Other Sites in the North-Eastern Sector of Caesaromagus*, Chelmsford Archaeological Trust Report 9, CBA Research Reports 75, Chelmsford Museums Service and the CBA.

12 A Severed Head. Prolegomena to a Study of the Fragmented Body in Roman Archaeology and Art

Iain Ferris

Next was a bunch of half a dozen men all blown to bits, an archipelago of corrupt fragments...

Arthur Graeme West. *'Night Patrol'*, March 1916

Introduction

In Sigmund Freud's London house in Maresfield Gardens, Hampstead, is a collection of archaeological objects that includes a number of pieces of Greek and Roman sculpture. One of the criteria set by Freud for acquiring such items for his collection was apparently that they should be complete (Forrester 1994, 227), a condition imposed by him for purely aesthetic purposes, rather than through any concern about the perhaps ambiguous state of the fragmentary image.

There is something almost seductively unreal about complete objects to many archaeologists, and a great deal of time and effort in our profession goes into reconstructing the wholeness of the past, in sticking broken pots back together, in estimating vessel equivalents from a pottery assemblage of individual sherds, and in honing sampling strategies that will allow us to believe we can understand a whole site or a whole landscape from our supposedly scientifically-selected samples. Perhaps, as some academics have suggested, under the influence of the psychoanalytical theories of Jacques Lacan and Melanie Klein, we need to return to the whole in this way in order to understand our own lives, to fulfil some inner need, some innate desire buried deep within us (Dubois 1996; 1998; Ellis 2000).

But while so much of the evidence for the past is all too often fragmentary, broken, damaged, or incomplete, a certain amount of this material was in this state before it entered the archaeological record, so that any biographies of such fragments must include consideration of both their once complete state as artefacts and their existence as fragmented objects. Fragmentation may have taken place immediately prior to these fragments being disposed of or buried, or the fragments may themselves have been employed or used in some way, in some way other than in their previous form, before fragmentation took place. The process of fragmentation and the significance of the fragment have been the subject of academic enquiry in prehistoric archaeology for some time, and is best exemplified by the work of John Chapman (Chapman 2000). While Chapman's work dealt principally with Balkan prehistory, Roman archaeologists should be able to engage with many of Chapman's themes and bring new lines of enquiry into play on their own data.

This paper will deal specifically with images of fragmented bodies, although many of the methods of enquiry employed could equally be applied to artefact studies. While in Greek society and art the body remained an almost inviolable whole, in Roman art the body became something that could sometimes be portrayed simply by representing the head or bust of an individual. The cropping of images of people often occurred in wall paintings and on gemstones. Body parts of statues were sometimes intentionally interchangeable by design. Portrait heads could be recarved, sometimes out of economic necessity, other times for more political reasons. The sick could represent themselves at healing shrines with *ex votos* portraying their diseased or affected body parts. The human body in these instances was not simply modified, it was transformed into a series of unrelated parts. There was evidently a tension between beliefs in Roman society, mirrored in Roman culture, of the body as an ideal form and the body as a flexible image.

This fragmentation of the body, when it occurred, perhaps reflected a permeability of boundaries in Roman society and culture, particularly between life and death, and sickness and health. The social body in certain contexts condoned and acquiesced in this dismemberment of the corporeal body into images. In some instances the corporeal body was reduced to the status of an artefact, and it is this process which will be examined in this paper.

This paper takes the form of an outline for a fuller study of the fragmented body in the Roman world and, by extension, of the process of fragmentation itself. Inevitably, it will touch upon some of the issues previously raised in an earlier paper on the subject of fragmentation (Ferris 2003b) and, equally inevitably, it will put forward some ideas and arguments which are not yet fully developed or which at least are in the early stages of development.

Theorising the body

There has been a considerable amount of attention paid to the body in antiquity and perceptions of the human body in the ancient world, not only by archaeologists but also by ancient historians, classicists, and art historians (see, for example, Brown 1988; Bynum 1992; Hallett and Skinner 1997; Halperin *et al.* 1990; Kampen 1996; Kampen *et al.* 2002; Koloski-Ostrow and Lyons 1997; Meskell 1998; 2000; Montserrat 1998; 2000; Rautman 2000; Rouselle 1988; Wyke 1998). Perhaps rather tellingly, the majority of work on the body in the ancient world was undertaken in the body-conscious, not to say body-obsessed, 1990s and much of it was concerned with issues of gender identity. A more recent strand of research has concentrated on male identity and the male body in particular (*e.g.* Burrus 2000; Kampen *et al.* 2002; Kuefler 2001; Walters 1997)

Many of the previous studies of the classical body have dealt with the whole body, with issues of gender and representation, health and medical practice, or exclusion through disability or other perceived differences. How studies of the classical body fit into a wider 'body history' has been neatly summarised by Amy Richlin (Richlin 1997), though the balance of this historical overview of the field of study is not without its own inbuilt biases. Richlin interestingly argues against what she sees as a false historical watershed, around 1800, when many body historians, including Michel Foucault, see fundamental changes in attitudes to sexuality and homosexuality as having taken place, or even indeed for these concepts only to have emerged around about that time (Richlin 1997, 27–8). She also quite rightly questions the idea that pornography only came to be associated with obscenity in relatively recent times, that is, after 1500 (Richlin 1992; 1997, 28).

In thinking about analysing the fragmented body, consideration needs to be given to psychoanalytical approaches to the viewing and reception of fragmented and fragmentary images of the body, approaches principally championed by Melanie Klein and Jacques Lacan, and in the field of classics by Page Dubois (Dubois 1996; 1998). The psychoanalyst and social theorist Julia Kristeva has been involved in an art historical research project, centred on the exhibition 'Visions Capitales' held at the Louvre in 1998 and its accompanying catalogue of the same name (Kristeva 1998). Through an exploration of the image of the severed or disassociated head from prehistoric contexts up to its inclusion in the art of Andy Warhol in the 1960s, the project provides a broad context for perhaps understanding the varying cultural situations in which the image has been employed. A great deal of relevant material can also be found in writings on the subject of the fragment by the art historian Linda Nochlin (Nochlin 1994; though also see: Elsen 1969; 1969–70; Pingeot 1990), and by the artist Kurt Schwitters (Elderfield 1985). Together, these sources can perhaps help provide a theoretical framework for looking at such images in the context of the classical and Roman world. While Nochlin's work on fragmentary images, principally in painting, is of great relevance to this study, it is again a study that by tying the use of fragmented images to the birth of modernism-she actually subtitles her paper 'The Fragment as a Metaphor of

Modernity' – creates another possibly false watershed in body history.

Images of ancestors

The creation, display and use of wax masks – *imagines* – of noteworthy male ancestors who had held magisterial office was a well-attested aspect of social display among the aristocratic classes of Rome from the early Republic onwards and may have had its origins in Etruscan or pre-Roman Italic social practices (Flower 1996; Dupont 1987; Rambaud 1978), though the tradition of using masks in a purely theatrical context obviously goes back to the Greeks. Discussion of the display of such masks in the home (Dwyer 1982) and their more active use in funeral processions (Bodel 1999), where they were worn by mourners playing the role of the deceased ancestors, has centred on their origins and significance as status symbols and their possible influence on the development of Roman portraiture, with its concentration on the head and face, at the expense of the whole person (see Ferris 2003b for a fuller discussion). The use of such masks at Roman funerals was both a piece of social bonding with the idea of the ancestors and, of course, a piece of political theatre (Bodel 1999).

In Roman art, from the time of the Republic onwards, portrait heads and busts proliferated as a medium for the representation and commemoration of the individual, both men and women, at first in sculptural form only (Barr-Sharrar 1987) but subsequently in two dimensions on funerary reliefs (Figure 12.1), sarcophagi, mosaics and gemstones. This truncated representation of the human body probably owed its origins wholly, or in part, as has just been mentioned, to the Roman aristocratic tradition of commissioning wax ancestor masks as a form of social display, although the Etruscan and Italic traditions of manufacturing terracotta heads was also an undoubted influence on developments in Roman portraiture (Beard and Henderson 2001, 227–32; Flower 1996; Gazda 1973; Huskinson 2000; Nodelman 1975; Walker 1985; 1995). It can be assumed that sculptural portrait busts of ancestors were common in the houses of the aristocracy in the same way that the wax *imagines* had been, although portraiture became an artistic medium not confined to aristocratic patrons alone. A good depiction of a pair of ancestral busts on display in a wooden cabinet appears on a cylindrical funerary altar from Brescia, northern Italy (Stella *et al.* 1998, 71).

The origins, development and use of Roman portraits in the form of busts and heads are again linked to funerary situations, not only at Rome and more broadly in Italy, but also further afield within the Empire, as in Egypt where the painted Fayum mummy portraits represent a significant and vibrant variation on this practice (Doxiadis 1995). As has been pointed out by Koortbojian (1996), many portrait busts were intended for display on the outside of tombs and one must try to remember that in this context their

Fig. 12.1. Grave monuments with portrait busts. Museo Romano, Brescia (Photo: I. M. Ferris)

viewing was only a small part of the overall sensory experience of walking down a street of tombs, looking at the structures themselves, viewing portraits and reading the biographical detail given in the accompanying inscriptions. The same would have applied to the display of busts in niches inside *columbaria* such as those at Vigna Codini in Rome (Della Portella 1999, 124–9). Perhaps accessing all this information together allowed the viewer to reconstruct the life and appearance of the deceased ancestor from these fragmented commemorations of their lives.

Portrait busts also appear in later, Christian, contexts such as on the fourth-century mosaic in the Basilica at Aquilea by the so-called 'Master of Portraits' where ten portrait depictions in roundels of men and women, cut off mid-torso, appear. These portraits probably represent affluent members of the Christian community in the city and benefactors of the Church.

Alchemy of suffering

Anatomical *ex votos*, models of human body parts made of various materials, were widely dedicated as offerings at healing shrines and religious sanctuaries throughout the Roman world (Figures 12.2 and 12.3; van Straten 1981; Ferris 1999). In an earlier paper on the subject of fragmentation (Ferris 2003b) I compared *ex votos* from the Republican healing sanctuary at Ponte di Nona, near Rome (Potter 1985), with those from the Gallo-Roman religious site at the Source of the Seine, near Dijon (Deyts 1994), and consideration was given to the differences between these sites as reflected in the relative numbers and types of body parts represented at each. The role played by anatomical *ex votos* in the process of seeking a cure at such sites and the significance of the representative

body parts themselves – heads, torsos, eyes, ears, hands, arms, legs, feet, sexual and internal organs – must be viewed in the context of the special position of the sick in the classical world (Sigerist 1977).

At Ponte di Nona the huge collection of mainly terracotta *ex votos* of body parts – over 8,000 were recovered by excavation in the mid-1970s – represented all the most common body parts found at such sites – heads (1,365), feet (2,368), limbs (971), hands (604), eyes (377), ears (44), male genitals (160) and breasts (8) – but also included numbers of uteri (27), models of intestines (7), a tongue, a mouth, hearts, kidneys and vaginas (Potter 1985, 28–33), which suggests a much deeper knowledge of human anatomy than seen at many other healing shrines.

Portrayals of individual body parts cannot, though, always be taken at face value, as can be demonstrated in the case of a stone *ex voto* from Rosinos de Vidriales, Spain, and in the Museo Provincial de Zamora (Arce *et al.* 1997, 408). On it are depicted the soles of two pairs of feet, the right-hand pair with toes facing downwards and the left-hand pair with them facing upwards. Rather than being an anatomical *ex voto* of the kind dedicated at healing shrines this may in fact represent a dedication by a gladiator, a gladiator trainer, or an organiser of gladiatorial games at a Nemeseion, signifying entering and leaving on good feet, that is, surviving in the arena in a gladiatorial contest.

Brief consideration should also be given here to some instances where individual body parts of deities appear in Roman art, in contexts where the healing power of the deity is being invoked. The most common, though still relatively rare, example of such an image is connected to the cult of Sabazios, a deity most often represented *in*

Plate I A. The context of finds: the radius and ulna of a Roman burial with bracelets and bangles at the wrist; the Whitefriars excavation, Canterbury. (Photo: Canterbury Archaeological Trust)

Plate I B. The context of excavation: an excavator at work at the Whitefriars dig, Canterbury; the pottery vessel contains a cremation of 2nd century date. (Photo: Canterbury Archaeological Trust)

Plate II A. A group of surface collected finds from ploughsoil, within a 10m by 10m square, at a Roman roadside settlement at Nettleton, Lincolnshire. (Photo: Spencer Scott)

Plate II B. A group of excavated finds from a single context associated with a Roman town house at the Church of Our Lady site, Tongeren. The excavations for the Flemish Heritage Institute were directed by Alain Vanderhoeven. (Photo: Steven Willis)

Plate III A. Part of the site at Shiptonthorpe, East Yorkshire, during excavations, showing site features and the individual heaping of spoil per context. (Photo: Martin Millett)

Plate III A. inset: Scanning of topsoil spoil with a metal detector at Shiptonthorpe, East Yorkshire. (Photo: Martin Millett)

Plate III B. Fine-mesh dry-sieving of excavated contexts for finds, at the Iron Age and Roman complex at Hayton, near Shiptonthorpe; part of the Lowland East Yorkshire Project directed by Martin Millett and Peter Halkon. Note the individual spoil heaps per context. (Photo: Steven Willis)

Plate IV. Well preserved site features at the late Roman 'Saxon Shore' fort at Oudenburg, near Ostend, being the context of the finds in Plate V.
These shots, of the Spegelaere site, show the line of the stone wall defences, a building with distinct rooms and a surface with various cultural remains. The excavations were directed by Sofie Vanhoutte for the Flemish Heritage Institute. (Photos: Steven Willis)

Plate V. A range of finds from the Spegelaere site at the late Roman 'Saxon Shore' fort at Oudenburg, near Ostend, during a 'open day' in 2004. (Photos: Stéphanie van der Maas)

Plate VI A. A range of Roman copper alloy objects from the Whitefriars excavations at Canterbury. (Photo: Canterbury Archaeological Trust)

Plate VI B. An in situ *pottery vessel containing a group of copper alloy objects at the Grijpenveld site, Tienen. The excavations were directed by Marleen Martens for the Flemish Heritage Institute.* (Photo: Harrie Spelmans, the Museum het Toreke, Tienen)

Plate VII A. A pit of the Flavian period at the Kielenstraat site, Tongeren, containing in situ *faunal remains, being the refuse of marrow, grease and glue production.* (Photo: The Flemish Heritage Institute)

Plate VII B. Detail of the faunal remains subject to industrial processing from a pit of the Flavian period at the Hondsstraat site at Tongeren; the photo shows a sample of the remains subsequent to lifting and washing. (Photo: The Flemish Heritage Institute)

Plate VIII A. A Dressel 20 amphora bound round and roped having been lifted out of the ground; this vessel, which had had its neck, rim and handles removed in antiquity had been re-used to house a cremation burial in the east London cemetery at Mansell St., site G. The excavations were undertaken by DGLAN for the Museum of London. (Photo: Steven Willis)

Plate VIII B. A Drag. 27 samian cup with a section of the rim and wall missing (perhaps deliberately broken off in antiquity) and an unusual closed form in local greyware, found together in a pit dating to the pre-Boudiccan colonia *phase at The Gilberd School site, Colchester. The excavations were directed by Don Shimmin for Colchester Archaeological Trust.* (Photo: Steven Willis)

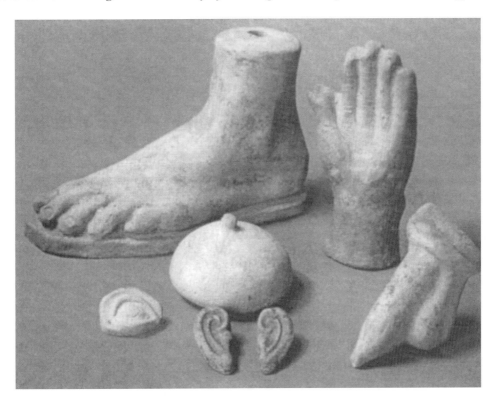

Fig. 12.2. Anatomical ex votos *from Ponte di Nona (Photo: after R. Jackson 1988* Doctors and Diseases in the Roman Empire*, Fig 43)*

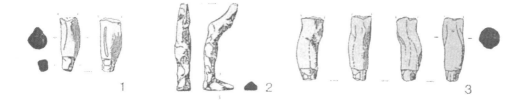

Fig. 12.3. Anatomical ex votos *in the form of legs from West Hill, Uley (Photo: after A. Woodward and P. J. Leach 1993* The Uley Shrines: The excavation of a Ritual Complex on West Hill, Uley, Gloucestershire 1977–79*)*

absentia by his hand only, a good example of such a 'mano panthea' coming from Brescia and on display in the Museo della Citta, Santa Giulia (Stella *et al.* 1998, 48). Again, the right hand, palm outwards and with fingers splayed out, depicted on a stone votive from Quintanilla de Somoza, León, Spain, and now in the Museo de León, may similarly be linked to Zeus-Serapis, as indicated by a Greek inscription on the stone, rather than being a depiction of the hand of a dedicatee seeking a cure. Finally, in a Christian context, the hand of God appears twice emerging from out of the clouds on one of the apse mosaics in Sant Apollinare in Classe, Ravenna.

Body politics

The barbarian enemies of Rome were common subjects in Roman art from the Republic to the late Empire (Ferris 1994; 1997; 2000; 2001; 2003a; Zanker 1998; 2000; 2002). From the reigns of the emperors Marcus Aurelius and Commodus onwards there was a growing trend towards the dehumanisation of the barbarian in Roman art, as most dramatically exemplified by the images of slaughtered and beheaded barbarians on the Column of Marcus Aurelius in Rome and a similar scene of the beheading of a prisoner, his hands tied behind his back, which occurs on the Bridgeness legionary distance slab from the Antonine Wall in Scotland (Ferris 1994; 2000, 114–15). These gruesome images must be examined, along with earlier headhunting scenes on Trajan's Column, again in Rome, and the historically-attested appalling post-mortem treatment of the severed head and hand of the Dacian king Decebalus (Ferris 2000, 80–1), in order to try to understand the significance of these acts of ritualised bodily dismemberment in the context of the wider study of fragmentation of the body in Roman art. That there was not a trend among the Romans for depicting themselves in a similar way suggests that they may have had made some distinction between the bodies of Romans and of non-Romans.

The issue must be raised as to whether any of these images of mutilation of barbarian bodies represents a strain of pornographic or sexual violence, and whether there was some element of sadism inherent in these depictions. The common Graeco-Roman sculptural subject of the punishment of the satyr Marsyas, who had the temerity, or foolishness, to challenge Apollo to a musical contest, could also be seen as perhaps being part of such a strain, although in this case the subject matter was purely mythological. Having lost the musical contest, Marsyas had to submit himself to Apollo's chosen forfeit, for the satyr to be flayed alive by his Scythian servant. While pre-Hellenistic representations of this story generally concentrated on the musical contest, leaving the appalling aftermath to the imagination of the viewers, Hellenistic and Roman sculptures, perhaps all derived from the Hellenistic original known today as the 'Hanging Marsyas', depicted the distressed and anguished Marsyas strung up in a tree, hanging by his hands, positioned above and behind his head, and awaiting the cut of the Scythian's knife (Pollitt 1986, 118–19).

These headhunting scenes and scenes of beheadings should perhaps be seen in the wider context of Roman attitudes towards the games (Barton 1989; 1993) and towards judicial punishment (Coleman 1990; MacMullen 1986).

A particularly gruesome example of a beheading scene during a gladiatorial combat can be seen on a relief from Due Madonne, Bologna (Figure 12.4), dated to the second half of the first century BC (Govi and Vitali 1988, 344). On the left of the surviving part of the relief is a gladiator with raised right arm looking to strike at an opponent who must have appeared on the now-missing part of the relief. But it is the scene on the right-hand side of the stone that is of relevance here. A third gladiator, clad in a short skirt-like garment held in place with a thick belt, boots, a wrist-guard and a helmet, holds up an oval shield in his left hand and moves his right, sword hand down towards his waist, having just struck a swingeing blow to behead a fourth gladiator who kneels on the ground to his right. The kneeling figure, hands held passively behind his back, is headless. His head, still encased in his helmet, falls to the ground to his right, his shield discarded behind him.

The subject of Roman judicial savagery has been considered by Ramsay MacMullen who has noted that the number of crimes for which capital punishment was to be meted out rose considerably in the period after AD 200 (MacMullen 1986, 209), and that some crimes that had previously merited decapitation now were subjected to supposedly harsher punishments such as 'crucifixion,

Fig. 12.4. Relief depicting gladiatorial combat from Due Madonne, Bologna. Museo Civico Archeologico di Bologna (Photo: I. M. Ferris)

burning, or wild beasts'. MacMullen also alludes to Eusebius' accounts of the judicial mutilation of Christians by the breaking of legs, the cutting out of an Achilles tendon, the putting out of an eye or the cutting off of an ear or the nose (MacMullen 1986, 210). Under Constantine some corrupt officials could have their hands amputated (MacMullen 1986, 211), punishment also recorded as commonplace under Valentinian and in the army under Theodosius (MacMullen 1986, 211–2). Mutilation was not a formal judicial penalty before AD 300. 'Amputation, whether loss of a foot for a deserter, of a hand for the destroyer of public buildings, or of sexual organs for the pederast (under Justinian)', proclaimed 'symbolically the particular evil being punished' (MacMullen 1986, 212).

Metaphor and metamorphosis

A very specific type of fragmentation is the destruction associated with the concept of *damnatio memoriae* (Kinney 1997; Nylander 1998; Varner 2000). Pliny, in his panegyric to Trajan, related the feelings of those who had attacked images of the emperor Domitian: 'it was our delight to dash those proud faces to the ground, to smite them with the sword, and savage them with the axe, as if blood and agony could follow from every blow' (Pliny *Panegyric* 52.4). Such vandalisation of images in the Roman world, principally of statuary, is relevant both in terms of this official and overt political process of *damnatio memoriae* (the condemnation of an emperor by the Roman senate, leading to the destruction, mutilation or alteration of his images) and the more covert activities of iconoclasts whose motives are less susceptible to generalised analysis (Besançon 2001; Sauer 2003). Both strains of destruction must be considered in terms of

investigating how and why such acts of vandalism were organised, how they were carried out, and particularly which parts of the images were targeted, and in what ways.

In his paper on the fragmentation of Roman statues in Britain Ben Croxford does not specifically address the possible differences of motive and motivation that may have led to the destruction of religious statues as opposed to political statues (2003). Croxford does, though, demonstrate quite conclusively that there are statistically significant biases in the archaeological record towards the survival of certain parts of the bodies of statues, implying in some cases a careful and deliberate targeting of specific parts of some statues and a marked process of selection, even curation, of broken statue fragments. The problem lies in how to interpret individual finds of parts of statues and place them in a convincing explanatory structure of interpretation, as the next four diverse examples may help to demonstrate.

An example used by Croxford was the fate of the cult statue of Mercury from the temple complex site of West Hill, Uley, Gloucestershire, portions of which were found during excavations in the 1970s. The head of the cult statue was found carefully deposited in a pit sealed beneath a rubble platform outside the very late Roman or post-Roman Structure VIII of excavation Phase 7 (Figure 12.5; Woodward and Leach 1993, 71–2), while other parts of the statue were also found in the same phase, in a clay spread. There can be no doubt that these fragments, especially the statue's head, were treated with some degree of post-fragmentation respect; indeed, that they were curated, ending in their careful burial.

The second example concerns a cache of sculptural material excavated from Sector 16–P in Antioch (Padgett

Fig. 12.5. The stone head of the cult statue of Mercury from West Hill, Uley (Photo: A. Woodward and P. J. Leach)

2001, 92–3), consisting of twenty-five fragments of arms and hands in white marble and twelve legs and feet in the same material: 'along with several other [unspecified] statue fragments' (Padgett 2001, 92). The catalogue publication of this material notes that the material came apparently from a sculptor's workshop: 'in the immediate area of…an oven that may have functioned as a lime-kiln…and [they] may have been destined for destruction in the limekiln or for reuse by the sculptor.' (Padgett 2001, 251). Such an explanation hardly seems credible, given the biased composition of the assemblage of statuary body parts. Some conscious selection of statue body parts had clearly taken place here and been caught *in stasis* in the archaeological record.

The third example is a bronze head of Augustus, obviously cut off a full-size statue of the emperor, found at Meroë in the Sudan, and now in the collections of the British Museum. This was obviously booty of some sort, it has been suggested, perhaps from the capture of Roman Syene by Ethiopian forces in 24 BC (Kleiner 1992, 67), and was found under the entrance staircase into a temple of victory probably dedicated a few years after the victory at Syene. In this case the destruction of the original, complete statue of the emperor was motivated by anti-Romanism, though the carrying off the head of the statue shows a recognition of the power of images, a power then presumably further insulted by a ceremonial burying of the broken image.

A fourth example is provided by a head and single foot from a more-or-less life size bronze statue excavated from the same level in Zone C, Ercavica, Castro de Santaver, Canaveruelas, Cuenca, Spain (Arce *et al.* 1997, 370). Bronze statue fragments are, of course, much more likely to be recycled, by melting down, than are stone statue fragments. The survival of just these two body parts therefore once more implies selection and curation, post-fragmentation of the original statue.

While political and religious motives probably account for most of the destruction or mutilation of statues, images, and inscriptions in the Roman world, other motives may equally have applied. Andrew Gregory has pointed out that 'the harming of people through private magic by the mutilation (or binding, or burying) of images of them was one manifestation of the widespread and well-known habit of… enchantment… in the ancient world.' (Gregory 1994, 96). Indeed, the texts of curse tablets are often composed in such a way as to target enemies' bodies, and quite often specific parts of those bodies, commonly the eyes.

Real bodies

Burial in the Roman world represented an arena in which the inert body was transformed by cultural practice and custom into a signifying artefact, whether by cremation (Musgrave 1990) or by inhumation. It can be argued that mortuary ritual and the post-mortem treatment of the body may sometimes have mirrored the processes of fragmentation of the body into disassembled images, as seen in Roman funerary art, and which perhaps had its origins in Etruscan society (Bruni 2000; Damgaard Andersen 1993).

It must be asked, though, whether there was not in parts of the Roman world a distinct process of post-mortem manipulation of human body parts before in-humation burial. Certainly in prehistoric Britain there may well even have been a cult of human relics, as identified by Ann Woodward (1993), that could have continued in some form into the Roman period or have been revived then. As well as examining such links, consideration also needs to be given to the significance of the Christian cult of relics (Biddle 1986; Brown 1981; Butler and Morris 1986; Rollason 1986; 1989) that developed in the later Empire and which spawned its own accompanying decorated artefacts, in the form of reliquaries, to house bones and other relics of the saints.

When General Franco died he was clutching the relic arm of Saint Teresa of Avila. This is one of the more high-profile and later examples of the cult of relics which had its origins in late antiquity and perhaps reached its height in the figure of Philip II of Spain, who amassed a collection of over 7,000 holy relics, including 144 heads, 306 arms and legs and 10 whole bodies. Philip, as he lay on his death-bed in his palace at El Escorial, selected the arm of St Vincent and the knee of St Sebastian from his collection to bring him solace (Blom 2002).

Collecting and curation of body parts is attested in many other cultures, and for many different reasons. In the mid-seventeenth century the Dutch artist Albert van der Eeckhout, in his painting 'A Tarairiu or Tapuya Woman' (in the National Museum, Copenhagen), recorded a cannibal woman in Brazil, naked save for a strategically-placed piece of vegetation probably added by Eeckhout, calmly looking towards the viewer. She holds in her right hand a severed human hand, while sticking out of the basket held by a strap over her head is a human foot.

Robert Philpott, in his survey of grave treatment and furnishing in Roman Britain, has discussed the phenomenon of decapitation as a burial rite (Philpott 1991, 77–89), and has recognised three variations in the rite across a sample of 70 individual sites on which decapitation has been recorded. These variations are: burials with the head missing or buried separately nearby; burials with the head placed in the correct position at the neck of the torso; and examples where the head has been placed in the grave but usually by the feet or lower legs. Though there are one or two isolated earlier examples, Philpott dates this rite to the later third century, with most examples being of a fourth-century date. Slightly more women than men are represented in Philpott's catalogue of 98 decapitated burials, with older women being well represented. He concluded that the linking factor must be 'social status, caste or kinship affiliations' (Philpott 1991, 79–80). Geographically, most are found in rural cemeteries. When such burials occur in urban contexts they are at the peripheries of the cemeteries, as is indeed also the case in rural locations. In a very few cases mutilation of the body seems to have taken place along with the decapitation. Philpott cites examples where skull and body parts had been moved and replaced in the grave, and one instance at a cemetery in Dunstable where a right foot had been removed but still buried with the body (Philpott 1991, 82).

Skulls are often found in non-burial contexts, as are other stray body parts. As part of a paper on special deposits at Roman Heybridge, Essex, given at the Durham conference, Mark Atkinson briefly alluded to the discovery of the articulated remains of a human arm in the fill of a ditch. The arm had obviously been carefully buried, but no other possible explanation for this unusual burial was given, other than the supposition that the arm might have been torn off in an agricultural or industrial accident.

Raphael Isserlin (Isserlin 1997) has quite convincingly argued that human sacrifice may have taken place in Roman Britain, and that in such circumstances it would have been part of a process of placation that may have replaced a more symbolic act of controlled violence, including 'the smashing of pots, the bending of weapons, and the killing of animals' (Isserlin 1997, 92). Isserlin discusses a number of examples of possible human sacrifice where the excavated remains have been of partial bodies only, though he does not discuss the implications of this possible additional evidence for dismemberment as, on occasions, part of the process of sacrifice.

It is worth briefly considering here the question of how familiar the Romans were with the human skeleton and whether the appearance of skeletons and skulls in Roman art represents part of the same phenomenon of fragmentation of the body being discussed in this paper, with the unfleshed body being seen as distinct and divorced from the live body. Almost certainly there was a developed medical knowledge of human anatomy, much of it derived from dissection carried out in Alexandria (Lloyd 1973, 75–90) or from chance opportunities for doctors to study uncovered skeletons. In later antiquity it would appear that anatomy lessons centred on a study of human cadavers were ubiquitous, one such scene being portrayed in a fresco on one of the catacombs in Via Latina in Rome.

A useful survey of the skeleton in Graeco-Roman art has been compiled by Katherine Dunbabin (1986) who came to the conclusion that the skeleton was a relatively common motif in classical art, particularly in the context of the appearance of skeletons at a feast or banquet, in scenes which were principally intended to remind diners of their own mortality. This trend led to a relatively short-lived liking for comic images of animated skeletons, best exemplified by their appearance on the Boscoreale silver cups and to the limited use of skeletons in funerary art starting in the first century BC (Dunbabin 1986, 237). Of the few examples of Roman art where the skeleton can be taken as representing the dead body, Dunbabin cites a second- or early third-century relief from Rome itself, now in the British Museum, in which a skeleton is laid out full length under a panel containing an inscription (Dunbabin 1986, 245).

The Epicurean theme identified by Dunbabin's extensive research certainly would appear to account for the vast majority of appearances of skeletons in Roman art, though one or two other appearances are worthy of further discussion here. She notes that: 'a realistic rendering of the condition of a decaying corpse is indeed inconceivable within the limits of pre-Hellenistic Greek art. But even in Hellenistic and Roman art, with their interest in realism, such a representation is by no means common as a way of rendering the dead in general. The question of the origin of the image of the dead as a skeleton is therefore... inseparably tied up with that of the uses to which such images were put' (Dunbabin 1986, 189). There can be identified, though, a distinct use of the image of the skeleton in funerary art. Almost all instances of the skeleton in Graeco-Roman art are late-Hellenistic, Republican, Augustan or early imperial (Dunbabin 1986, 193). As with the skeleton, so with the skull motif, most famously appearing along with a mason's level and other items as the *emblema* of a mosaic pavement from Pompeii and on tombstones being contemplated by a philosopher.

Sexual fragments

The phallus was one of the most common motifs in Graeco-Roman art, appearing in numerous artistic media across the Roman world (Johns 1982; Turnbull 1978). While it was most often probably used as a protective or apotropaic symbol, it was also, nevertheless, a ubiquitous reminder of the dominant social position of the sexualised male in Roman society (Kellum 1996). The phallic motif needs to be discussed in terms of its numerous meanings and its contexts of use, but it must also be considered from the point-of-view of its more provocative role in representing a generalised male dominance (Bevan 1994; Clarke 1996; 1998). Amy Richlin has noted that 'walking down a city street in Pompeii, you would have been surrounded on all sides by images of the erect penis – stamped on walls and paving stones, decorating shop signs, worn as amulets by children' (1997, 33). The same impression comes from a perusal of the study of Pompeian street signs by Ling (1990).

Studies of sexual symbolism in the Graeco-Roman world have perhaps too often placed discussion of the use of the phallus completely beyond the issue of sexuality by categorising all such imagery as part of a broader category of erotic art (*i.e.* Johns 1982). This has, of course, helped to move the definition of such material away from nineteenth- and earlier twentieth-century views of its being obscene but in so doing has perhaps created a false dichotomy itself. It can surely no longer be sustainable to argue that the motif of the phallus was not largely concerned with the construction of maleness and the place of men in Roman society. Ideas relating to fertility and protection, linked to the phallus, are nevertheless also linked to male sexuality and being.

While certain strategies were employed at different times to emphasise the power and potency of emperors – Augustus appearing with numerous children on the Ara Pacis, the ever-youthful portrait types of Augustus and Trajan, Trajan as 'the father' of his country on the Benevento arch, the bull-necked coin portraits of some of the third-century military emperors – the employment of the image of the phallus in an imperial context did not take place. Nevertheless, many examples of such sexualising of rulers' bodies in other ancient societies can be found (*e.g.* Winter 1996).

While the phallus was undoubtedly a ubiquitous symbol and motif in the Graeco-Roman world, female genitalia were also employed as images in certain contexts, though such uses were nowhere near as numerous as those of the phallus (Johns 1982, 72–5) and, indeed, Johns is almost guilty of special pleading to account for this rarity. Mention has already been made of models of female genitalia being found at healing sanctuaries as anatomical *ex votos*, but it is true to say that female sexuality and fertility is more usually represented in the Roman world by the portrayal of the female breast, often the suckling breast.

Sometimes body parts could be conflated, as in an example of a small bronze amulet from Palencia and in the Museo de León, Spain, in the form of a winged phallus at one end of which is a hand making the obscene gesture known as the *fica* (Arce *et al.* 1997, 414). Another amuletic bronze from Lancia, again in the León museum collection, has one end formed as a pair of testicles and the other by a hole in the object which may represent a stylised portrayal of a female sexual organ. Again, the phallus and the so-called evil eye were also often conflated, as in the case of a small terracotta, in the British Museum, depicting two animated phalluses sawing an eye in half (Johns 1982, 68, Plate 51).

Conclusions

It can be argued that while the various case studies presented above do not represent a coherent, all-encompassing theory for understanding the widespread use of the fragmentary or partial image of the human body in Roman art, nonetheless there are many linking threads between these contexts and situations which could be further investigated and illuminated by the introduction of analagous material from other chronological periods and different cultural contexts.

In a short paper such as this there has only been space to touch upon a number of issues relating to fragmented remains. I have chosen to look principally at the fragmented body as an image in Roman art and so have perhaps already restricted discussion of wider issues relating to the conception of the body in Roman society and in Romanised societies. The broad-brush approach adopted here also makes it difficult to identify temporal and chronological difference and, importantly, temporal and chronological change. The focus on art means that language and literature have been necessarily omitted, although it is quite obvious that conceptions of the body in any society will be reflected in many aspects of that culture, and not just in its art.

In his study of sexual ambivalence in the Graeco-Roman world Luc Brisson notes that in classical mythology there are a number of examples of severed heads coming back to life in their own right and delivering prophecies (Brisson 2002, 18–22). He recounts the story of Polyclitus who, after his death, returned to Aetolia as a ghost and killed his recently-born hermaphrodite child (Brisson 2002, 8–18). Having torn the child apart and eaten most of its body, Polyclitus departed, leaving only the child's head intact. The head then begins to speak and deliver an oracle to the assembled people of Aetolia. Of course, the best known story of such a talking head is that of Orpheus (Deonna 1925; Brisson 2002, 18–21), but the Polyclitus story is particularly noteworthy in terms of its intertextual references to cannibalism – the eating of human body parts – and hermaphroditism – the physical state of having what were viewed as the wrong set of sexual body parts. As Natalie Boymel Kampen has noted, in discussion of two faience vessels in the form of sleeping or reclining possibly hermaphroditic figures, 'the ongoing fascination with the hermaphrodite speaks…to a sometimes unconscious concern with boundaries, for the objects make the distinction between male and female as unclear as those between childhood and maturity.' (Kampen *et al.* 2002, 73).

A strain of interest in a 'rhetoric of dismemberment' has been identified in Neronian poetry (Most 1992), particularly in the works of Seneca and Lucan. As Most has noted 'there is not a single tragedy in the Senecan corpus in which the mutilation and amputation of human bodies does not play a significant role, even at moments where neither the literary tradition would seem to require it nor common sense to tolerate it' (1992, 395–6). While there are individual passages in Greek tragedies and early Roman epics which describe mutilations, these tend to be isolated incidents and ones that are few and far between (Most 1992, 400). Most sees the only real precursor to the Neronian trend as being found in the *Metamorphoses* of Ovid. In trying, though, to find an explanation as to why the Neronian period should mark a zenith of literary interest, even obsession, with dismemberment, Most has looked to the Stoic beliefs of many of the writers and their interest in the boundaries between human behaviour and that of animals, perhaps centred on the games in the arena (Most 1992, 401–5). Stoic writers on philosophical science like Galen and Philo saw the body, both human and animal, as being an accumulation of parts 'held together by a sustaining force' (Most 1992, 405–6; Sedley 1982). Seneca's 'choppy' style of composition may even have mirrored, or been mirrored by, the dimemberments of human bodies in his text (Most 1992, 407–8).

Literary and linguistic evidence, however, for the broken body being used as a metaphorical device is not restricted to the canonical writings of the Neronian period, as has been demonstrated, for instance, by Terry Wilfong, who has examined the language used in Coptic texts which suggest, through the use of metaphor, 'the disjoining and fragmenting of the body along gender lines' (1998, 116). Consideration will also need to be given to the Latin sexual vocabulary in any fuller study of the fragmented body (Adams 1987; Parker 1992; Richlin 1992).

At a more demotic level there can perhaps be seen in the *graffiti* caricatures from the walls of Pompeii another explicit trend towards the reduction of the human body to a set of signifying, disconnected parts, though here we may be seeing humour and spite as the driving forces behind these creations, rather than any complex philosophical reasoning. Most of the caricatures relied upon the exaggeration of certain features, almost always, though not completely exclusively, on facial features, particularly 'hair, beard, eyebrow, lips, jaw, nose, ear and neck' (Funari 1993, 138), each of which, according to Funari's analysis, had connotations relating to aspects of laughter, power and authority (1993, 138–9). Interestingly, Funari sees many of the caricatures as being reactions to the Neronian era's 'culture of nouveau-riche freedmen' and 'introspection by local elites' (1993, 142). 'These people', he notes, 'not only did criticise people in power but also used their own stylistic and symbolic creativity to carry on this critique' (Funari 1993, 143). The broad contemporaneity of the creation of the Pompeian *graffiti* images and the poetic images of dismemberment mentioned above provides an interesting potential insight into views on the body in the Neronian period.

The ideas expounded in this paper about the processes behind the fragmentation of the human body into images of partial bodies in Roman art should not be seen as being esoteric art historical musings, of no relevance to the study of Roman artefacts, the theme of this volume and of the conference from which it originated. Rather, it should be stressed that essentialising statements about the experience of the body being culturally unmediated, often found in studies of the classical world, ignore the simple concept that a study of the fragmented body – this archipelago of corrupt fragments – as with a study of fragmented objects, is fundamentally a study of ideas and concepts underpinning Roman culture and society, possibly contributing towards an understanding of the way in which the Romans differed from the Greeks in their conceptions of the body and of the world.

Bibliography

Adams, J. N. (1987) *The Latin Sexual Vocabulary*. London, Duckworth.

Arce, J., Ensoli, S. and La Rocca, E. (eds) (1997) *Hispania Romana. Da Terra di Conquista a Provincia dell'Impero*. Milan, Electa.

Barr-Sharrar, B. (1987) *The Hellenistic and Early Imperial Decorative Bust*. Mainz, Verlag Philipp Von Zabern.

Barton, C. A. (1989) The scandal of the arena. *Representations* 27, 1–36.

Barton, C. A. (1993) *The Sorrows of the Ancient Romans. The Gladiator and the Monster*. Princeton, Princeton University Press.

Beard, M. and Henderson, J. (2001) *Classical Art. From Greece to Rome*. Oxford, Oxford University Press.

Besançon, A. (2001) *The Forbidden Image; an Intellectual History of Iconoclasm*. Chicago, University of Chicago Press.

Bevan, L. (1994) Powerful pudenda: the penis in prehistory. *Journal of Theoretical Archaeology* 3/4, 41–57.

Biddle, M. (1986) Archaeology, architecture, and the cult of saints. In L. A. S. Butler, and R. K. Morris (eds), 1–31.

Blom, P. (2002) *To Have and to Hold: An Intimate History of Collectors and Collecting*. Harmondsworth, Allen Lane.

Bodel, J. (1999) Death on display: looking at Roman funerals. In B. Bergmann and C. Kondoleon (eds) The art of ancient spectacle. Studies in the history of art 56, 259–82. *Center for Advanced Study in the Visual Arts Symposium Papers XXXIV*. Washington, National Gallery of Art.

Brisson, L. (2002) *Sexual Ambivalence. Androgyny and Hermaphroditism in Graeco-Roman Antiquity*. Berkeley, University of California Press.

Brown, P. (1981) *The Cult of the Saints. Its Rise and Function in Latin Christianity*. Chicago, Student Christian Movement.

Brown, P. (1988) *The Body and Society; Men, Women and Sexual Renunciation in Early Christianity*. New York, Columbia University Press.

Bruni, S. (2000) Sculpture. In Torelli, M. (ed.) *The Etruscans*, 365–91. London, Thames and Hudson.

Burrus, V. (2000) *'Begotten, Not Made'; Conceiving Manhood in Late Antiquity*. Stanford, Stanford University Press.

Butler, L. A. S. and Morris, R. K. (eds) (1986) *The Anglo-Saxon Church: Papers on History, Architecture and Archaeology in Honour of Dr H. M. Taylor*. CBA Research Report 60. London.

Bynum, C. W. (1992) *Fragmentation and Redemption: Essays on Gender and the Human Body in Medieval Religion*. New York, Zone Books.

Chapman, J. (2000) *Fragmentation in Archaeology*. London, Routledge.

Clarke, J. R. (1996) Hypersexual black men in Augustan baths: ideal somatypes and apotropaic magic. In Kampen, N. B. (ed.), 184–98.

Clarke, J. R. (1998) *Looking at Lovemaking. Constructions of Sexuality in Roman Art 100 BC–AD 250*. Berkeley, University of California Press.

Coleman, K. M. (1990) Fatal charades: Roman executions staged as mythological enactments. *Journal of Roman Studies* 80, 44–73.

Croxford, B. (2003) Iconoclasm in Roman Britain? *Britannia* 34, 81–95.

Damgaard Andersen, H. (1993) The Etruscan ancestor cult – its origin and development and the importance of anthropomorphization. *Analecta Romana Instituti Danici* 21, 7–66.

Della Portella, I. (1999) *Subterranean Rome*. Cologne, Konemann.

Deonna, W. (1925) Orphée et l'Oracle à la Tête Coupé. *Revue des Études Grecques* 28, 44–69.

Deyts, S. (1994) Un peuple de pelerins. Offrandes de pierre et de bronze des Sources de la Seine. *Revue Archeologique de l'Est et du Centre-Est, Treizieme Supplement*. Dijon.

Doxiadis, E. (1995) *The Mysterious Fayum Portraits. Faces from Ancient Egypt*. London, Thames and Hudson.

Dubois, P. (1996) Archaic bodies in pieces. In N. B. Kampen (ed.), 55–64.

Dubois, P. (1998) *Sowing the Body: Psychoanalysis and Ancient Representations of Women*. Chicago, University of Chicago Press.

Dunbabin, K. (1986) Sic erimus cuncti…the skeleton in Graeco-Roman art. *Jahrbuch des Deutschen Archaologischen Instituts* 101, 185–255.

Dupont, F. (1987) Les morts et la mémoire: le masque funèbre. In F. Hinard (ed.) La mort, les morts et l'au-delà dans le monde Romain. *Actes du Colloque de Caen 1985*, 167–72. Caen.

Dwyer, E. (1982) *Pompeian Domestic Structures; a Study of Five Pompeian Houses and Their Contents*. Rome.

Elderfield, J. (1985) *Kurt Schwitters*. London, Thames and Hudson.

Ellis, P. (2000) Sexual metaphors in the Neolithic. In L. Bevan (ed.), 56–63.

Elsen, A. E. (1969) Notes on the partial figure. *Artforum* 8, 58–63.

Elsen, A. E. (1969–1970) *The Partial Figure in Modern Sculpture: from Rodin to 1969*. Baltimore, Baltimore Museum of Art.

Ferris, I. M. (1994) Insignificant others; images of barbarians on military art from Roman Britain. In S. Cottam, D. Dungworth, S. Scott and J. Taylor (eds) *TRAC 94. Proceedings of the Fourth Annual Theoretical Roman Archaeology Conference, Durham 1994*, 24–31. Oxford, Oxbow Books.

Ferris, I. M. (1997) The enemy without, the enemy within: more thoughts on images of barbarians in Greek and Roman art. In Meadows *et al.* (eds.), 22–8.

Ferris, I. M. (1999) Alchemy of suffering: hope and faith beyond the healing arts in Roman Britain. In A. Leslie (ed.) *Theoretical Roman Archaeology and Architecture, The Third Conference Proceedings*, 1–13. Glasgow, Cruithne Press.

Ferris, I. M. (2000) *Enemies of Rome. Barbarians through Roman eyes*. Stroud, Sutton Publishing.

Ferris, I. M. (2001) The body politic: the sexuality of barbarians in Augustan art. In L. Bevan (ed.), *Indecent Exposure. Sexuality, Society and the Archaeological Record*, 100–9. Glasgow, Cruithne Press.

Ferris, I. M. (2003a) The hanged men dance. Barbarians in Trajanic art. In S. Scott and J. Webster (eds) *Roman Imperialism and Provincial Art*, 53–68. Cambridge, Cambridge University Press.

Ferris, I. M. (2003b) An empire in pieces. Roman archaeology and the fragment. In G. Carr, E. Swift and J. Weekes (eds) *TRAC 2002. Proceedings of the Twelfth Theoretical Roman Archaeology Conference, Canterbury*, 14–28. Oxford, Oxbow Books.

Flower, H. I. (1996) *Ancestor Masks and Aristocratic Power in Roman Culture*. Oxford, Clarendon Press.

Forrester, J. (1994) Freud and collecting. In J. Elsner and R. Cardinal (eds.) *The Cultures of Collecting*, 224–51, London, Reaktion Books.

Funari, P. P. A. (1993) Graphic caricature and the ethos of ordinary people at Pompeii. *Journal of European Archaeology* 1:2, 133–50.

Gazda, E. K. (1973) Etruscan influence in the funerary reliefs of Late Republican Rome: a study of vernacular portraiture. *Aufstieg und Niedergang der Römischen Welt 1,4*, 855–70.

Govi, C. M. and Vitali, D. (1988) *Il Museo Civico Archeologico di Bologna*. Bologna, Bologna University Press.

Gregory, A. P. (1994) 'Powerful images': responses to portraits and the political uses of images in Rome. *Journal of Roman Archaeology* 7, 80–99.

Hallett, J. P. and Skinner, M. B. (eds) (1997) *Roman Sexualities*. Princeton, Princeton University Press.

Halperin, D., Winkler, J., and Zeitlin, F. (1990) *Before Sexuality: The Construction of the Erotic Experience in the Ancient Greek World*. Princeton, Princeton University Press.

Huskinson, J. (2000) Portraits. In R. Ling (ed.) *Making Classical Art. Process and Practice*, 155–68. Stroud, Tempus.

Isserlin, R. M. J. (1997) Thinking the unthinkable: human sacrifice in Roman Britain? In K. Meadows *et al.* (eds), 91–100.

Johns, C. (1982) *Sex or Symbol. Erotic Images of Greece and Rome*. London, British Museum Publications.

Kampen, N. B. (ed.) (1996) *Sexuality in Ancient Art*. Cambridge, Cambridge University Press.

Kampen, N. B., Marlowe, E., and Molholt, R. M. (2002) *What is a Man? Changing Images of Masculinity in Late Antique Art*. Portland, Douglas F. Cooley Memorial Art Gallery, Reed College.

Kellum, B. (1996) The phallus as signifier: the forum of Augustus and rituals of masculinity. In N. B. Kampen (ed.), 170–83.

Kinney, D. (1997) Spolia: Damnatio and Renovatio Memoriae. *Memoirs of the American Academy in Rome* 42, 117–48.

Kleiner, D. E. E. (1992) *Roman Sculpture*. Yale, Yale University Press.

Koloski-Ostrow, A. O. and Lyons, C. L. (eds.) (1997) *Naked Truths. Women, Sexuality and Gender in Classical Art and Archaeology*. London, Routledge.

Koortbojian, M. (1996) *In Commemorationem Mortuorum*: text and image along the 'Streets of Tombs'. In J. Elsner (ed.) *Art and Text in Roman Culture*, 210–34. Cambridge, Cambridge University Press.

Kristeva, J. (1998) *Visions Capitales*. Paris, Reunion des Musées Nationaux.

Kuefler, M. (2001) *The Manly Eunuch: Masculinity, Gender Ambiguity, and Christian Ideology in Late Antiquity*. Chicago, University of Chicago Press.

Ling, R. (1990) Street plaques at Pompeii. In M. Henig (ed.) *Architecture and Architectural Sculpture in the Roman Empire*, Oxford University Committee for Archaeology Monograph 29, 51–66. Oxford..

Lloyd, G. R. (1973) *Greek Science after Aristotle*. London, Chatto and Windus.

MacMullen, R. (1986) Judicial savagery in the Roman Empire. Reprinted in R. MacMullen (1990) *Changes in the Roman Empire. Essays in the Ordinary*, 204–17. Princeton, Princeton University Press.

Meadows, K., Lemke, C., and Heron, J. (eds) (1997) *TRAC 96. Proceedings of the Sixth Annual Theoretical Roman Archaeology Conference Sheffield 1996*. Oxford, Oxbow Books.

Meskell, L. M. (1998) The irresistible body and the seduction of archaeology. In D. Montserrat (ed.), 139–61.

Meskell, L. M. (2000) Writing the body in archaeology. In A. E. Rautman (ed.) *Reading the Body. Representations and Remains in the Archaeological Record*, 13–21. Philadelphia, University of Pennsylvania Press.

Montserrat, D. (ed.) (1998) *Changing Bodies, Changing Meanings. Studies on the Human Body in Antiquity*. London, Routledge.

Montserrat, D. (2000) Reading gender in the Roman world. In J. Huskinson (ed.) *Experiencing Rome. Culture, Identity and Power in the Roman Empire*, 153–81. London, Routledge.

Most, G. (1992) The rhetoric of dismemberment in Neronian poetry. In R. Hexter and D. Selden (eds) *Innovations of Antiquity*, 391–419. London, Routledge.

Musgrave, J. (1990) Dust and damn'd oblivion: a study of cremation in ancient Greece. *Annual of the British School at Athens* 85, 271–99.

Nochlin, L. (1994) *The Body in Pieces. The Fragment as a Metaphor of Modernity*. London, Thames and Hudson.

Nodelman, S. (1975) How to read a Roman portrait. *Art in America* 63, 26–33. Reproduced with postscript in E. D'Ambra (ed.) (1993) *Roman Art in Context. An Anthology*, 10–26.

Nylander, C. (1998) The mutilated image. 'We' and 'they' in history and prehistory? *Kungl. Vitterhets Historie och Antikvitets Akademien Konferenser* 40, 235–51. Stockholm.

Padgett, J. M. (ed.) (2001) *Roman Sculpture in the Art Museum, Princeton University*. Princeton, Princeton University Press.

Parker, H. (1992) Love's body anatomized: the ancient erotic handbooks and the rhetoric of sexuality. In A. Richlin (ed.) *Pornography and Representation in Greece and Rome*, 90–111. Oxford, Oxford University Press.

Philpott, R. (1991) *Burial Practices in Roman Britain. A Survey of Grave Treatment and Furnishing A.D. 43–410*. British Archaeological Report (British Series) 219. Oxford, British Archaeological Reports.

Pingeot, A. (ed.) (1990) *Le Corps en Morceaux*. Paris, Musée d'Orsay.

Pollitt, J. J. (1986) *Art in the Hellenistic Age*. Cambridge, Cambridge University Press.

Potter, T. (1985) A Republican healing sanctuary at Ponte di Nona near Rome and the Classical tradition of votive medicine. *Journal of the British Archaeological Association* 138, 23–47.

Rambaud, M. (1978) Masques et imagines. Essai sur certains usages funéraires de l'Afrique noire et de la Rome ancienne. *Les Études Classiques* 46, 3–21.

Rautman, A. E. (ed.) (2000) *Reading the Body. Representations and Remains in the Archaeological Record*. Philadelphia, University of Pennsylvania Press.

Richlin, A. (1992) *The Garden of Priapus: Sexuality and Aggression in Roman Humour*. Second edition. Oxford, Oxford University Press.

Richlin, A. (1997) Towards a history of body history. In M. Golden and P. Toohey (eds.) *Inventing Ancient Culture. Historicism, Periodization, and the Ancient World*, 16–35. London, Routledge.

Rollason, D. (1986) The shrines of the saints in later Anglo-Saxon England: distribution and significance. In L. A. S. Butler and R. K. Morris (eds), 32–43.

Rollason, D. (1989) *Saints and Relics in Anglo-Saxon England*. Oxford, Blackwell.

Rousselle, A. (1988) *Porneia. On Desire and the Body in Antiquity*. Oxford, Blackwell.

Sauer, E. (2003) *The Archaeology of Religious Hatred in the Roman and Early Medieval World*. Stroud, Tempus.

Sedley, D. (1982) The Stoic criterion of identity. *Phronesis* 27, 255–75.

Sigerist, H. E. (1977) The special position of the sick. Originally published 1960, reprinted in D. Landy (ed.) *Culture, Disease and Healing. Studies in Medical Anthropology*, 388–94. London, MacMillan.

Stella, C., Valvo, A., and Morandini, F. (1998) *L'Età Romana, La Città, Le Iscrizioni*. Brescia, Santa Giulia Museo della Città. Milan, Electa.

van Straten, F. T. (1981) Gifts for the gods. In H. S. Versnel (ed.) *Faith, Hope and Worship. Aspects of Religious Mentality in the Ancient World*, 65–151. Leiden, Brill.

Turnbull, P. (1978) The phallus in the art of Roman Britain. *Bulletin of the Institute of Archaeology* 15, 199–206.

Varner, E. R. (2000) *From Caligula to Constantine. Tyranny and Transformation in Roman Portraiture*. Atlanta; Michael C. Carlos Museum, Emory University.

Walker, S. (1985) *Memorials to the Roman Dead*. London, British Museum Press.

Walker, S. (1995) *Greek and Roman Portraits*. London, British Museum Press.

Walters, J. (1997) Invading the Roman body: manliness and impenetrability in Roman thought. In J. P. Hallett and M. B. Skinner (eds), 29–43.

Wilfong, T. (1998) Reading the disjointed body in Coptic: from physical modification to textual fragmentation. In D. Montserrat (ed.), 116–38.

Winter, I. (1996) Sex, rhetoric, and the public monument: the alluring body of Naram-Sîn of Agade. In N. B. Kampen (ed.), 11–26.

Woodward, A. (1993) The cult of relics in prehistoric Britain. In M. O. H. Carver (ed.) *In Search of Cult. Archaeological Investigations in Honour of Philip Rahtz*, 1–7. Woodbridge, The Boydell Press.

Woodward, A. and Leach, P. J. (1993) *The Uley Shrines; Excavation of a Ritual Complex on West Hill, Uley, Gloucestershire 1977–1979*. London, English Heritage.

Wyke, M. (ed.) (1998) *Gender and the Body in the Ancient Mediterranean*. Oxford, Blackwell.

Zanker, P. (1998) Die Barbaren, der Kaiser und die Arena. Bilder der Gewalt in der Römischen Kunst. Reprinted in translation as: I barbari, l'imperatore e l'arena. immagini di violenza nell'arte Romana. In P. Zanker (2002), 38–62.

Zanker, P. (2000) Die Frauen und Kinder der Barbaren auf der Markussäule. Reprinted in translation as: Le donne e i bambini sui rilievi della colonna Aureliana. In P. Zanker (2002), 63–78.

Zanker, P. (2002) *Un'arte per l'impero. Funzione e intenzione delle immagini nel mondo Romano*. Milan, Electa.

13 Artefacts, Contexts and the Archaeology of Social Practices

Andrew Gardner

Perspective

This paper will examine the essential role that finds studies can play in the integration of theory and practice in Roman archaeology. I shall argue that detailed contextual analysis of artefacts of all types is well suited to addressing interpretative questions raised by the recent development of a range of 'practice theories' in the social sciences. The concept of practices – more or less routine 'ways of doing' things – appears in the work of a number of writers, including Archer, Bourdieu and Giddens, and has penetrated archaeology in a number of guises, particularly with reference to technology (*e.g.* Dobres 2000). Here I will take a broad view of this idea and use it to define a series of activities – such as dwelling, eating and appearing – which can be interpreted from the relationships between different kinds of finds and different kinds of contexts on archaeological sites. In this way, practice becomes a linking concept between the patterning of the archaeological record and past human social life, structured as this was by similarities and differences between 'ways of doing'. As such, it offers great potential for deepening our understandings of cultural change and interaction in the Roman world.

Introduction: data and interpretative optimism

This paper concerns the role of practice in Roman archaeology, both as an interpretative framework for the study of the past, and as an aspect of that study in the present. Both of these dimensions necessarily entail a consideration of the relationship between practice and theory. My essential standpoint – that these are inseperable elements of Roman finds work, as with any other human activity – will be argued for more explicitly later in the paper. Before reaching that point, though, I hope to make the case for such a position by interweaving data-studies and discussions of wider issues in a more intimate way than is often attempted. I will thus begin by introducing the idea of practice in the context of some small-scale artefact analyses and then widen this context with a consideration of the general relationships between practices and social institutions, and with some larger-scale finds studies. These will lead, in turn, to a broader consideration of the relationship between theoretical and practical

attitudes in all human action in my final section. Overall, I hope to demonstrate not only the interpretative potential of finds work for addressing major questions of social interaction and change in the Roman period, but also the absolute necessity of acknowledging the theoretical dimension which such work involves.

This is not simply for reasons of academic trendiness, but in order to make the most of the material which has been collected and analysed thus far and which will be in the future. If finds catalogues are not simply to remain examples of a particular approach to classifying the world (Allison 1997; Foucault 1970 [2002], xvi), they need to be harnessed to broader goals. This, in turn, requires a degree of optimism about the interpretative value of archaeological material. In subsequent sections of this paper a series of interpretative steps will be taken to link patterns of artefact distribution in space and time to particular ways of doing things, thence to social institutions (especially social identities) and from there to an understanding of specific trajectories of social continuity and transformation. This chain is held together by the notion of context and, as will be shown, this can accommodate factors like poor data resolution or redeposition, which might otherwise be held to inhibit our interpretative ambition (cf. James 2001, 89). The importance of the idea of context lies in its flexibility. As Shanks and Tilley have argued, contexts are: 'sets of relationships which bestow meaning' (1992, xix). Building up such meaningful sets of relationships requires us to integrate multiple finds specialisms and multiple scales of analysis, but will pay dividends in terms of generating the kinds of social understanding of past human life that should be our goal as archaeologists. In what follows I hope to demonstrate that such optimism is not misplaced.

Finds and practices at the micro scale

The initial step in the interpretative chain referred to above requires a focus on the analysis of artefactual material from a pair of late Roman sites at small scales of resolution (cf. Gardner 2002 for further examples). This kind of study, as will become clear later on, is vital not only for illustrating the main points of a practice framework but also for underpinning larger-scale interpretations within such a framework. The first site I would like to consider is Birdoswald. Recently published excavations in the area of the main west gate (*porta principalis sinistra*) of the fort have provided a good deal of high-resolution data (Wilmott 1997) which allows finds to be situated within a range of spatial, temporal and typological contexts. These, in turn, permit us to think about the artefacts (and, indeed, the stratigraphic sequence) in terms of activities. This is not in itself a great departure from current debates about stratigraphic description (Lucas 2001, 152–62), or from now well-established developments in finds classification (by function rather than material; Crummy 1983, 4–6). If we define these activities more precisely as *practices*, however, that is, as routinized ways of doing things (Dobres 2000, 147–8), then we open up more potential to interpret

them socially (see below) at the same time as anchoring these interpretations in elementary features of the archaeological record, namely similarity and difference, or *patterning*.

This connection is discernible at Birdoswald. Even a fairly crude use of GIS software allows us to pick out patterns in the distribution of the artefacts deposited in the west gate area (Fig. 13.1). The most immediately obvious activity which can be treated as a 'practice' is deposition itself: dumping of refuse was clearly an important aspect of action in this environment at particular times (*e.g.* the later fourth-century phase of the northern *horreum*, Building 198), and must be treated as potentially meaning-

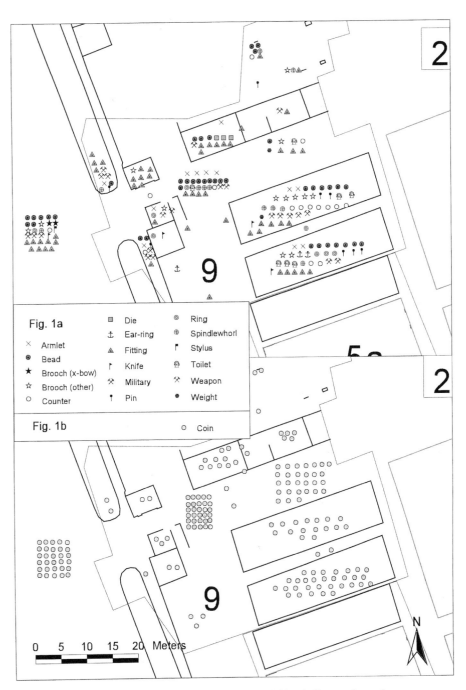

Fig. 13.1. Plans showing distributions of small finds (1a) and coins (1b) of all periods in the west gate area at Birdoswald, arranged in approximate area of excavation. (Data and background plan after Wilmott 1997, 10–11; Summerfield et al. 1997)

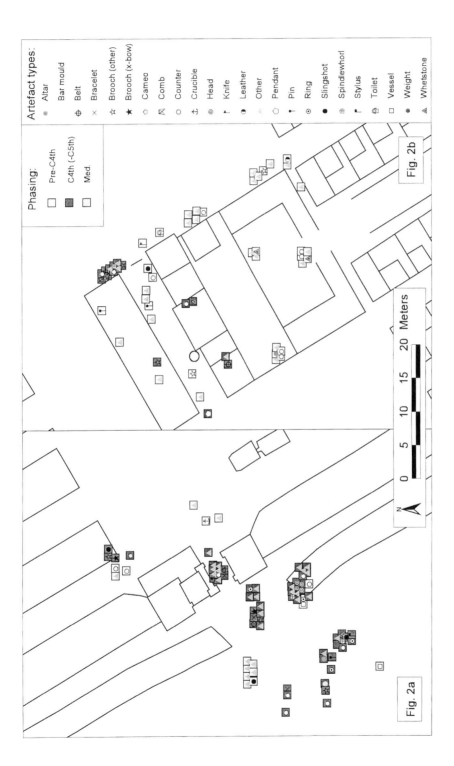

Fig. 13.2. *Plans showing small finds in the west gate (2a) and principia (2b) areas at South Shields, arranged in approximate area of excavation, and with an indication of the phasing of the contexts from which they were recovered. (Data and background plan after Bidwell and Speak 1994, 34; Croom et al. 1994)*

ful (cf. Thompson 1979). Other activities which can all be treated as persistent elements of a generalized practice of *dwelling* include movement through the gateway (important well into the 'sub-Roman' phases of the site) and maintenance – for instance, of the southern *horreum* (Building 197). The apparently changing purpose of the latter building (to more domestic occupation), however, indicates that there is transformation as well as continuity in this category of practice. The artefacts themselves speak of a different range of actions. Concentrating on the small finds and coinage (pottery and animal bone from this and other sites will be discussed separately below), we can suggest that the latter were associated with practices of *exchanging* and that the majority of the other finds, comprising 'personalia' of one kind or another (armlets, beads, brooches, *etc.*), were associated with practices of *appearing*. While the dating of the latter categories of material is often problematic, there are indications of conservatism in their use from the presence of old artefacts in some of the later deposits (not necessarily to be dismissed as residual) and fairly slow typological change. At the same time the presence of such artefacts at all is notable as evidence of differentiated identities within the fort community.

That we can chart the persistent importance of certain basic practices over considerable periods of time is in itself a product of their routinized nature. This connection between practices and routine takes on a more specifically meaningful aspect if we turn to the second site I would like to consider at this scale, South Shields. Here, material from recent excavations in the area of the *principia* and the south-west gate provides similar opportunities for analysis to that from Birdoswald (Bidwell and Speak 1994; Fig. 13.2). The most notable feature of the distributions here is that the finds types occurring in the area of the *principia* are essentially limited to miscellaneous fittings and a few counters, while there is more variety in the material coming from the south-west gate site (where there are also greater quantities of coins, not illustrated). Moreover, there are differences in the kinds of context concerned, with the gate material largely deriving from late ditch deposits and the *principia* material from construction deposits; it is noteworthy here that the one later dump does contain a wider range of objects. At this site, then, we again have evidence for routine practices of dwelling – in the way the *principia* was kept clean compared to the open areas in the gateway and in the patterns of dumping in the ditch, at least some of which was highly structured (an early fourth-century group of objects relating to heads was noted in one ditch terminal by the excavators; Snape 1994, 136–7). The maintenance of the gate into the fifth century further reflects the continuity of such practices, though the encroachment of refuse disposal into the vicinity of the *principia* also suggests change. The evidence of the artefacts themselves indicates practices of appearing and exchanging, as at Birdoswald.

These kinds of observation do not mean a great deal in isolation, but when they are compared with a wider range of sites a fuller picture begins to emerge of the ways in which different practices develop through this period; in other words, whether they change more quickly or more slowly, and how these dynamics fit together at local, regional or provincial levels. In this, it is the description of small-scale patterns in terms of *practices* like dwelling, exchanging or appearing, which form part of a loose typology that I shall expand below, that is crucial. Without pre-judging the meaning-content of the specific artefacts concerned, or their associations with specific identities, talking about practices foregrounds the temporal dimension of human life – the doing of things in particular ways through time. It is then in comparing these 'ways of doing' that we *can* begin to say something about those identities and their role in social change. This is because, as we will see in the next section, it is through the balance of routine and transformation in daily practices that larger-scale social and cultural formations are made or unmade. Even working with just the two sites discussed here, the ordering of dwelling practices at a site like South Shields can be seen, from its context, to relate to the institution of the military, but there are also clearly differences within that institution, manifest in the various practices of appearing represented in the artefacts, and transformation too, in changing habits of dumping (and of building use at Birdoswald). The interpretative chain connecting artefact patterns to practices to identities depends upon detailed contextual finds work and, in turn underpins interpretations of major social dynamics. In order to proceed further with this latter step, however, we do need to consider more of the theoretical background to these issues.

Theories of practice and society

A number of approaches to the relationship between routine practices and broader social structures have been developed within the social sciences (cf. Turner 1994). Most take Marx as their point of departure, both for his emphasis on sensuous, material practice in distinction to the 'theoretical attitude' (1845 [1983], 155), and for his dictum that 'men [sic] make their own history, but not spontaneously, under conditions they have chosen for themselves' (1852 [1983], 287). The latter statement, in particular, encapsulates what is at issue here: the relationship of different kinds of individual action to the social structures which surround us. This is arguably the defining problem of modern social theory (Jenkins 1996, 25–6; Parker 2000, 14–5). The two writers who are most commonly associated with developing the notion of practice to address this problem are Anthony Giddens and Pierre Bourdieu. For Giddens, social reproduction and transformation hinges upon the capacity of individuals (or human 'agents') for reflexive, routine action, that is practice (1984, 1–37). It is primarily through such action that the 'rules and resources', which are the

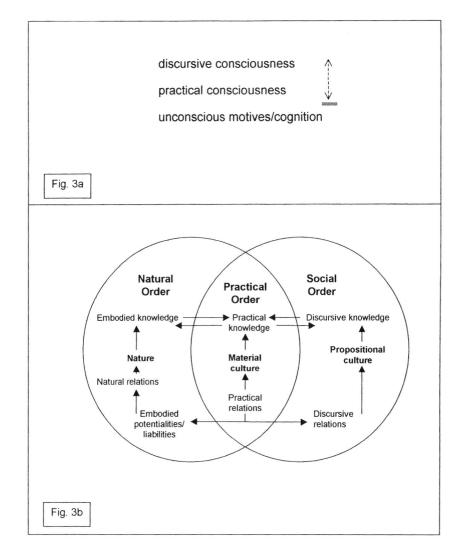

Fig. 13.3. Diagrams illustrating Anthony Giddens' stratified model of human consciousness (3a; after Giddens 1984, 7) and Margaret Archer's more elaborate division of human experience into natural, practical and discursive orders of reality (3b; after Archer 2000, 162)

fundamental elements of social structures, are both drawn into daily life and, simultaneously, maintained as features of social reality. This is the process of 'structuration': the (re-)generation of large-scale social formations through small-scale activities.

Giddens emphasises the routine, habitual nature of the actions which are most instrumental in this process by differentiating human consciousness between the unconscious, practical consciousness and discursive consciousness (Fig. 13.3a; 1984, 4–8). While the unconscious retains a Freudian aspect of repressed motivations, distinguishing practical and discursive consciousness allows us to differentiate, for example, between the actions of driving a car and the way we talk about the methods involved in driving. While the latter is necessary in learning to drive, it is only by converting such discursive knowledge into habitual practical knowledge that one can really make a success of driving on a road without causing an accident. Routine actions are thus vital in reproducing social norms

– whether these be of road use or of identity categories in Roman-period Britain. Giddens has been criticized for over-stressing this aspect of human knowledge and action at the expense of the discursive or theoretical (*e.g.* Cohen 1994, 21; Mouzelis 1995, 119–21), and I shall pursue this argument further below. For now, the connection between routine activity and social structures is sufficiently demonstrable to be of use in relating small-scale archaeological patterns to larger-scale identity groups.

This much is also clear from the work of Bourdieu and Archer, though the former can also be criticised for mystifying the role of practical consciousness (*e.g.* Archer 2000, 179–80; Parker 2000, 106–7). In Bourdieu's terms, this is the '*habitus*', the culturally-shared depositary of shared dispositions which actors live by. While Bourdieu is successful in emphasising the embodied, material dimensions of this kind of practice in his writing, which is generally better grounded in anthropological case studies than that of Giddens (Bourdieu 1990, 66–79; Parker 2000,

Making a *Raki* in Araypallpa

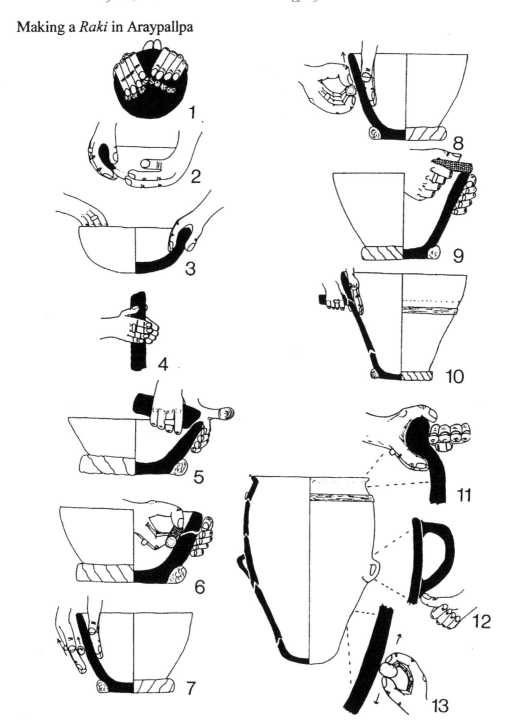

Fig. 13.4. An example of a chaîne opératoire – *a processual model of the production of an artefact which highlights opportunities for choice – based on the manufacture of one type of Andean pottery (Sillar 2000, 166)*

40–1), he provides a concept which is even less open to discussion and to transformation than 'practical consciousness' (Jenkins 1992, 97). As will be seen in what follows, this constitutes an important shortcoming. This is much less of a problem for Margaret Archer, who asserts – in spite of her disagreement with Giddens and Bourdieu on a number of major issues – the primacy of the practical order in human life, but accommodates it with a clear understanding of the natural and discursive orders (Fig.

13.3b; Archer 1995, 93–134; 2000, 121–90; see Parker 2000 for an excellent summary of these various positions). Her insistence on the priority of practice over language in the development of personal identity is an important additive to many social theories which tend to overplay the linguistic at the expense of the practical and material (Archer 2000, 22–50, 86–117; cf. also Crossley 1996, 49–65; Dant 1999; Mead 1934, 237), acting as a corrective to much post-structuralist influence. Her association of social interaction almost exclusively with language use (*e.g.* 2000, 318–9), however, does somewhat misdirect her from exploring the *social significance of practices*; this is something we will be exploring in the next section.

To conclude this review of approaches to practice, though, it is worth noting certain aspects of the way the idea has been imported into archaeology. Increasingly, a stress on 'ways of doing things' as a vital element in social reproduction is found in a range of contexts, not least in the study of various aspects of identity, as pursued in this paper (*e.g.* Jones 1997; cf. Gardner 2002). It is, however, useful to examine an earlier manifestation of this concept, as a way of illustrating its particular relevance to finds work. This is in the field of 'technological choices', influenced more by the French anthropological tradition than any Anglophone social theorists, and typified in the work of Pierre Lemonnier (1993) and, more recently, of Marcia-Anne Dobres (2000; cf. also Sillar and Tite 2000). The key goal of this work is to break technology studies out of a functionalist deadend by using the details of the production process of an artefact to understand the choices taken in the practice of making it (Fig. 13.4). This accommodates the relationship discussed above between the social and the individual, by considering the connection between the practical routines involved in making something, which reproduce existing social conventions and institutions, and discursive choices which might generate change. Clearly, this manifestation of practice theory is very much applicable to Roman material, where detailed aspects of production techniques can be understood from a range of technical, textual and contextual evidence. In this paper, however, I am trying to take a broad view of the concept of practice, applying it to other kinds of 'doing' than making things. Some of these were aired in the small-scale studies described above and this list can now be expanded through the consideration of larger-scale patterns.

Aggregation of finds and practices

In this section I want to examine different categories of material to those used in the case-studies above, by looking at patterns in bulk finds, specifically pottery and animal bone, through the prism of practice theory. This distinction between 'small' and 'bulk' finds is of course largely artificial, both in terms of past practices of use (*e.g.* of a spoon with a vessel), and of present analytical practices: distributions of sherds of different vessel types could be incorporated profitably into micro-scale studies of the kind discussed above, while the more aggregative approach to be explored in this section is certainly applicable to functional categories of personal objects or to coins (*e.g.* Cooper 2000, 82–5; Gardner 2002, 327–31; Reece 1991). It is also the case that, even at a broad scale, interpretation of finds like faunal remains in terms of practices still requires a certain degree of temporal and spatial resolution. Nonetheless, providing we are

sensitive to the flexibility of the concept of context in looking for similarities and differences across wider expanses of space and time, then such interpretation is certainly possible. One way of approaching this for both pottery and faunal remains is to consider them as elements in practices of *eating* (cf. Hawkes 1999; Meadows 1994). While other practices are clearly involved in the biographies of these kinds of artefact, such a general category can, as I hope to show, still be useful, in a similar fashion to the idea of dwelling.

In addition, then, to the kinds of small-scale studies already illustrated, my research into military institutions and identities in fourth-century Britain (Gardner 2001; 2002) has entailed a much broader survey of settlements, with highly variable bulk finds data. This variation, which is largely due to differences in recording practices, presents some problems to do with the comparability of assemblages, but these can be overcome to a considerable extent by taking care as to the nature of comparisons attempted, seeking groups of similarly-excavated sites for more specific problems or aggregating sites to explore broad trends. These strategies do, I believe, allow us to interpret patterns of 'eating' in a meaningful way. For this practice, and speaking in the most general terms, we can detect a generalized norm across provincial Britain in the fourth century, but with some important movement towards increasingly localized variation. If we focus on pottery supply, for instance, we can compare the range of fabrics at different kinds of sites over time by plotting graphically the percentages of these in different stratigraphic phases (*e.g.* Fig. 13.5).

These charts emphasize the importance of local wares to most supply throughout the Roman period, though these are commonly influenced in terms of vessel types by larger industries, particularly of course BB1 (Tyers 1996, 67; see also Evans 2001 on the importance of large-scale typological comparisons). In the late fourth century this pattern of local manifestations of a wider continuity in practice remains, despite the decline of the inter-regional movement of fabrics (which was always more important for urban sites; Cooper 2000, 77–82). Thus, for instance, different calcite- or shell-gritted fabrics become popular across a number of different local areas (cf. Tyers 1996, 77–8). In terms of the questions concerning military identity which I have pursued so far, this kind of pattern cuts across divisions between site types, such as forts and towns and even some farms. Taken on its own, this evidence might suggest that local community identities within a wider – albeit perhaps largely unacknowledged – norm were more likely to be manifest in practices of eating than those relating to a specific kind of institution like the military, and that this likelihood increased through the second half of the fourth century.

If we look at the other category of material that I would like to include under the heading of 'eating' – animal bone – then this picture is generally confirmed, but there are also signs of some persistent institutional traditions.

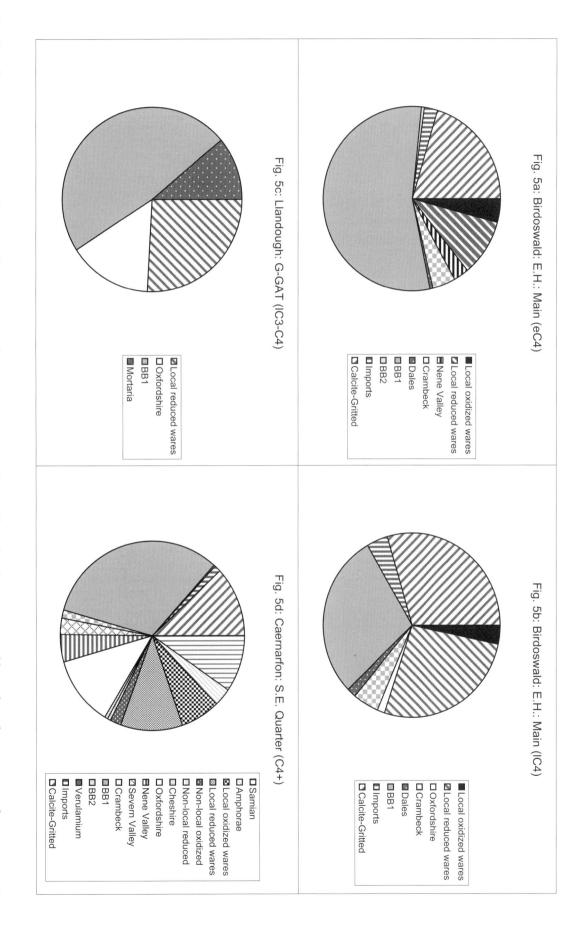

Fig. 5a: Birdoswald: E.H.: Main (eC4)

■ Local oxidized wares
▨ Local reduced wares
□ Crambeck
▨ Dales
■ BB1
▨ BB2
▥ Imports
□ Calcite-Gritted

Fig. 5b: Birdoswald: E.H.: Main (lC4)

■ Local oxidized wares
▨ Local reduced wares
□ Oxfordshire
□ Crambeck
▨ Dales
■ BB1
▥ Imports
□ Calcite-Gritted

Fig. 5c: Llandough: G-GAT (lC3-C4)

▨ Local reduced wares
□ Oxfordshire
■ BB1
▨ Mortaria

Fig. 5d: Caernarfon: S.E. Quarter (C4+)

□ Samian
□ Amphorae
▨ Local oxidized wares
▨ Local reduced wares
▨ Non-local oxidized
▨ Non-local reduced
□ Cheshire
□ Oxfordshire
■ Nene Valley
▨ Severn Valley
□ Crambeck
▨ BB1
▨ BB2
▨ Verulamium
▥ Imports
□ Calcite-Gritted

Fig. 13.5. Comparative pottery supply charts. There are clear changes between the earlier and later fourth-century assemblages from the main area of recent excavation at Birdoswald (1987–92). In the later phase, this site also compares more closely to the farm of Llandough, near Caerwent, than with the fort at Caernarfon, which is in turn more similar to some towns (cf. Cooper 2000, 79–82). (Data from Hird 1997, 234 [Birdoswald; coarse ware only, % by weight]; King and Millett 1993: 244; Webster 1993, 252 [Caernarfon; % MNV]; Hartley 1988, 171; Webster 1988, 161–70 [Llandough; coarse ware only, % MNV])

Andrew Gardner

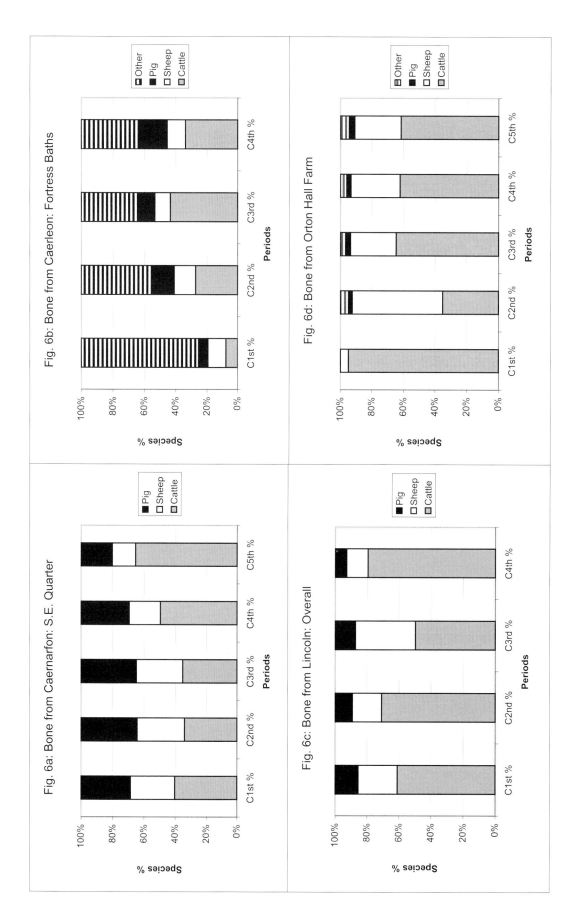

Fig. 13.6. Comparative charts showing percentages of different species in the faunal remains assemblages from selected sites. In addition to the general importance of cattle, and the secondary significance of pig at Caernarfon, it is worth noting the effect of the particular depositional environment of the baths at Caerleon, with the higher proportion of 'other' species attesting to a wider range of 'snacks' (O'Connor 1986: 225–9). (Data from Noddle 1993 [Caernarfon; % MNI]; O'Connor 1986 [Caerleon; % MNI]; Dobney, Jaques and Irving 1995, 20–61, 132–3 [Lincoln; % fragment numbers]; King 1996 [Orton Hall Farm; % bone numbers])

Here, again, we can quantify the different major species for different stratigraphic phases from a range of sites (Fig. 13.6). Notwithstanding important issues to do with the movement of animals, it is clear that cattle is the dominant species found on many sites (cf. Grant 1989). Again, therefore, we have a widespread area of common practice. Still, within this there is variation, which can be related in part to more localized patterns of supply. This includes, for instance, one tendency which might indicate military distinctiveness in the kind of food eaten, even if it is consumed in more commonplace vessels. Many of the assemblages from military sites, like Caernarfon and Caerleon in the west or Portchester in the south, have pig as the major species behind cattle, while in towns and farms this secondary species is more often sheep. If genuine, this pattern suggests that, while military communities had much in common with others in the manner of serving food – and perhaps its preparation – the constitution of their diet may have been slightly different (cf. King 1999). This is the kind of practice that, within a military community, might be implicitly accepted as a routinized manifestation of tradition, only becoming articulated as distinctive when discursively noticed during interaction with someone from a different background.

As noted earlier, in isolation, this kind of pattern of practice doesn't mean very much. Taken in combination, however, the use of different kinds of artefact studies to explore different kinds of practice allows us to gain more purchase on the identities constructed through them and the times when these were discursively contested or in flux, as against the times when they were simply being reproduced in a routine fashion. Based on a range of analyses along the lines of those presented here (see Gardner 2002 and forthcoming for a fuller exposition), it is clear that through the fourth-century in Britain the importance of localized routines increased (especially in dwelling practices). This made the local community – as a 'community of practice' (Wenger 1998) – the main axis along which difference might be discursively noticed, as opposed to broader, more abstract categories like 'military' or 'civilian'. Nonetheless, such change was gradual and, as we have seen, some traditions did persist. Overall, these patterns suggest that the more historically-salient developments at the beginning of the fifth century need not be taken as a sudden collapse, but rather as a further stage in the ongoing transformation of social life in Roman-period Britain.

Conclusions: theory and practice

To summarise the main argument that I have tried to develop through the preceeding case studies, I believe that thinking about practices provides a fruitful way of connecting artefact patterns to social interpretations. This is because the identities which structure social relations are built upon similarities in ways of doing things on a routine basis and these routine patterns of daily life are often quite clearly discernible in archaeological contexts. Equally, though, social change and transformation, which occupy much of our attention in attempting to understand the impact of Roman imperialism on Iron Age Britain, are typically associated with the contact between noticeably different ways of doing things and this is, again, something that archaeologists are in a relatively good position to address. This distinction between routine actions and those that are noticeable is therefore of vital importance in linking patterning in the archaeological record – that is, in the simplest of terms, similarities and differences – with dynamic social relations in the past. As such, it draws heavily upon the theories discussed above which posit separate practical and discursive dimensions to human consciousness and, in the final part of this paper, I want to return to this idea and draw out some of its further implications for the nature of archaeological, and particularly artefactual, work in the present.

Although I have suggested that archaeologists can successfully explore the difference between routinized and discursively noticeable practices in many contexts, it must be acknowledged that these are less likely to include the most transitory shifts between these modes of thinking, which do in fact occur very commonly in daily life. If we synthesize the concepts discussed so far, we can distinguish between a 'practical attitude' of absorbed, habitual engagement in an interaction and a 'theoretical attitude', which entails some degree of objectification, of taking something out of the flow of practice and making it a discursive problem or focus of analysis. Two important points must be made here. One is that these attitudes can be assumed in all kinds of interaction – whether with people, ideas or objects (Crossley 1996, 1–23; Dreyfus 1991, 61–83; Shanks and Tilley 1992, 111). This distinction does not, therefore, correspond to any separation of the material and the ideal, but rather assumes that these are fundamentally intertwined in the way that humans engage with the world (Archer 2000, 188–90; Heidegger 1962, 78–86; Mead 1934, 347). Secondly, we frequently move between them in the course of the use of a single artefact, in the progress of a single conversation or in the conduct of a single activity.

While fluctuation at this level will clearly be difficult to address specifically with archaeological patterns (requiring aggregation and generalization, as illustrated above), this latter point is nonetheless vital in re-establishing the dynamics of the relationship between theory and practice in archaeology. This relationship has been discussed overtly at least since the advent of the New Archaeology, when David Clarke, among others, called for the nurturing of critical self-consciousness amongst practitioners of the discipline (Clarke 1973). While the notion that theory is separable from practice seems doggedly persistent, many have argued against such a cleavage, perhaps increasingly in the last 15 years (*e.g.* Johnson 1999, 102; Shanks and Tilley 1987, 1–28). I would certainly add my own voice to this chorus, precisely because – and this may seem perverse – of the distinction I have drawn between theoretical and practical attitudes. While we certainly can identify times when an activity is routine and unproblematic, and others when it is the subject of discussion, these situations are highly fluid and completely intertwined – in short, they are *both* applicable to all human activities, as vital elements of the way humans live in the world around them.

Thus, whilst digging often involves a practical attitude to the routine, habituated rhythm of mattocking, for instance, this may switch to a theoretical attitude if the tool breaks, or if a new kind of soil demands that it be used in a different way. Archaeology as a discipline necessarily entails a theoretical attitude – by making 'the past' an object of analytical enquiry – as well as practical attitudes to activities like digging. Similarly, finds work involves a theoretical attitude, inasmuch as pieces of pottery, for example, are not used to hold water or to cook with but are probed and analysed – are taken as problematic and talked about. At the same time, this work involves a practical attitude too, most obviously in the routines of recording and quantifying. In summary, then, understanding the relationship between theoretical and practical attitudes will not only help us to think about the significance of different activities in the past, but will benefit the communicability of our work in the present by expanding the range of problems it can be seen to address. The interconnection of theoretical and practical attitudes in all human activities means that, for archaeologists as much as anyone else, separating theory and practice is simply not an option.

Acknowledgements

The core of this paper is drawn from my doctoral thesis, and I owe a continuing debt to Mark Hassall, Richard Reece, Stephen Shennan, Jeremy Tanner, Simon James and Matthew Johnson for their roles in the successful completion of that project, which was funded by the AHRB. I am also grateful to Richard Hingley and Steve Willis for the invitation to participate in the Durham conference, to J. D. Hill and Steve Townend for comments on the paper's content, to Bill Sillar for permission to use an illustration of his as my Fig. 13.4, and to my other friends and colleagues in London, Leicester and Reading, for their continued support.

Bibliography

Allison, P. M. (1997) Why do excavation reports have finds catalogues? In C. G. Cumberpatch and P. W. Blinkhorn (eds) *Not So Much a Pot, More a Way of Life: current approaches to artefact analysis in archaeology*, 77–84. Oxbow Monograph 83. Oxford, Oxbow Books.

Archer, M. S. (1995) *Realist Social Theory: the morphogenetic approach*. Cambridge, Cambridge University Press.

Archer, M. S. (2000) *Being Human: the problem of agency*. Cambridge, Cambridge University Press.

Bidwell, P. and Speak, S. (1994) *Excavations at South Shields Roman Fort: Volume 1*. Monograph Series 4. Newcastle, Tyne and Wear Museums/Society of Antiquaries of Newcastle upon Tyne.

Bourdieu, P. (1990) *The Logic of Practice*. Cambridge, Polity Press.

Clarke, D. (1973). Archaeology: the loss of innocence. *Antiquity*, 47, 6–18.

Cohen, A. P. (1994) *Self Consciousness: an alternative anthropology of identity*. London, Routledge.

Cooper, N. J. (2000) Rubbish counts: quantifying portable material culture in Roman Britain. In S. Pearce (ed.) *Researching Material Culture*, 75–86. Leicester Archaeology Monographs 8. Leicester, Leicester School of Archaeological Studies

Croom, A. with contributions by Allason-Jones, L., Griffiths, W. B., Hooley, A., McLean, S. and Snape, M. E. (1994) Small finds. In P. Bidwell and S. Speak *Excavations at South Shields Roman Fort: Volume 1*, 177–205. Monograph Series 4. Newcastle, Tyne and Wear Museums / Society of Antiquaries of Newcastle upon Tyne.

Crossley, N. (1996) *Intersubjectivity*. London, Sage.

Crummy, N. (1983) *The Roman Small Finds from Excavations in Colchester 1971–9*. Colchester, Colchester Archaeological Trust.

Dant, T. (1999) *Material Culture in the Social World*. Buckingham, Open University Press.

Dobney, K. M., Jaques, S. D. and Irving, B. G. (1995) *Of Butchers and Breeds: report on verterbrate remains from various sites in the City of Lincoln*. Lincoln Archaeological Studies 5. Lincoln, City of Lincoln Archaeology Unit.

Dobres, M.-A. (2000). *Technology and Social Agency*. Oxford, Blackwell.

Dreyfus, H. L. (1991) *Being-in-the-World: a commentary on Heidegger's* Being and Time, *Division I*. Cambridge, Massachusetts, MIT Press.

Evans, J. (2001) Material approaches to the identification of different Romano-British site types. In S. James and M. Millett (eds) *Britons and Romans: advancing an archaeological agenda*, 26–35. Council for British Archaeology Research Report 125. York, CBA.

Foucault, M. (1970 [2002]) *The Order of Things*. London, Routledge.

Gardner, A. N. (2001) *'Military' and 'Civilian' in Late Roman Britain: an Archaeology of Social Identity*. PhD thesis, Institute of Archaeology, UCL (University of London).

Gardner, A. (2002) Social identity and the duality of structure in late Roman-period Britain. *Journal of Social Archaeology*, 2.3, 323–51.

Gardner, A. (forthcoming) *An Archaeology of Social Practices: soldiers and society in later Roman Britain*. London, UCL Press.

Giddens, A. (1984) *The Constitution of Society*. Cambridge, Polity Press.

Grant, A. (1989) Animals in Roman Britain. In M. Todd (ed.) *Research on Roman Britain: 1960–89*, 135–46. Britannia Monograph 11. London, Society for the Promotion of Roman Studies.

Hartley, K. F. (1988) Mortaria. In H. S. Owen-John, Llandough – the rescue excavation of a multi-period site near Cardiff, South Glamorgan, 171. In D. M. Robinson (ed.) *Biglis, Caldicot and Llandough*, 123–78. British Archaeological

Reports (British Series) 188. Oxford, British Archaeological Reports.

Hawkes, G. (1999) Beyond Romanization: the creolization of food. A framework for the study of faunal remains from Roman sites. *Papers from the Institute of Archaeology*, 10, 89–95.

Heidegger, M. (1962) *Being and Time*. Oxford, Blackwell. (Translated by J. Macquarrie and E. Robinson).

Hird, L. (1997) The coarse pottery. In T. Wilmott *Birdoswald: Excavations of a Roman fort on Hadrian's Wall and its successor settlements: 1987–92*, 233–54. English Heritage Archaeological Report 14. London, English Heritage.

James, S. (2001) Soldiers and civilians: identity and interaction in Roman Britain. In S. James and M. Millett (eds) *Britons and Romans: advancing an archaeological agenda*, 77–89. Council for British Archaeology Research Report 125. York, CBA.

Jenkins, R. (1992) *Pierre Bourdieu*. London, Routledge.

Jenkins, R. (1996) *Social Identity*. London, Routledge.

Johnson, M. (1999) *Archaeological Theory: an introduction*. Oxford, Blackwell.

Jones, S. (1997) *The Archaeology of Ethnicity*. London, Routledge.

King, A. (1999) Animals and the Roman army: the evidence of the animal bones. In A. Goldsworthy and I. Haynes (eds) *The Roman Army as a Community*, 139–49. Journal of Roman Archaeology Supplementary Series 34. Portsmouth, RI.

King, A. and Millett, M. (1993) Samian ware. In P. J. Casey, J. L. Davies and J. Evans, *Excavations at Segontium (Caernarfon) Roman Fort, 1975–1979*, 234–49. Council for British Archaeology Research Report 90. London.

King, J. (1996) The animal bones. In D. F. Mackreth, Orton Hall Farm: a Roman and early Anglo-Saxon farmstead, 216–18/mf.9. *East Anglian Archaeology*, 76. Manchester, Nene Valley Archaeological Trust.

Lemonnier, P. (1993) Introduction. In P. Lemonnier (ed.) *Technological Choices: transformation in material cultures since the Neolithic*, 1–35. London, Routledge.

Lucas, G. (2001) *Critical Approaches to Fieldwork*. London: Routledge.

Marx, K. (1845 [1983]) Theses on Feuerbach. In E. Kamenka (ed.) *The Portable Karl Marx*, 155–58. Harmondsworth, Penguin.

Marx, K. (1852 [1983]) The Eighteenth Brumaire of Louis Napoleon. In E. Kamenka (ed.) *The Portable Karl Marx*, 287–323. Harmondsworth, Penguin.

Mead, G. H. (1934) *Mind, Self and Society, from the Standpoint of a Social Behaviorist*. Chicago, University of Chicago Press. (Edited with an Introduction by C. W. Morris).

Meadows, K. (1994) You are what you eat: diet, identity and Romanisation. In S. Cottam, D. Dungworth, S. Scott and J. Taylor (eds) *TRAC 94: Proceedings of the Fourth Annual Theoretical Roman Archaeology Conference, Durham, 1994*, 133–140. Oxford, Oxbow Books.

Mouzelis, N. (1995) *Sociological Theory: What Went Wrong? Diagnosis and remedies*. London, Routledge.

Noddle, B. (1993) Bones of larger mammals. In P. J. Casey, J.

L. Davies and J. Evans, *Excavations at* Segontium *(Caernarfon) Roman Fort, 1975–1979*, 97–118. Council for British Archaeology Research Report 90. London, CBA.

O'Connor, T. P. (1986) The animal bones. In J. D. Zienkiewicz *The Legionary Fortress Baths at Caerleon, II: The Finds*, 225–48. Cardiff, National Museum of Wales/CADW.

Parker, J. (2000) *Structuration*. Buckingham, Open University Press.

Reece, R. (1991) *Roman Coins from 140 Sites in Britain*. Cotswold Studies Vol. IV. Cirencester.

Shanks, M. and Tilley, C. (1987) *Social Theory and Archaeology*. Cambridge, Polity Press.

Shanks, M. and Tilley, C. (1992) *Re-Constructing Archaeology: theory and practice*. London, Routledge (Second Edition).

Sillar, B. (2000) *Shaping Culture: making pots and constructing households. An ethnoarchaeological study of pottery production, trade and use in the Andes*. British Archaeological Reports (International Series) 883. Oxford, British Archaeological Reports.

Sillar, B. and Tite, M. S. (2000) The challenge of 'technological choices' for materials science approaches in archaeology. *Archaeometry*, 42.1, 2–20.

Snape, M. (1994) The southwest gate, *intervallum* street and fort ditches. In P. Bidwell, and S. Speak, *Excavations at South Shields Roman Fort: Volume 1*, 107–44. Monograph Series 4. Newcastle, Tyne and Wear Museums/Society of Antiquaries of Newcastle upon Tyne.

Summerfield, J. with contributions by Allason-Jones, L., Bayley, J., Coulston, J. C. N., Davies, J., Edwards, G., Henig, M., Lloyd-Morgan, G., Mould, Q., Price, J., Cottam, S., Riddler, I. and Tomlin, R. S. O. (1997) The small finds. In T. Wilmott *Birdoswald: Excavations of a Roman fort on Hadrian's Wall and its successor settlements: 1987–92*, 269–362. English Heritage Archaeological Report 14. London, English Heritage.

Thompson, M. (1979) *Rubbish Theory: the creation and destruction of value*. Oxford, Oxford University Press.

Turner, S. (1994) *The Social Theory of Practices: tradition, tacit knowledge and presuppositions*. Cambridge, Polity Press.

Tyers, P. A. (1996) *Roman Pottery in Britain*. London, Batsford.

Webster, P. V. (1988) Coarse pottery. In H. S. Owen-John, Llandough – the rescue excavation of a multi-period site near Cardiff, South Glamorgan, 161–70. In D. M. Robinson (ed.) *Biglis, Caldicot and Llandough*, 123–78. British Archaeological Reports (British Series) 188. Oxford: British Archaeological Reports.

Webster, P. V. (1993) Coarse pottery. In P. J. Casey, J. L. Davies and J. Evans, *Excavations at* Segontium *(Caernarfon) Roman Fort, 1975–1979*, 250–316. Council for British Archaeology Research Report 90. London.

Wenger, E. (1998) *Communities of Practice: learning, meaning and identity*. Cambridge, Cambridge University Press.

Wilmott, T. (1997) *Birdoswald: Excavations of a Roman fort on Hadrian's Wall and its successor settlements: 1987–92*. English Heritage Archaeological Report 14. London, English Heritage.

Applications of Method and Theory

14   Contexts in Colchester

Hella Eckardt

Material culture, social practice and identity

The relationship between the social practice of consuming material culture and the expression of identity is central to our understanding of the Roman world. At present, however, all too often there still seems to be a significant gap between theoretical concepts of identity and the difficult business of dealing with the complex record of Roman material culture. This paper does not promise any neat and tidy solutions to this dilemma but advocates a *contextual* approach, using a case study from Colchester.

Traditionally, research on Roman material culture has been very strongly dominated by a focus on chronology, spatial distribution and the economy, resulting in some very fine-grained data. The degree of definition in terms of both the artefacts and their contexts is therefore superior to many other archaeological periods. In recent years some interesting theoretical work has also been done on the relationship between consumption and identity (cf. Miller 1995 for a convenient summary). The impact of the concept of agency (cf. Barrett 2001) in particular has led us to view material culture not just as a passive reflection of a society; rather, artefacts are used by knowledgeable agents and play a crucial and active part in the construction and maintenance of social, cultural and personal identity. As part of this theoretical debate we have begun to think much more carefully and explicitly about the concept of identity (cf. Hill 2001; Meskell 2001).

Identity is now seen as heterogeneous rather than homogenous, open to change rather than static, situational rather than universal, and actively created rather than given (Hill 2001, 12). In short, our concepts of identity have become significantly more complex and fluid. As a consequence, the traditional focus on a Roman–native dichotomy is beginning to be replaced by research on a much wider range of identities (such as regional identity, gender, age and class: cf. Hill 2001, 15). While these emerging approaches to identity are central to future work, I would argue that it is now vital to consider fully their methodological implications. However attractive as a concept, is it really possible to trace these fluid and subtle identities in the fragmentary and partial archaeological record? Rather than employing 'identity' as a catch-all label, we need to think much more about which material culture patterns might relate to which specific aspects of identity. This paper will focus primarily on how status

may be reflected in the social practice of consumption.

Status is taken to include not just wealth but also the potential contrasts between Roman versus native as well as military versus civilian uses of material culture. An interest in identity should not tempt us to abandon or belittle research into the complexities of function, supply, chronology and taphonomy; in fact it becomes even more important to 'peel apart' the many factors (including 'identity') that have affected the objects we study (cf. Cool and Baxter 1999).

To address issues of identities, it is probably less important to consider what is being used than where, how and by whom something is used. In other words, we ought to reconsider the concept of 'context' as an investigative tool (Hodder 1987; 1992). While generally agreed to be 'a good thing', context is all too often used either in the narrow sense of 'feature' or as a very vague general term. Nevertheless, archaeology (and in particular Roman archaeology with its rich datasets) is often able to identify the broad cultural context in which objects were used and can easily distinguish between sites of differing character (military, urban, rural, *etc.*) as well as between specific site activities (domestic, industrial, ritual, *etc.*) This paper argues that we should exploit this broadly defined contextual data more systematically in the analysis of Roman material culture. Finally, if we are serious about situational and changing identities and about the multiple meanings attributed to the same object (both in the past and in the present), it is also necessary to study context on many different levels, with the scale of analysis ranging from sites to whole provinces. Thus, a site such as Balkerne Lane may display a very 'Roman' consumption pattern when viewed against the province of Britain as a whole but within the context of Colchester there may still be discernable differences between it and inter-mural sites.

Illuminating Roman Colchester

This paper will explore this notion, using Colchester as a case study (Fig. 14.1). Beginning with a particular group of artefacts (lighting equipment), the context of use will be studied both in terms of intra-site variation and in terms of Romano-British consumption practices in a wider sense. The contextual study of sites within Colchester will then be broadened to include the proportional representation of other groups of material culture.

I would argue that it is important to choose objects

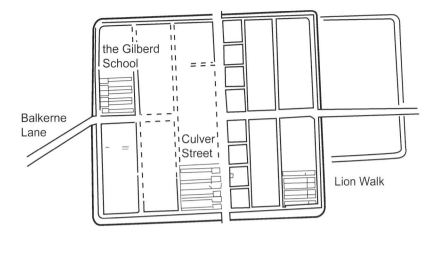

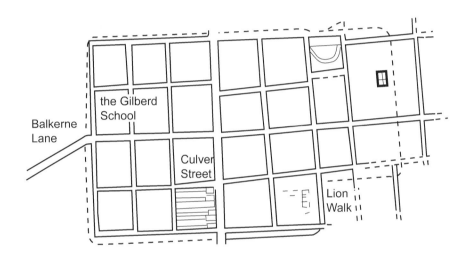

*Fig. 14.1. The Colchester sites discussed in the text. Period 1 (legionary fortress) and Period 2 (*colonia*). After Crummy 1997, 61. Drawn by M. Matthews*

with a clear social or cultural significance and objects where we can identify and clearly compare the factors which have potentially influenced their use, deposition and survival. With regard to an object's cultural significance and relevance to the expression of identity, the concept of 'front-stage' activity is useful. Weatherill (1988; see also Goffman 1971) in her study of early modern consumption suggests that changes to the expression of cultural identity are often particularly marked in front-stage activities, that is, consumption taking place in relatively public arenas and also in the display and use of objects related to particular skills, activities or attitudes to life (in her case, for example, teacups, books, clocks and mirrors). She suggests that consumption hierarchies are not always identical with social hierarchies and that the adoption of new goods, especially when consumption is very 'socially visible', is often governed by attitudes to consumption rather than simply wealth and emulation.

I have argued elsewhere (Eckardt 2000, 8–9) that lighting equipment as a category is socially meaningful and perhaps related to a very 'Roman' identity. Using artificial light has obvious economic implications as it requires a constant supply of fuel but, more importantly, the very desire for artificial light is significant in terms of social practice. Lamps are probably indicative of culturally-laden activities such as reading and writing or Roman-style dining. Compared to the continent, lighting equipment is rare overall in Roman Britain; in the first century AD it is also virtually limited to large military and urban sites (cf. Eckardt 2002a). There is thus a marked cultural bias in the context of consumption and use of these particular objects. Comparison with other forms of imported ceramic artefacts, which appear to be much more widely distributed across the province, suggests that the decisive factors are not simply wealth and access to objects but consumer choices related directly to social practice.

My case study is Colchester, the site on which most Roman lighting equipment has been found (322 lamps and candlesticks out of a Romano-British total of *c*. 2600). I will examine how the use of the two most common forms of pre-Flavian lamps varies on a detailed contextual level across the site (Fig. 14.2). Most of the lamps were unpublished and I would like to thank Nina and Philip Crummy who allowed me access to the lamps and to the site archives.

Picture lamps (Fig. 14.3) are relatively delicate, mould-made objects with a decorated top or discus; in Britain their use peaks in the period *c*. AD 43–70, although some types continue in use in the later Roman period (cf. Eckardt 2002a; Bailey 1980, 126–376). Picture lamps would have burned oil, albeit not necessarily olive oil as is usually assumed (Rottländer 1992). Open lamps (Fig. 14.3) can be either mould produced or handmade; they are not usually decorated, although in Colchester there is good evidence for the local production of open lamps with base decoration (Eckardt 2002a). In Britain the type can be dated to the period from AD 43 into the second century, with a marked pre-Flavian bias (Eckardt 2002a). Open lamps would have burned animal fat or tallow.

Both types of lamps fulfilled essentially the same function. Both are ceramic but they vary in terms of production technique, level of decoration and type of

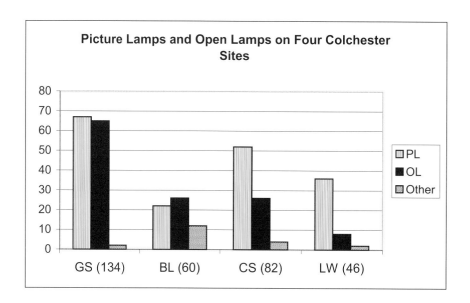

Fig. 14.2. A comparison of picture lamps and open lamps from four sites in Colchester

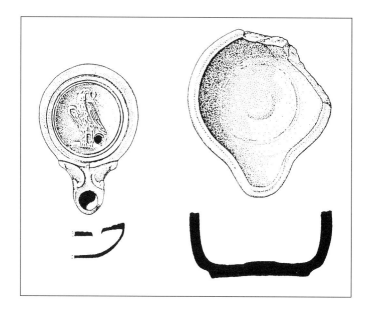

Fig. 14.3. A picture lamp and an open lamp from Colchester. After Crummy 1992, fig. 5.20, 599 (PL) and 605 (OL)

fuel. These differences may relate to status and wealth and perhaps also to other aspects of social practice, an issue explored in more detail below.

I will begin by exploring the proportional relationship between these two forms of lighting equipment across four contexts in Colchester, namely the three intra-mural sites at Lion Walk, Culver Street and the Gilberd School, as well as the extra-mural site at Balkerne Lane. Strictly speaking, no wall existed from *c*. AD 50 till after the Boudican revolt, as famously recorded by Tacitus. Nevertheless, it seems likely that differences in social practice and in the status of inhabitants between the *canabae* and the fortress/*colonia* persisted.

Although many of the lamps were found in residual contexts, the contextual analysis will concentrate on Colchester Periods 1 and 2 (the pre-Boudican legionary fortress and *colonia*) as virtually all these lamps can be dated to those periods on typological grounds. Comparing the proportional relationship between types rather than absolute numbers between sites avoids some of the pitfalls of sample size and quality (see below).

It is encouraging that the relationship between the two lamp types is not uniform, indicating that use, or at least rubbish disposal practices, varied between our four sites (Fig. 14.2). Two sites (Lion Walk and Culver Street) appear to show a bias towards picture lamps while the relationship between the two lamp types appears to be more equal at the Gilberd School site. By contrast, there are more open lamps than picture lamps at Balkerne Lane. Issues of sampling, taphonomy and chronology are discussed in more detail below.

Contexts in Colchester

Contextual information from our four Colchester sites can be used to explain why two sites appear to have a picture lamp bias while open lamps are more strongly represented on two other sites. The available contextual information about the four sites is strongly biased towards Period 1 (the legionary fortress) because it is easier to summarize and interpret structures relating to the initial military construction and occupation rather than the subtle and complex pattern of subsequent re-use and reconstruction on these sites. It seems likely, however, that some status differences (such as the extra/intra-mural contrast and differences in the size and elaboration of buildings) continued into the colonial period. Most finds specialists do not attempt to distinguish between Period 1 and Period 2 material in Colchester as not all contexts can be allocated with precision to one period and changes in the bulk material culture are subtle (pers. comm. N. Crummy). Disentangling consumption practices between the two periods must therefore remain a priority for future research.

At first sight the Gilberd School, Culver Street and Lion Walk sites are quite similar, as all three are situated within the fortress/*colonia* and all contained military buildings which were subsequently reused or replaced in various ways. There are, however, significant differences.

The Lion Walk excavations (Crummy 1984) focused particularly on the centurion's quarters and it could be suggested that the status of the commanding officer is reflected not only in more spacious accommodation but perhaps also in access to high status goods. The excavations at Culver Street (Crummy 1992) uncovered the barracks of the first cohort, an élite unit of double strength, as well as a possible tribune's house; again, the observed picture lamp bias could be interpreted in terms of the higher status of troops and officers.

By contrast, 'ordinary' barracks were discovered at the Gilberd School site (Crummy 1992). The fourth site, at Balkerne Lane, is located to the west of the fortress/*colonia* (Crummy 1984). The *canabae* contained a series of strip buildings, some of which appear to have been associated with iron-working. The very presence of lamps distinguishes this site from smaller civilian sites elsewhere in Britain but the bias towards open lamps may suggest that its inhabitants had less access to (and less desire for) picture lamps.

We next have to consider whether factors such as supply, function or survival rather than social practice could have created this pattern. In terms of their survival in the archaeological record, it should be noted that although both lamp forms are ceramic, the more robust open lamps may have been differentially affected by breakage and fragmentation. As lamps were only quantified by a simple sherd count, this factor could have boosted the numbers of picture lamps. There was no modern selection in the archaeological recovery of lamps as all sites were excavated by professional teams. The large sample includes mainly unpublished fragments, many of which were only found during pottery processing in post-excavation.

In terms of ancient deposition practices and subsequent activity, our four sites of course have different post-Boudican histories; I have examined this question in detail elsewhere (Eckardt 2002a), by studying the lamps' chronological profile and degree of fragmentation, but there appears to be no clear link between the emerging chronological patterns and a preference for either picture lamps or open lamps.

Supply, availability and cost may well have been more important factors. While both forms were clearly available in Colchester, most of the picture lamps were probably imported while many of the open lamps were locally made (Eckardt 2002b). The difference between locally produced and imported products could relate to the relative cost of lamps. While there are no obvious functional differences, their relative prices might also have been affected by the type of fuel and the differing degree of elaboration and decoration.

Differences in the cost of lamps and in the wealth of lamp users might therefore be a significant factor in the differing context pattern in Colchester. Put simply, sites with proportionally more picture lamps are 'richer'. Wealth and status are important areas of identity but there is more to consumption than mere economic ability – clearly it is a question of how different social groups *chose* to invest their funds. The differences lie in varying social expectations and varying perceptions of the 'appropriate' ways of spending wealth (cf. Weatherill 1988).

Essentially, therefore, we are dealing with aspects of social practice: the use of lighting equipment is in itself a very 'Roman' and perhaps mainly military cultural practice, and in terms of lamp consumption Colchester as a whole is a unique and outstanding site. On a broad cultural context level it is evident that different social groups seem to vary in their consumption choices and in whether or not they view lighting equipment as useful and desirable. This paper suggests that these choices may be more subtle than either use or non-use of lighting equipment and extend to differences in the kind of lamps used. Thus the use of the more elaborate picture lamps appears to be especially pronounced on the higher-status military intra-mural sites. Picture lamps may not just simply indicate wealth but act as a cultural signifier, perhaps relating to an 'officer material culture package'.

Context patterns in other forms of material culture

Due to the small numbers of lamps on most Romano-British sites, it is difficult to extend this contextual comparison using only lighting equipment. It might, however, be helpful to examine how other forms of material culture (such as pottery, animal bone, coins and small finds) are behaving across the four Colchester sites. It is difficult to obtain such data from traditional finds reports but it is hoped that future publications will present their material in a way that lends itself to a more holistic and synthetic approach, which aims to examine the interlinking use of different forms of material culture. Only when we draw all the material culture information together can we write a truly 'thick description' (Geertz 1973, 3–30) of the social practice of consumption on these four sites.

It has already been argued that investment in lamps distinguishes Colchester from many other Romano-British sites but we can attempt to identify more specifically how investment in lamps (of all types) compares to investment in other 'high status and imported ceramic goods' across the four Colchester sites. I have used pre-Flavian South Gaulish samian stamps and mould-decorated fragments (Dannell 1999; Dickinson 1999) for this purpose as they are published individually and can therefore be directly compared against lamp fragments, which were also individually recorded. Such a simple comparison also serves to highlight differences in sample quality and size between sites.

As expected, more samian ware than lamps is found on most sites. This difference is perhaps especially marked on the extramural site of Balkerne Lane (Fig. 14.4). Again, we can identify consumption choices, which relate directly to social practice, in this case with a higher likelihood of investment in tableware rather than lamps. Rather surprisingly, this comparison also shows that the Gilberd School site is not just different in terms of having significant numbers of open lamps but that in general the quantities of lamps are very high compared to contemporary samian (Fig. 14.4). This could be the result of specific choices related to the types of samian used but quantified data on undecorated and non-stamped samian from the Gilberd School site is unfortunately not available from the published report. In general, this result nevertheless serves as a useful example of how contextual analysis of finds can reveal patterns which can then alert us to site-specific activities and consumption practices and which should be fed back into the interpretation and analysis of those sites.

We can further broaden our contextual analysis to incorporate other forms of material culture unrelated to lighting equipment. Cool and Price (1995) published the proportional representation of functional categories within the glass assemblage from Colchester and suggested (1995, 229) that first-century containers, as opposed to serving and drinking vessels, are under-represented in Balkerne Lane. This might be linked to a specifically military consumption pattern (cf. Cool and Baxter 1999, 83–87) and supports the intra/extra-mural contrast already identified. In general, we are once again observing the reflection of differences in social practice. Glass is used on all four sites but varying economic ability or wealth and, more importantly, a varying willingness or desire to invest in particular forms associated with either front-stage activities such as dining or back-stage activities such as storage may be reflected in the proportional representation of functional forms.

Luff (1993, 45–7, 128–36), in her analysis of the animal bone from Colchester, suggests that the bone assemblage from the extra-mural area at Balkerne Lane is dominated by cattle (followed by sheep) and therefore varies from the intramural sites where pig and cattle are very strongly represented. She suggests that the intramural dietary pattern relates to a very 'Roman' or, perhaps more particularly, Gallo-Roman military identity. The strong representation of cattle and pig is thought to be characteristic of Roman Britain, in particular of military and urban sites (King 1991, 16–17; 1999). The relatively high representation of pigs has been linked to high status and Gallo-Roman consumption practices (Dobney 2001, 36–7).

Another interesting zoo-archaeological pattern is the unusually high proportion of roe deer bones on the Gilberd School site (Luff 1993, 45), which has already been identified as different in terms of the lamp and samian assemblages. The presence of deer may be interpreted in terms of high status, with hunting as a leisure pursuit, or conversely as a sign of low status, where the site's inhabitants are forced to rely on hunting to supplement their diet (Luff 1993, 135–6).

Coins, as probably the most closely dated artefacts on

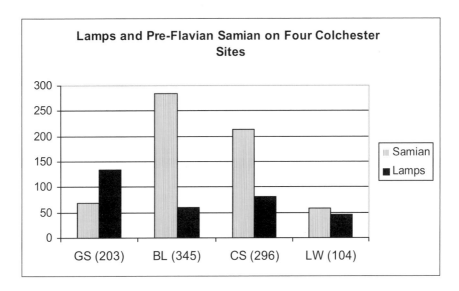

Fig. 14.4. A comparison of pre-Flavian Samian and lamps from four sites in Colchester

Context patterns and small finds

a site, can also be used to highlight differences between our sites. Reece (1987, fig. 10) illustrates coin loss patterns across Colchester sites compared to the mean values from towns in Britain. He identifies differences in site activities as well as an overall high early coin loss pattern in Colchester, indicating its elevated early position when compared to other Romano-British towns. The high status of Colchester in the pre-Flavian period when compared to the rest of the province has already been highlighted with regard to lamps and other forms of material culture. The relationship between regular issues and Claudian copies amongst the pre-Flavian coins also varies across our four sites (Fig. 14.5). Thus Davies (1992, 293; cf. Kenyon 1987) suggests that the Gilberd School site has yielded an unusually high proportion of Claudian copies. A similar pattern may be evident in Culver Street as well. The Gilberd School site is also characterised by a predominance of low denomination issues. Such differences in the value and origin of the coins used may well relate to differential coin supply and use.

Context patterns and small finds

The number of small finds dated to the first century is too small to allow for meaningful comparisons between the Colchester sites and I shall therefore consider material from the whole of the Roman period in order to identify potential differences between our sites.

Cool, Lloyd-Morgan and Hooley (1995, 1626–7) and Cool and Baxter (2002) argue that the proportional representation of functional categories can be related to site activities and 'identity' while Cooper (2000, 82–4) suggests that the result is often too blurred by patterns of ancient loss, of survival in the archaeological record and of modern recovery. It might therefore be more helpful to focus on the proportional relationship between *selected*

artefacts rather than whole assemblages in order to compare sites. Examples could include objects of similar size and material (*e.g.* number of writing equipment items out of the total bronze and iron assemblage) or objects serving the same function but differing in their materials. Thus Cooper (2000, 84–5) uses the relative proportions of bronze and bone hairpins as an indicator of wealth and access to expensive materials. This approach appears to indicate some differences between sites on the provincial level, with a suggested ratio between bronze and bone hairpins of about 1:7 in Colchester but about 1:10 in Leicester. Examining only our four domestic settlement sites, the ratio for Colchester is in fact similar to that in Leicester at about 1:10. This would therefore indicate that the relative representation of bronze and bone hairpins at about 1:10 acts as a benchmark across urban sites (*i.e.* the average frequency with which these objects reach the archaeological record) rather than as an indicator of differential investment into female status objects. Further work is now needed to identify whether differences exist between more broadly defined contexts (*e.g.* urban, military and rural). There may nevertheless be slight differences between our four sites (Table 14.1). All four assemblages are dominated by bone hairpins but while three have the expected ratio of about 1:10, Lion Walk has a ratio of about 1:6. This may be related to the presence of substantial high status court-yard houses at Lion Walk (cf. Crummy 1984, 52–66).

In future work, it will be important to conduct such comparisons between sites of more strongly differentiated character (military *versus* urban *versus* rural) and sites from different parts of the Roman Empire to establish whether patterns relate to specific social practices or to general factors such as taphonomy or regional patterns of supply.

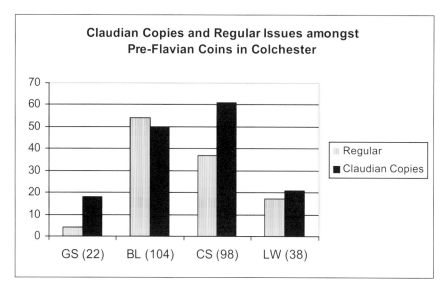

Fig. 14.5. A comparison of pre-Flavian coins from four sites in Colchester

Table 14.1. Hairpins of different materials on four sites in Colchester

	Gilberd School	*Balkerne Lane*	*Culver Street*	*Lion Walk*
Bone	30	191	227	75
Metal	3	21	19	12
Totals	33	212	249	87

Conclusion

In conclusion, the emerging context patterns are clearly very complex and this should be the expected result. Identities and site activities are multi-layered, potentially contradictory and interwoven in ways which may be difficult to disentangle in the archaeological record.

Thus, in first-century Colchester, the use of lighting equipment, samian ware, glass, bone and coins varies between sites, highlighting differences between intra- and extra-mural areas and even between the intramural sites. For each category of data recent work is available to place these patterns into their broader province-wide context (Reece 1995; Willis 1998; Cool and Baxter 1999; 2002; King 1999; Eckardt 2002a). Our understanding of consumption practices at the Balkerne Lane site changes depending on whether the site is viewed in terms of the province (where it looks 'Roman' and military) or in terms of Colchester, where the *canabae* appear to be of 'lower status' and characterised by differing social practices and consumption choices. Different areas of material culture tell slightly different stories. It is important to attempt to relate the use of various forms of material culture and there is clearly a need for future finds reports to develop a more synthetic approach to the material culture found on a site. Consumption of different things may

change at different speeds (cf. Weatherill 1988) and we should anticipate a complex tapestry of material culture, not all of which conforms to one uniform cultural meaning or identity. It is argued that if we wish to paint a richer and more holistic picture of Romano-British society, 'context' is a useful way of bridging the divide between theoretical concepts and the material record.

Roman archaeology is in a privileged position with regard to context information and sites of differing character (military, urban, rural, *etc.*) can be distinguished with relative ease, but it is now time to exploit this data systematically. At present, this general context information, which in contrast to prehistoric archaeology is easily available, is still under-used in material culture studies. The same contextual method could be used to investigate more specific context patterns and consumption practices (*e.g.*: military *versus* civilian, officer *versus* men, extramural *versus* intra-mural) and specific site activities (domestic, industrial, ritual) but even in Roman archaeology this is of course extremely difficult in practice. Often, studying the proportional relationship between selected types can be sufficient to illuminate varying consumption practices. If we are to take ideas about the complexity and fluidity of social practice and identity seriously we need to try to use context on many different levels, ranging from intra-site variation to empire-wide comparisons. It is only in this way that we can hope to identify the multiple and shifting meanings, contexts and identities postulated by recent theoretical work. In conclusion, I would therefore argue that if we are to write social histories of the Roman world we need to go beyond the *temporal and spatial distribution of Roman objects* and think about the *social distribution of material culture* and this can only be achieved through a contextual approach.

Acknowledgements

I would like to thank Nick Cooper, Nina Crummy and Vicki Cummings for their comments. Many thanks also to Margaret Matthews who produced Fig. 14.1 at very short notice.

Bibliography

Bailey, D. M. (1980) *A Catalogue of Lamps in the British Museum. Vol.2: Roman lamps made in Italy*. London, British Museum Publications.

Bailey, D. M. (1988) *A Catalogue of Lamps in the British Museum. Vol.3: Roman provincial lamps*. London, British Museum Publications.

Barrett, J. C. (2001) Agency, the duality of structure, and the problem of the archaeological record. In I. Hodder (ed.) *Archaeological Theory Today* 141–64. Cambridge, Polity Press.

Cool, H. E. M. and Baxter, M. J. (1999) Peeling the onion: an approach to comparing vessel glass assemblages. *Journal of Roman Archaeology* 12, 72–100.

Cool, H. E. M. and Baxter, M. J. (2002) Exploring Romano-British Finds Assemblages. *Oxford Journal of Archaeology* 21.4, 365–380.

Cool, H. E. M., Lloyd-Morgan, G. and Hooley, A. D. (1995) *Finds from the Fortress. The Archaeology of York: the small finds 17/10*. York, York Archaeological Trust.

Cool, H. E. M. and Price, J. (1995) *Roman Vessel Glass from Excavations in Colchester, 1971–85*. Colchester, Colchester Archaeological Trust.

Cooper, N. J. (2000) Rubbish Counts. In S. Pearce (ed.) *Researching Material Culture*, 75–86. Leicester Archaeology Monograph 8, Leicester, School of Archaeology.

Crummy, N. (1992) The Roman Small Finds from Culver Street. In P. Crummy *Excavations at Culver Street, The Gilberd School and Other Sites in Colchester, 1971–85*, 140–205. Colchester, Colchester Archaeological Trust.

Crummy, P. (1984) *Excavations at Lion Walk, Balkerne Lane and Middleborough, Colchester, Essex*. Colchester, Colchester Archaeological Trust.

Crummy, P. (1992) *Excavations at Culver Street, The Gilberd School and Other Sites in Colchester, 1971–85*. Colchester, Colchester Archaeological Trust.

Crummy, P. (1997) *City of Victory: the story of Colchester – Britain's first Roman town*. Colchester, Colchester Archaeological Trust.

Dannell, G. B. (1999) Decorated South Gaulish samian. In R. P. Symonds, and S. Wade *Roman Pottery from Excavations in Colchester, 1971–86*, 13–74. Colchester, Colchester Archaeological Trust.

Davies, J. A. (1992) Overview of the Culver Street and Gilberd School coins. In P. Crummy *Excavations at Culver Street, The Gilberd School and Other Sites in Colchester, 1971–85*, 290–4. Colchester, Colchester Archaeological Trust.

Dickinson, B. (1999) Samian stamps. In R. P. Symonds and S. Wade *Roman pottery from excavations in Colchester, 1971– 86, 120–36*. Colchester, Colchester Archaeological Trust.

Dobney, K. (2001) A place at the table: the role of vertebrate zooarchaeology within a Roman research agenda. In S. James and M. Millett (eds) *Britons and Romans: advancing an archaeological agenda*, 36–45. York, Council for British Archaeology.

Eckardt, H. (2000) Illuminating Roman Britain. In G. Fincham, G. Harrison, R. Holland and L. Revell (eds) *TRAC 1999, Proceedings of the ninth Theoretical Roman Archaeology Conference, Durham 1999*. Oxford, Oxbow Books, 8–21.

Eckardt, H. (2002a) *Illuminating Roman Britain*. Montagnac, Instrumentum.

Eckardt, H. (2002b) The Colchester lamp factory. *Britannia* 33, 77–94.

Geertz, C. (1973) *The interpretation of cultures: selected essays*. New York, Basic Books.

Goffman, E. (1971; first published 1959). *The Presentation of Self in Everyday Life*. London, Pelican Books.

Hill, J. D. (2001) Romanisation, gender and class: recent approaches to identity in Britain and their possible consequences. In S. James and M. Millett (eds) *Britons and Romans: advancing an archaeological agenda*. CBA Research Report 125, 12–18. York, Council for British Archaeology.

Hodder, I. (1987) The contextual analysis of symbolic meanings. In I. Hodder (ed.) *The Archaeology of Contextual Meanings*, 1–10. Cambridge, Cambridge University Press.

Hodder, I. (1992) *Theory and Practice in Archaeology*. London and New York, Routledge.

Kenyon, R. (1987) The Claudian coinage. In N. Crummy (ed.) *The Coins from Excavations in Colchester 1971–9*, 24–41. Colchester, Colchester Archaeological Trust.

King, A. (1991). Food production and consumption – meat. In R. F. J. Jones (ed.) *Britain in the Roman Period: recent trends*, 15–20. Sheffield, J. R. Collis Publications.

King, A. (1999) Diet in the Roman world: a regional inter-site comparison of the mammal bones. *Journal of Roman Archaeology* 12, 168–202.

Luff, R. (1993) *Animal Bones from Excavations in Colchester, 1971–85*. Colchester, Colchester Archaeological Trust.

Meskell, L. (2001) Archaeologies of identity. In I. Hodder (ed.) *Archaeological Theory Today*, 187–213. Cambridge, Polity Press.

Miller, D. (ed.) (1995) *Acknowledging Consumption: a review of new studies*. London, Routledge.

Reece, R. (1987) The Roman coins. In N. Crummy (ed.) *The Coins from Excavations in Colchester 1971–9*, 17–23. Colchester, Colchester Archaeological Trust.

Reece, R. (1995). Site finds in Roman Britain. *Britannia* 26, 179–206.

Rottländer, R. C. A. (1992) Der Brennstoff römischer Beleuchtungskörper. *Jahresberichte aus Augst und Kaiseraugst* 13, 225–9.

Weatherill, L. (1988) *Consumer Behaviour and Material Culture in Britain 1660–1760*. London, Methuen.

Willis, S. (1998) Samian pottery in Britain: exploring its distribution and archaeological potential. *The Archaeological Journal* 155, 82–133.

15   Creating Order in Waste: Structured Deposits in Roman Tienen

Marleen Martens

Introduction

From 1997 up to the beginning of 2003 a large part of the southwestern periphery and the southwestern cemetery of the Roman small town of Tienen (Belgium) has been excavated (Figs. 15.1 and 15.2). In total 18 hectares have been explored. From the settlement more than 3,500 features and in the cemetery approximately 1,100 tombs were excavated. The size of the excavation and the nature of the features and finds gradually led to the formulation of a series of research aims. Next to the traditional questions of technological, economic and social organization, we would also like to study human behaviour with an emphasis towards material culture (*e.g.* waste deposition) and towards the supernatural. For these purposes the design of a customised method of post-excavation study was necessary. In this paper I would like to elaborate on a recently developed methodology to analyse archaeological contexts. The development of the research methodology was to be ready and tested before the beginning of the post-excavation study in 2003. Before elaborating on the research method a characterisation of the town will be presented in a brief overview of the archaeological investigation in Tienen.

The Roman 'small town' of Tienen

The small town or *vicus* of Tienen is situated in the fertile loess area of the *civitas* Tungrorum, in the province of Germania Inferior. The town developed on the road from Cologne to Boulogne about 30 kilometres from the *civitas* capital Tongeren. The settlement stretches out over a plateau, bordered on three sides by small rivers. The extent of the settlement can be estimated at 60 ha. and can therefore be classified as quite a large 'small town'.

In the seventies a systematic study by Mertens (1972) of the accidental finds in the settlement offered evidently quite an accurate description of the general characteristics of the Roman small town. Since the eighties three excavation campaigns have brought to light a lot of information on the socio-economic development and character of the town. During the first campaign in 1982 a team from the museum of Tienen (Thomas 1983) excavated a Claudian cellar and a third-century pottery kiln in the southern part of the town. In 1995–6 a team from the Institute of Archaeological Heritage of Flanders

excavated a site in the western part of the town (Vanderhoeven *et al.* 2002: 133–60). On each side of a pebbled road leading to the small town of Elewijt a granary of at least 60 m in length and a bathhouse of the Flavian period were laid out. At the beginning of the second century these buildings were demolished and replaced by houses with a common portico facing the street. Around the houses, pits with iron slag and waste of copper-alloy production were found. Other pits contained waste of the processing of animal bone into secondary products such as marrow or fat. Apart from its obvious residential deployment this area clearly also fulfilled both artisanal and commercial functions. Between 1997 and the beginning of 2003 a large area of the southwestern periphery, as well as the complete southwestern cemetery, of the *vicus* has been excavated on a site called Grijpenveld. Although only a few contexts have been studied until now, it is possible to give a short overview of the different periods of occupation in the settlement.

In the Tibero-Claudian era a large ditched enclosure of 60m by 60m (Martens *et al.* 2003:401–16) dominated the area. The enclosure had an entrance to the north, facing a road and the centre of the town. In the northwest corner of the enclosure a building of between 9 and 25m in length was situated. What is remarkable about this enclosure is that, apart from some animal teeth, the ditch was completely empty except for a very rich deposition to either side of the entrance. Here lay a very dense layer consisting of burnt clay, charcoal, burnt bone, a mass of ceramic debris and some small finds (cf. Tuffreau-Libre 1994). In order to study the deposition process of the material we have wet-sieved the complete layer per square metre. Because of the special nature of this collection we will briefly sum up the finds.

The ceramic remains can be divided into two groups by function: tableware and ceramic containers. The minimum number of individuals are counted based on the rims, bases, handles and decoration, except for the salt containers for reasons which will become clear further on. The tableware consists of 18 pieces of samian ware of Italo-Gaulish origin and from the South of Gaul, 8 fine ware cups from the workshops of Cologne or Neuss, 55 pieces of *Terra Nigra*, 9 pieces of *Terra Rubra* and three jugs in local ware. The category of ceramic containers consists of 9 pieces of dolia and 38 pieces of the so-called *kurkurnes*

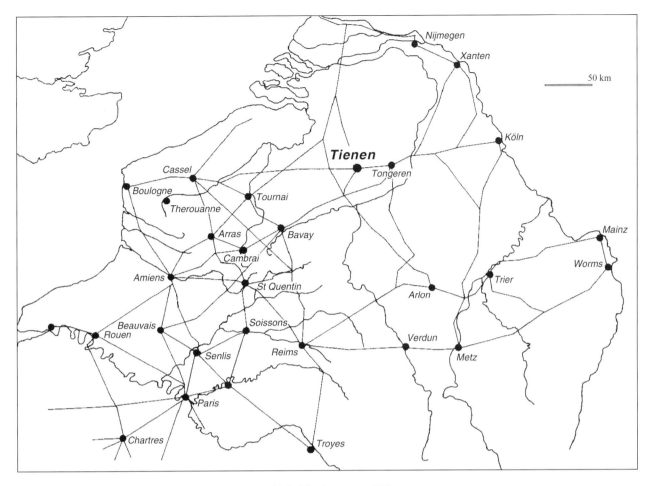

Fig. 15.1. The location of Tienen

(handmade calcite-tempered ware from the Ardenne-Eifel region) known elsewhere to have contained a preparation of thrushes (specifically in an example from Nijmegen), though they may also have simply been cooking vessels. Thanks to the sieving operation we have been able to collect no less than 32,862 fragments of salt containers, corresponding to a weight of 39.86 kilograms. We estimated that there are a minimum number of 40 individual examples of these vessels. This number was obtained by dividing the total weight by the weight of an almost complete example found in Kesteren, in the province of Gelderland, The Netherlands; the type is known as 'thin-walled orange-red ware' (Van den Broeke 1996).

Among the other objects, we have fragments of bracelets and beads of glass, an intaglio of 3–coloured glass with traces of gold, 4 fibulae and a palmet in copper-alloy, a total of 10 Augustan copper-alloy coins and a large amount of iron objects including 250 fragments of shoe nails.

The interpretation of this deposit will be discussed only briefly. The uniform layer and the distribution of the material in the ditch indicate that we are dealing with a one-event deposition. Furthermore, the presence of mostly imported tableware and ceramic containers seems to indicate that we are dealing with the remnants of a feast. Some items in the finds could be dated a few generations

earlier than the rest of the material: the Italian samian ware, the Augustan coins and the La Tène bracelets. These could be heirlooms, reminders of certain events in the past. We have good reasons to believe that this enclosure was a large ceremonial complex. The indications are that the founders had contacts with many regions of the Roman Empire: the kurkurnes are associated with the *civitas* of the Treveri, the salt originates from the Menapii or Morini, the fine ware cups from the Ubii and the coins, samian ware, sandals and intaglio from various other areas of the empire. The founders must also have had considerable political or economic power to be able to organise such a labour-intensive project. Moreover, there are strong indications that the enclosure was a key factor in the foundation of the small town.

In the Flavian period two roads were laid out, parallel with the side-ditches of the enclosure but leaving the enclosure space untouched. Next to the roads Roman pottery kilns were installed; in both the workshops contained two kilns (Hartoch and Martens 2000: 29–39; Martens 2001: 217–219). Around the ovens we excavated pits with production waste (Martens and Willems 2003: 331–43). In the second century artisanal activities continued to take place in the quarter. A glass production workshop with a glass oven was installed along with a series of water pits. In the third century a temple dedicated to Mithras (Martens 1999: 244–51; Martens 2004: 25–56; Lentacker *et al.* 2004: 57–80) was erected next to one of the roads. The building was dug approximately 1.2 m below the ground level. The superstructure of the temple was built in timber framing. Throughout the area a multitude of pits and ditches from the second and third centuries were excavated. Most of the contexts have yet to be studied. During the excavation some of the depositions in these pits were especially eye-catching (cf. Petit 1988). *Some* examples of these special deposits can be outlined here. In one case a statue of Fortuna and a bowl with copper-alloy objects were deposited on the bottom of a pit. The upper layer of this pit consisted of a concentration of tiles. Nearby, three mortaria were placed at the bottom of a deep pit. In another deep pit a huge amount of intact ceramic objects was discovered; this pit was covered with a very thick layer of tiles and big stones. In the immediate surroundings of this pit another square shallow pit contained three complete dog skeletons and a horse skull. Not far from this a further pit contained a statue of the goddess Venus, bone hairpins, a ring in copper-alloy with a blue stone intaglio depicting a horse, 13 coins, while in samian ware we have a bowl decorated with erotic scenes, two mortaria, and goblets in colour-coated ware; locally-produced ware comprised goblets, cooking pots, incense burners, mortaria and plates (Thomas 1983: 273–75). Very recently a large pit was studied containing the remains of six dogs, many complete ceramics and a terracotta statue from the workshop of Servandus in Trier (Martens, *et al.* 2203: 43–90). Also in the cemetery, intact ceramics and complete or partial animal skeletons were intentionally deposited in pits as well as in the bordering ditch. In the same bordering ditch too a series of inhumation burials were excavated. We have also uncovered horse burials in the cemetery. In the autumn of 2002 the wooden grave chamber of a Roman burial mound was excavated at the edge of the settlement. The complete context has been wet-sieved but the finds have yet to be studied. The grave contained cremated human remains and a human skeleton which had not been burned, as well as complete ceramics, various valuable objects, a statue of Dyonisus, dog skeletons, dog foetuses, remains of sheep and a horse skeleton. Most of these depositions provide strong evidence for the ritual character of the contexts (cf. Fulford 2001). The common elements in these contexts are mostly intact objects (ceramics, animal skeletons and small finds) in combination with the remains of a feast (animal bone, plates, beakers, cooking pots, *etc.*).

Research potential

The size of the Grijpenveld site, the number of features, the nature of the depositions and the excavation strategy are all factors determining the high research potential. The research questions (apart from the traditional ones) were all decided upon during the excavation. Since the discovery of the first structured depositions we were constantly wondering if it is possible to "objectively" distinguish ritual from rubbish depositions. Closely related to this is the issue of how Gallo-Roman society dealt with waste. The importance of finding an answer to these questions is crucial for various reasons. First of all, if we mistake ritual depositions for rubbish, or *vice versa*, this would lead to a completely different interpretation of Gallo-Roman society. Furthermore, ignoring the presence of ritual depositions on a site would, depending on the frequency of their occurrence, bias the archaeological assemblage as a representative sample of the ancient population of products. All of this depends on how the Gallo-Roman inhabitants of the *vicus* dealt with waste (Thüry 2001). Was most of the rubbish lying around on the surface and only occasionally thrown in pits, or was the reverse the case? Why did they throw rubbish into a pit? Was it to fill up the pit or to get rid of the rubbish or a combination of these? How far did rubbish travel on a site? How long did it stay on the surface before it was buried? Can we distinguish different categories in rubbish depositions? Which behaviour is represented by these different categories? All of these questions have to be answered before we can distinguish ritual from rubbish deposition. The motivation to develop a method to resolve these basic questions grew steadily over recent years. The interpretation of the genesis of a context is as important as the identification of the material in it. By producing lists of categories and types of ceramics and other objects in archaeological features only a part of the research potential of a pit is used. The analysis of the formation process of many archaeological records can provide information on behaviour patterns of Gallo-Romans (cf. Kimpe *et al.* 2002; Martens and Vilvorder in press). This subject has rarely been thoroughly examined in past archaeological studies.

Textural analysis of contexts

It is clear that in order to attempt to find an answer to these questions, traditional post-excavation study methods would not suffice. A customised methodology is necessary. To reconstruct the formation process of an archaeological context, the structure of the context needs to be examined. For this, the individual elements constituting the layers of that context should be identified and characterized. Finally, the interconnection and interdependence of these individual elements should be examined. In other words, what we suggest is to perform a textural analysis of the stratigraphically different layers in an archaeological feature. The method is comparable with the textural analysis of ceramics. Textural analysis will reveal the internal structure of a deposit and this should hint at the deposition history of the pit, or other feature. In other words, we have to analyse how and with what kind of material it was filled. At the fieldwork level this means two things. First of all we have to understand the

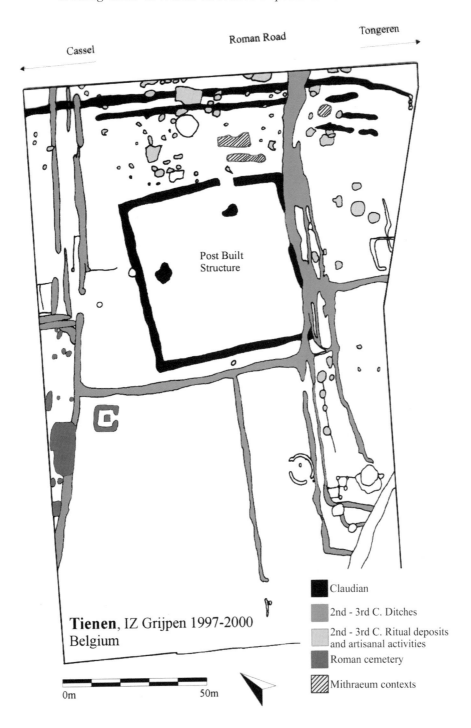

Fig. 15.2. Excavated areas at Tienen 1997–2000

stratigraphy or formation process of the pit and we have to be able to assess possible post-depositional processes. Secondly, while we were still at an early stage of the excavation we had to evaluate if our excavation and registration techniques were sufficient to record the necessary information for this kind of analysis. Of particular interest for the development of our methodology was of J. D. Hill's publication (1995) on the Iron Age of Wessex. The work of Grant (1984; 1991), Derks (1998),

Fauduet (1993) and Simon Clarke (2000) also greatly influenced the way in which the fieldwork was adapted as well as providing input for the methodology of the post-excavation study.

Some examples of adaptations of the fieldwork to collect adequate data for contextual analysis can be outlined here. During the excavation special attention is paid to animal bone. Before lifting it we verify if we are dealing with complete skeletons or associated/articulated bone groups.

If this is the case, they are located and registered in detail within the context. The same is true for complete or nearly complete ceramic pots and small finds. More attention is paid to the fact that all finds should be recovered from a context, including ecofacts like pebbles. When we notice layers with dense concentrations of stones or tiles we expect special depositions underneath it and adapt the excavation strategy by digging with extra care so as not to damage the objects or their associations. From every stratigraphically distinct unit a soil sample was systematically taken. In some cases we decided to dry- or wet- sieve complete deposits or half of them.

Relational database

In order to attempt to answer some of the complicated research questions a specific research strategy was developed. It became obvious that we would never resolve the complicated structures of deposition with human intellect alone. Based on field experience and study of the literature, we decided that the solution was to design a database with variables containing objective information on the feature, the stratigraphical components of the feature and the finds. For each find category a 'Fill in' list of objective variables, not too detailed but also not too superficial, had to be created. For each material category a specialist was consulted. The concept and aim of the database was also discussed with colleagues who had some experience with setting up databases. In order to design the right structured database several days of discussion with the information technology specialist were necessary, as were several testing sessions. Finally, we chose to create a relational database in which the data are placed in matrices that can be interlinked. Logically, the structure of the database reflects very well the aim of the research. At the top we have the entity of the site itself and at the bottom we have the entity of the layers, between which we have the contexts as linked entities or layers. The layer entity acts as a pivot between the data of the site and the data of the finds. As we have already mentioned, the variables or attributes of the database were carefully selected as a function of the research questions. A separate 'Fill in' list is made for ceramics, glass, animal bone, metal, stone, and organic remains. The advantage of this database is that it can be interrogated in all directions. It can serve as a database for traditional research questions as well as for more 'controversial' aims. For example, we could request finds per context or in which contexts South Gaulish samian ware occurs or the proportions of local to imported wares throughout the Roman era. More important for the subject of this paper is the fact that this database is designed to be screened for patterns in the deposition of the different materials in order to examine the treatment of waste in Roman times. Another important goal is to identify the different structured or ritual depositions. As a result we could define the different characteristics of ritual depositions on the one hand and waste on the other. In other words, which are the non-coincidental patterns of structured depositions? For example, we could look for a link between the occurrence of square-shaped features, dog bones, and pots with a completeness of more than 75%; or in which third of a pit is the average sherd weight of ceramics the smallest: the upper the middle or the bottom. The fragmentation of ceramics seems very important for the analysis of the behaviour of deposition. For this reason we started to weigh all the sherds individually; they were all weighed during periods of bad weather and at the same time that the inventory number was allocated. We then quantified the ceramics by counting the minimum number of individuals. This is important for evaluating the completeness of the pots which in turn can be used effectively to determine the freshness of the waste in a context, *e.g.* was the rubbish lying around on the surface for many years or were broken pots immediately thrown into a pit? A ritual deposition could contain more complete (not intact!) pots than a layer of waste that has been lying around at the surface and finally ends up in a pit. The average sherd weight would also be higher in the first case. Of course, great care should be taken while interpreting these results. A fresh pottery dump can also contain high average sherd weights and many complete pots. If an individual pot consists of fragments spread over different layers or features, this is also registered in the database. This method is very useful for examining the spread and movement of objects and waste over the site and what this could reveal. The aim of the database is to uncover the structure of depositions and, if possible, to make a classification of different types of layers of depositions, each with its own definition. This would involve average sherd weight, the degree of completeness of pots, the type of pots, the minimum number of individuals (MNI) of pots, the occurrence of fragmented animal bone, articulated bone groups or complete carcasses and the presence or absence of different categories of small finds. This information, in combination with the shape of the feature and the layer, could provide more insight about the context, how it was formed and what happened to different objects before they were deposited, completely or partly. The contribution of the integration of the sieved samples still remains to be examined.

The excavation on the Grijpenveld in Tienen seems to be a good opportunity to test this methodology. In the settlement we have excavated more than 3,500 features and in the cemetery we have more then 1,100 graves. These numbers should be sufficient to ensure statistical relevance. Another advantage is that we have already defined some characteristics of ritual depositions, which we can then refine.

As a conclusion we would like to formulate a critique to our research. First of all, the database is still in its design stage, as is the methodology to interrogate it. The research aims are very ambitious and may not be achievable. The subject of research is very delicate and open to criticism. However, we will attempt to categorise and identify different categories of waste and at the same time expose possible ritual depositions. The different categories of ritual depositions should be identified in turn, so it could become possible to reconstruct different types of ritual behaviour in Gallo-Roman Tienen. These patterns should be compared with patterns in other regions and also with different settlement categories: towns, villas and small-scale rural settlements. The integration of the data of the Iron Age site in our excavation area could also bring to light possible continuities in the behaviour of ritual deposition.

Conclusion

The research into the behaviour of the Gallo-Roman people towards waste on the one hand and ritual on the other hand should take up a more important place in Roman archaeological studies. These contexts deliver the material we work with and interpret every day. We study Roman finds as a direct reflection of Roman material culture without fully understanding the processes which made it possible for the objects to end up in our hands on the excavation. One of the aims of archaeology is to understand and reconstruct Roman society and one of the aspects of that research must be to explain how these finds became part of a context. This would undoubtedly lead us to a greater insight into lifestyle and culture in Roman times.

Bibliography

Clarke, S. (2000) In search for a different Roman period: the finds assemblage at the Newstead military complex. *TRAC 99. Proceedings of the Ninth Annual Theoretical Roman Archaeology Conference Durham 1999*, 22–9. Oxfrod, Oxbow.

Derks, T. (1998) Gods, temples and ritual practices. The transformation of religious ideas and values in Roman Gaul. *Amsterdam Archaeological Studies* 2. Amsterdam.

Fauduet, I. (1993) *Les temples de tradition celtique en Gaule Romaine*. Paris.

Fulford, M. (2001) Links with the past: persuasive "ritual" behaviour in Roman Britain. *Britannia* 32, 199–218.

Grant, A. (1984) Survival or sacrifice? A critical appraisal of animal burials in Britain in the Iron Age. In C. Grigson and J. Clutton-Brock (eds.) *Animals and Archaeology 4: Husbandry in Europe*. British Archaeological Reports International Series 602, 221–27. Oxford.

Grant, A. (1991) Economic or symbolic? Animals and ritual behaviour. In P. Garwood, D. Jennings, R. Skeates and J. Toms (eds.) *Sacred and Profane*, 109–14. Oxford, Oxford University Committee for Archaeology.

Hartoch, E. and Martens, M. (2000) La production de céramiques dans le vicus de Tirlemont (Belgique). Composition des pâtes liée à la fonction des céramiques, *SFECAG, Actes du Congrès de Lille-Bavay*, 29–39.

Hill, J. D. (1995) *Ritual and Rubbish in the Iron Age of Wessex. A Study on the Formation of a Specific Archaeological Record*. British Archaeological Reports. British Series 242. Oxford.

Kimpe, K., Martens, M. and Jacobs, P. A. (2002) *Influence of Mixing Different Food Sources in Ceramic Pots of the Gallo-Roman Site of Tienen, Belgium*. Leuven.

Lentacker, A., Ervynck, A. and Van Neer, W. (2004) The symbolic meaning of the cock. The animal remains from the Mithraeum at Tienen. In M. Martens and G. De Boe (eds) *Roman Mithraism: the evidence of the small finds*. Archeologie in Vlaanderen Monografie 4, 57–80. Brussels.

Martens, M. (1999) Een tempel voor Mithras in de vicus van Tienen, *Hermeneus* 73/3, 244–51.

Martens, M. (2001) De pottenbakkerswijk in de zuidwestelijke periferie van de vicus van Tienen. In A. Schrijvers and L. Van Impe (eds) *Op het spoor van het verleden. Archeologie op de hogesnelheidslijn*, 117–19. Herent.

Martens, M. (2004) The Mithraeum of Tienen. Small finds and what they can tell us. In M. Martens M. and G. De Boe (eds) *Roman Mithraism. The evidence of the small finds*. Archeologie in Vlaanderen Monografie 4, 25–36. Brussels.

Martens, M., Debruyne, T. and Vanderhoeven, A. (2003) La céramique d'un enclos claudien dans le vicus de Tirlemont et la commercialisation du sel au début de l'époque romaine en Gaule du Nord. *Société Française de l'Etude de la Ceramique Antique en Gaule, Actes du Congrès de Bayeux*, 401–16. Marseille.

Martens, M., Hanut, F., Ervynck, A., Lentacker, A., Cosyns, P., Van Heesch, J. and De Beenhouwer, J. (2003) Ensemble détritique ou contexte cultuel? Etude du matériel archéologique et des restes fauniques d'une grande fosse (S 082) du *vicus* de Tirlemont (Tienen, Belgique), 43–90. *Revue du Nord*. Lille.

Martens, M. and Willems, S. (2003) La production et la diffusion de céramiques locales. Les exemples de Tirlemont et de Tongres. *Société Française de l'Etude de la Ceramique Antique en Gaule, Actes du Congrès de Bayeux*, 331–44. Marseille.

Martens, M. and Vilvorder, F. (in press) La céramique à glaçure plombifère et sa fonction cultuelle. *Rei Cretariae Romanae Fautores Acta* 38.

Mertens, J. (1972) Tienen, een Gallo-Romeinse nederzetting. *Acta Archaeologica Lovaniensa* 5, 119–27. Leuven.

Petit, J.-P. (1988) *Puits et fosses rituels en Gaule d'après l'exemple de Bliesbruck (Moselle) I–II*. Bliesbruck.

Thomas, S. (1983) *Vicus Tienen. Eerste resultaten van een systematisch onderzoek naar een Romeins verleden*. Tienen.

Thüry, G. E. (2001) *Mull und Marmorsaulen Siedlungshygiene in der Römischen Antike*. Mainz.

Tuffreau-Libre, M. (1994) La céramique dans les sanctuaires gallo-romains. In C. Goudineau, I. Fauduet and G. Coulon (eds.) *Les sanctuaires de tradition indigène en Gaule romaine. Actes du colloque d'Argentomagus, 8–10 octobre 1992*. Paris.

Van den Broeke, P.W. 1996. Southern sea salt in the Low Countries. A reconnaissance into the land of the Morini, in M. Lodewijckx (ed.) *Archaeological and Historical Aspects of Western-European Societies*. Acta Archaeologica Lovaniensia Monographiae 8, 193–205.

Vanderhoeven, A., Vynckier, G. and Wouters, W. (2002) Het oudheidkundig bodemonderzoek aan de Zijdelingsestraat van Tienen (prov. Vlaams-Brabant). Interimverslag 1995–1996, *Archeologie in Vlaanderen* VI, 133–60. Zellik.

16   Not in My Back Yard? The Industry of Secondary Animal Products within the Roman Civitas Capital of Tongeren, Belgium

Alain Vanderhoeven and Anton Ervynck

Introduction

Functional interpretations of Roman towns have for a long time been the hostage of the theoretical debates amongst historians and archaeologists over their nature. That ancient towns were considerably different from medieval and modern ones is obvious. But how we should estimate their role within ancient society and economy is the subject of a long and ongoing debate. On one side are the advocates of the theory of the consumer city, suggesting that the towns lived off the land, that urban wealth was generated by rural rents and that the towns were at most in a very limited way contributing to craft, manufacturing or industrial production (Finley 1973; 1981; Kuhnen 1995). On the other side are the followers of the theory of the producer city, arguing that, instead, towns were organising the surrounding countryside (Leveau 1983) and playing an important economic and monetary role by 'turning low value high bulk goods into high value low bulk goods' and, as a consequence of this, by generating the tax cycle (Hopkins 1978; Whittaker 1990).

The extreme idea of a consumer city as a parasite town, living from the land, now seems to have been abandoned. Over the last few years more and more researchers have pointed to the role that ancient towns were playing in the field of trade and the production of goods (Wallace-Hadrill 1991; Hopkins 1978). The impact of towns on the organisation of the land and on the development of the Roman economy seems to have been larger than the consumer city model suggests, although the scale of urban manufacturing or industrial production and the assessment of its monetary and economic impact, are still matters of debate (Whittaker 1990; Duncan-Jones 1994). Most arguments are drawn from literary, epigraphical and numismatic sources, and where archaeological arguments are invoked there is a tendency to minimise the volume of urban production (Whittaker 1990, 112–13; Wierschowski 1991; Schalles 2001, 446–8).

Following this line of argument, it is also understandable how the public's perception of the environmental nature of habitation within a Roman town in Northern Gaul is strongly biased by incomplete information and modern prejudices. Traditionally, in many people's minds, a medieval town is depicted as a crowded, chaotically structured place, polluted by foul odours, fumes and the garbage of many working places. People

were living in the town but, most importantly, were also working there. In contrast, the Roman town is believed to be a clean, well-structured place, grouping monumental residences and public buildings along the spacious orthogonal street plan. People lived in town but did not seem to work there, at least not in industrial enterprises. While medieval archaeologists will argue that this traditional picture of the poor hygienic conditions and industry in a medieval town is at least exaggerated, it is up to Roman archaeologists to test the rightness of the traditional image of the Roman urban environment.

To get out of the impasse about the function of Roman towns, and in order to gain important new information about the nature of their environment, two important steps need to be taken as part of the abandonment of our traditional viewpoints. The first step concerns Roman society as a whole and is already proposed by Whittaker (1990) and Woolf (1998, 126–9). It consists of abandoning the concept of linking economic functions and settlement types. As an alternative, it can be proposed that, in Roman times, a specific type of craft, manufacturing or industrial activity is not necessarily linked to a particular settlement type, but can be done at all kinds of sites, ranging from rural settlements, to rural centres and towns. These activities were generally financed and organised by the élite and were carried out by more or less dependent workers in places that were technically the most appropriate, whether in a rural or urban setting. It remains for the rest to be estimated how much room there was for small independent entrepreneurs in the economic environment of northern Gaul. The second step specifically concerns the ancient town and consists of a more careful study and evaluation of the archaeological record. Until now, when archaeological arguments are used to discuss the nature of ancient towns, these are generally based on public monuments, (rich) urban dwellings and their social spacing, luxury goods and consumption patterns (Brulet 1996; Rollet *et al.* 2001). Building structures excavated in former Roman agglomerations are often more easily interpreted as houses instead of working places, whilst the purpose and meaning of many less monumental structures remain obscure. Until recently hardly any attention was paid to these less monumental features or to the inconspicuous finds categories they contain. The refuse associated with these smaller structures is often not studied in sufficient detail, which is especially true when dealing with organic material (Dobney 2001). As a result, many aspects of Roman urbanisation remain unclear and its role within the economy of the Empire, a province or even a region is difficult to define adequately (Burnham *et al.* 2001; Millett 2001).

This article pleads for a more careful analysis of the numerous less monumental features, predominantly pits, and of the often countless finds (frequently the waste of craftmanship or industrial production) they contain, and for doing this against the background of the theoretical debate on the function and nature of ancient towns. Of course, it is taken into account that the relation between pits and the finds they contain is already a complicated matter. Indeed, the waste encountered in excavated features often does not say anything about the primary function of these structures. Although it generally comes from elsewhere, it is, however, unusual to move waste over long distances and one may thus assume that in many cases it originates from a nearby place and can thus possibly bear a relationship with the excavated area or its nearby vicinity. In this respect it resembles the spread of the so-called background noise of archaeological plant remains (Jones 1985). Another complicating factor is formed by the (often unknown) patterns of waste disposal within a Roman town. There are, for example, many known cases of Roman dumping-grounds (Thüry 2001, 31–45), which could lead to the conclusion that, within a Roman town, all relationships between waste and waste production centre must have been lost. One day of excavation in any Roman urban agglomeration, however, is enough to realise that refuse never was collected and removed completely and in a systematic way. It is a safe assumption that a lot of waste material can still be found close to the spot where it originated. At the Roman town of Augusta Raurica (Augst, Switzerland) experience has shown that there is often a real connection between the function and status of rooms within excavated houses and the refuse deposited (Deschler-Erb pers. comm.) Finally, it has to be taken into account that waste depositions are not always the result of rational, for us understandable, behaviour. It is now known that arguments that are in our view irrational led to the structuring of depositions within individual features as well as within whole settlements (Hill 1995; Clarke 1997; 1999; Fulford 2001 and the numerous contributions in this volume).

In the following pages we will concentrate on the reconstruction and location of industrial activities in the Roman town of Tongeren, based on the analysis of the internal compositions of finds assemblages of severely fragmented cattle bones and of dug features. We hope that the analysis can sufficiently show that the finds and features are at least indirectly related to each other, notwithstanding the complicating factors mentioned above, and that it is still possible to reconstruct social and economic processes in spite of all the difficulties caused by cultural transformation processes. It is the authors' belief that the case study presented, concerning possible urban economic activities in Tongeren of a kind that was hitherto difficult to grasp, can ultimately bear relevance for the assessment of the organisation and scale of the regional economy in northern Gaul.

Tongeren: a case study

Tongeren (Fig. 16.1) was founded *c.* 10 BC as the *civitas* capital of the Tungri. The *civitas Tungrorum* was created under Augustus in the eastern part of a territory formerly occupied by the *Germani Cisrhenani*, a collective noun given by Caesar to a group of more or less obscure tribes, situated along the left bank of the Rhine and on both sides of the Meuse. Of these tribes the Eburones unexpectedly became famous for their victory over an important part of Julius Caesar's army in the winter of 54 BC and for the subsequent attempts by Caesar to annihilate them in revenge. The origins of the Tungri are unknown (Timpe 1993). They may be partly descendants of the Eburones and partly descendants of a population transferred from over the Rhine. In general, the ethnogenesis of the Tungri and the constitution of the *civitas Tungrorum* still need to be studied. Although written sources are contradicting themselves, it is now generally admitted that the *civitas Tungrorum* was part of the province of *Gallia Belgica* until the creation of the Germanic provinces, after which it was transferred to *Germania Inferior*. In the fourth century it was undoubtedly part of *Germania Secunda* (Raepsaet-Charlier 1995).

Remains of the capital of the *civitas Tungrorum* extend over an area of more than 150 ha, mostly under the present town of Tongeren. The ancient town was founded along both sides of the strategic road from Boulogne to Cologne, on the watershed between the basins of the rivers Meuse and Scheldt. The ancient urban area can be subdivided into four sectors (Fig. 16.2) (Vanderhoeven 2001 159–61; Vanderhoeven *et al.* 2001b, 60–1). The first is situated in the northern, most elevated part of the town. It was dominated by a monumental temple and was probably the official centre of the *civitas* capital. The second sector surrounds the first one to the west, south and east, more or less occupying the northern slope of the valley of the river Jeker. This sector seems to have mainly functioned as a residential area, based on the finds of numerous parts of urban dwellings, often in the form of ground plans of luxurious courtyard houses. The third sector covers the alluvial plain of the Jeker; it probably contained a small harbour, since in the second century a considerable effort was made to incorporate the reach of the Jeker within the town wall. Perhaps this sector also contained industrial quarters, an assumption not based upon extensive excavations within this sector but upon the seeming scarcity of traces of industrial activities in the other sectors of the town (but see now this article). The fourth sector unites the cemeteries to the north-east and south-west of the urban centre.

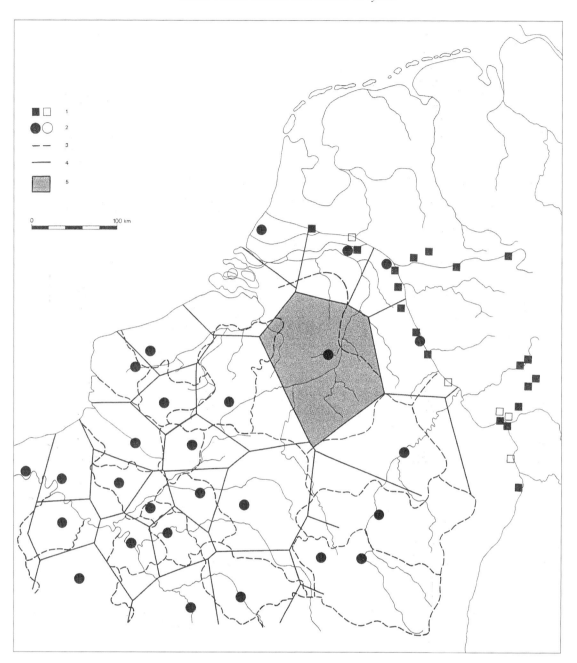

Fig. 16.1. The location of the civitas Tungrorum *and its capital Tongeren within (early) Northern Gaul: 1: army camps (black: certain, and white: hypothetical) (after Schönberger 1985); 2:* civitas *capitals (black: certain, and white: hypothetical); 3:* civitas *borders based on medieval diocesan borders (after Bloemers 1983 and Haselgrove 1990); 4:* civitas *borders based on Thiessen polygons (after Bloemers 1983 and Haselgrove 1990); 5:* civitas Tungrorum

In the löss area around Tongeren, animal bones are generally not preserved, due to the acidification of the soil since the end of the last Ice Age. As an exception to this situation, however, the soil of the town of Tongeren offers good conditions for the conservation of animal bones, thanks to the use (and spill) of large quantities of calcareous mortar during Roman times and the following periods, and due to the presence of a large quantity of bones already in the soil (assuming that the calcium from decaying bones protects the others close by). Since we may assume that the bones excavated in Tongeren predominantly

originate from domestic and wild animals from the surrounding area, we have an unexpectedly rich data set for the study of the relation between man and animal in the countryside of the *civitas Tungrorum*. Up to the present this rich source of information has hardly been used. In the past animal bones were generally not even collected during excavation. Only incidentally were selected finds put at the disposal of palaeontologists (Gautier 1975; Vanvinckenroye 1984). The systematic collecting of animal remains started at Tongeren in the mid-1980s, but, after almost two decades of constant excavation activities, the

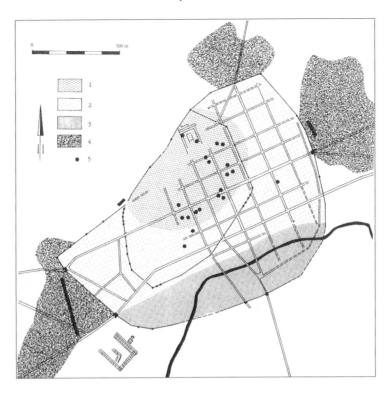

Fig. 16.2. The Roman urban agglomeration of Tongeren, with indication of the major sectors within town (1: official centre, 2: residential area, 3: industrial quarters, perhaps including a small harbour, 4: cemeteries, 5: the black dots indicate the find-spots of monumental architecture or sculpture)

overwhelming majority of the finds still needs to be studied.

Regarding the use of animal products, the zooarchae-ological study of a limited number of samples has already revealed interesting patterns (Vanderhoeven *et al.* 1987; 1991; 1992; 1993; 1994; 1996a; 1996b). It became clear that, in contrast to the Iron Age situation, soon after the town's short foundation period cattle became by far the most important animal for the urban meat supply (Ervynck and Vanderhoeven 1997) and that the slaughtering of animals (mainly cattle) and the preparation of meat (particularly smoked ham) took place within town, and on a scale far beyond the level of domestic needs (Vander-hoeven *et al.* 1991). Moreover, the conviction grew that, in the wake of the intensification of cattle husbandry, the production of a series of secondary cattle products became important and was soon also organised on a large scale within the town (Van Neer 1994; Vanderhoeven *et al.* 1996a; Daniëls 2001). Regarding the disposal, in and around the *civitas* capital, of the resulting organic waste, a synthetic study is still lacking, although the existence of a dumping ground has been described (Vanvinckenroye 1989). Generally, however, the excavations at Tongeren show the common pattern of all Roman agglomerations, *i.e.* the deposition of waste widely scattered throughout the town. Structural depositions resulting from 'irrational' behaviour also continuously occur in the soil archive of Roman Tongeren, in visible and less visible ways but, apart from some rare cases at the Veemarkt site (Vander-

hoeven *et al.* 1993), none of them have ever been published.

In what follows we will deal with features and finds from the 'Elisabethwal' site and the 'Hondsstraat' site, both excavated in the second, so-called residential, sector of Roman Tongeren (Fig. 16.3). These features and finds date from the Flavian period to the first half of the second century. Considering the possible urban economic activ-ities at these locations, attention is focused upon industries based on secondary (non-meat) animal products. The features concerned are large pits, sometimes lined with clay or wood. The finds consist of animal remains, more precisely the raw material gained after slaughtering cattle. For a good understanding of the situation, the chain of events that reduced a slaughtered animal to many finished products will first be described.

From carcass to finished products

It is often noted that, in contrast to Iron Age dwelling places, Roman sites frequently contain archaeozoological contexts illustrating a systematic, large-scale processing of cattle bones. Specific types of bone refuse can be recognised and structures with very similar contents can be recovered from a large number of sites. This pattern is traditionally linked with the shift from a small-scale subsistence economy in pre-Roman times to a large-scale market-oriented economy during the Roman occupation (Roymans 1996). Additionally, it is striking that Roman-

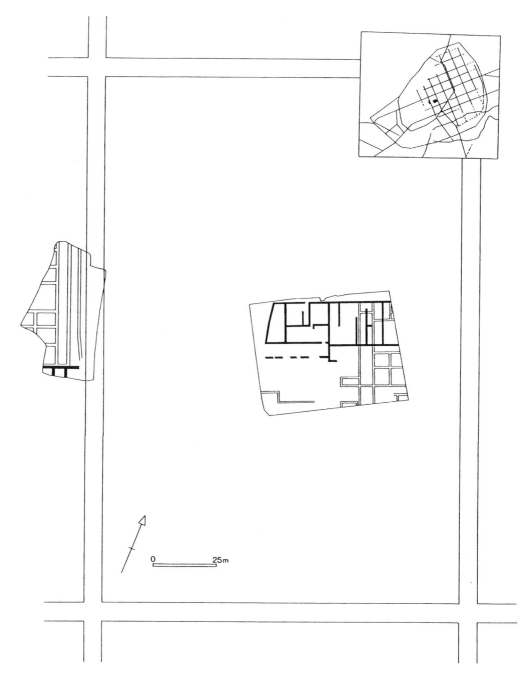

Fig. 16.3. The location of the 'Elisabethwal' (west) and 'Hondsstraat' (east) sites within the Roman town of Tongeren, showing that they belonged to the same neighbourhood (inset: town plan showing the location of the sites)

period cattle bone assemblages frequently show characteristics that cannot be understood by only referring to culinary or slaughtering practices. On the contrary, it has recently been established that industrial purposes must be invoked in order to explain, for example, the high degree of fragmentation of certain cattle bone contexts. While such an assemblage from Zwammerdam (the Netherlands) was originally described as representing the refuse from a 'soup kitchen' (Van Mensch 1974), it is now strongly suggested that the material is the refuse of the industrial extraction of a wide range of products,

including marrow, marrow oil, fat, bone grease and glue (Stokes 2000, see below). In fact, the industrial context of these refuse assemblages had already been postulated much earlier (Askew 1961; Schmid 1972: 48–9) but it was Stokes (2000) who experimentally illustrated the multipurpose nature of the activities associated with the origin of the bone deposits.

Figure 16.4 introduces a scheme representing a hypothetical chain of events describing the reduction of a cattle carcass into a series of finished products desired by the Roman consumers. This scheme is based upon ethnological

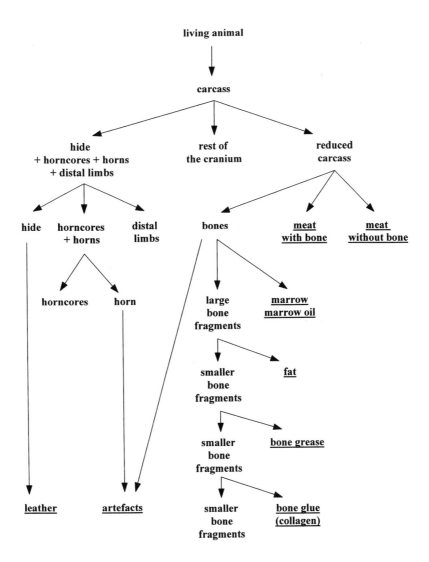

Fig. 16.4. Scheme describing the reduction of a cattle carcass into finished products and specific production refuse (see text) (underlined: finished products)

data (Vehik 1977), published archaeological literature (Rackham 1991; Stokes 2000; Dobney *et al.* 1996; Dobney 2001), the authors' (unpublished) experience with excavated contexts (both in the field and from laboratory work) and especially upon experimental work, reproducing and evaluating the possible acts involved within each production activity. One of the authors' experience with the subject comes from a session organised in 1997 by Stokes and Dobney, during which results were repeated from the extensive experimental work performed by Stokes during previous years.

The starting point is the slaughtering of the animal, a process most probably started by a blow on the forehead, fracturing the frontal bone and sedating the animal. Evidence of this action can often be observed from excavated material (*e.g.* Lentacker *et al.* 1993, fig. 126). Subsequently, the animal is killed and flayed, a process during which the horns, as a pair, are broken away from the skull, making it possible that horns and hide stayed

together to be transported to a tannery. Eventually, the horns are separated from the hide, before or during the tanning process. The horn must then be detached from the horncore to serve as raw material for hornworking. This separation of horn and bone can have taken place at the tannery or at the hornworkers' workshop. It is sometimes suggested that the bones from the extremities of the limbs (complete metapodials or their distal parts, and phalanges) also stayed attached to the hide, and that the fat content of these skeletal elements was used to make oil that served as leather dressing (Serjeantson 1989).

After flaying the next step involves the splitting up of the carcass. In some cases, the meat stays attached to the bone (ribs, scapula), in others the meat is cut away from it (see *e.g.* Maltby 1989; Lignereux and Peters 1996 for a detailed account). Finally, bare bones are left behind at the processing place, in the case of the long bones from the limbs mostly in complete form. However, these long bones are almost never found intact at archaeological sites. A part of them (especially the metapodials or the radius) could have been used for the production of artefacts, an activity witnessed by refuse contexts containing regularly chopped or cut bone fragments (*e.g.* Van Neer 1993; Vallet 2000). A major part of the cattle long bone fragments are broken rather randomly, indicating that they were processed in order to extract marrow. Experimental work shows that a fragmentation of the shaft is sufficient to achieve this extraction. Heating the diaphysis of the bone can facilitate this action and has the additional advantage that (the fat content of) the marrow becomes liquid. When heated, this 'marrow oil' can easily be poured out of the fragmented shaft. It can be used as a top quality product to produce lamp oil, soap, cosmetics or medicines (Dobney 2001). The marrow itself must most probably have been used for consumption and, after heating, easily comes out of the long bone shaft.

Contexts from many Roman sites have been described that contained heavily fragmented cattle bones, much more broken up than is necessary only for the extraction of marrow (see the references below). It has been hypothesised that the bones broken for marrow extraction were subsequently broken up into smaller pieces and boiled, after which the 'superficial' fat coming from the bones was skimmed off. Further boiling could have allowed the bone grease to be released, consisting of the fat fraction *within* the bone. After cooling the liquid, this grease could again be skimmed off. Finally, the remaining liquid, containing collagen from the bones, could be heated again and reduced. Before the boiling liquid became too thick, the bone fragments must have been taken out and the liquid was then completely reduced. The crystallised end result was bone glue (collagen), a product that could be liquidated again by adding tepid water (Stokes 2000 and pers. comm.) Within this chain of events, the extra fragmentation after the marrow extraction must have been done in order to augment the total bone surface, facilitating the extraction of fat and collagen from the bone.

The scheme described above is hypothetical and necessarily remains vague. It does not, for example, explain where the different processes took place (was the removal of the horn from its core done at the tannery, did one boil the bones at the slaughter place or at some specialised workshop?) The craftsmen responsible for these activities also remain unknown. Despite some detailed and confident schemes published in literature (*e.g.* Lignereux and Peters 1996, 70), a more cautious approach is taken here, stressing the fact that, due to the absence of written sources for northern Gaul, it is impossible to be certain about the chain of events within the processing of the animal products. It is even less possible to gain insight into the internal organisation of the workshops. Moreover, it is plausible that differences occurred as a result of local traditions or needs. Certainly, an analysis of the classical texts is not sufficient as a basis for a reconstruction of these kinds of activities. More seems to be expected from careful analyses of internal compositions of finds assemblages, of features linked with industrial activities and of their intrasite distribution patterns.

The Elisabethwal site: evidence for a horner's workshop and a tannery?

The excavation of the Elisabethwal site (Fig. 16.2), carried out in a period of six months in 1997, covers an area of *c.* 600 m². The excavated plot is situated in the eastern part of the residential area of the Roman town, just inside the medieval town wall built in the 13th century. The site's Roman occupation history can be subdivided into six phases: *1* a military occupation dating to *c.* 10 BC (the so-called Oberaden horizon) and consisting of a series of shallowly dug pits and ditches; *2* an Augustan–Tiberian two-ailed stable house of the so-called 'Alphen–Ekeren' type (De Boe 1988; Slofstra 1991) surrounded by pits; *3* a series of Claudian and Neronian wooden constructions of an unknown type, a wooden construction (possibly an aquaduct) and pits filled with settlement waste pointing out the presence of nearby habitation; *4* a Flavian stone building, presumably a courtyard house, almost completely demolished at the end of the first or at the beginning of the second century; *5* a second-century stone building, perhaps a track house, constructed to the south of the demolished Flavian house, with a concentration of at least 16 pits dug on the site of the demolished former Flavian building; and *6* a small number of third-century pits (at least 2) situated in the same area. Although some late Roman stray finds were recorded during the excavation, no features could be dated to the fourth century.

A detailed overview of the pre-Flavian features is published in Vanderhoeven (2001) and Vanderhoeven *et al.* (2001b). The Flavian period and the second-century occupation history of the site (phases 4 and 5) will now be described in more detail, the features and finds from that period being of central importance for the subject of this article. During this period a NNE–SSW-oriented street belonging to the urban street grid was situated in the eastern part of the excavated area. The Flavian courtyard house was build shortly after the destruction by fire of the Claudian and Neronean constructions, an event traditionally related to the Batavian revolt (AD 69–70). While the street gradually slopes from the north to the south, the courtyard house, of which less than half of its ground plan could be recorded, had to be built on an artificial terrace. That terrace was constructed along the street and kept in place by a wooden wall later replaced by a stone one. The house had a gallery oriented towards the street. A few decades after its construction the building was systematically demolished. Even the foundations were completely dug out and removed, the reason for which is unknown. Shortly after, a new construction was built to the south of the previous one, of which we only have the north-eastern corner. In the area formerly occupied by the Flavian courtyard house at least 16 pits were dug. Of these, at least six (labelled A, B, C, D, G and H) are of Flavian date (Fig. 16.5). Although, for security reasons, we were not able to reach the bottom of pit A, we tend to consider this structure to be a well. Pits F and J, the latter showing traces of wood lining, were dug during the first half of the second century. Pits F, G and H showed traces of clay lining. Additionally, on the bottom of pit F a number of large flint blocks were found. A series of other pits (K, L, M, N and O) contained only a few finds. They must have been dug after the demolition of the first, Flavian house and before the construction of the second, second-century house. They represent a short activity, which is of no further importance to the subject of the present article. Pits I, P and possibly also pit E date from the third century and are therefore also of no further relevance to our subject. In what follows, the finds from the four Flavian pits B, C, D and the second century pit F, will be analysed in more detail.

Pit B is a square structure of *c.* 180 cm by *c.* 180 cm and is *c.* 180 cm deep. Its filling consists of a thin layer of charcoal on the bottom of the pit and two greyish layers of sandy loam, each covered by dark greyish brown layers with charcoal and mineralised organic material. These primary fills of the pit are covered by a thin layer of white mortar and lime. Above this stratigraphy are several sagged layers of yellow loam mixed with small fragments of white mortar.

Pit C has a rectangular plan of *c.* 280 cm by *c.* 240 cm. It is *c.* 175 cm deep. From the bottom to the top it is successively filled with a thick dark grey layer of sandy loam, a thick gray layer of sandy loam, a thin black layer of charcoal and a gray layer of white mortar, comprising the primary fill of the pit. On top of it are sagged layers of yellow loam mixed with fragments of white mortar, light grey loam, white sand, black charcoal and, again, yellow loam mixed with fragments of white mortar.

Pit D is a rectangular excavation of *c.* 180 cm by *c.* 120 cm and is *c.* 135 cm deep. Its primary fill consists of a grey layer of sandy loam and a grey layer with fragments of white mortar and tegulae. This fill is covered by a thin black layer of charcoal, a yellow layer of loam, a second black layer of charcoal and a second yellow layer of loam mixed with burnt clay.

Pit F is a more or less square excavation of *c.* 430 cm by *c.* 460 cm and has a depth of *c.* 155 cm. Its fill mainly consists of two considerably thick layers. The lower one is a mixture of greyish sandy loam and green coloured clay, the remains of the clay lining of the pit, and contains a large number of flintstone blocks. The upper layer is yellow-brown and mixed with charcoal and small fragments of burnt clay. During a later period at least three stone pillar foundations were dug into its fill. They presumably supported the front wall of a construction of which no other traces were left.

These structures, located to the north of a house dating from the first half of the second century, are all rather

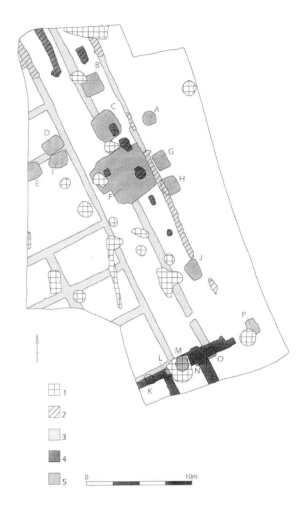

Fig. 16.5. Tongeren, the 'Elisabethwal' site: 1: post-Roman features; 2: foundations (partly) preserved; 3: robber trenches of the first stone building (Flavian to the beginning of the second century); 4: robber trenches of the second stone building (second century to third century); 5: pits dug after the demolition of the first stone building

large, deep and have, at first sight, an unknown function. The characteristics of one of them (pit F), *i.e.* the presence of clay lining and of large flint blocks in the fill, may indicate the presence of a tannery at the excavated spot, but this interpretation is hazardous given the scarcity of the evidence. The clay lining could have been applied in order to make the pit waterproof, for the soaking of hides, for example, while the large stones could have served to keep the hides submerged. Other structures excavated on the site do not add to this interpretation, although it is worth mentioning that in the same period of the origin of the fill of pit F (the second century AD) a construction, founded on pillars, stood in the centre of the area where the pits were dug. This construction could represent a sheltered working area, but unfortunately this cannot really be proven. The presence of a well (pit A) could have had an industrial significance, but it may have been dug for domestic purposes only.

In order to further evaluate the functional interpretations the small finds from the pits were examined more closely. The artefacts from the pits' fills, mostly pottery sherds, only consist of stray refuse. They did not reveal anything about their function, but did provide a dating for the origin of the fill. The animal remains, however, preserved in larger quantities, had a more specific composition. The archaeozoological analysis of the material from the four pits was carried out by the authors during the preparation of the present report. The animal remains from the other contexts from the Elisabethwal site had already been studied earlier (Seuntjens 1999). The four pits discussed here in detail are distinguished from the other assemblages of bone from the site by the large number of cattle horncores found in them. It should, however, be noted that small numbers of horncores were also found in other contexts on the site, amounting to about a hundred specimens excavated outside of the pits, but never found in any real concentrations (see Seuntjens 1999).

The inventory of animal remains from the pits can be summarised as follows. All contexts contain a dominant majority of cattle bones (Table 16.1). The remainder of the bones comprise the remains of goose, domestic fowl, roe deer, sheep or goat, pig, horse and dog. The latter two species presumably represent animals that were not consumed, while the remains of the other species must be consumption refuse. Horncores were present amongst the cattle remains from all four pits. Cattle was also the only species from which this skeletal element was found. Given the fact that it is the authors' experience that cattle horncores are only rarely encountered in consumption refuse contexts from Roman Tongeren (see the inventories in the publications referenced above), this is already a remarkable pattern. In total, around one thousand horncores or horncore fragments have been found in the pits, most of them in pit C (Table 16.2), and, as already mentioned, an additional hundred outside the pits. This represents at least 550 animals, since both left and right horncore specimens are present in equal frequencies.

Calculating the frequencies of the horncores within the category of cattle bones reveals that these vary, reaching 50% in pit C but only 4% in pit F (Table 16.2). When the frequencies are evaluated in more detail, at the level of the individual layers within each pit, it can be demonstrated that in pit B a concentration of horncores occurred in the middle part of the fill. In pits C and D the

Table 16.1. *Inventory of the species present in the bone collections from four pits at the Elisabethwal site (n: finds numbers, %: percentages calculated without taking into account the unidentifiable fragments)*

Pit	B	C	D	F	B	C	D	F
	n	n	n	n	%	%	%	%
Goose	2	0	0	6	0,6	0,0	0,0	1,7
Domestic fowl	4	5	2	4	1,1	0,2	1,1	1,1
Roe deer	0	0	1	2	0,0	0,0	0,6	0,6
Cattle	303	1841	121	225	86,1	91,5	69,5	63,9
Sheep or goat	14	66	10	33	4,0	3,3	5,7	9,4
Pig	29	95	39	81	8,2	4,7	22,4	23,0
Horse	0	0	1	1	0,0	0,0	0,6	0,3
Dog	0	4	0	0	0,0	0,2	0,0	0,0
Indet.	338	213	314	364				
Sum	690	2224	488	716	100	100	100	100

Table 16.2. *Frequency of horncores among the cattle remains for four pits from the Elisabethwal site*

Pit	B	C	D	F	B	C	D	F
	n	n	n	n	%	%	%	%
Horncores	63	915	15	10	20,8	49,7	12,4	4,4
Other bones	240	926	106	215	79,2	50,3	87,6	95,6
Total	303	1841	121	225	100	100	100	100

majority of horncores was found at the bottom of the structure, although only in the first case was a very large number of these skeletal elements present. In pit F a small number of horncores was recovered, dispersed throughout the fill. For conciseness' sake, the exact inventories per structure and per layer are not represented here. Instead, Tables 16.3 and 16.4 present a detailed account of the largest concentration: the bottom layer of pit C (find n° TO97EL/001/509). The observations made on the basis of this subset of material have also proven to be valid for the horncores in the other structures.

Table 16.3 shows that within the bottom layer of pit C almost all bones represent cattle (96%). Table 16.4 gives a detailed list of the skeletal elements from cattle. When counting the horncores, a subjective distinction was made between more or less complete specimens and fragments. The 325 complete ones represent 27% of the cattle remains, the 440 fragments 37%. Taking into account that the 190 cranial fragments (16%) are mostly parts of the frontal, the parietal or the occipital bones broken away from the horncore, it can be inferred that 80% of the cattle remains from the layer consists of 'horncores'. The remainder of the cattle bones are derived from all parts of the skeleton, without a clear selection.

The horncores from pit C are, except for one case, all preserved as single finds and never as a pair. The cranial bones surrounding the base of the horncore are always limited in extent, if not absent. In a few instances, clear cutting or sawing marks have been found at the horncore base. Three fragments from the pits (one each from pits C, D and F) come from horncores sawn into pieces (Fig. 16.6). Following the criteria of Armitage and Clutton-Brock (1976), the morphology of the horns illustrates a large variety of cattle types, with animals of all ages (and without doubt of both sexes) present.

The concentrations of horncores must be related to the craft of hornworking. The traces of cutting around the base of some of the finds, and the fact that the horn was sometimes sawn into pieces while still attached to the bone, are clear references to the activities of a workshop. Similar finds from Augst have led to the same conclusion (Schmid 1972, 47–8). That the majority of finds from the Elisabethwal site does not show cutting or sawing traces around the base does not argue against this, because the easiest technique of detaching the horn from the bone consists of allowing the tissue between bone and horn to putrefy by soaking the horns in water for a few days. After this, the horn can be removed without cutting and the horncore will show no traces.

Strictly speaking, however, the presence of the horncore assemblage is not sufficient to prove the existence of a horner's workshop at the site, because it remains possible that we are dealing with a secondary deposit of refuse originating from a locality at some distance away; for example somewhere in the supposed industrial quarters in the alluvial plain of the Jeker or elsewhere on the edge of the town. Yet such an explanation seems rather unlikely

Fig. 16.6. Sawn cattle horncores from the 'Elisabethwal' site

Table 16.3. Inventory of the species present in the bone collection from the bottom layer of pit C at the Elisabethwal site (find n° TO97EL/001/509) (n: finds numbers, %: percentages calculated without taking into account the unidentifiable fragments)

	n	*%*
Cattle	1191	96,2
Sheep or goat	23	1,9
Pig	21	1,7
Dog	3	0,2
Indet.	12	
Sum	1250	100

because this would imply that a house in town was used as a dumping ground for industrial waste produced at a distance and that the hundreds of horncores have all been transported through a major part of town.

Van Driel-Murray (2001) stressed the fact that the formation processes of contexts associated with industrial sites should be studied in more detail, and that often material found in structures associated with industrial production only represents secondary filling that bears no relation to the industry itself. The fact that the horncores in pit B are only in the middle part of the fill suggests that the collection indeed represents a secondary, displaced deposit. That a real concentration of hundreds of horncores is found at the bottom of pit C and a smaller one at the bottom of pit D, however, can be seen as evidence for a close association between the horncores and these pits. At least it can be assumed that the (primary) accumulation of the horncores was contemporaneous with the construction and use of the pits. Finally, the presence of about a hundred horncores dispersed over the site creates the impression that the horner's workshop must have been nearby. Shortly after the abandonment of the pits, the whole site must have been cleaned and perhaps levelled, a process during which most of the primary refuse from the hornworkers was dumped in pit C, while the rest of the wasted horncores was left on the surface or disappeared in shallowly dug ditches and pits.

Medieval and post-medieval examples illustrate that concentrations of horncores are often found at the location of tanneries (MacGregor 1989; 1998; Shaw 1996; Ervynck *et al.* 2003). The question must therefore be asked whether the horncores from the Elisabethwal site also provide evidence for the presence of a tannery in Roman times. The answer is problematic. In the literature the association between horncores and tanneries is always made upon the basis of the assumption that the horns stayed attached to the hides until they arrived at the tannery (Serjeantson 1989). However, can we be certain that in Roman Tongeren horns did stay attached to the hides, just like in medieval times?

Even if the horncores are rejected as evidence for a tannery, the presence of the clay- and wood-lined pits and of the flint blocks at the bottom of one of them (pit F) cannot be disregarded. It could be stated that perhaps the pits were only used for soaking the horncores, an argument also developed by Morel (1991) for the interpretation of a number of structures at the *vicus* of Vitudurum. Morel described horncores from an arrangement of vats, set in clay and waterproofed on the inside with pitch or resin, but pointed out that these vats were probably only used for soaking the horns and had no function within the tanning process. Other parts of the site, however, showed clear evidence of tanning activities (Martin-Kilcher 1991). The pits described from Tongeren are large and deep, and could have had the right dimensions for soaking cattle hides. One can even state that these structures seem to have been too elaborate only for soaking horns. Moreover, the flint blocks would not have been needed to keep the horns under water but were necessary to keep hides in place during tanning, a process that may well have lasted several months, perhaps even more than a year (van Driel-Murray 2001). The provisional conclusion, therefore, remains that at some time at the end of the first century or at the beginning of the second, a tannery and a hornworker's shop were active near the house at the Elisabethwal site. Most probably, there was a functional relationship between the two, *i.e.* one providing the raw material for the other.

The fact that no large concentrations of (distal) metapodials and phalanges from cattle, skeletal elements that are traditionally thought to have stayed attached to the hides (see above and Serjeantson 1989), have been found at the Elisabethwal site is not necessarily in contradiction with the above interpretations. There are examples of well documented medieval tanneries (*e.g.* at Bruges, Belgium; Ervynck *et al.* 2003) where only horncores and no other cattle bones have been found. It can thus not be excluded that in Roman times too the distal limb bones ended up somewhere else. In the case of the metapodials, for example, the destination could have been the boneworkers' shops (see earlier). Finally, it must be remarked that tail vertebrae are present in find n° TO97EL/001/509, in the bottom layer of pit C (Table 16.4). Traditionally, tails are also thought to have stayed attached to the hides after flaying.

When the conclusion is accepted that a horners' workshop and a tannery were located in the *insula* near the centre of town, regardless of the relationship between the two, this implies that within Roman Tongeren industrial activities were undertaken in an area that, because of the nature of the building remains, would have been attributed only to housing. As a result, this part of the town must have suffered from air pollution caused by the odours produced by the work of the tanners and hornworkers. The water used during production was of course also polluted and had to be discarded through the town towards the River Jeker. It has also to be stressed that the production activities at the site were not on a small scale. A minimum of 1,100 horns have been processed, which could correspond with the tanning of at least 550 hides.

This location is rather unexpected since tanneries, because of environmental concerns, are thought to be located outside the habitation centres (van Driel-Murray 2002). Indeed, at Augusta Raurica, the location of a tannery has been excavated on the edge of the Roman town. Structures found include pits and connecting channels, and the interpretation as a tannery is also based upon a concentration of sheep and goat horncores recovered from the same parcel (Schmid 1969). In another part of that town, however, a tannery seems to have been located within a house in the Schmidmatt area, in the transition zone between the lower and the upper town (Müller 1985). Moreover, within different parts of the upper town there is possible proof for the location of other tanneries (*i.e.* insulae 15, 23, 30 and 31, and near the theatre: Deschler-Erb 1992, 391; 1998, 269–74). Strangely enough, except for Augusta Raurica, and perhaps Tongeren, the central and north-western European parts of Roman Empire seem not to have provided conclusive examples of tanneries located in or just outside of a Roman town. In the Walbrook area of London a Roman tannery has been excavated and even part of a (cattle?) hide, still staked out, has been found. This site has not yet been published, however, and is only mentioned in a popular account (Milne 1995).

Finally, it could be questioned whether the location of a tannery at the Elisabethwal site, uphill from the river, was indeed a practical option. The need for water, however, could also have been accommodated by the presence of the aqueduct nearby or by the use of the well (pit A).

The Hondsstraat site: industrial production of marrow, grease and glue

The excavation at the Hondsstraat site took place in 1989 and 1990. Over a period of 8 months, an area of *c.* 1,200 m² was excavated in the eastern part of the residential sector of the Roman town. A NNE–SSW-oriented street of the Roman street grid was situated *c.* 20 m east of the western side of the excavation. The Roman habitation history of the site can be subdivided into 5 periods: *1* a military presence *c.* 10 BC (the so-called Oberaden horizon); *2* an Augustan–Tiberian two-aisled stable house

Table 16.4. Inventory of the skeletal elements from cattle present in the bone collection from the bottom layer of pit C at the Elisabethwal site (find n° TO97EL/001/509) (n: finds numbers, %: percentages, pf: proximal fragment, sf: shaft fragment, df: distal fragment)

	n	*%*
processus cornualis ('complete')	325	27,3
processus cornualis (fragm.)	440	36,9
cranium	190	16,0
maxilla	8	0,7
maxillar tooth	6	0,5
mandibula	29	2,4
mandibular tooth	6	0,5
hyoid	2	0,2
vertebra (cervical + thoracal + lumbal)	44	3,7
sacrum	2	0,2
vertebra (caudal)	5	0,4
rib	51	4,3
sternum	0	0,0
scapula	9	0,8
humerus pf	1	0,1
humerus sf	0	0,0
humerus df	0	0,0
radius pf	2	0,2
radius sf	1	0,1
radius df	3	0,3
ulna	0	0,0
carpalia	1	0,1
metacarpus	4	0,3
pelvis	13	1,1
femur pf	0	0,0
femur sf	2	0,2
femur df	0	0,0
patella	0	0,0
tibia pf	3	0,3
tibia sf	4	0,3
tibia df	2	0,2
calcaneus	0	0,0
astragalus	2	0,2
other tarsalia	0	0,0
metatarsus	14	1,2
metapodalia	0	0,0
sesamoid bones	0	0,0
phalanx I	6	0,5
phalanx II	5	0,4
phalanx III	11	0,9
Sum	1191	100

Fig. 16.7. Tongeren, the 'Hondsstraat' site: 1: post-Roman features; 2: foundations (partly) preserved; 3: robber trenches of the first stone building (Flavian to the first half of the second century); 4: robber trenches of the second stone building (second half of the second century to third century); 5: pits from the Flavian period, the second and third centuries (the one discussed in this article is indicated with 'A')

of the Alphen–Ekeren type (see De Boe 1988 and Slofstra 1991); *3* a Claudian–Neronian courtyard house, burned down during the Batavian revolt (AD 69–70); *4* a Flavian square courtyard house constructed partly in stone and partly in timber shortly after the Batavian revolt, and finally burned down around the middle of the second century; and *5* a rectangular track house, built shortly after the middle of the second century and demolished at the end of the third or at the beginning of the fourth century. The excavated plot lies within the fourth century town wall, but, apart from some stray finds in the upper layers of the stratigraphy, no traces of a late Roman occupation were encountered.

Of this history of Roman occupation only the Flavian period and the subsequent first half of the second century (phase 4) are of interest here. The pre-Flavian occupation sequence has already been presented in Vanderhoeven (2001) and Vanderhoeven *et al*. (2001b). Only the back of the rich urban courtyard house, dating from the Flavian period and the first half of the second century, could be

excavated. The front, overlooking the street, lies outside the excavation plot. The excavated part of the house consists of a complex of rooms built around a courtyard. Behind these rooms was a gallery *c*. 19 m long with a mosaic floor, behind which there seems to have been an open space where several pits and ditches were dug during the occupation of the courtyard house (Fig. 16.7). One of these pits contained a layer with an unusually large amount of heavily fragmented animal bones (find n° TO89HO/ 001/259) and is therefore of central importance to our subject. The construction seems to have had an irregular shape, with a diameter of *c*. 8.40 m. More than half of the pit was already destroyed at the time of the excavation, partly by the construction of foundations for the second Roman stone building of the second half of the second century, partly by post-medieval pits, and partly by the construction of foundations for a school building in the first half of the 20th century. The pit, with a preserved depth of *c*. 1 m, was filled with a complex sequence of layers. On the bottom a dark grey layer was found, containing a large amount of fragmented animal bones. It was covered by a grey layer of sandy loam, a dark grey layer with charcoal, a yellow-brown layer of sandy loam, another dark grey layer with charcoal, a layer of white sand and a grey layer of sandy loam. The layer with fragmented animal bones probably dates to the Flavian period; the others contained a mixture of material from the first and second centuries and were presumably thrown into the pit at the time of the construction of the second Roman building (in the second half of the second century). At that time the old Flavian pit must still have been visible as a depression in the ground surface.

The bottom layer from the fill of the pit was sieved (using a 10 mm mesh width), yielding an approximate volume of 0.5 m^3 of bone. It was decided to concentrate on a sample of about one-fourth of these finds. This sample represented a volume of approximately 120 dm^3 of bone. Except for a very small number of bones from birds, red deer, pig, sheep or goat, dog and horse, almost all bone fragments from the pit represent cattle. In fact, a vast majority could not be identified to species level with a hundred percent certainty because of a possible confusion between the small fragments of the bones from cattle, red deer and horse. Within the category of finds that were identified with absolute confidence (within this group of three species), however, only one skeletal element from red deer was found, two from horse, and 750 from cattle (see below). This strongly suggests that almost all unidentifiable large mammal bones from the pit also come from cattle. Moreover, it is striking that, except for a few examples, the cattle bones are all heavily fragmented, while this is never the case for the remains of the other species (including those of red deer and horse).

The fragmentation of the cattle remains is so severe that most of them could not be attributed to a skeletal element. Additionally, the bones are not preserved in excellent condition. They have become brittle and the bone surfaces are flaky and, therefore, especially the smaller shaft fragments from long bones, posed problems for identification. Nevertheless, identification of the skeletal element could be achieved for 750 cattle bones. The remaining cattle bone fragments from the sample (of which the position within the skeleton remained unknown) have not been counted but represent a volume that is three times that of the 'identified' cattle bones (three quarters of the sample volume of 120 dm, which in its turn represents one-fourth of the total volume of bones). Expressed in finds numbers, this evaluation must be much higher because the 'unidentifiable' fragments tend to be considerably smaller than the 'identified' ones. Certainly, at least 3000 or perhaps 4000 cattle bone fragments must have been present in the sample volume studied, suggesting an estimation of at least 12000 to 16000 finds for the preserved part of the pit.

The inventory in Table 16.5 shows that fragments of all the long bones were present in roughly equal numbers. Epiphyses were recognised in equal frequencies as dia-physes, and most elements came from adult animals (with epiphyses fused). It is striking, however, that some bones are completely (or virtually) absent from the collection. This is the case for horncores, maxillae or maxillar teeth, hyoid bones, sacral and caudal vertebrae, the sternum, the patella, sesamoid bones and the phalanges II and III. In comparison with the long bones cranial fragments are rare (only two fragments of the occipital condylae were found) as are the metacarpus, the calcaneus (of which only three small parts of the articulation surface with the astragalus were recovered), the metatarsus, and the metapodalia in general. Of course, the effects of differential preservation, fragmentation and recognisability have influenced the inventory, but these factors are not sufficient to explain the complete absence or rarity of the elements listed. An additional check of the 'unidentified' cattle bone fragments, with special attention for the 'missing' elements, did not yield extra finds. The strong impression remains that a clear selection has acted upon the collection (see below).

It is clear that the pit from the Hondsstraat site must be related with the industrial activities of marrow, marrow oil, bone grease and glue production described earlier. Its contents, and the characteristics of the cattle bone fragments, are clearly similar with the Romano-British contexts reviewed by Stokes (2000): Little Chesters (Askew 1961), York (O'Connor 1988) and Piercebridge (Rackham and Gidney, unpublished data). Additional comparison is found in the published Roman assemblages from Zwammerdam (Van Mensch 1974), Xanten (Waldmann 1967; Berke 1995), Köln (Berke 1989; 1996), Arras and Beaumont-sur-Oise (Lepetz 1996) and Augst (Schmid 1969). An early medieval context from Carlisle (Rackham 1991) is the only example known from a site younger than the Roman period. A similar Roman context had already been published from Tongeren (Van Neer 1994) but the bone collection was only roughly and very selectively collected by hand, making an elaborate study impossible. It should be noted that a quantitative comparison of all similar contexts known from the literature is beyond the scope of this paper (but will perhaps be included in a future study). In order to attempt this, the pit from the Hondsstraat should first be analysed completely, and a number of other unpublished contexts from Tongeren and elsewhere in Belgium should be studied. It is clear already, however, that differences in sampling and recovery strategies, together with differences in the level of detail with which the inventories are prepared for publication, will severely hamper any comparison.

Industrial activity at the site can explain the severe fragmentation of the cattle bones but, because it seems that all types of bones present were used without distinction, it cannot provide reasons for the absence or rarity of some of the skeletal elements. Most probably, the missing bones went to some other destination. Horncores, sacral and caudal vertebrae perhaps went to the tannery (see the finds at the Elisabethwal site). The hyoid bones could

Table 16.5. Inventory of the skeletal elements from cattle present in the pit from the Hondsstraat site (n: finds numbers, %: percentages, pf: proximal fragment, sf: shaft fragment, df: distal fragment)

	n	%	fused	non fused
processus cornualis	0	0,0		
cranium	2	0,3		
maxilla	0	0,0		
maxillar tooth	0	0,0		
mandibula	24	3,2		
mandibular tooth	40	5,3		
hyoid	0	0,0		
vertebra (cervical + thoracal + lumbal)	88	11,7		
sacrum	0	0,0		
vertebra (caudal)	0	0,0		
rib	28	3,7		
sternum	0	0,0		
scapula	24	3,2		
humerus pf	40	5,3	37	3
humerus sf	65	8,7		
humerus df	57	7,6	57	0
radius pf	23	3,1	23	0
radius sf	16	2,1		
radius df	14	1,9	13	1
ulna	13	1,7		
carpalia	20	2,7		
metacarpus	2	0,3	1	1
pelvis	38	5,1		
femur pf	37	4,9	33	4
femur sf	39	5,2		
femur df	46	6,1		
patella	0	0,0		
tibia pf	12	1,6	9	3
tibia sf	29	3,9		
tibia df	29	3,9	29	0
calcaneus	3	0,4		
astragalus	39	5,2		
other tarsalia	16	2,1		
metatarsus	1	0,1		
metapodalia	2	0,3		
sesamoid bones	0	0,0		
phalanx I	3	0,4		
phalanx II	0	0,0		
phalanx III	0	0,0		
Sum	750	100		

have stayed attached to the tongue that was sold directly to the consumers. The metacarpus and metatarsus were presumably used to produce artefacts. An unpublished site from Roman Tongeren contained a collection of half-products of bone artefact production, consisting of metapodials that were split up longitudinally (Daniëls 2001).

Some bones perhaps were lost during the flaying and splitting up of the carcass, or were deliberately left at the slaughter place (cranial fragments, maxillae, sternum, patella, sesamoid bones and the phalanges II and III). Remarkably, at the Sir John Cass School site in London, which was interpreted as a Roman butcher's shop, only skeletal elements from the head and feet were found (Milne 1995). Globally, the skeletal composition of the cattle remains from the pit at the Hondsstraat seems to illustrate the interdependence of all crafts using parts of cattle carcasses, and not a selection exercised by the producers of grease and glue.

Some idea about the scale of the industrial activity at the Hondsstraat can be obtained from an estimation of the minimum number of individuals (MNI) represented by the bone fragments. Of course, this is an extremely doubtful exercise given the severe fragmentation and bad preservation condition of the bones. Still, on the basis of the astragalus (a compact, rather robust bone often preserved more or less complete) the MNI could be estimated at 20 for the sample studied, making a total of 80 for the preserved part of the pit. Taking into account that more than half of the structure was destroyed after the deposition of the bone material, the MNI for the whole of the pit must be at least 160, perhaps even more. This means that the skeletons of between 100 and 200 animals were processed at the site. It must be emphasised that the estimation of the MNI is based upon the assumption that all bones from a carcass not used in another craft ended up at the glue workshop.

The Hondsstraat site thus provides another example of an industrial activity located within an urban habitation area. The processing may have taken place within the courtyard house or an unexcavated annex, but the waste certainly ended up in the back yard. Comparable examples of a location of this type of context within an urbanised zone are found at York, Tanners Row (O'Connor 1988) and at Xanten (Berke 1995). At Köln, a clear context of similar bone processing was excavated just outside the walls of the Roman town (Berke 1989), while more waste from similar cattle bone chopping was found amongst other types of refuse at another location, this time within the town (Berke 1996). At Augst, examples are known situated at the edge of the town (Schmid 1969) and at Zwammerdam a similar context has been found in a ditch surrounding a military occupation (Van Mensch 1974). It seems now that we are dealing with a widespread type of industrial activity.

Discussion and conclusion

Over the last years an increasing number of archaeologists have pointed out the complicated relation between features and finds (*e.g.* van Driel-Murray 2001) and between ritual and rubbish (Hill 1995). These warnings seem to bear fruitful results for researchers of practices and ritual behaviour, of ideology and identity. But they also cause some pessimism amongst some of us who try to reconstruct social and economic processes by studying material culture. This last feeling is misplaced. It seems rather that, thanks to the warnings we become equipped with better analytical tools to unravel the complicated relations between finds, the historical contexts in which they were used in the past

and the archaeological contexts in which they are nowadays encountered. Our analysis of the internal composition of a specific finds category, cattle horns and severely fragmented cattle bones, and of a series of seemingly insignificant structures, their distorted relation and intrasite distribution within a context of a provincial Roman town led us to several conclusions. These conclusions may have relevance for our perception of the scale and organisation of urban industrial activities, which became a spin off of the stock breeding system. They make us also think about the urban environment and the nature of ancient cities. Finally they may stimulate a more careful excavation and detailed analysis of less visible features and finds.

From the beginning of the Roman period the stock-breeding regime of the *civitas Tungrorum* changed from a domestic mode of production to a market-oriented system by focusing on cattle raising. At least since the Flavian period, and perhaps even earlier, a variety of secondary products such as objects in bone, leather and horn, marrow, marrow oil, fat, bone grease and glue were processed in a systematic and organised manner. Most importantly, it could be demonstrated that at least a substantial part of these activities was situated in the so-called residential sector of Roman Tongeren (Fig. 16.2), on the site of a demolished élite residence and in the back yard of an existing one, located at the Elisabethwal site and the Hondsstraat site respectively. This implies that the local élites of the Tungri were involved, if not in the actual working process then at least in its organisation. In terms of socio-economic meaning, we must speak of urban industries instead of homecrafts. The volume of production leftovers is simply too large to suggest production only for domestic needs. This implies that, most probably, the richer part of urban society made a considerable amount of money out of these industries, and not only out of their rural enterprises as is traditionally thought. The alternative idea, stating that rich house owners sub-rented a part of their living place to a sort of 'urban middle class' of craftsmen, is more difficult to substantiate. We would expect this middle class to settle in less luxurious dwellings, perhaps even in their own urban quarters. In fact we know of track houses in the *vici* of the *civitas Tungrorum*, associated with the same kind of industrial waste as was described in this article (Vanderhoeven *et al.* 2001a; 2002).

The finds from the Elisabethwal and Hondsstraat sites suggest that production activities were not on a small scale and must therefore have had a considerable environmental impact upon the neighbourhood (producing noise, smell, and other forms of pollution). This observation must now be taken into account within our perception of the nature of Roman towns and can perhaps also lead to renewed attention being paid to historical data about environmental concerns in ancient towns, such as the inscriptions about pollution on monuments (Hanoune 2001–2) or the classical texts on pollution in cities (Goguey 2001–2). Even considering Tongeren alone, the question must be asked whether the presence of industrial activities was perceived as a nuisance or was largely tolerated. Perhaps the present-day attitude of 'not in my back yard!' was not valid within Gallo-Roman urban society? It is possible that the industrial waste was systematically removed and that the material we encounter was simply the rubbish of the last production, left on the site after the abandonment and/or destruction of the working facilities. This does not, however, alter the fact that the production process itself must have caused a great deal of nuisance, at least according to our present-day perceptions. The Elisabethwal and Hondsstraat sites in Tongeren were thus more than just living areas, in contradiction to the idea that most industrial activities must have been situated at the edge of town or even at some distance from it (see *e.g.* van Driel-Murray 2001 for tanneries). If the large-scale urban industries that we have observed in the so-called residential sector of Tongeren turn out to be a part of more widespread practices, they may then shine new light on the nature of provincial Roman towns. Of course, the sites from Tongeren do not provide the first archaeological evidence for the presence of industry in Roman towns (see *e.g.* Richmond 1966 for workshops in Romano-British towns; Poulter 1992 for the location of workshops in Nicopolis ad Istrum, Bulgaria; and Rüger 1969 and Rieche and Schalles 1987 for Xanten) but the gradual accumulation of examples and case studies will make the mixture of industrial and other activities within Roman habitation quarters a widespread and acceptable idea. Indeed, in a recent popularising reconstruction of a Roman town house from Augusta Raurica, a great deal of attention is paid to the workshops (Rütti and Aitken 2001).

Finally, from the outcome of the two case studies it is clear that most probably, in the past, a lot of information has simply escaped our attention during and after the excavation of Roman urban sites. It is now realised that the archaeological visibility of many industrial processes can be very low. Given that most (historically better known) medieval crafts are very difficult to grasp archaeologically (Verhaeghe 1995), we can be sure that we have overlooked much evidence for the less well known Roman urban industrial activities. This is true, considering the structures, since an honest archaeologist will admit that for a majority of the 'pits' excavated at a Roman site no clear function can be hypothesised. Considering the small finds, a large category of material, certainly including the organic remains, is simply not recognised as production waste. Often this is due to the absence of taphonomical analysis or to the lack of detailed study. With the adoption of a more global and interdisciplinary approach, however, it can be foreseen that in the future more and more archaeological information about former industrial activities will become available.

Acknowledgements

The authors wish to thank Paul Stokes and Keith Dobney, of the University of Durham (UK), with whom one of us conducted a series of (small-scale) bone-smashing experiments. Frédéric Hanut (Centre de Recherches d'Archéologie nationale, Université Catholique de Louvain) kindly provided the dating of the features of the Elisabethwal site, on the basis of his analysis of the ceramics. André Detloff, Monique Vanvinckenroye and Marijke Willaert (Institute for the Archaeological Heritage of the Flemish Community) took care of the illustrations, while photo 16.6 was taken by Guido Schalenbourg (Gallo-Romeins Museum Tongeren). Sabine Deschler-Erb (University of Basel) must be thanked for commenting upon an earlier version of this text and for providing essential information.

Bibliography

Armitage, P. and Clutton-Brock, J. (1976) A system for classification and description of the horn-cores of cattle from archaeological sites. *Journal of Archaeological Science* 3, 329–48.

Askew, S. (1961) An excavation on the Roman site at Little Chester. *Derbyshire Archaeological Journal* 81, 107–108.

Berke, H. (1989) Funde aus einer Römischen Leimsiederei in Köln. *Kölner Jahrbuch für Vor- und Frühgeschichte* 22, 879–92.

Berke, H. (1995) Reste einer spezialisierten Schlachterei in der CUT, Insula 37. In A. Riehe and S. Kraus (eds) *Grabung – Forschung – Präsentation. Xantener Berichte* 6, 301–6. Köln, Rheinland Verlag.

Berke, H. (1996) Die Tierknochenfunde aus den Ausgrabungen an der Jahnstrasse in Köln. *Kölner Jahrbuch für Vor- und Frühgeschichte* 22, 879–92.

Bloemers, J. H. F. (1983) Acculturation in the Rhine/Meuse Basin in the Roman Period. A preliminary survey. In R. Brandt and J. Slofstra (eds) *Roman and Native in the Low Countries. Spheres of interaction.* British Archaeological reports. International Series 184, 159–209. Oxford.

Brulet, R. (1996) La maison urbaine en Gaule belgique et en Germanie inférieure. In La maison urbaine d'époque romaine en Gaule narbonnaise et dans les provinces voisines. *Actes du colloque d'Avignon. 11–13 novembre 1994; Documents d'Archéologie Vauclusienne* 6, 73–97. Avignon.

Burnham, B. C., Collis, J., Dobinson, C., Haselgrove, C. and Jones, M. (2001) Themes for urban research, *c.* 100 BC to AD 200. In S. James and M. Millett (eds) *Britons and Romans: advancing an archaeological agenda.* Council for British Archaeology Report 125, 67–76. York.

Clarke, S. (1997) Abandonment, rubbish disposal and 'special' deposits. In K. Meadows, C. Lemke and J. Heron (eds) *TRAC 96. Proceedings of the Sixth Annual Theoretical Roman Archaeology Conference Sheffield 1996*, 73–81. Oxford.

Clarke, S. (1999) In search of a different Roman period: the finds asemblage at the Newstead military complex. In G. Fincham, G. Harrison, R. Holland and L. Revell (eds.) *TRAC 99. Proceedings of the Ninth Annual Theoretical Roman Archaeology Conference Durham 1999*, 22–9. Oxford.

Daniëls, I. (2001) Analyse van de collectie Romeinse en vroegmiddeleeuwse voorwerpen uit been en gewei van het Provinciaal Gallo-Romeins Museum Tongeren. Unpublished thesis; University of Leuven, Belgium.

De Boe, G. (1988) De inheems-Romeinse houtbouw in de Antwerpse Kempen. In F. Brenders and G. Cuyt (eds) *Van beschaving tot opgraving. 25 jaar archeologisch onderzoek rond Antwerpen*, 47–62. Antwerpen, Antwerpse Vereniging voor Romeinse Archeologie.

Deschler-Erb, S. (1992) Ostelogischer Teil. In A.R. Furger and S. Deschler-Erb (eds) *Römische Beinartefakte aus Augusta Raurica. Rohmaterial, Technologie, Typologie und Chronologie. Forschungen in Augst,* 15, 355–445. Augst, Römerstadt Augusta Raurica.

Deschler-Erb, S. (1998) Römische Beinartefakte aus Augusta Raurica. Rohmaterial, Technologie, Typologie und Chronologie. *Forschungen in Augst* 27. Augst, Römerstadt Augusta Raurica.

Dobney, K. (2001) A place at the table: the role of vertebrate zooarchaeology within a Roman research agenda for Britain. In S. James and M. Millett (eds) *Britons and Romans: advancing an archaeological agenda.* Council for British Archaeology Report 125, 36–45. York.

Dobney, K., Jaques, D. and Irving, B. (1996) Of butchers and breeds. Report on vertebrate remains from various sites in the City of Lincoln. *Lincoln Archaeological Studies* 5. Lincoln, City of Lincoln Archaeology Unit.

Duncan-Jones, R. (1994) *Money and Government in the Roman Empire.* Cambridge, Cambridge University Press.

Ervynck, A., Hillewaert, B., Maes, A. and Van Strydonck, M. (2003) Tanning and horn-working at late and post-medieval Brugge: the organic evidence. In P. Murphy and P. Wiltshire (eds) *The environmental archaeology of industry. Symposia of the Association for Environmental Archaeology No 20,* 60–70. Oxford, Oxbow.

Ervynck, A. and Vanderhoeven, A. (1997) Tongeren (Belgium): changing patterns of meat consumption in a roman *civitas* capital. In M. Kokabi and J. Wahl (eds) *Proceedings of the 7th ICAZ Conference. Anthropozoologica* 25–6, 457–64. Paris, L'Homme et l'Animal.

Finley, M. I. (1973) *The Ancient Economy.* London, Chatto and Windus.

Finley, M. I. (ed.) (1981) *The Ancient City: From Fustel de Coulanges to Max Weber and beyond.* Cambridge, Cambridge University Press.

Fulford, M. (2001) Links with the past: pervasive 'ritual' behaviour in Roman Britain. *Britannia* 32, 199–218.

Gautier, A. (1975) De dierlijke skeletresten. In J. Mertens and W. Vanvinckenroye (eds) *Een Romeins gebouwencomplex extra-muros te Tongeren. Publicaties van het Gallo-Romeins Museum Tongeren* 22, 53–4. Tongeren, Gallo-Romeins Museum.

Goguey, D. (2001–2) Nuisances urbaines selon les auteurs latins. Confrontation avec les données de quelques villes gallo-romaines. In R. Bedon (ed.) *Amoenitas urbium. Les agréments de la vie urbaine en Gaule romaine et dans les régions voisines. Caesarodunum* XXXV–XXXVI, 255–73. Limoges, Presses Universitaires de Limoges.

Hanoune, R. (2001–2) *Amoenitas urbium?* Quelques textes en réaction. In R. Bedon (ed.) *Amoenitas urbium. Les agréments de la vie urbaine en Gaule romaine et dans les régions voisines. Caesarodunum* XXXV–XXXVI, 287–93. Limoges, Presses Universitaires de Limoges.

Haselgrove, C. C. (1990) The Romanization of Belgic Gaul. Archaeological perspectives. In T. F. C. Blagg and M. J. Millet (eds) *The Early Roman Empire in the West,* 45–71. Oxford, Oxbow Books.

Hill, J. D. (1995) *Ritual and Rubbish in the Iron Age of Wessex: A Study of a Specific Archaeological Record.* British Archaelogical Reports British Series 242. Oxford, BAR.

Hopkins, K. (1978) Economic growth and towns in classical antiquity. In Ph. Abrams and E. A. Wringley (eds) *Towns in Societies. Essays in Economic History and Historical Sociology,* 35–77. Cambridge, Cambridge University Press.

Jones, M. (1985) Archaeobotany beyond subsistence reconstruction. In G. Barker and C. Gamble (eds.) *Beyond Domestication in Prehistoric Europe. Investigations in Subsistence Archaeology and Social Complexity. Studies in Archaeology,* 105–28. London, Academic Press.

Kuhnen, H.-P. (1995) Max Weber – die römische Stadt und die Provinzialrömische Archäologie. Archäologische Anmerkungen zur Diskussion um die antike Stadt. In W. Czysz, C.-M. Hüssen, H.-P. Kuhnen, C. S. Sommer and G. Weber (eds) *Provinzialrömische Forschungen. Festschrift für Günter Ulbert zum 65. Geburtstag,* 253–60. Espelkamp.

Lentacker, A., Van Neer, W. and Desender, K. (1993) Archéozoologie. In R. Brulet (ed.) *Braives Gallo-Romain V. La fortification dus Bas-Empire. Publications d'Histoire de l'Art et d'Archeologie de l'Université Catholique de Louvain* LXXXIII, 284–339. Louvain-la-neuve, Université Catholique de Louvain.

Lepetz, S. (1996) L'animal dans la société Gallo-Romaine de la France du Nord. *Revue Archéologique de Picardie* n° spécial 12. Amiens, Centre de Recherche Archéologique de la Vallée de l'Oise.

Leveau, Ph. (1983) La ville antique et l'organisation de l'espace rurale: villa, ville, village. *Annales Economies, Sociétés, Civilisations* 4, 920–42.

Ligneureux, Y. and Peters, J. (1996) Techniques de boucherie et rejets osseux en Gaule Romaine. *Anthropozoologica* 24, 45–98.

MacGregor, A. (1989) Bone, antler and horn industries in the urban context. In D. Serjeantson and T. Waldron (eds) *Diet and crafts in towns. The evidence of animal remains from the Roman to the Post-Medieval periods.* British Archaeological Reports British Series 199, 107–28. Oxford.

MacGregor, A. (1998) Hides, horns and bones: animals and interdependent industries in the early urban context. In E. Cameron (ed.) *Leather and fur. Aspects of early medieval trade and technology,* 11–26. London, Archetype Publications.

Maltby, M. (1989) Urban-rural variations in the butchering of cattle in Romano-British Hampshire. In D. Serjeantson and T. Waldron (eds) *Diet and Crafts in Towns. The evidence of animal remains from the Roman to the post-medieval periods.* British Archaeological Reports British Series 199, 75–106. Oxford.

Martin-Kilcher, S. (1991). *Vitudurum 5. Berichte der Züricher Denkmalpflege Archäologische Monographien 10.* Zürich, Züricher Denkmalpflege.

Millett, M. (2001) Approaches to urban societies. In S. James and M. Millett (eds) *Britons and Romans: advancing an archaeological agenda.* Council for British Archaeology Report 125, 60–6. York, CBA.

Milne, G. (1995) *Book of Roman London. Urban archaeology*

in the nation's capital. London, B. T. Batsford / English Heritage.

Morel, P. (1991) Die osteologischen und anthropologischen Untersuchungen. In: S. Martin-Kilcher (ed.) *Vitudurum 5. Berichte der Züricher Denkmalpflege Archäologische Monographien* 10, 79–176. Zürich, Züricher Denkmalpflege.

Müller, U. (1985) Die römischen Gebäude in Kaiseraugst – Schmidmatt. *Archäologie der Schweiz* 8 (1), 15–29.

O'Connor, T. P. (1988) The animal bones from the General Accident site, Tanner Row. *The Archaeology of York. The animal bones* 15/2. York, Council for British Archaeology.

Poulter, A. G. (1992) Nicopolis ad Istrum: the anatomy of a Graeco-Roman city. In H.-J. Schalles, H. von Hesberg and P. Zanker (eds) *Die Römische Stadt im 2. Jahrhundert n. Chr. Der Funktionswandel des öffentlichen Raumes. Xantener Berichte* 2, 69–86. Köln, Rheinland Verlag.

Rackham, D. J. (1991) The animal bone from post-Roman contexts. In M. R. McCarthy (ed.) *The structural sequence and environmental remains from Castle Street, Carlisle. Excavations 1981–2.* Cumberland and Westmorland Archaeological and Architectural Society Research Series n° 5, 85–8. Kendal.

Raepsaet-Charlier, M.-Th. (1995) Municipium Tungrorum. *Latomus* 54, 361–69.

Richmond, I. (1966) Industry in Roman Britain. In J. S. Wacher (ed.) *The Civitas Capitals of Roman Britain*, 76—86. Leicester, Leicester University Press.

Riehce, A. and Schalles, H. J. (1987) Arbeit. Handwerk und Berufe in der römischen Stadt. *Führer und Schriften des Archäologischen Parks Xanten* 10. Köln, Rheinland and Verlag GmbH Köln.

Rollet, Ph., Balmelle, A., Berthelot, F. and Neiss, R. (2001) Reims – Marne – Le quartier gallo-romain de la rue de Venise et sa réoccupation à l'époque Moderne. *Archéologie Urbaine 4, Bulletin de la Société Archéologique Champenoise* 2–3, 2001.

Roymans, N. (1996) The sword or the plough. Regional dynamics in the romanisation of Belgic Gaul and the Rhineland area. In N. Roymans (ed.) *From the sword to the plough. Three studies on the earliest romanisation of Northern Gaul.* Amsterdam Archaeological Studies 1, 9–126. Amsterdam, Amsterdam University Press.

Rüger, C. B. (1969) Zur Rekonstruktion der Handwerker-Viertel in der Colonia Ulpia Traiana bei Xanten. In *Das Rheinische Landesmuseum Bonn* 3, 36–8. Dusseldorf, Rheinland Verlag.

Rütti, B. and Aitken, C. (2001) *Domus romana. Das Römerhaus. Augster Museumhefte* 26. Augst, Römermuseum Augst.

Schalles, H.-J. (2001) Die Wirtschaftskraft städtischer Siedlungen am Niederrhein: Zur Frage der wirtschaftlichen Beziehungen des römischen Xanten mit seinem Umland. In Th. Grünewald (ed.) *Germania inferior. Besiedlung, Gesellschaft und Wirtschaft an der Grenze der römisch-germanischen Welt, Reallexikon der germanischen Altertumskunde. Ergänzungsband* 28, 431–63. Berlin and New York, Walter de Gruyter.

Schmid, E. (1969) Knochenfunde als archäologische Quellen. In J. Boessneck (ed.) *Archäologie und Biologie. Deutsche Forschungsgemeinschaft* 15, 100–11. Wiesbaden, Franz Steiner Verlag.

Schmid, E. (1972) *Atlas of Animal Bones. For prehistorians, archaeologists and Quaternary geologists.* Amsterdam, Elsevier.

Schönberger, H. (1985) Die römischen Truppenlager der frühen und mittleren Kaiserzeit zwischen Nordsee und Inn. *Berichte der Römisch-Germanischen Kommission* 66, 321–497. Mainz, Philipp von Zabern.

Serjeantson, D. (1989) Animal remains and the tanning trade. In D. Serjeantson and T. Waldron (eds) *Diet and crafts in towns. The evidence of animal remains from the Roman to the Post-Medieval periods.* British Archaeological Reports British Series 199, 129–42. Oxford.

Seuntjens, G. (1999) Archeozoölogisch onderzoek van de Romeinse vindplaats 'Elisabethwal' te Tongeren. Unpublished thesis, University of Ghent, Belgium.

Shaw, M. (1996) The excavation of a late 15th- to 17th-century tanning complex at The Green, Northampton. *Post-Medieval Archaeology* 30, 63–127.

Slofstra, J. (1991) Changing settlement systems in the Meuse-Demer-Scheldt area during the early Roman period. In N. Roymans and F. Theuws (eds) *Images of the past. Studies in Pre- and Protohistorie* 7, 131–99. Amsterdam.

Stokes, P. R. G. (2000) The butcher, the cook and the archaeologist. In: J. P. Huntley and S. Stallibrass (eds) *Taphonomy and interpretation. Symposia of the Association for Environmental Archaeology* 14, 65–70. Oxford, Oxbow.

Thüry, G. E. (2001) *Müll und Marmorsäulen. Siedlungshygiene in der römischen Antike.* Mainz, Philipp von Zabern.

Timpe, D. (1993) Der Namensatz der taciteischen Germania. *Chiron* 23, 325–52.

Vallet, C. (2000) Le travail de la matière animale à l'époque Romaine. Le travail de l'os à Augustoritum (Limoges, Haute-Vienne). In I. Bertrand (ed.) *Actualité de la recherche sur le mobilier Romain non céramique. Actes du colloque de Chauvigny (Vienne, France) 23 and 24 octobre 1998 (Mémoire XVIII de l'Association des Publications Chauvinoises)*, 195–214. Chauvigny.

Vanderhoeven, A. (2001) Das vorflavische Tongeren: Die früheste Entwicklung der Stadt anhand von Funden und Befunden. In G. Precht (ed.) *Genese, Struktur und Entwicklung römischer Städte im 1. Jahrhundert n.Chr. in Nieder- und Obergermanien. Xantener Berichte* 9, 157–76. Mainz, Verlag Philipp von Zabern.

Vanderhoeven, A., Ervynck, A. and Van Neer, W. (1993) De dierlijke en menselijke resten. In A. Vanderhoeven, G. Vynckier and P. Vynckier (eds) Het oudheidkundig bodemonderzoek aan de Veemarkt te Tongeren (prov. Limburg). Eindverslag 1988. *Archeologie in Vlaanderen* III, 177–86.

Vanderhoeven, A., Martens, M., Ervynck, A., Cooremans, B. and Van Neer, W. (2001a) Interdisziplinäre Untersuchungen im römischen Vicus von Tienen (Belgien). Die Integration von ökologischen und archäologischen Daten. In M. Frey and N. Hanel (eds.) *Archäologie. Naturwissenschaften. Umwelt. Beiträge der Arbeitsgemeinschaft "Römische Archäologie" auf dem 3. Deutschen Archäologiekongress in Heidelberg. 25.5.–30.5.1999.* British Archaeological Reports International Series 929, 13–31. Oxford, BAR.

Vanderhoeven, A., Martens, M. and Vynckier, G. (2001b) Romanization and settlement in the central part of the Civitas Tungrorum. In S. Altekamp and A. Schäfer (eds) *The Impact on Settlement in the Northwestern and Danube Provinces. Lectures held at the Winckelmann-Institut der Humbolt-Universität zu Berlin in winter 1998/99.* British Archaeological Reports International Series 921, 57–90. Oxford, BAR.

Vanderhoeven, A., Van de Konijnenburg, R. and De Boe, G. (1987) Het oudheidkundig bodemonderzoek aan de Kielenstraat te Tongeren. *Archaeologia Belgica* III, 127–38.

Vanderhoeven, A., Vynckier, G., Ervynck, A. and Cooremans, B. (1992) Het oudheidkundig bodemonderzoek aan de Kielenstraat te Tongeren (prov. Limburg). Interimverslag 1990–3. Deel 1. De vóór-Flavische bewoning. *Archeologie in Vlaanderen* II, 89–145.

Vanderhoeven, A., Vynckier, G., Ervynck, A., Cooremans, B. and Wouters, W. (1996a) Het oudheidkundig bodemonderzoek aan de Koninksemsteenweg te Tongeren (prov. Limburg). Eindverslag 1995. *Archeologie in Vlaanderen* V, 69–84.

Vanderhoeven, A., Vynckier, G., Ervynck, A., Van Neer, W. and Cooremans, B. (1994) Het oudheidkundig bodemonderzoek aan de Minderbroederstraat te Tongeren (prov. Limburg). Eindverslag 1991. *Archeologie in Vlaanderen* IV, 49–74.

Vanderhoeven, A., Vynckier, G. Vandenbruaene, M. and Ervynck, A. (1996b) Het oudheidkundig bodemonderzoek aan de Jaminéstraat te Tongeren. Eindverslag 1995. *Archeologie in Vlaanderen* V, 85–96.

Vanderhoeven, A., Vynckier, G. and Vynckier, P. (1991) Het oudheidkundig bodemonderzoek aan de Kielenstraat te Tongeren. Interimverslag 1987. *Archeologie in Vlaanderen* I, 107–24.

Vanderhoeven, A., Vynckier, G. and Wouters, W. (2002) Het oudheidkundig bodemonderzoek aan de Zijdelingsestraat te Tienen (prov. Brabant). Interimverslag 1995–6. *Archeologie in Vlaanderen* VI, 133–60.

van Driel-Murray, C. (2001) Technology transfer: the introduction and loss of tanning technology during the Roman period. In M. Polfer (ed.) *L'artisanat romain: évolution, continuités et ruptures (Italie et provinces occidentales). Actes du 2e colloque d'Erpedange (26–28 octobre 2001)*, 55–67. Montagnac, Séminaire d'Études Anciennes du Centre Universitaire de Luxembourg and Instrumentum.

van Driel-Murray, C. (2002) The leather trades in Roman Yorkshire. In P. Wilson and J. Price (eds) *Aspects of Industry in Roman Yorkshire and the North*. Oxford, Oxbow.

Van Mensch, P. J. A. (1974) A Roman soup-kitchen at Zwammerdam? *Berichten van de Rijksdienst voor het Oudheidkundig Bodemonderzoek* 24, 159–65.

Van Neer, W. (1993) Le travail de l'os et du bois de cervidés. In J. Gillet (ed.) *L'artisanat en Gaule Romaine*, 45–50. Rixensart, Archeolo-J.

Van Neer, W. (1994) Het dierlijk beendermateriaal. In: W. Vanvinckenroye (ed.) *Een bijdrage tot het stadskernonderzoek van Romeins Tongeren. Publicaties van het Gallo-Romeins Museum Tongeren* 46, 28–36. Tongeren, Gallo-Romeins Museum.

Vanvinckenroye, W. (1984) De Romeinse zuidwest-begraafplaats van Tongeren. *Publicaties van het Provinciaal Gallo-Romeins Museum te Tongeren* 29. Tongeren.

Vanvinckenroye, W. (1989) Terra sigillata uit een Romeinse stortplaats te Tongeren. *Publicaties van het Provinciaal Gallo-Romeins Museum te Tongeren* 41. Tongeren.

Vehik, S. C. (1977) Bone fragments and bone grease manufacturing: a review of their archaeological use and potential. *Plains Anthropologist* 22, 169–82.

Verhaeghe, F. (1995) Industry in medieval towns: the archaeological problem. An essay. In J.-M. Duvosquelle and E. Thoen (eds) *Peasants and townsmen in medieval Europe. Studia in honorem Adriaan Verhulst*, 271–93. Gent, Snoek-Ducaju en Zoon.

Waldmann, K. (1967) Die Knochenfunde aus der Colonia Ulpia Traiana, einer römischen Stadt bei Xanten am Niederrhein. *Archaeo-Physica* 3. Köln, Rheinland Verlag.

Wallace-Hadrill, A. (1991) Elites and trade in the Roman town. In J. Rich and A. Wallace-Hadrill (eds.) *City and Country in the Ancient World*, Leicester-Nottingham Studies in Ancient Society 2, 241–71. London and New York, Routledge.

Whittaker, C. R. (1990) The consumer city revisited: the vicus and the city. *Journal of Roman Archaeology* 3, 110–18.

Wierschowski, L. (1996) Handels- und Wirtschaftsbeziehungen der Städte in den nordwestlichen Provinzen des römischen Reiches. In W. Eck and H. Galsterer (eds) *Die Stadt in Oberitalien und in den nordwestlichen Provinzen des römischen Reiches. Kölner Forschungen* 4, 121–39. Mainz, Philipp von Zabern.

Woolf, G. (1998) *Becoming Roman. The origins of provincial civilization in Gaul*. Cambridge, Cambridge University Press.

17   Styles of Pottery Deposition at a Roman Rural Site in Hampshire

J. G. Evans

Introduction

The work described in this paper from Bossington in the Test Valley, Hampshire, is part of a study of the Holocene environmental history of chalkland river valleys in central southern England, in which my co-researcher is Professor Charlie Harris of the Department of Earth Sciences, Cardiff University. Earlier work in the nearby Wallop Brook and Anton Valley has already been reported on (Williams and Evans 2000), while slightly further afield relevant sequences have been discussed from the Itchen and Wylye Valleys (Evans *et al.* 1992; Davies 2003). To the north, in the Kennet Valley, fuller publication has shown the quality of information and analysis aimed at for Bossington (Evans *et al.* 1993).

Bossington in the Test Valley (Fig. 17.1) has proved a significant location in terms of long sequences of sediments in which there is good archaeology. Excavations, close to the Roman road from Old Sarum to Winchester (Fig. 17.1), revealed a stratified sequence of Roman materials. The excavation was designed specifically to look at the stratigraphy at the edge of the valley and more broadly as

part of a section across the valley to investigate its Holocene history.

Archaeologically, the site is one of about 18 in the 100 square kilometres around Bossington of concentrations of Roman material suggestive of small settlements (Fig. 17.1, B). Most of these are plateau sites on clayey soils (*e.g.* Rogers and Walker 1985). Only Bossington itself and another settlement directly opposite it on the other side of the Test are in valley edge locations, and these presumably related to the river crossing of the Roman road. In our work, towards the centre of the valley, we found the flint-cobbled surface of what may have been this road crossing the floodplain between two arms of the River Test and associated with Roman pottery and a Greensand rotary quern. It was overlain by a thin layer of alluvium. There are also 25 small collections of single finds of pottery, tile, stone, glass, coins and a few other items like an inscribed lead pig and quern fragments (Test Valley Archaeological Trust SMR). In addition there are many Celtic fields which could be Roman. More widely (Fig. 17.1, A), Bossington lies at the south-west

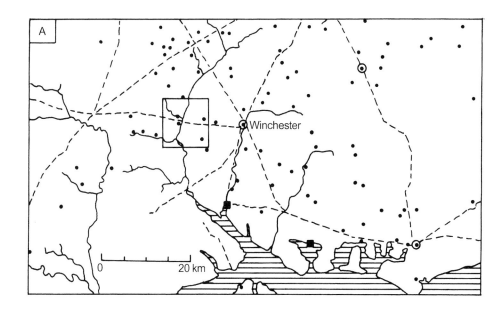

Fig. 17.1. A. Central southern England (east Wiltshire and south Hampshire) showing the distribution of Roman settlements (villas, substantial buildings and settlements) (dots), towns (dots in circles), forts (squares) and roads (after Johnston 1981: Fig. 15).

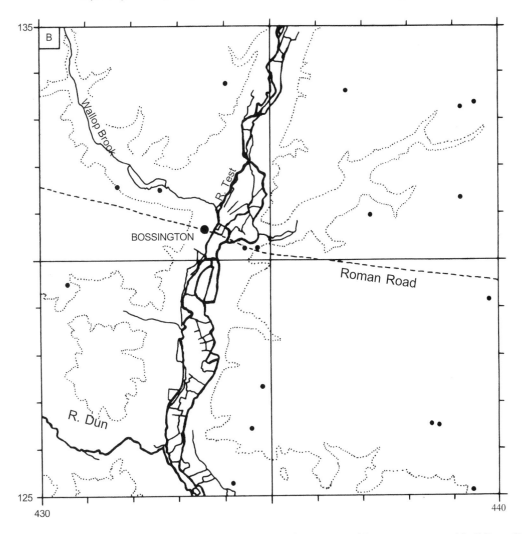

Fig. 17.1. B. Location map of the Bossington Roman site and significant sites of Roman pottery and buildings (Test Valley Archaeological Trust SMR). National grid at 1 km intervals, 50–m contour, based on the Ordnance Survey 1:25,000 series, Crown Copyright).

edge of a significant spread of villas and substantial buildings, to the south of which is the blank area of the New Forest (Johnston 1981: Fig. 15). We will refer to these somewhat singular aspects of the location of Bossington later in relation to the visuality of the site.

Deliberate deposition of materials

The locality at Bossington discussed here (Fig 17.1, C) consists of several small pits ('pits' here being the excavations, not ancient archaeological features) at the western edge of the floodplain where alluvium, hillwash and buried soils interfingered. The immediate context is the edge of a field or settlement where material had been dumped against banks of flint and chalk. The sequence ran from the first to the fourth centuries as indicated by the pottery. The simplicity or low diversity of the pottery and the undecorated nature of the samian indicated that this was a rural site, while daub, box-tile and smithing debris indicated some buildings including one with a hypocaust and another that was a smithy.

Several features suggested that the material-cultural deposition at the valley edge might have been deliberately structured. This was exhibited through the re-use of materials, as in the manufacture of roundels and the incorporation of grog. It also occurred in the taking in of native styles. Thus some of the pots, although Roman, were significantly similar to Iron Age forms, as seen, for example in the Atrebatic pottery (ceramic phase 8) at Danebury (Cunliffe 1984), in Belgic and early Roman forms from Silchester (Boon 1969) and in the 'Iron Age C' of Wessex, specifically Hengistbury and Rotherley (Brailsford 1958). Lisa Brown, reporting on some of the pottery from the lowest levels at Bossington, identifies residual Iron Age material amongst the early (first-century AD) Roman assemblage (in litt.). The floodplain edge location of these depositions may also be a continuation of the native Iron Age practice of depositing materials in natural and artificial watery places, including rivers (Cunliffe 1991), although it must be cautioned that this may also be a significant Roman development in its own right (Webster 1997).

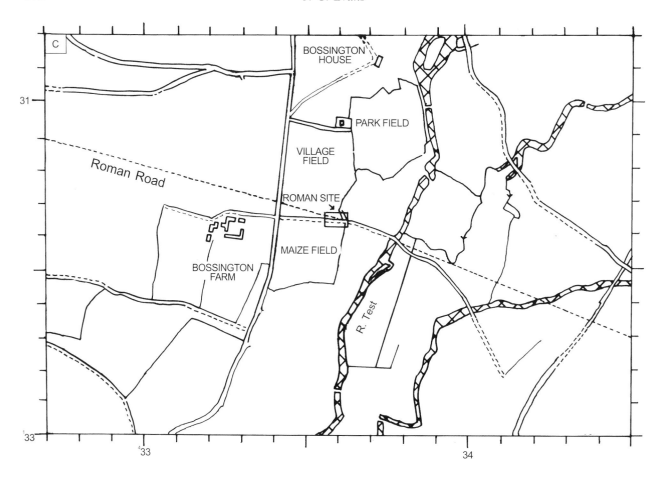

Fig. 17.1. C. Detailed location map of Bossington Roman site, grid at 100 m intervals

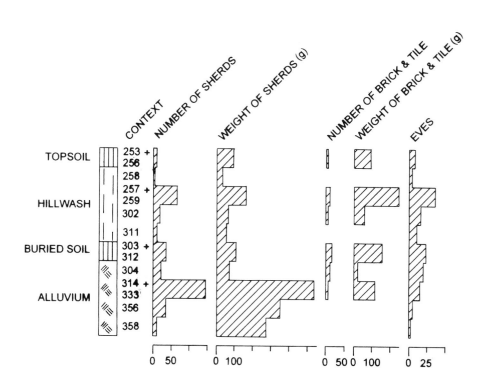

Fig. 17.2. Numbers and weights of pottery and tile in Pit 252

Visual display was an important part of the process. Significant aspects include the following:

1. Deposition of complete vessels

In one part of the sequence (Pit 252), about 50 m into the flood-plain from the valley edge, there were three bowls, two complete and one in fragments but probably complete when deposited, which lay close to the base of the alluvium (Fig. 17.2, contexts 356 and 358). The bowls were first-century AD Roman, but were Iron Age in style (Figs. 17.3 and 17.4). The floodplain context of these finds suggests that the Iron Age practice of depositing materials in swamps and lakes was here continuing into the Roman period and with the use of native pottery styles.

2. Fragmentation through the sequence

In the lower part of the sequence the pottery sherds were quite large, and there were some half or even complete, albeit broken, vessels. This occurred in the area of the floodplain referred to above (Pit 252), and further towards the dryland at its edge (Pit V). Often several large sherds from different vessels were closely associated. In one area, there was a more or less complete small black-burnished ware jar; three larger grey-ware bowls of coarser fabric, one of which was quite complete although broken in four parts; and more than half of a black shallow dish. All this material was present on a chalk bank beneath alluvium or close to the base of the alluvium, and had been deposited at the start of a period of alluviation.

Moving up through the sequence, the number of vessels (as estimated from rims/EVEs) increased while the quantity of pottery (as numbers of sherds and total weight) decreased (Fig. 17.2), indicating much greater fragmentation in these upper levels. The situation is complex and there are many influences here, but I suspect the changes are partly due to the action of ploughing in the upper levels and partly to the deliberate incorporation of the large sherds and complete vessels in the lowest part of the sequence.

3. Modification of pots and sherds

Modification had taken place in several ways. There was an amphora neck that had been mostly sawn through transversely and then snapped off (Fig. 17.5).

About fifteen broken sherds had been modified into circular discs. Some of these were the tops of lids which had been chipped around, and some were jar bases which had been similarly treated (Fig. 17.6). Two of the bases had central holes in them (although these may have been original) and one had a cross on one side (Fig. 17.7). A samian base with the makers name on it, 'Laxtucisf', had been chipped deliberately and was particularly distinctive (Fig. 17.8). Some of these pieces could be interpreted as gaming pieces, but most of them were

pretty crude and it is more likely that it was the sheer secondary use and working of the pottery that was important rather than the pieces themselves. Half of the neck of a flagon had been knapped into a series of embayments (Figs. 17.9 and 17.10).

A large number of sherds at various levels had been secondarily burnt, often after the vessels had been fragmented, as could be seen by the way the burning covered broken edges. It was particularly apparent with many of the black-burnished sherds and some of the greywares, both types of pottery acquiring a brick red cortex and a flaky exterior. Some of the New Forest Ware sherds had also been similarly burnt, and in these there was a distinctive exfoliation of the surface (Fig. 17.11).

4. The use of grog

Some of the pottery (from storage vessels or jars) was pretty thick and tempered with a variety of colours of reused pottery or tile – reds, yellows, whites and greys (grog-tempered ware) – giving a particular impression of the deliberate incorporation of an earlier cycle of pottery manufacturing and decay (Fig. 17.12). Although grog-tempered wares are particularly common on some Roman sites, the presence of this kind of pottery at Bossington is worth mentioning here since in the context of the other examples of pottery re-use it takes on more significance.

5. Change of style through the sequence

As one moved up through the sequence, the style of the pottery changed, and this was especially clear in Pit V, close to the valley edge (Fig. 17.13). Black-burnished wares which were common in the lower levels, declined somewhat and were replaced by local coarse wares. Even some of the expected BBI later types with flared projecting rims were present as copies in a coarse pink or red fabric which was probably local.

In the uppermost deposits of ploughwash, which contain only Roman and no later pottery, there is a succession of fine wares – Nene Valley, New Forest and Oxford Wares. The New Forest sherds are all quite small yet extremely hard and angular. It is almost as if they have been added to the ploughsoil deliberately to entexture it with some kind of meaning.

Brick and tile, absent from the very lowest layers, as also in Pit 252 (Fig. 17.2), are present in abundance in the upper deposits, although these probably have a different origin and meaning; yet they were still pretty visually obvious, in a way more so than the pottery, and would certainly have been so on the fields and as dumps of waste.

6. General visuality of materials

More generally through the sequence as a whole, there was considerable quantity of oyster, another very visual

Fig. 17.3. Virtually complete first-century AD bowl from the base of the alluvium in Pit 252, context 358

Fig. 17.6. Base of a quartz-gritted, dark fabric, chipped into a roundel

Fig. 17.4. Partially complete first-century AD bowl from the base of the alluvium in Pit 252, context 358

Fig. 17.7. Base of a grey-ware fabric, chipped into a roundel and inscribed (after firing) with a cross

Fig. 17.5. Sawn and snapped-off neck of an amphora, view of the cut surface

Fig. 17.8. Base of a Samian ware pot, with maker's name 'Laxtucisf', and chipped into a roundel

Fig. 17.9. Half of a flagon neck in a pale yellow fabric tempered with orange grog, reworked around the flange from the inside with seven flake removals

Fig. 17.11. Base of New Forest Ware vessel from the inside, showing exfoliation due to secondary (i.e. post-firing) burning

Fig. 17.10. As for Fig. 17.9, from the outside

Fig. 17.12. Sherd of grog-tempered ware

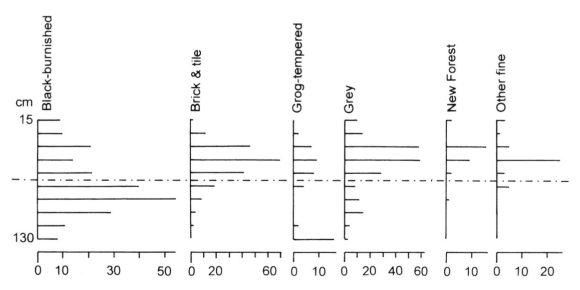

Fig. 17.13. Pit V East, selected profiles of numbers of sherds and brick and tile through the sequence. In the vertical scale, each sample is from one excavation level, varying from 5 to 20 cm in thickness; depth measurements are from below the modern surface. The dashed and dotted line is the approximate junction between occupation deposits (below) and ploughwash (above). Other fine wares are mainly Nene Valley and Oxford wares

manifestation of Romanisation, and one that is un-fortunately being ignored in some recent excavation reports, *e.g.* at Fosse Lane (Leach 2001), although not in others, *e.g.* Silchester (Fulford and Timby 2000) where there is an interesting late Iron Age usage of oysters. There was also a large quantity of smithing debris which in its redness and glinting flecks of hammer scale was visually striking.

The meaning of visuality

My general impression is one in which people were using pottery as a means of creating visuality. This was done not just through the complete pot but through sherds, discarding of broken pots, and the modification and reworking of pots and sherds. There was a sense of the incorporation of the past into contemporary lives, even in their creation as with the incorporation of grog into new pots, the strewing of sherds onto fields on a wider scale, and the more prescribed deposition of whole pots in wet areas at the valley edge.

It seems certain that people were entexturing the land and their lives at the edge of the floodplain in various ways. Much of this was visual, especially in the colours and textures of the materials, and this would make sense, too, adjacent to a major road and river crossing, at the edge of the floodplain where people would need to slow down if not stop altogether. It was a sensible place to display. Even the location with reference to the junction of dry land and floodplain has a visuality on its own (Fig. 17.1, B), while the marginal location of Bossington in relation to the wider distribution of Roman settlements in the region may be of similar relevance (Fig. 17.1, A).

It is likely, too, that this visuality is about social worlds, and connected with personal, individual, ease and identity as much as that of the community or people as a whole. Scales and purpose could vary. At one level, there might have been the deposition of the partly broken and complete pots in clusters as an appeasement for the alluviation of land. At a more general level, the novel and highly visual oysters and tile would have served well as a signal of Romanisation. At the community scale, identity and land ownership were perhaps referenced through the strewing of the distinctive and durable sherds of New Forest Ware and other fabrics. At the individual scale there was the hearth waste of the smith.

The taking in of earlier materiality in the creation of lives is a familiar theme in prehistory, as with the fragmentation of pottery and its further use in 'enchain-ment' in south-east Europe (Chapman 2000), and the way Iron Age people appropriated Neolithic monuments (Hingley 1996). It is also a feature of the historical periods, as where people in the early Middle Ages used Roman spolia in their churches, even mundane materials like tile being used in a really imaginative and visual way (Eaton 2000). Similarly, the re-use of pottery at Bossington is paralleled in the manufacture of roundels and spindle-whorls at Silchester in the Roman period (Timby 2000), while the selective collection of Roman fabrics and pot parts and their re-use (as spindle-whorls, discs or reels) at West Stow in Suffolk continues the pattern into Anglo-Saxon times (Plouviez 1985). In another style, the appropriation of Roman estates in the early Middle Ages, as Wendy Davies (1979) has argued, may be a similar way of taking over the past, along with property donations and other sorts of transfers, and bringing it into contemporary lives for legitimation or just easing one's way in life. Also, in the precise location of Roman Bossington against the flood-plain edge, which seems singularly expressive, I am reminded of the close buttressing of Medieval settlements in these chalkland valleys in just such situations.

This is an increasingly fashionable theme. The walls and bastions of towns like Caerwent and maybe even the fortresses are coming to be seen in terms of their monu-mentality (Guest 2002), rather than of defence, even though defence is being referenced here. The old *fora-basilicae* were brought into a newer monumentality, perhaps as a symbolic means of controlling the movement of native people and their livestock. Likewise, strict layout of fields in the Gwent Levels in the second and third centuries AD (Allen and Fulford 1987) is in striking contrast to the irregularity of adjacent Iron Age fields and perhaps more of an opposition to them; more of a boundary delineation of Romanisation, than a source of drainage and of areas for keeping horses. It could also have broken up old transhumance routes between uplands and the coastal saltmarshes, just as the fields today make it quite difficult to get to the unenclosed foreshore and the saltmarsh.

Even the conquest of Britain by Rome in the first place was a personal socio-political construct designed to keep Claudius in power, a reinforcement of his boundaries rather than those of the Roman Empire, while at a still greater scale of relevance, the pattern of frequency of replacement of Roman Emperors (Fig. 17.14) rather than mapping raw politics or economics can be seen as referencing socio-cultural style. We can hardly have been the first people to experience a Post-modern world, a point made precisely by Golden and Toohey (1997).

Implications

The implications of these ideas are far-reaching and I will mention three areas.

First, pottery and tile distributions revealed by field-walking and excavation may be about the active entexturing of the land as a means of social expression. The data need interpreting, not just as a mapping of old settlements, rural activities, or rubbish put on the fields with manure but in a wider and more socially imaginative way – a way which acknowledges their active role in social reproduc-tion. It is easy to understand how the pottery and tile fragments could have been experienced in this way: people lived very close to the surface of the land, not just in farming activities, like weeding, harrowing and gleaning,

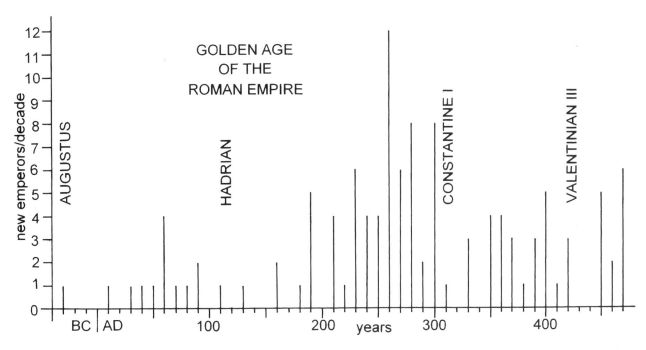

Fig. 17.14. Numbers of new emperors per decade in the Roman empire as an index of socio-cultural style. Data from Salway (1997, pp. 571–4), with much simplification in the later centuries

but in other areas like the collecting of iron ore (Hingley 1997). The visuality of the land surface and its texture were intimately encountered. In addition, the adding of midden material to the field increases fertility thus creating a better surplus which would be seen as a success in ritual terms.

All field surveys, however, have failed to take into account the way the materials were used in the active creation of visualities. It is not so much a question of looking at the manuring problem (Alcock *et al.* 1994; Bintliff and Snodgrass 1988) but of thinking about pottery and tile in a wider, actively created, social world – from manufacture, into the privacy of the household, out onto the rubbish dumps, and into the public arena of the fields. A significant part of the interpretation of pottery on the land lies in an understanding of its social meaning. In the household and settlement, there is a need to investigate how pottery is deposited, as has been done by Ault (1999) for the Classical Greek city of Halieis on *koprones*, or how cereal grain and processing materials are distributed, as Kooistra (1991) has done for the Roman villa at Voerendaal in the Netherlands. Similar work has been done on distributions and depositions in Iron Age houses and settlements in southern England, as at Winnall Down (Fasham 1985) and in the wider implications of this and other sites by Hill (1995). The social meaning of pottery in its use in the household, however, also needs tracking into the primary depositional contexts of the middens and waste-pits and then onto the fields if its deeper significance in these domains is to be understood. Work like that of Moore (1986) on the meaning and use of materials like broken pottery, chaff and slag in modern people in Kenya

needs to be applied to archaeological sites. This should be possible with careful contextual and multi-variate analysis: archaeological sites are, ultimately, open to the same detail and depth of analysis as ethnographic ones.

A second point is that in terms of environmental archaeology similar caveats apply (Evans 2003). For example, it may not be just potsherds but weeds of cultivation that were actively encouraged in their own right as a means of entexturing the soil surface and signalling some kind of community boundary. That would put a whole new meaning on the botanical evidence of plant remains as indicators of intensity of cultivation and style of cropping (van der Veen 1992). At a larger scale, other environmental variables, such as the siting of settlements, may have been as much about expressing community identity as about resource use. In relation to river valleys, the core theme of the current project, curation of land surfaces and the prevention of erosion as a means of display can have had significant consequences for floodplain style and for our interpretation of their sediment histories (Howard and Macklin 1999).

Finally, a third area of relevance is in delayed curation and scavenging (Cameron and Tomka 1993). The nature of surface assemblages in caches left behind in temporarily abandoned settlements or of waste material in middens can be related to the length of time they have been exposed and the kinds of materials present. This has been shown by the work of Tomka (1993) on agro-pastoralists in the Bolivian Andes. Sites permanently abandoned might be expected to have poorer assemblages in terms of quality and completeness of artefacts than those irregularly left, and these in turn poorer than those only seasonally abandoned. But this is to see things in a normative, Binfordian, way, and it may well be that the particular style of site abandonment – even the fact of different styles at all – is an active creation of social expression. This could be about family or community identity, or just a means of easing life in the knowledge of a diversity of materials and sites as people criss-crossed the land.

Acknowledgements

The work was done in conjunction with Prof. Charlie Harris in the Department of Geology, Cardiff University, partly supported by the SERC. I am grateful to Richard Hingley and Steve Willis for inviting me to present this paper and include it in their volume. Peter Guest kindly discussed his work on Caerwent and some of the ideas with me. Niall Sharples has discussed ideas about the use of pottery on land surfaces in a visual role. Lisa Brown very kindly reported on some of the pottery from the earliest levels. I am grateful to my students for their work on the Roman pottery from Bossington, particularly Charlotte Baxter, Sian Mather and Amy Seadon. The survey and excavations there are to be published in due course, but it is fitting here to acknowledge the help I have received from John Fairey, the land owner of Bossington, for practical assistance during the work. Finally I must thank Peter Webster for his patience in instructing me in the fascinating world of Roman pottery.

Bibliography

Alcock, S. E., Cherry, J. F. and Davis, J. L. (1994) Intensive survey, agricultural practice and the classical landscape of Greece. In I. Morris (ed.) *Classical Greece: ancient histories and modern archaeologies*, 137–70. Cambridge, Cambridge University Press.

Allen, J. R. L. and Fulford, M. G. (1987) The Wentlooge Level: a Romano-British saltmarsh reclamation in south-east Wales. *Britannia* 17, 91–117.

Ault, B. A. (1999) *Koprones* and oil presses at Halieis: interactions of town and country and the integration of domestic and regional economies. *Hesperia* 68, 549–73.

Bintliff, J. and Snodgrass, A. (1988) Off-site pottery distributions: a regional and inter-regional perspective. *Current Anthropology* 29, 506–13.

Boon, G. C. (1969) Belgic and Roman Silchester: the excavations 1954–8 with an excursus on the early history of Calleva. *Archaeologia* 102, 1–81.

Brailsford, J. (1958) Early Iron Age 'C' in Wessex. *Proceedings of the Prehistoric Society* 24, 101–19.

Cameron, C. M. and Tomka, S. A. (eds) (1993) *Abandonment of Settlements and Regions: ethnoarchaeological and archaeological approaches*. Cambridge, Cambridge University Press.

Chapman, J. (2000) *Fragmentation in Archaeology: people, places and broken objects in the prehistory of south-eastern Europe*. London, Routledge.

Cunliffe, B. (1984) *Danebury: an Iron Age hillfort in Hampshire.*

Vol. 2, The Excavations 1969–1978: the finds. London, Council for British Archaeology.

Cunliffe, B. (1991) *Iron Age Communities in Britain*. London, Routledge.

Davies, P. (2003) The interpretation of Mollusca from Holocene overbank alluvium: progress and future directions. In A. J. Howard, M. G. Macklin and D. G. Passmore (eds) *Alluvial Archaeology in Europe*, 291–302. Lisse, A.A. Balkema.

Davies, W. (1979) Roman settlements and post-Roman estates in south-east Wales. In P. J. Casey (ed.) *The End of Roman Britain*, 153–73. Oxford, British Archaeological Reports.

Eaton, T. (2000) *Plundering the Past: Roman stonework in Medieval Britain*. Stroud, Tempus.

Evans, J. G. (2003) *Environmental Archaeology and the Social Order*. London and New York, Routledge.

Evans, J. G., Davies, P., Mount, R. and Williams, D. (1992) Molluscan taxocenes from Holocene overbank alluvium in central southern England. In S. Needham and M.G. Macklin (eds) *Alluvial Archaeology in Britain*, 65–74. Oxford, Oxbow.

Evans, J. G., Limbrey, S., Máté, I. and Mount, R. (1993) An environmental history of the Upper Kennet Valley, Wiltshire, for the last 10,000 years. *Proceedings of the Prehistoric Society* 59, 139–95.

Fasham, P. J. (1985) *The Prehistoric Settlement at Winnall Down, Winchester*. Winchester, Hampshire Field Club.

Fulford, M. and Timby, J. (2000) *Late Iron Age and Roman Silchester: excavations on the site of the forum-basilica 1977, 1980–86*. London, Society for the Promotion of Roman Studies.

Golden, M. and Toohey, P. (eds) (1997) *Inventing Ancient Culture: historicism, periodization and the ancient world*. London and New York, Routledge.

Guest, P. (2002) Manning the defences: the development of Romano-British urban boundaries. In M. Aldhouse-Green and P. Webster (eds) *Artefacts and Archaeology: aspects of the Celtic and Roman world*, 76–89. Cardiff, University of Wales Press.

Hill, J. D. (1995) *Ritual and Rubbish in the Iron Age of Wessex*. British Archaeological Reports, British Series 242. Oxford.

Hingley, R. (1996) Ancestors and identity in the later prehistory of Atlantic Scotland: the re-use and reinvention of Neolithic monuments and material culture. *World Archaeology* 28, 231–43.

Hingley, R. (1997) Iron, ironworking and regeneration: a study of the symbolic meaning of metalworking in Iron Age Britain. In A. Gwilt and C. Haselgrove (eds) *Reconstructing Iron Age Societies*, 9–18. Oxford, Oxbow Books.

Howard, A. J. and Macklin, M. G. (1999) A generic geomorphological approach to archaeological interpretation and prospection in British river valleys: a guide for archaeologists investigating Holocene landscapes. *Antiquity* 73, 527–41.

Johnston, D. E. (1981) Hampshire in the Roman period. In S. J. Shennan and R. T. Schadla-Hall (eds) *The Archaeology of Hampshire: from the Palaeolithic to the Industrial Revolution*, 46–55. Winchester, Hampshire Field Club and Archaeological Society.

Kooistra, L. I. (1991) Arable farming in the hey-day of the Roman villa at Voerendaal (Limburg, The Netherlands). In I. E. Hajnalová (ed.) *Palaeoethnobotany and Archaeology*, 165–75. Nitra, Archaeological Institute of the Slovak Academy of Sciences.

Leach, P. (2001) *Excavation of a Romano-British Roadside Settlement in Somerset: Fosse Lane, Shepton Mallet 1990*. London, Society for the Promotion of Roman Studies.

Moore, H. L. (1986) *Space, Text and Gender: an anthropological study of the Marakwet of Kenya*. Cambridge, Cambridge University Press.

Plouviez, J. (1985) The late Romano-British pottery. In S. West *West Stow: the Anglo-Saxon village, vol. 1*, 82–85. Ipswich, Suffolk County Planning Department.

Rogers, J. and Walker, J. S. F. (1985) A detached Romano-British bath-house at Braishfield, near Romsey, Hampshire. *Proceedings of the Hampshire Field Club and Archaeological Society* 41, 69–80.

Salway, P. (1997) *A History of Roman Britain*. Oxford, Oxford University Press.

Timby, J. (2000) Objects of fired clay. In M. Fulford and J. Timby *Late Iron Age and Roman Silchester: excavations on the site of the forum-basilica 1977, 1980–86*, 392–4. London, Society for the Promotion of Roman Studies.

Tomka, S. A. (1993) Site abandonment behavior among transhumant agro-pastoralists: the effects of delayed curation on assemblage composition. In C. M. Cameron and S. A. Tomka (eds) *Abandonment of Settlements and Regions: ethnoarchaeological and archaeological approaches*, 11–24. Cambridge, Cambridge University Press.

van der Veen, M. (1992) *Crop Husbandry Regimes: an archaeobotanical study of farming in northern England, 1000 BC–AD 500*. Sheffield, University of Sheffield.

Webster, J. (1997) Text expectations: the archaeology of 'Celtic' ritual wells and shafts. In A. Gwilt and C. Haselgrove (eds) *Reconstructing Iron Age Societies: new approaches to the British Iron Age*, 134–44. Oxford: Oxbow.

Williams, D. and Evans, J. G. (2000) Past environments in river valley bottoms around Danebury. In B. Cunliffe *The Danebury Environs Programme: the prehistory of a Wessex landscape. Vol. 1, introduction*, 39–43. Oxford, Institute of Archaeology.

18   Deposit or Withdrawal?

Raphael M. J. Isserlin

B. R. H. in memoriam

Introduction

The year in which this paper was delivered marked the centenary of W. H. D. Rouse's *Greek Votive Offerings: an essay in the history of Greek religion*. That appeared in 1902, just when scholarly interest in ritual and folklore was getting off the ground. J. G. Frazer had just published an annotated edition of Pausanias' *Guide to Greece* – which among other things gives an unequalled insight into the centrality of cult and ritual in communities – and was busy working on his *Golden Bough*. The study of classical texts, architecture, artefacts and social anthropology were all working hand in-hand and were enjoying something of a Golden Age. Rouse's work is now rather out of date, and Romano-British archaeology was to pursue a somewhat different track, especially in studying cult and ritual deposits, eschewing an holistic archaeology for much of the last century.

Richard Bradley (1985; 1998) and J. D. Hill (1995) have recently shown just how pertinent concepts and terms derived from the study of pre- and proto-historic ritual deposits of Britain and north-west Europe are. It would be foolish to define the phrase 'ritual deposits' ('special deposit' is an alternative); but I take it we all know broadly what we think we are talking about. The transition from Briton to Roman is important without a doubt, and here ritual deposits have a part to play in the study of change. Their contribution, however, to our understanding of the effective functioning of cult and religion *during* the ensuing period (*i.e.* 'Roman Britain proper') is no less so, as Martin Henig has reminded us (1984; 2002). He has also pointed out that we should not lose sight of the Classical world if we are to maximise the potential of our material, for it has many Mediterranean overtones. As even the briefest reading of Pausanias' *Guide to Greece* reminds us, culture is cumulative, with homage being paid in the Roman period to religious practices in Classical Greece, so we might profit by learning from what the Hellenists are doing, for their investigation of cult is not to be neglected (*see below*). In short, Roman Britain is too important to leave to the prehistorians.

Having said that, perhaps I might be permitted an aside here on the need for 'joined-up' thought – taking on board their deliberations. Richard Bradley offered some valuable suggestions concerning Roman votive miniatures in his *The Passage of Arms: An Archaeological Analysis of Prehistoric Hoard and Votive Deposits*, instantly recognised as a classic work, yet the (Romanist) community at large has apparently ignored them (1998, xxx). To give one specific example of the consequences, some years after the first edition of his book appeared in 1990, excavation of a waterlogged pit associated with a temple in an extremely large rural settlement site in south-east England produced pewter vessels. It had been pointed out by the time this was excavated that there seems to be some sort of relationship between pewter and water (Poulton and Scott 1993). This same pit also produced what has been considered to be a child's toy wooden sword. A better example of a miniature votive one cannot reasonably hope to get, and in a material and of a category preserved entirely by chance. The implications for our understanding of ritual deposits are considerable, yet the hints the archaeological record offered were ignored. To place matters miniature in perspective, Miranda Green's *corpora*, the standard works on the subject, appeared 20 or so years before the site was excavated (1976; 1978; 1981), although her work deals mostly with items of metal. One looks forward with interest to the final report – and a *correct* interpretation, taking on board the idea of skeuomorphism – and a holistic, more informed approach. But let us return to broader principles.

In some ways the overall differences between prehistorians, Romanists, and Hellenists might not prove insurmountable were we to look at the sub-disciplines more closely – a task beyond my present remit. In this piece I shall first of all be considering aspects of ritual deposits in Roman Britain, against some potential points of *contact* with practice in the 'Classical world' (a practice now unfashionable in Romano-British studies) and also (in lesser measure) some potential points of *departure*. I shall do this by reference to a specific site, namely Bath; as it is commonly held to be 'classical', my remarks will be biased towards points of *contact*. The text will be mainly (but not exclusively) concerned with the internal structure of the deposit.

Four points to ponder

My own views are conditioned by research over some years into aspects of public building in Roman Britain, especially their phasing and stratification. Whilst pursuing this topic I came across some related problems that I thought needed highlighting, *viz.* chronology (Isserlin 1995) and the incorporation of human remains into structures as foundation rituals (Isserlin 1997). This led me to pondering upon ritual deposits, from which I would single out two general points for your consideration.

– *Quantity.* To quote a recent review '… for more than a century votive deposits have been a chance find in many parts of central Italy. Deposits provide huge groups of finds often thousands of objects within a few cubic meters …' (Ginge 1993, 286). As a result a corpus of Roman votives is being prepared for all of Italy.

– *Chronology.* Many sites in Classical Greece also produce large quantities of votives. Archaeologists have devised and refined *chronologies for* these ritual-deposits, and are able to define *sorts of events* from them. As Professors Boardman and Snodgrass have shown, there is more to chronology than dating (see below).

Here is an immediate point of departure – we seem to have rather fewer items per cubic metre than in Italy. I shall return to that theme of absence of material evidence again later on. Whether the people of Roman Italy or Classical Greece are grossly profligate or those of Britain particularly miserly is a matter on which I shall withhold judgement, because it implies the existence of a norm and I do not want to say what the norm is. But we do treat ritual deposits in particular ways, subconsciously or otherwise, and here I would single out two further general points for your consideration.

– *Context and significance.* What historical events or social processes produced material for us to describe as votive? Were they normative or exceptional, the products of, for example, social change or stress? At Sparta, Samos, Olympia, and elsewhere this has been identified not least through the study of quantified assemblages (Boardman 1963; Snodgrass 1990). Incidentally, the study of military material deposited in watery conditions in the marshes of Jutland has led to speculation about social processes in a way that totally bypasses Roman Britain (Randsborg 1995). In Roman Britain, inscriptions on altars, *etc.* have led the way in providing statements (but about what?) for many years; few actually say what was given. No Romano-British *civil* site excavated to modern standards has produced *both* an inscription from a stratified context stating a donation *and* an identifiable sealed ritual deposit, with one exception that I shall come to shortly. One military site – namely, Coventina's Well, Northumberland – meets these criteria (Allason-Jones and McKay 1987); though *reported* to modern standards, this excavation was carried out long ago. Maryport, Cumbria, has produced altars that used to be considered as being ritually deposited, but if there were other finds they have not really been considered. In any case there has recently been severe doubt concerning the ritual deposition of the altars (Hill 1997, 98–103).

– *Quality.* We catalogue, even categorise, what we have got. We don't really consider what we *haven't* got or do not seem to have, or ask why this is so.

In short, we have the deposits but we are in many ways ignorant of the rituals that produced or preserved them

and few conclusions have been drawn from them about the 'history' or 'society' of Roman Britain. Where to begin?

Bath: a special site for studying special deposits

In the remainder of this paper I shall use Bath (the exception mentioned above) as a case study to examine how the four points that I have highlighted interrelate, and how they can be exploited. Though neither the most everyday religious site nor fully excavated, Bath is a useful tool for thinking. It is a pity that its potential is still not fully realised by many in the academic community for, as recent reviews have shown, it is a site of more than provincial importance and *seems to be* pretty much the closest Britain gets to 'prolific' by 'classical' standards (Blagg 1990; Davies 1990 and Jordan 1990; see also Reynolds and Volk 1990). It *should* therefore be able to tell us something about the 'history' of Roman Britain and social trends therein. For various reasons, discussed below, that appearance may be illusory, hence the *caveats* 'seems to be' and 'should'; note that Lydney produced 300 votive bracelets (Wheeler and Wheeler 1932, 42). So far, Bath has yielded none.

A reading of the Bath excavation reports with an eye to structural phasing and chronology sparked off specific questions on phasing and chronology of ritual deposition. What is here offered builds on the solid achievement of other people. It involves a degree of speculation inappropriate to the impeccable texts of Cunliffe, Davenport, Henig, Walker and Tomlin. Their deliberations are contained in three volumes: analysis of material from old and new excavations up to the 1960s (Cunliffe 1969, 66–85); presentation of finds from the temple precinct in the 1980s (Cunliffe and Davenport 1985); and the publication and (re)analysis of all available sacred spring material (Cunliffe 1988).

Two points in particular require explicit answers:

1. When does the ritual deposit in the sacred spring actually *date to*?
2. If Bath is the richest temple site in the province, why is its finds assemblage *so poor*?

To solve these problems would be well on the way towards solving many others, not just at Bath. Here I take a distinctly unconventional viewpoint about the importance of Bath. I happen to believe that it, like the temple of Claudius in the *colonia* of Colchester, was probably one of the touchstones of imperial architectural policy in the province, especially, but not exclusively, as a result of imperial visits, and that traces of official intervention, imperial or otherwise, can be seen in the structural sequence. This premise is explained further in my forthcoming book *Towns and Power: Public Building in Roman Britain*.

To revert to our questions concerning finds from the

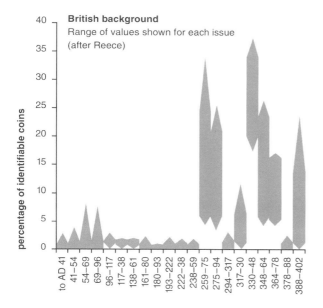

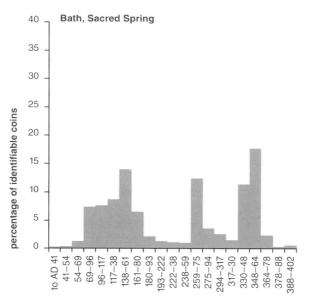

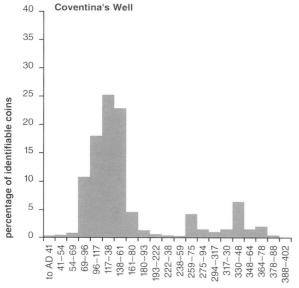

'sacred spring', several additional points may be noted, though it should be stressed that arguing from negative evidence has its risks. Nevertheless, so far:

– In general terms, the most common items *present* are non-organic and metallic – coins and curse tablets. There are also items of metal tableware, some of which can be dated. Almost all are of pewter; two are of silver; none are of gold.
– The earliest intrinsically datable items are Iron Age coins and the latest are Roman coins of AD 402 – a wide time span. One might expect a 'Poisson-curve' for the frequency of coinage in the deposit as it waxes and wanes through time. Yet when John Davies plotted the coinage by issue period, the curve showed distinct oscillations (Fig. 18.1). These reflect the nature of coin usage and money supply, and give an insight into economic and fiscal policy. They do *not* reflect rates of deposition in the sacred spring for reasons that will be discussed below (p.189). These are two very different phenomena.
– There are only 6 Roman gold coins.
– Not a single votive plaque has been found, yet these occur in votive deposits elsewhere, and the curse tablets attest to literacy of a sort at Bath. A key criterion for votive activity appears to be absent.
– Apart from a washer from a catapult and what may be a boss from a helmet crest, though that is not fully certain, there is a dearth of armour or weaponry. It is quite possible, as at Bourbonne-les-Bains, that the soldiers deposited many coins (Sauer 1999). The soldier:civilian ratio at Bath awaits further determination: though inscriptions repeatedly attest a military presence, their numbers need not have been substantial. Even if the ivory breasts (Cunliffe 1984, 8 no.4) are in fact portions of a sword pommel (Greep 1998, 267), the quantity of militaria remains low. (See also next point).
– There are very few anatomical *ex votos*, none of limbs, and no medical instruments. Again, there is a contradiction with the epigraphic evidence, this time for Bath's role as a healing shrine. If re-identification of one piece as a sword pommel is correct (see previous point) the numbers are even lower. Contrast, for instance, the shrine at Ponte di Nona in Italy with its plethora of limbs (Potter 1985). Healing is implied in the text of several monumental inscriptions (e.g. *RIB* 138–40), but not explicitly stated. The only possibility of anatomical *ex votos* is if some of the twigs present are supposed to represent limbs. But they seem pretty impromptu and might conceivably represent the poorer sorts of supplicant. In Cologne too there were wooden anatomical *ex votos* (Gregory of Tours, *Liber Vitae Patrum*, 6.2).
– There is a near-total absence of pottery, especially samian, apart from a few shards of Oxfordshire Colour-Coated Wares; and little, if any, glass.

Fig. 18.1. Deposits at Bath and Coventina's Well, sorted by issue period, and viewed against the British background; Source: Davies 1990, 435, used with permission. It is suggested that the values for Bath may be attenuated due to clearance to fund construction on several occasions, and could originally have been higher. See also Fig. 18.3.

There are very few organic finds. Items of cloth and human or animal bones are absent. This must be significant, as waterlogging creates conditions favourable to their preservation. The pH of the water might have affected preservation of artefacts differentially, as at Bourbonne-les-Bains (cf. Sauer 1999).

– The sacred spring assemblage is 'open' in terms of hoarding behaviour. Items could be added to or removed from it, and it has no clear date of closure.

Mind the gaps...

I would now like to deal with some of the finds from Bath thematically and chronologically, that is to say, according to internal dating evidence.

Pre-Roman material

The excavated portion of the 'sacred spring' at Bath has yielded 18 pre-Roman coins (Mays in Cunliffe 1988, 279). By contrast, 1,041 pre-Roman and 34 Roman coins were excavated from a looted hoard at a much less architecturally prominent Roman temple at Wanborough, Surrey. The original scale of the hoard there has been put at 20,000–30,000 coins (Bird and O'Connell 1994, 32 and table 11). Were more than 18 pre-Roman coins *originally* deposited at Bath? If so, what happened to them? This matter becomes even more pressing since the terminus of a pre-Roman causeway lies under the Roman precinct remains at Bath (Cunliffe 1988, 1). This suggestion has been restated (Cunliffe 2000, 12) and deserves serious consideration. The concept of a jetty or causeway leading to a sacred marsh or river is reminiscent of Bronze Age and Iron Age practice as at La Tène and at Fiskerton, Lincolnshire (Field and Parker Pearson 2003) and even (according to recent research) at Llyn Cerrig Bach – so where are the Bronze Age and Iron Age finds? The site, though 'sacred', yields no Iron Age coin moulds – significant? If so, of what?

A possible answer is to assume that there was originally more material and that the spring was dredged at some time. Was it plundered as an act of conquest *c.* AD 43/7 and sent off to Rome as booty (as Caepio did to the sacred pond near Toulouse in 106 BC: Strabo, IV, 1,3, quoting Posidonius), or kept in the ritual sector of the local economy and recycled as cash devoted to the construction of the cult-complex? We cannot say on internal evidence, as it depends on the local politics of the time. Like Martin Henig, I believe that Tiberius Claudius Togidubnus was involved – Henig was dealing with this from an art-historical point of view (2000). I have already published a preliminary note on some epigraphic evidence that I believe supports his view decisively (Isserlin 2000). If our interpretation, reached by separate means is correct, it begs questions about the Classical rituals at Bath – I think they had a very specific

flavour because Togidubnus was trying to be a Hellenistic-style client king. I deal with this matter further in my book. Suffice it to say here that it has a profound impact that reaches way beyond our understanding of cult in Bath.

Whether or not this view of patronage and control be accepted, one can quite legitimately ask not just *if* the site was cleared, but also *when*. The stratigraphic and structural sequence, in particular the chronology of architectural fragments, suggests that building work started under Nero or Vespasian. A date-range of AD 65–75 has been offered for the earliest construction levels (Cunliffe and Davenport 1985, 178f.) So we can anticipate at least one episode of clearing-out, possibly more than one if the site was used continuously before building work finished. Much depends on the rate of deposition and access to ritual features in a potentially busy construction site. Was the site fenced off meanwhile – who knows?

Roman material

We have to date 89 small finds, 34 intaglios, 130 curse tablets and 12,595 coins from the sacred spring at Bath. This total is rather puny, compared with the watery shrines of early Roman Gaul: 300 wooden figures recovered from the source of the Seine; 5,000 from Chamalières in the *Massif Central*; several hundred *fibulae* from Nuits-St-Georges in the *Côte-d'Or* (Wells 2001, 99). The marshes of the Jutland penninsula are even more productive of Roman (military) material in 'wet' contexts, with as many as 15,000 items being deposited at a single site (Randsborg 1995; Ilkjaer 2000) – but that is another matter, as this was the work of Barbarians. What might the original volume of material deposited by civilised provincials at Bath have been?

Let us concentrate on one class of identifiable material, the coins, and leave aside the question of entire classes of evidence apparently absent from Bath's sacred spring though, being waterlogged, it is quite capable of preserving wooden sculptures. Strictly speaking, there is no way of telling how many coins might have been deposited at Bath, but if *for the sake of argument* a daily average of 10 people visited Bath while it was flourishing, each of whom deposited a coin (of whatever value you like) in the spring over the 350 years of its lifetime, 127,750 coins should have been excavated. By comparison (perhaps not the right word) Coventina's Well yielded perhaps as many as 16,000 coins on discovery (Allason-Jones and McKay 1987, 50). There are other options of course, such as offerings of liquids into the spring, for example wine or beer (Walker 1988, 286), but even that would have cost money. Animal blood, mixed with wine and flowers, is another altogether nastier possibility (Horace, *Odes* III, XIII).

To repeat, *in actual fact* only 12,595 Roman coins were found in the spring at Bath (Walker in Cunliffe and Davenport 1985, 281). This is a retention rate of under

10% in the archaeological record – quite a high proportion of our *theoretical assemblage* is missing, perhaps *again in theory* up to 90% – this is no slur on the high level of skill of the excavators who employed sieving through 3 sizes of mesh, not just manual recovery. Even though they excavated only *part* of the deposit within the sacred spring and the rest of the coins could lurk elsewhere or have been removed by earlier excavators, I do not think that this is the whole story. Now it has been suggested that opening the sluice gates to drain the sacred spring would flush some coins out (Walker 1988, 283). I am not sure that this is solely responsible either. The spring drains into the Great Bath and it is into that vast receptacle that they would presumably have been deposited if the process of flushing were unchecked. Taking this suggestion at face value, that in turn would mean that the Great Bath would ultimately become chock-full of coins, perhaps other votives too – an awful prospect I simply do not wish to contemplate! But perhaps we *should* be more positive about what might have been – Posidonius says the Roman general Caepio auctioned off the 15,000 talents of gold and silver bullion deposited in the temple enclosure and sacred lakes at Toulouse (Strabo IV,1,3). The veracity of his figure cannot be ascertained but, as a talent weighs 25.86 or 37.80 kg depending whose standard you are using (*OCD*³, *s.v.* 'Weights'), it was a lot, even in 105 BC. In *modern* Rome the Fontana di Trevi is an example of 'watery cult': tourists toss in coins, which are duly retrieved at daybreak by a man with a rake six days a week for which he receives €500 (= £315) per day for 20 minutes work (*The Independent*, 29.7.02, 8). This level of tourism is truly exceptional, of course, and activity peaks during 'the season', no doubt – but it shows what can be done.

But returning to Bath, the sluice must have been responsible for catching a lot of material: how much? Is it the only control on accumulation of the deposit? I would argue not. For treating the 12,595 coins we *do* have as a chronologically undifferentiated mass; we get the incredibly low average figure of about 3 coins a month being deposited over the notional 350 years of the life of the site. One way or another, money was flowing into Bath in quantity, I am pretty sure. The artefactual record does not seem to recognise this. As we have been reminded in the Wanborough report, the role of temples as banks in the ancient world should not be underestimated (Bird and O'Connell 1994, 33f.) In medieval Europe, badges were produced on site at Christian shrines as souvenirs for pilgrims to take back home. Sales of 12,500 are documented, even a daily sale of 9,285; churches guarded the moulds as a valuable source of income (Spencer 1968; Stopford 1994, 57). It is surely no accident that at Roman Bath we have stone moulds for the casting of metal vessels from the sacred spring. Mass marketing of souvenirs or votives at shrines like Bath is almost certain – a forum was set up for this purpose at the temple of Vendoevre-en-Brenne (*ILS* 9361; Frere 1975, 6).

I would like to leave numismatic matters at this stage and to turn to the well-known second-century renovation and expansion of the site. Its architectural implications will not be commented on here. I believe it is worth saying that it was pretty certainly Hadrianic in date. A coin of this period was mortared into the piers in the Great Bath – a votive deposit and potentially dating evidence – its potential as a historic indicator has been underplayed. I believe that Hadrianic intervention affected the composition of the ritual deposit in the sacred spring: it was dredged out and that is why we may have a *potential gap* in the sequence of finds and/or a *reduction in volume*. Whether we can clearly see such a gap is another matter.

We should now consider another religious site, the temple of Lanuvium in Etruria, which Hadrian repaired. He says in an inscription that he found 3 lbs. of gold and 206 lbs. of silver there (*CIL* XIV 2088). These were not stray ingots but metal votive offerings, possibly even coin. They were weighed as a preliminary to melting them to fund rebuilding of the temple at Lanuvium – and he probably did the same thing at Bath. I am not fully sure how this clearing-out would affect the picture of coin circulation at Bath: I suspect that if the coin assemblage were smaller, it would still be subject to the same economic trends as a larger one. Indeed, when John Davies reviewed Walker's Bath coins text, he said that an '…unquantifiable number of coins would have been dredged from the well at intervals by priests, during its period of use. Fortunately the size of the Bath assemblage is so substantial that the effects of such distortions in the recovery record will have been minimized…' (1990, 436). After each clearance the *volume* of coin would be less; that after it is probably disproportionately high; that before it probably lower, both undetectably so – but the volume-ratio of issue-periods during the time between clearances should be fixed. I offer this thought with one qualification, that I am not a numismatist. To return to a point made at the outset, I do wonder why it is that there are so few silver and gold coins. No gold coin before the reign of Marcus Aurelius – the first coin is of Lucilla, AD 164–9, and thereafter they appear sporadically; and no silver coin appears in the assemblage before AD 353–60 (Walker 1988, 306, 309). Why? Are the variables of coin-supply operating here? Is this an indication of poverty, with only small donations from poor people? Or were there more valuable coins in the assemblage originally? If so, were they dredged from the spring shortly after deposition, or were they kept elsewhere? I suspect the answer to all these questions is the same – yes.

Are there any more episodes to affect the deposit? The next major phase of building work is Severan (Cunliffe 1988, 359); again, I believe, through direct personal intervention of the emperor. Here I would refer you to the curse tablets and in particular to their chronology. Their content gives few clues regarding dating but, on the style of writing, most of those executed in *Old Roman Cursive* fall in the period AD 175–275 and, more specifically, AD 200–50 (Tomlin 1988, 88, 97). Little is known of the preceding period. Either religious/cult practice changes around AD 200 or most pre-existing items were cleared out from the sacred spring. In either case, this is much the same time as on independent grounds Severan building activity seems likely. There are a very few *defixiones* that might be regarded as early second-century in date, suggesting, again, survivors from a Hadrianic clearance and also implying that deposition (re)started after a Severan dredging of the spring *c.* AD 200. We do incidentally have some mid-second-century coins from the deposit which would seem *prima facie* to argue *against* a Severan clearance; how else would they survive it? But they seem originally to have been in containers such as bags (Walker 1988, 310) and so they could have been deposited as individual groups in mud that accumulated in the spring *anytime after* the suggested Severan dredging and merely sunk. Severus' rather austere views on oracles and that sort of thing may also affect the artefactual record; they certainly affected Egypt *c.* AD 198/9 (Lane-Fox 1986, 213).

Let us stay with the curse tablets and turn to conjecture again. If the whole deposit from the sacred spring at Bath was excavated (we have 130 *defixiones* in lead or pewter) it might contain 780 *defixiones* in all. Over the 350 years of occupation this would imply an annual deposition rate of 2.22 *defixiones*. This is clearly unrealistic – a rate that is a mere twelfth that of the coins! At Uley, Gloucestershire, 140 *defixiones* are known, slightly more from what was, as far as we know, a fairly remote and relatively minor site (Woodward and Leach 1993, 113). Potentially, something is badly adrift here. How badly? Let us turn to Classical Greece for further illumination. The excavations at the shrine of Sparta undertaken by the British School during the early part of last century (Wace 1929) yielded 99,502 lead figurines over the 550 years of its occupation – an average deposition rate of 180/year, or 1 lead figurine deposited every 2 days or so. This varied considerably through time, as reassessment has shown (Boardman 1963). The quantity of figurines expressed in terms of annual deposition rates is shown in Fig. 18.2. Though it may also be an underestimate (could any establishment run on such a paltry income?), it is much nearer the order of approximation one might have in mind for a high status shrine such as Bath.

One way or another, the implication is by now I think fairly clear: there are whole swathes of evidence absent from the material record at Bath at the time building work starts. I suspect that this was no coincidence, that it was siphoned off to fund the work and this has clear implications for deposits at other sites. Even when we do have fairly high numbers of finds, as for instance the 300 bracelets, possibly votive, from Lydney, Gloucestershire (Wheeler and Wheeler 1932, 42), we should remember how little we really have. That number seems high at first glance. It amounts to only a few per year. This in actual fact *low* figure is particularly important because here *we know* for certain from epigraphic evidence that

the material assemblage is deficient *because the proceeds of offerings were devoted to the building itself* (*RIB* 308).

There are grounds to believe the flavour of the deposit changes again under Constantine. We have to look at the general context. AD 325 is a potential key date for Bath, not AD 313 when Constantine became a Christian. In AD 325 Constantine delivered the *Oration to the Saints* at Antioch. It refers to the mysteries of hot springs provided by Providence (Lane-Fox 1986, 645). Copies of the speech almost certainly went to every province (Eusebius, *V.C.*, III, 19, 20, 54–8). British officials would certainly be aware of the likely consequences if they did not claim another prominent cult centre for Christianity; the treatment of temples in Phoenicia and Cilicia provided an instructive object lesson in how to go about things. So we might expect items to cease accumulating in AD 325. I am not so sure about coinage, but it so happens that one of the few pewter items that *can* be dated is a bowl with a cast of a coin of Constantine at its base, which is stylistically contemporary with the 'Munich Hoard' of silver plate deposited *c.* AD 324. Several pieces in the Munich hoard were made to order in AD 321/2 for Licinius and Constantine at towns in the Eastern Empire (Nicomedia, Antioch and Nyssa) for a high-ranking recipient (cat. no 14: Cunliffe 1985, vol. II, 11; Kent and Painter 1977, 20ff.). The Bath bowl surely implies an imperial donation, *c.* AD 321/2, either to a high-ranking official or to the temple itself – if it was still functioning as a temple. It or premises nearby could have been converted into a church and that is how some of the material dating to pre AD 325 could have entered the archaeological record, as 'pagan rubbish'.

Comment on fluctuations after Constantine must be reserved for another occasion (see Postscript). It is likely that worship of Sulis Minerva was interrupted, for an undated inscription refers to the wrecking of a holy place (*locum religiosum*) and its subsequent cleansing perhaps in the time of Julian the Apostate (*RIB* 152; Cunliffe 1969, 4; 2000, 130). We may infer the arrival of Christianity at some stage before the traditional cult later

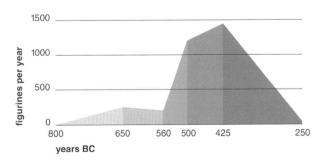

Fig. 18.2. Deposition rates of lead figurines at Sparta. Source: Whitley 2001, table 12.2. Not all periods are of equal length. Did rates of deposition at Bath also vary through time?

resumed. We do not know if the people who wrecked the *locum religiosum* were Christians (it is a reasonable guess) and if so whether they were local residents acting under orders or officials, perhaps visitors, brought in to alter the interior and fittings of the place. Possibly the temple-complex underwent a change of use, namely conversion to a church. So far, however, we have no explicit structural evidence to suggest this other than a resurfacing of the temple forecourt *c.* AD 300 or sometime after (Period 4: Cunliffe and Davenport 1985, 65ff., 75). Any alterations to the temple may have taken place above ground, or Christian foci such as a *martyrium* may lie outside the limits of excavation. Nor need this have been the only transformation in the vicinity. If (as *RIB* 152 implies) there was another temple opposite that of Sulis Minerva, in which emperor-worship took place, this too is likely to have undergone significant alterations. It may be no coincidence that Bath Abbey overlies these remains. Possibly temple and church ultimately co-existed in an uneasy relationship. A curse tablet from the sacred spring adjoining the temple of Sulis Minerva in New Roman Cursive contains a reference to Christians (*Tab. Sul.* 98), but lacks internal dating evidence (Tomlin 1988, 88, 97). It need not be fourth-century – some Christians could have been active before their religion was made legal in AD 313.

Ritual deposition of coinage at the sacred spring at Bath was in decline from *c.* AD 350 (Walker in Cunliffe and Davenport 1985, 361). What seem to be the last

coherent traces of formal ritual activity occur with the burial of pots, including fourth-century Black-Burnished Ware, at the top of the temple steps and in the temple forecourt area where cattle bone, perhaps from the last pagan sacrifices, was also deposited (Davenport 1991, 146). Theodosian coinage from ill-understood stratification in the temple forecourt shows some form of activity as late as AD 388–402 (Period 5C: Cunliffe and Davenport 1985, 74ff.). What either of these indicators means is anyone's guess. Did the pots on and by the stairway contain pagan offerings – or candles on the steps of a church?

In brief, the sacred spring deposit underwent a cycle. Every major phase of construction was accompanied by a major phase of clearance of the spring; in between, deposits accumulated. Expressed graphically, the revised sequence of building activity and clearance (if you believe my premise that building campaigns can be linked to emperors) is very simply this (Fig. 18.3).

What is not in the deposit?

We don't know what we are missing, but can guess at the possibilities:

– *Liquid offerings.* The evidence of jugs and ladles suggests this. There may have been other loci for making liquid offerings to the spring deity. We could expect *bothroi*, sacred pits or trenches *within* the precinct, perhaps sealed beneath the paving as at the forum in Rome.

– *Faunal remains.* There are no animal or human bones

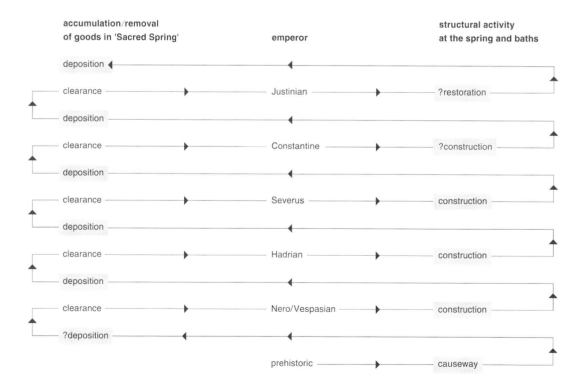

Fig. 18.3. Cycles of artefact deposition, clearance and architectural construction at the 'sacred spring', displayed chronologically as a 'switchback'. The sequence can be read by following the arrow. Source: author

from the spring. That this may not be a correct picture is becoming increasingly clear from the study of ritual pits and shafts. Coventina's Well represents institutionalised cult activity at the source of a spring and it produced a wide range of faunal remains. There should be dumps of waste from *centuries* of sacrifices or burnt offerings somewhere at Bath unless all the remains were consumed or flushed into the River Avon – an offering to Sabrina perhaps? There could equally well be dump or discard zones off site, in the town ditch or *temenos* – or beyond it.

— *Other organic material.* There are a few twigs and hazel nuts. These are sacred in terms of 'Celtic' religion: are we looking at votives (a category of find that seems entirely absent), as at the source of the Seine, or at material fallen from a tree nearby? Does that in turn imply a sacred grove? Or were branches ritually carried by a guild of *dendrophoroi*, as a graffito from the territory of Verulamium shows (Frere 1983, 13)? If so, where from? The existence of ivory and leather objects hint that organic wooden votives could have survived had they entered this micro-environment. So where were they?

— *Other non-organic material, e.g.* jewellery. There are 2 earrings, 5 rings, 4 bracelets, 4 brooches (one pennanular) and 34 intaglios. This seems a rather low amount for a total of *personalia* from the complex!

— *Placements on the ground.* Caesar himself describes the Gaulish habit of piling material on the ground; it was considered inviolate (*BG* VI, 17). At Wanborough, a relatively minor site, there were considerable quantities of material deposited on the ground, *under the temple* (Bird and O'Connell 1994).

— A temple treasury (*arca*) that held material is likely to have been above ground. We know of an *arkarius* (treasurer or cashier) at Chichester (Hassall, in Down 1981, 88), which also implies a repository for sacred objects. What might it have contained? Probably the more important objects. Wanborough, for instance, has at least 1,063 pottery vessels (Bird and O'Connell 1994, 133). The clue for Bath is the deposit in the temple courtyard reported separately – it contains a wide range of material including artefacts and coins (Cunliffe and Davenport 1985, 66–75). None of it need necessarily be ritual – but some of it probably was. Significantly, most of it was deposited in the fourth century or later, and the earliest surviving coins were of AD 270 (Period 5). But where had it been before then?

So whose cult was it anyway... and what was the sacred spring for?

These are not easy questions, and my answer is divided into several parts.

We may posit a phase of initial contact with a local and non-Roman deity. One inscription refers merely to a *genius loci* (*RIB* 139). When did either element of Sulis Minerva appear? We have no early reference for the name Sul before *c.* AD 121/2 (*RIB* 143). This may be significant in some way not immediately clear to us. Ptolemy, writing in the time of Hadrian, still refers (II, 3, 28) to Bath as *Aquae Callidae* ('hot springs'), not *Aquae Sulis*; the conflated name Sulis Minerva only occurs in the Antonine Itinerary (486, 3). But he could be working from outdated sources. We are so conditioned to thinking of Sulis Minerva as definitive that we forget the cult of Sul Minerva was possibly formalised (Romanised) as Sulis Minerva, but we do not know when conflation of Roman and local deity took place. How does this relate to gaps in the artefactual record? I am not sure that it necessarily does. The real promotion of Minerva/Athene *could* but *need* not be a relatively late creation. The pre-Hadrianic lack of name is the only hint of the cult of a 'native' deity – the material remains do not show this because they were dredged from their context.

Bath functioned as a site of pilgrimage for healing and incubation. This is assumed but needs to be spelt out – there is more proof than we think. The ivory and bronze breast votives from the sacred spring suggest a dedication to Sulis as a Romanised healing goddess, Minerva Medica (Henig, in Cunliffe 1988, nos. 4, 5). This was a female healing goddess – were the sexes, their healing gods and their votive deposits separated? If so, one might expect a shrine to the male healing deity Aesculapius elsewhere – stones suggest that this was at the Cross Bath spring, in the south-west quarter of the town (Cunliffe 2000, 115). The spring drains towards the Hot Baths. A building nearby is very reminiscent of a mansio in form. An inscription from the United Hospital site suggests the erection of a structure after someone, a man, had a vision (*RIB* 153). Incubation is implied, and therefore accommodation, but the site of this inscription is in the north-west quarter of the town.

Alas, the separation by gender is not so simple. Quite a few soldiers (and male civilians) dedicated altars to Sulis and they occur at the temple there. We know of a *sacerdos* (priest) from a tombstone (*RIB* 155) and of a *haruspex* who dedicated a statue (*JRS* 56 1966, 217 no.1). There is no evidence of female participation. One gets the impression that males controlled the cult; as so often elsewhere in the Roman Empire a female priesthood was ruled out.

Other deities besides Sulis Minerva were worshipped at Bath in the town or actually on the same complex. A sculpted stone from Cleveland Walk depicts the three *matres*. The sacrificial altar from the temple area depicts Bacchus, while gems from the spring depict other deities, including Cupid, Jupiter, Mercury, Minerva, Diana and Fortuna. So where were *their* shrines? We do not know for the most part. There is, however, an altar to Diana from the hot bath (*RIB* 138) so perhaps separate areas were set aside for the worship of different deities. An altar to Mars Loucetius and Nemetona may suggest a shrine adjacent to the precinct of the temple of Sulis Minerva (*RIB* 140; Cunliffe 2000, 132). It chimes with the theme of several martial offerings from the sacred spring such as the ballista washer and helmet crests. The hazel remains in the spring suggest the presence of a sacred grove – *nemeton*. Some of this may be rather late.

We have the *luna* pediment, the precise location of which is not known, beyond fringing on the main precinct to the north. Presumably it would, in theory, be balanced by worship of the sun deity S*ol*) fringing on the main precinct to the south (Cunliffe and Davenport 1985, 126–8; Cunliffe 2000, 60, 67). This indicates a worship of a moon deity, similar perhaps to the Semitic/Phoenician Astarte, and we might anticipate votives from either cult. I suspect that this was Severan. A correlate of this may be a mould for the manufacture of amulets, with a cross on the base of the sort associated with solar religion (Henig, in Cunliffe 1988, 24, cat. no. 60). Was there a *capitolium* at Bath and, if so, where?

There is one complicating factor. Was there a temple of the Imperial Cult in Bath? 'Consideration of the size of the surviving pieces [of architectural stonework] shows that…Bath…had another richly decorated building similar in size to the Maison Carrée at Nîmes and, if it too was a temple, one considerably large and grander than Sulis Minerva's' (Blagg 2002, 100). If so, where was it? The first epigraphic signs of emperor-worship appear at the Cross Bath AD 161–9+ (*RIB* 146) and at Stall Street, perhaps AD 208+ (*RIB* 152). Architecturally the first signs may appear rather earlier. We know of a circular *rotunda* or *tholos* from unstratified stone fragments. It was probably east of the temple forecourt, on a podium

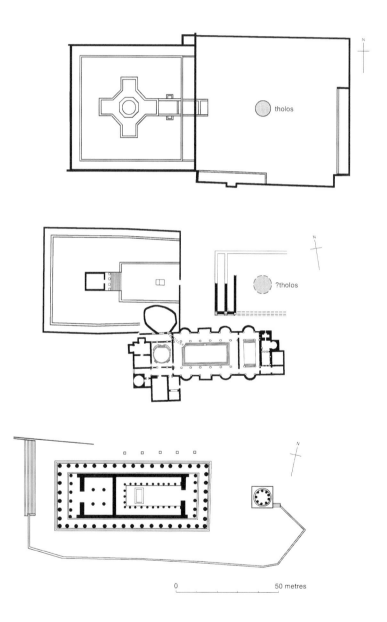

Fig. 18.4. Shrines with circular tholoi; from top to bottom: at Sanxay (Haute-Poitou), France; Bath, England; and Athens, Greece. The tholos-like feature E of the Parthenon, often interpreted as a temple to Rome and Augustus, has been reinterpreted as an altar of the Imperial Cult. Sources: Cunliffe 1989; and Hurwit 1999, fig. 3. Where was the temple of the Imperial Cult at Bath, if the tholos there is actually an altar?

now underneath the medieval Bath Abbey. This podium lay on a common principal axis with the doorway and altar of the temple of Sulis Minerva, and this too has parallels in Gaul (Cunliffe 1989, 66f; 2000, 110). The circular *tholos* recalls not only the Temple of Vesta in Rome but also the *monopteros* adjacent to, and on the principal axis of, the Parthenon on the Acropolis in Athens. That round structure, usually interpreted as a shrine to Rome and Augustus, has plausibly been reinterpreted as an altar of the imperial cult (*IG* II² 3173; Camp 2001, 186f.) It is worth noting that in AD 61/2, an inscription honouring Nero was added to the eastern architrave of the Parthenon itself (*IG* II² 3277; Hurwit 1999, 280f.), suggesting an imperial statue in or near the temple.

The ritual we *think* we know most about in Bath is cursing (Reynolds and Volk 1990). This is an illusion. We do not know *how often* consultations resulted in execration – nor how often a curse was subsequently *lifted* (and the *defixio* removed). We know less still of any archaeological indication of the opposite of curses – blessings. Cursing is clearly *over-represented* in the ritual record, thanks to various processes of deposition and clearance and (thank goodness) reportage, but the relation between actual rituals and the archaeological record is not straightforward as shown in this paper. Understandably, archaeologists have concentrated more on what went into the sacred spring (archaeologically visible material) than what came out of it – steam.

The aspect we actually know least about is Bath's *role as an oracle*. No doubt Bath was in large measure devoted to healing, but the steam welling up is reminiscent of Classical sites like Cumae, Lake Avernus, and Delphi – renowned oracles all. It is as well to recall that the iconography of the temple pediment depicts a gorgon – a creature depicted on the temple of Jupiter Ammon at Avenches in *Helvetia* (Henig 2000, 126f. and pers. comm.) and suggesting links all the way back to the oracle of Ammon at the Oasis of Siwah in Egypt which Alexander the Great consulted in 332 BC (Isserlin, in preparation). A well-known work of divination, the *Fates of Astrampsychus*, had come into being by the mid-first century. Shortly afterwards Bath came first into the Roman sphere of interest as a curiosity, and then into being as a shrine. Both Astrampsychus and Bath persisted into the Christian era (Lane-Fox 1986, esp. 207, 210f., 677). The walling-in of the sacred spring at Bath would create a heady sinister atmosphere and it would be quite possible for Romans to consider that they could speak to the gods of the underworld in this cavernous ambience. This is *the* context for the consigning of curse tablets to the depths. Being of lead or pewter, they sunk. What we do not know is the chain of processes that lead to their creation – namely the consultation of an official at the oracle. Divining the future was at least part of the function of the complex at Bath – there was a *haruspex*. The oracle would have been consulted by means of *sortes* – wooden slips cast to foretell the future, rather like the

Chinese *I-Ching*. If they were made of wood, they have either decayed or floated away. Surely, only as a result of an official's decision could an officially sanctioned curse be made and a *defixio* deposited in the spring. The fame of Bath as an oracle is indirectly attested in the writings of Solinus (*de rerum memorabilium*) who describes the use of coal on an altar; this curiosity is probably a snippet copied out from a larger (and missing) anonymous work, either on oracles or on the province as a whole.

Conclusions:
points of contact and of departure

My initial conventional definition was that sacred spring material is an open, single-aspect deposit – essentially inorganic and mostly metallic. It is correct as far as it goes; I now think we can say a bit more than that. There are several points that we can come away with:

At the very least, we cannot take it on trust that what we have really is a simple votive or ritual deposit, or a true representation of simple cult activity at or around the sacred spring. By way of concrete documented analogy, the main temple at the source of the river Clitumnus in Italy was surrounded by a sacred grove; it contained *sortes* oracular tablets (probably wooden); coins were thrown in to the spring; separate deities had their own shrines clustered around the main one; inscriptions or graffiti are notable too (Pliny *Letters*, viii, 8). Precisely the sorts of features we might expect at Bath. The Fonti di Clitunno, near Spoleto is being investigated by the British School at Rome, together with Filippo Coarelli of Perugia University and the Soperintendenza Archeologica dell'Umbria (http//:www.bsr.ac.uk).

Deposition need not necessarily be a primary purpose of the sacred spring during the Roman period – it was only one aspect. The assemblage now in its silts is only part of a wider spectrum of rituals that have changed with time, which relied on processes of *structured deposition* or *placement* in *properly organised repositories*. We should probably think of other repositories like a temple treasury as at Nîmes, on which the temple of Sulis Minerva is supposedly modelled and which it is said, probably correctly, had internal shelving, possibly for a library (MacDonald 1986, 116). Sacred books, organic and inorganic votive items, including quantities of clothing, weapons, furniture, and human hair would probably be stored there in their prescribed places, as epigraphically attested elsewhere in the Graeco-Roman world. They would be labelled with the date of their acquisition or donation and a register kept of their condition and shelf location (Macmullen 1981, 34f.; Camp 2001, 81f.). Similar items at Bath (including organic items, miniatures, and votive plaques) will have been stored *above ground*.

The 'sacred spring' deposit (dump?) is a window into these other cults with their deposits. But we cannot 'read off' information from it about these cults as easily as we think. The correlation is not direct. When the various temples of Minerva, Diana, Luna, Sol, or the Emperor came to an end, material such as ivory breasts, military catapults or pewter plates entered the sacred spring *from a variety of separate sources, not just one*. Unwanted pagan rubbish assemblage was dumped in the spring or scattered in the temple courtyard, probably as a result of, for example, Christian looting of temple treasuries. Very few items are *in situ* in their primary context and the original locus of deposition may be elsewhere. We have, for instance, five wooden combs and a miniature wooden spear, an attribute of Athena/Minerva. Most intriguing of all is a piece of leather(?) carefully rolled into a cylinder (Cunliffe 1988, 24–7, nos. 67–71, 80 and 82), perhaps a miniature scroll or petition. They are probably inappropriate to single-aspect 'watery deposits'. A lot more was probably carted away and burned, buried or melted down (*e.g.* gold and silver plate) in this final Christianising stage. It is not surprising then that what we have is unspectacular – the local bishop probably considered it to have been comparatively harmless or worthless. If many of the coins present were originally offerings on behalf of the emperor as at Bourbonne-les-Bains (Sauer 1999), this would go some way to confirming the suggestion that there was also a temple of the Imperial Cult nearby, with its own separate treasury.

There are significant and real gaps in deposition, as goods were recycled into temple architecture throughout the lifecycle of the building. This is accepted practice in Gaul and Britain. At Yverdon: *dona venibunt et ex stipibus ponentur*. Votive letters were sold at the extensive pilgrimage centre at Lydney. One building was built from offerings (*ex stipibus*) in the AD 360s (Wheeler and Wheeler 1932, 103; RIB 308; RIB 2488.3; Wright 1985). In other words, we do have the votives, or rather the proceeds from their sale, *transformed into something else.* Prehistorians such as Richard Bradley have correctly observed that there is a relationship between artefact deposition and prehistoric monument construction (1985). To put it more classically, *si monumentum requiris, circumspice*.

I only became aware of Dr Eberhard Sauer's publications after my paper was delivered (Sauer 1999; 2000; forthcoming), and have tried to take account of them where possible. His suggestion that the Roman army played a major role in offering coins at springs should certainly be considered as a factor at Bath. He also points out (pers. comm., 4/3/04) that, on the analogy of Bourbonne-les-Bains, the high proportion of early imperial coins at Bath is hard to reconcile with my suggestion of a high proportion of the coins being removed at regular intervals from the sacred spring deposit (though it depends of course when and whence they were introduced into the deposit – they could have emanated from somewhere off-site, and need not have been there *ab initio*, in their primary context, near the date they were minted). His observation that there is virtually no firm evidence for Iron Age coin

offerings in springs anywhere else may cast doubts on the notion that Iron Age coins were removed from the deposit – though that general absence might equally well be interpreted to mean thorough removal. The Wanborough deposit placed at surface-level and sealed by a later temple is the potential indicator here. What – if anything – is the equivalent at Bath, one wonders?

The appearance, after the present text was submitted, in March 2004 of *World Archaeology* volume 36, entitled 'The Object of Dedication' is also to be noted. There are welcome signs of convergence: the editor of the thematic issue, a prominent Hellenist, also underscores the need for a holistic archaeology and the need to study votive deposits (Osbourne 2004), though he is possibly over-pessimistic so far as matters Roman are concerned, to judge by some developments in the north-western provinces. That issue also contains a useful paper devoted to the potential of votive shafts in Roman towns to indicate foundation rituals. The suggestion that deposits could be 'periodically cleared out' (Woodward and Woodward 2004, 79) is of course a tenet of the present paper. Readers of their paper are also referred to a treatment by the present author, of Roman votive shafts in ritual contexts, where the crucial principle of repetitive dedicated deposits being related to festivals that the authors espouse was, to the best of his belief, first expounded (Isserlin 1995). Neither of these two recent papers affects the present text, the style and substance of which remain unchanged.

Postscript

A study of the 4th-century silver coinage has led to the suggestion that, as at nearby Shapwick, the coins were deposited as a group as a single event – *along with the pewter items*. This would be at the earliest after AD 392, possibly in the pagan revival of Eugenius. It has also been suggested that this group of coins may not be complete; some of these were clipped as in the Patching hoard (deposited *c.* AD 465). Stylistic dating of one item of metalwork suggests a date-range of AD 450–550 is possible (Gerrard 2005, 372). Whether or not (all?) coins were (finally?) deposited *en bloc* in the Spring at the same time as (all?) the metalwork, this reinforces the point that the Sacred Spring Deposit was an open assemblage with many sub-components – each with their own history.

Acknowledgements

Thanks to the organisers for inviting me; to C. R. Wallace for reading this paper and bibliographical assistance; and to Hilary Cool for supplying a reference to the Bath sword pommel. I am most grateful to Eberhard Sauer for his penetrating observations at less than short notice, and to the anonymous referee for improving the paper considerably.

References

Allason-Jones, L. and McKay, B. (1987) *Coventina's Well: a shrine on Hadrian's Wall.* Chesters, Trustees of the Clayton Collection.

Bird, J. and O'Connell, M. G. (1994) The Roman temple at Wanborough, excavation 1985–1986. *Surrey Archaeological Collections* 82, 1–168.

Blagg, T. F. C. (1990) The Temple at Bath (*Aquae Sulis*) in the context of classical temples in the west European provinces. *Journal of Roman Archaeology* 3, 419–30.

Blagg, T. F. C. (2002) *Roman Architectural Ornament in Britain.* British Archaeological Reports, British Series 329. Oxford.

Boardman, J. M. (1963) Artemis Orthia and Chronology. *Annual of the British School at Athens*, 58, 1–7.

Bradley, R. (1985) *Consumption, change and the archaeological record. The archaeology of monuments and the archaeology of deliberate deposits. Two Munro Lectures given in the University of Edinburgh 27 and 28 November 1984.* Edinburgh, Department of Archaeology University of Edinburgh Occasional Paper 13.

Bradley, R. (1998) *The Passage of Arms. An Archaeological Study Of Prehistoric Hoards And Votive Deposits.* Oxford, Oxbow (2nd edition).

Camp, J. M. (2001) *The Archaeology of Athens.* New Haven and London, Yale University Press.

Cunliffe, B. W. (1969) *Roman Bath.* Report of the Research Committee of the Society of Antiquaries 24.

Cunliffe, B. W. (ed.) (1988) *The Temple of Sulis Minerva at Bath: Volume 2, the finds from the sacred spring.* Oxford, Oxford University Committee for Archaeology Monograph 16.

Cunliffe, B. W. (1989) The Roman Tholos from the sanctuary of Sulis Minerva at Bath, England. In Curtis, R. I. (ed.) *Studia Pompeiana & Classica in Honor of Wilhemina F. Jashemski, Volume II: Classica*, 59–71. New York, Orpheus Publishing.

Cunliffe, B. W. (2000) *Roman Bath.* Stroud, Tempus Publishing.

Cunliffe, B. W. and Davenport, P. (1985) *The Temple of Sulis Minerva at Bath. Volume 1, The site.* Oxford, Oxford University Committee for Archaeology Monograph 7, Oxford.

Davenport, P. (ed.) (1991) *Archaeology in Bath 1976–1985*, Oxford, Oxford University Committee for Archaeology Monograph 28, Oxford.

Davies, J. A. (1990) Coins from the Sacred Spring at Bath. *Journal of Roman Archaeology* 3, 431–6.

Down, A. (1981) *Chichester Excavations*, 5. Chichester, Phillimore.

Field, N., and Parker-Pearson, M. (2003) *Fiskerton: An Iron Age Timber Causeway with Iron Age and Roman Votive Offerings.* Oxford, Oxbow.

Frere, S. S. (1975) The origin of Small Towns. In W. J. Rodwell and R. T. Rowley (eds.) *Small Towns of Roman Britain*, 4–7. British Archaeological Reports 15. Oxford.

Frere, S. S. (1983) *Verulamium Excavations II. The Finds.* Oxford University Committee for Archaeology Monograph. Oxford.

Ginge, B. (1993) Votive deposits in Italy: new perspectives on old finds. *Journal of Roman Archaeology* 6, 285–88.

Green, M. J. (1976) *A Corpus of Religious Material from the Civilian Areas of Roman Britain.* British Archaeological Reports 24. Oxford.

Green, M. J. (1978) *Small Cult Objects from the Military Areas of Roman Britain.* British Archaeological Reports 52. Oxford.

Green, M. J. (1981) Model objects from military areas of Roman Britain. *Britannia* 12, 253–69.

Greep, S. (1998) The bone, antler and ivory artefacts. In H. E. M Cool and C. Philo (eds.) *Roman Castleford Excavations 1974–85.* I: *The Small Finds*, 267–85. Yorkshire Archaeology 4. Wakefield, West Yorkshire Archaeological Service.

Gerrard, G. (2005) A possible Late Roman silver 'hoard' from Bath. *Britannia* 36, 371–3.

Henig, M. (1984) *Religion in Roman Britain.* London, Batsford.

Henig, M. (1999) A new star shining over Bath. *Oxford Journal of Archaeology* 18.4, 419–25.

Henig, M. (2000) From Classical Greece to Roman Britain: some Hellenic themes in provincial art and glyptics. In G.R. Tsetskhaladze, A. M. Snodgrass and A. J. N. W. Prag (eds.) *Periplous: To Sir John Boardman from his pupils and friends*, 124–35. London, Thames and Hudson.

Henig, M. (2002) *The Heirs of King Verica: Culture and Politics in Roman Britain.* Stroud, Tempus.

Hill, J. D. (1995) *Ritual and Rubbish in the Iron Age of Wessex.* British Archaeological Reports British Series 242. Oxford.

Hill, P. R. (1997) The Maryport altars: some first thoughts. In R. J. A. Wilson (ed.) *Roman Maryport and its setting : essays in memory of Michael G. Jarrett*, 92–104. Kendal, Cumberland and Westmoreland Archaeological and Architectural Society.

Hurwit, J. M. (1999) *The Athenian Acropolis. History, Mythology and Archaeology from the Neolithic Era to the Present.* Cambridge, Cambridge University Press.

Ilkjaer, J. (2000) *Illerup Ådal: Archaeology as a Magic Mirror.* Moesgård, University Press.

Isserlin, R. M. J. (1995) A history of brief time: monuments and seasonality in Roman Britain. In S. Cottam *et al* (eds) *TRAC 94: Proceedings of the Fourth Theoretical Roman Archaeology Conference*, 45–56. Oxford, Oxbow.

Isserlin, R. M. J. (1997) Thinking the unthinkable: human sacrifice in Roman Britain? In C. Lemke *et al* (eds) *TRAC 96: Proceedings of the Sixth Theoretical Roman Archaeology Conference*, 91–100 Oxford, Oxbow.

Isserlin, R. M. J. (2000) Cogidubnus, Togidubnus – What's in a name? *Associate Lecturer Newsletter Department of Classical Studies*, 8–10. Milton Keynes, The Open University.

Isserlin, R. M. J. (in preparation) *Towns and Power.* Stroud, Tempus Publishing.

Jordan, D. R. (1990) Curses from the waters of Sulis. *Journal of Roman Archaeology* 3, 437–41.

Kent, J. P. C. and Painter, K. S. (eds) (1977) *Wealth of the Roman World: gold and silver AD 300–700.* London, British Museum.

Lane-Fox, R. (1986) *Pagans and Christians.* Harmondsworth, Penguin.

MacDonald W. M. (1986) *The Architecture of the Roman Empire II: An Urban Appraisal.* New Haven and London, Yale University Press.

Macmullen, R. (1981) *Paganism in the Roman Empire.* New Haven & London, Yale University Press.

Osborne, R. (2004) 'Hoards, votives, offerings: the archaeology of the dedicated object', *World Archaeology* 36(1), 1–10.

Potter, T. W. (1985) The Republican healing sanctuary at Ponte di Nona near Roma and the classical tradition of votive medicine. *Journal of the British Archaeological Association* 138, 23–47.

Poulton, R. and Scott, E. (1993) The hoarding, deposition, and use of pewter in Roman Britain. In E. Scott (ed.) *Theoretical Roman Archaeology: First Conference Proceedings*, 115–132. Aldershot, Avebury.

Randsborg, K. (1995) *Hjortspring: Warfare and sacrifice in Early Europe*. Aarhus, Aarhus University Press.

Reynolds, J. & Volk, T. (1990) Gifts, curses, cult and society at Bath. *Britannia* 21, 379–91.

Rouse, W. H. D. (1902) *Greek Votive Offerings*. Cambridge, Cambridge University Press.

Sauer, E. (1999) The Augustan army spa at Bourbonne-les-Bains. In A. Goldsworthy and I. Haynes (eds) *The Roman Army as a Community: Including papers from a conference held at Birkbeck College, University of London on 11–12 January 1997. Journal of Roman Archaeology Supplementary Series No 34*, 52–79. Portsmouth, Rhode Island.

Sauer, E. (2000) The Augustan coins from Bourbonne-les-Bains (Haute-Marne) – a mathematical approach to dating a coin assemblage. *Révue Numismatique 154*, 1999, 145–82.

Sauer, E. (forthcoming) *Coins, Cult, and Cultural Identity: Augustan coins, hot springs and the early Roman baths at Bourbonne-les-Bains*. Leicester, Leicester Archaeological Monographs 10.

Snodgrass, A. M. (1990) The economics of dedication at Greek sanctuaries. *Scienze dell'Antichità: Storia, Archeologia, Antropologia* 3–4 [1989–90], 287–94.

Spencer, B. (1968) Medieval pilgrim badges. In J. G. N. Renaud (ed.) *Rotterdam Papers: A Contribution to Medieval Archaeology*, 135–53.

Stopford, J. (1994) Some approaches to the archaeology of Christian pilgrimage. *World Archaeology* 26, 57–72.

Tomlin, R. S. O. (1988) The curse tablets. In B.W. Cunliffe (ed.) *The Temple of Sulis Minerva at Bath: Volume 2, the finds from the sacred spring,* 59–217. *Oxford University Committee for Archaeology Monograph* 16. (= *Tab. Sulis*). Oxford.

Wace, A. J. B. (1929) The lead figurines. In R. M. Dawkins (ed.) *The Sanctuary of Artemis Orthia at Sparta*. Supplement to the Journal of Hellenic Studies 5, 249–84.

Walker, D. R. (1988) The Roman coins. In B. W. Cunliffe (ed.) *The Temple of Sulis Minerva at Bath: Volume 2, the finds from the sacred spring,* 281–358. *Oxford University Committee for Archaeology Monograph* 16. Oxford.

Wells, P. S. (2001) *Beyond Celts: Germans and Scythians. Archaeology and Identity in Iron Age Europe*. London, Duckworth.

Wheeler, R. E. M. and Wheeler, T. V. (1932) *Report on the Excavation of the Prehistoric, Roman and Post-Roman site in Lydney Park, Gloucestershire*. London, Report of the Research Committee of the Society of Antiquaries 9.

Whitley, J 2001 *Archaeology of Ancient Greece* (Cambridge, CUP).

Woodward, A. & Leach, P. (1993) *Uley Shrines: Excavation of a ritual complex on West Hill, Uley, Gloucestershire, 1977–79*. London, English Heritage Archaeological Report 17.

Woodward, P. and Woodward, A. (2004) Dedicating the town: urban foundation deposits in Roman Britain, *World Archaeology* 36(1), 68–86.

Wright, R. P. (1985) A revised restoration of the inscription on the mosaic pavement found in the temple at Lydney Park, Gloucestershire. *Britannia* 16, 1985, 248–9.

19 The Detritus of Life: the Contribution of Small Finds to Understanding Smaller Military Installations

Sonja Jilek and David Breeze

Introduction

Studies of Roman small finds in the past have been largely concerned with observations on their style, function or manufacture. Such studies have concentrated on the interpretation of each object on an individual basis: seldom will one find a full discussion of the entire assemblage, even less a discussion of the small finds within the context of the results of the whole excavation. The presentation of material culture from excavations of Roman sites usually consists of the allocation of the small finds to specialists to write typological catalogues of each artefact category, with the objective of facilitating studies concerned with the production, distribution and dating of each category. In return, the excavators usually use the finds report to underpin their stratigraphy and date their building phases.

Yet small finds, as well as pottery, can be used to provide a fuller understanding of changing behaviour inside and around military installations, in the hinterland of frontiers, in villas, in roadside settlements, in civilian contexts and beyond the border of the *Imperium Romanum*. The focus here is upon Roman military sites, specifically smaller installations of the Roman army. Not so long ago archaeology was seen as failing to deal with many of the questions which scholars expected it to answer, particularly those relating to specific historical events and individuals, and there has been a lack of realisation of the fact that the real strength of the material lies in its capacity for allowing us to understand long-term processes. In recent years, however, things have begun to change; the true potential of archaeological data has begun to be recognised (Allison 1999; Spradley 2001; Allason-Jones 2002). This development has brought with it a consciousness of the potentially broad range of issues which can be studied using archaeological material. We are aware now that we have to explore the relationships within and between Roman provinces. We have not only to investigate the structure of the army itself but also the soldiers' relationships with broader communities in these provinces. A period of roughly four centuries requires to be covered, from the late Republican era to the fourth century, when army structure, administration and the whole of community life underwent major changes. We also need to assess the degree of change taking place over time, acknowledging that different periods produce different structures, each

deeply affected by the profound political changes taking place in the Roman world as a whole. For instance, the shift in power away from the central region in Rome and Italy towards the western and eastern provinces was linked to a change in the role played by the army within provincial societies. Furthermore, too many approaches have assumed that the army as a social formation remained static over long periods of time and this has also affected our understanding of the material culture in this complex field.

It is of special interest to us – each approaching this subject from different viewpoints – to acknowledge the close relationship between architecture, social institutions and material culture. These are closely locked together in that one cannot exist without the others. By taking a closer look at the architectural and material evidence relating to Roman fortlets as a case study, we shall seek to explore and emphasise the connections between built space, function and an individual social group, in this case the community of soldiers living within these structures. Although it is the archaeological information which forms the basis of this study, textual and also iconographic evidence is used to help construct an interpretative framework. To use and bring together all these different types of sources, where the remaining evidence is sometimes frustratingly poor, has turned out to be difficult at times; nevertheless, we hope that, whatever their remaining imperfections, the arguments presented here will stimulate debate on Roman finds – an area which has increasingly become a focus of interest for ancient historians as well as for archaeologists.

The interpretation of Roman military small finds

Small finds of military origin have the ability to tell us various stories about their owners and the places where they were stationed. Intense research during the last 30 years presents us with a definition of Roman military equipment in a general sense (Bishop and Coulston 1993; Feugère 2002). Because of the obvious nature of some artefacts there is no disagreement about the inclusion of distinctive finds, such as defensive or offensive weapons, in this category. Unfortunately, the interpretation of other material is often not as simple as that and becomes increasingly difficult when it concerns the interpretation of personal accessories, horse harness or various other items of equipment which are most frequently found in military contexts. The latest Roman military equipment conference in Switzerland in 2000, dedicated to the investigation of the role of military finds in civil contexts, clearly demonstrated that there is still a lively discussion in progress about the military nature of these objects (see the many articles in the *Jahresbericht Gesellschaft Pro Vindonissa* 2001). The debate, which has clearly not finished yet, is of the utmost importance when it comes to identifying a military presence in a particular place or context. Therefore, the given interpretation affects not only the artefacts themselves but our understanding of the military, social and administrative structures in the frontier provinces of the Roman empire.

There is a series of questions we can ask about the objects themselves and the answers will help us obtain a better understanding of the places where they were found, the nature of the troops who were stationed there and perhaps their purpose. It has previously been noted that military equipment can offer some help in identifying troops which in turn tells us something about the nature of the garrison. There is a common belief that *pilae* and heavy artillery are exclusively associated with legionary soldiers. Daggers and finds of *lorica segmentata* seem to hint at the presence of infantry. The iconographic evidence of soldiers' tombstones show that highly decorated belts were depicted only on infantry soldiers. Typical categories of weapons like archery equipment, sling shots or distinctive sorts of lances allow us to identify specially trained groups of soldiers. Finds of functional or elaborately decorated pieces of horse harness are generally explained by the presence of horsemen or cavalry units. If we review the well-known material evidence from many military sites and follow these assumptions, we are confronted with the fact that garrisons are much more diversely composed and organised than we would have thought before (Maxfield 1986).

Although we have no indication at all that the Roman army used uniforms in the modern sense, soldiers selectively emphasised their distinctiveness from the surrounding civilian society by a certain dress code. The finds illuminate the ways members of military communities expressed their collective identity, as in the wearing of specific types of equipment. This is first of all the sword and the sword-belt and, so long as a man wore both, he was identifiably a soldier. The importance of this special equipment is reflected in the decoration lavished on the sword-belts themselves and in their careful depiction on private monuments of soldiers not shown in battle-dress. But Roman soldiers, like those in modern armies, also had a ranking system: not all members were equal. The Roman army possessed a complex hierarchy of ranks, related to its command structure, which gave each soldier a specific status in the military community in which he lived. It is

still a difficult task for us to understand the complexity of badges of rank, costume accessories and military decorations. At the current stage of research we cannot identify a consequent sequence of badges of rank. If rank was not expressed in other ways, like in the colour of their clothes, the physical manifestation of the hierarchy might not have been as complex as in modern times. But we can clearly distinguish between certain ranks according to significant items of equipment. For instance, regimental standard bearers and musicians are clearly identifiable through the coats of wild animals, usually the pelt of a lion or a bear. Soldiers' tombstones show that centurions used to wear insignia like a helmet with a special transverse crest and carry the *vitis*, a short stick. Equestrian and senatorial officers are generally depicted in antiquated equipment of Hellenistic style with muscled-cuirass and *cinctorium*.

The army is seldom appreciated as a dynamic society in its own right. There are, however, clear signs that the Roman soldiers created and appreciated their own styles of fashion. New looks were maybe established by the soldiers in Rome and adopted and imitated by the men out in the frontier provinces. It is often stated that the moving around of the senior army officers brought the new fashion accessories even to the very far corners of the empire although we still lack evidence for this hypothesis. On parade, Josephus emphasised the splendour of the occasion and the pride the men took in their appearance, smartening themselves up and wearing their finest equipment (Josephus, *Bellum Judaicum* 5. 349–51). Through all this evidence we recognise pride in personal appearance and pride in membership, which of course at the same time created a unit identity.

Both officers and soldiers were subject to movement round the empire. Senior personnel and even entire regiments could be transferred from one end of the empire to another. So we would expect them to take all, or most, of their belongings with them. If we try to trace and prove this by the finds, we do not get far. Of course, there is some evidence, like the brooches in a typical Celto-British style on the Upper Rhine *Limes* (Böhme 1972, 30; cf. Swift 2000), assumed to have been brought by soldiers from Britain, or the Frisian and African style pottery recognised on various sites in northern Britain (Jobey 1979; Swan 1999). To explain this sparsity of evidence, it was argued that in practice these movements happened less and less frequently. Although the empire was bound together by the movement of people and ideas, only a relatively small proportion of well-equipped soldiers and their equestrian commanders would have served in both the East and the West. It is further argued that, as a result, armies developed regional or provincial attributes and allegiances when the individual units drew local recruits and were stationed in one place for generations and were mostly influenced by the community in which they were stationed. Although this theory is partly supported by the evidence, for instance, by the items of special third-century military equipment created and used by the armies of the Danube provinces, like belt-plates with *utere felix*-applications or little spearheads made out of bronze, which show up very seldom on sites in the western provinces, there are also some arguments against it. Roman politics and the military history of the later second and the third centuries clearly demonstrate that many troops were moved to fight against the serious threats and in lengthy wars in the East and on the Danube frontiers, or later on during the internal political conflicts of the third century. Beside the few exceptions mentioned above we have to emphasise the surprising fact that there was much uniformity across an area as diverse as the Roman empire and over an extended chronological period. The exceptions might be due to the high degree of independence of local government within the framework of the Roman imperial government, which has often been stressed. The interaction of imperial policy and provincial sub-policy is still a complex analytical problem because neither structure nor the boundaries between them are fixed.

The interpretation of find assemblages is difficult. In considering this material it is especially important to note and comment on the individual context, the specific place and stratigraphical level where each object was found. There are then various possibilities and models of interpretation which are not necessarily straightforward. We need to question the representativeness of the finds material from settlements and cemeteries. How did the objects find their way into the context? Equipment could have been lost during daytime activities inside the military installation or while on patrol, during training or when fighting away from the home base. Were soldiers sent away to undertake various tasks in the vicinity of their base or in other parts of the province, and indeed other provinces, always wearing their weapons and 'uniforms'? There is conflicting evidence in relation to the density of objects. Whereas some analysis of the distribution of the finds within military sites have shown considerable differential spread, others show a fairly consistent spread across most of the area examined (Zanier 1992, 104–56). Although one would assume that weapons and other military equipment were kept in the anterooms of the *contubernia* or in the *armamentaria*, the distribution pattern provides little support for this. Destruction levels tend to include more objects which are often, if not burnt, in good condition (for a wide ranging discussion of such matters see the Acta of the Roman Military Equipment Conference, Vienna 2003: *Archaeology of battlefields – militaria from destruction deposits, Carnuntum Jahrbuch* for 2003).

The army's day-to-day routine brought many soldiers into contact with civilians, both as individuals and in groups. We know that soldiers, detachments or regiments were not confined to narrow frontier zones or tightly delineated bases or forts; individual soldiers were frequently detached from their units for various reasons. The ordinary course of military duties required some soldiers

to travel far from their regiments. Such men feature repeatedly in papyri and writing tablets from the Roman world. The duty rosters from Dura Europos, Vindolanda and Vindonissa allow us to envisage the widespread movement necessitated by the working routines of ordinary soldiers. The organisation of supply within regiments was a matter of routine to the military in war as in peace; the maintenance and replacement of weapons and other equipment was vital. A special group of military personnel performed diverse administrative tasks for governors (see Davies 1989, 33–71 for a discussion of the soldiers' activities during peace time).

After their retirement it would appear that veterans were allowed to keep part of their equipment, if they wanted it and had paid for it. The evidence shows that only few of them actually did so during the first and second centuries, not least because it was financially remunerative for them, or their heirs, to sell their equipment back to the army (Breeze 1993b, 571–3). This situation changed rapidly during the late second and third centuries. Thence many pieces of military equipment as well as horse harness are found in the civil settlements and the villas in the hinterland of frontiers. This is also the first time that ornamented belts appear quite regularly in burials in the frontier zones. Most recently Thomas Fischer listed a series of arguments as to why weapons and military equipment are found in civilian contexts (Fischer 2002). This includes private ownership of weapons for self-defence; weapons for the chase, which are not so easily distinguished from weapons of the army; weapons lost during street fights or deposited in hoards in case of wartime; and workshops for weapons, which were produced mainly in civil settlements close to the frontier. Military objects in exclusively private or religious contexts tend to be more seldom considered in relation to this argument. Pliny's letters indicate that weapons were used as decoration or trophies, displayed in prominent positions within *villae rusticae* (Förtsch 1993, 40). Equipment like helmets or armour appear more frequently in sanctuaries or sacred areas where the majority of them represent votive offerings.

Weapons and various military equipment unearthed beyond the Roman frontiers in the *barbaricum* are very relevant and should not be excluded from a more general discussion. We do not need to stress the case of Roman swords, where the vast majority of pieces have come to light outside the empire, to emphasise this point. Excavations of native settlements and cemeteries often produce Roman artefacts (Hunter 2001 and this volume); although we must be aware of the significant differences in the quantity of the material revealed though time or from sites in different areas of Britain and on the Continent. While some regions, like the north of Britain, seem to be rather poor in evidence, others, like many sites north of the middle Danube frontier, have produced an incredible amount of all sorts of Roman artefacts, including military equipment. The reasons for this conflicting evidence are still unknown and need to be examined in a thoroughly based, comprehensive study. The most prominent Roman luxury items came to light in native upper class burials which clearly reflect the importance of these objects for the status of the chieftains of the tribes. Until most recently, scholars explained the origin of Roman finds in settlements and cemeteries in the *barbaricum* as the booty of war or – more often – as a result of the activities of Roman long-distance traders who exchanged Roman wares for products frequently mentioned by ancient authors such as meat, hides and salt. A new hypothesis by Michael Erdrich tries to link the occurrence of Roman artefacts in the *barbaricum* to diplomatic contacts between the Romans and the favoured native tribes during concrete historical events (Erdrich 2001; Erdrich, Giannotta and Hanson 2000). While this is not the right place to consider these divergent patterns in detail, it is important to note the introduction of new approaches to old evidence which should lead us to reflect upon our knowledge and understanding of Roman frontier policy generally and in detail.

Fortlets

No overall analysis of this special type of smaller fortified place exists. We lack specific knowledge about the type of troops stationed in such installations, about the military hierarchy operating at these sites and about the strength of the garrisons and their tasks. In general, small fortifications with a size less than 0.6 ha are called fortlets (Kleinkastelle). They appear in various sizes (see Table 19.1) ranging from very small sites with an internal space of 0.03 ha or less to larger enclosures which closely resemble the *numeri* forts which measure in general 0.6 to 1 ha (Baatz 2000, 40; Schallmayer 2001). The milecastles (and milefortlets) on Hadrian's Wall belong to the same group, because their structures are very similar to fortlets, albeit attached to the Wall (Breeze and Dobson 2000, 33).

Although the layout of the structures in fortlets do show a certain variety, they also have characteristic features in common (Figures 19.1–19.3). Few excavations have produced a complete plan of the internal structures together with details of the installations, *e.g.* milecastle 35 (Sewingshields), milecastle 48 (Poltross Burn), milefortlet 5 (Cardurnock), milefortlet 21 (Swarthy Hill), Barburgh Mill, Nersingen, Degerfeld, Haselburg, Holzheimer Unterwald and Rötelsee. Old excavations often lack this information, *e.g.* milecastle 9 (Chapel House), Saalburg Schanze A and B, Kemel and Hönehaus. Other more recently excavated sites provide us with some details on the interior structures but have not been fully excavated, *e.g.* milefortlet 1 (Biglands) and Neuwirtshausen. There are some sites known, like milecastle 39 (Castle Nick) on Hadrian's Wall or Bickenbach in Upper Germany (Göldner 1998), which have been completely excavated but not yet published.

Fortlets have either one or two gateways, which might be related to their function. Enclosures earlier than the

timber-built fortlet at Neuwirtshausen, which was constructed in Hadrianic times, tend to have two ditches, whereas most of the later examples built in stone are surrounded by one ditch only. In accordance with the existence of one or two gateways, the interior buildings are constructed as a U-shaped block of rooms arranged round a courtyard (Figure 19.4.3) or placed on each side of a central road (Figure 19.4.5): there are usually two such buildings, but three are known, for example at Haselburg. Exceptions from this are milefortlet 5 (Cardurnock), Barburgh Mill, Kemel period 2 and Degerfeld, which have only one gateway but contain two isolated buildings facing each other. The outline of the building-blocks in the fortlets of Kemel period 2 and Degerfeld seems to represent a hybrid because both ground plans show some indication that the rear side was closed in some way. The only site in Britain one might compare with this building type is Martinhoe in Devon (Fox and Ravenhill 1966), although the rear block is not directly attached to the adjacent rooms. Houses of the block type (Saalburg Schanze B, Kemel period 1, Neuwirtshausen and Rötelsee) seem to have a more regular layout with equally spaced rooms on both sides of the courtyard. The rooms in the central block to the rear often show different internal arrangements, so one can assume that the rooms on each side of the courtyard are barrack-blocks. The larger room(s) might have been for the commanding officer. In this type of fortlet we have no indication of storage facilities. Two hearths, excavated in the rear of the courtyard in Rötelsee, might have been used for cooking. A timber structure over the small channel, which was intended to drain off the water from the courtyard of this fortlet, was perhaps used as a latrine.

All other British fortlets and milecastles fall into the category which has one or two detached building blocks like the majority of the examples from Upper Germany. The excavation of the fortlet of the mid-second century at Barburgh Mill in southern Scotland in 1971 produced a complete plan of a fortlet of the double building type. The soldiers were accommodated in two buildings which faced each other within the narrow confines of the nearly square enclosure. Together, they contained two larger rooms and ten rooms of roughly equal size. If they had been arranged in a single building there would have been no doubt that they would have been designated as the accommodation of a single century. It seems that both blocks accommodated soldiers, which is also quite obvious from the ground plan in Degerfeld, while regularly-spaced rooms on one side of the road only, like the arrangements in Nersingen, remain the exception. It may be noted that in some sites the internal buildings were built up against the internal face of the enclosure wall: milecastle 37 (Housesteads), milecastle 39 (Castle Nick) and milefortlet 21 (Swarthy Hill) on Hadrian's Wall all contain such buildings (Daniels 1978; Crow 1989; Turnbull 1998). One of the internal buildings often contains a separate, slightly larger compartment or even several smaller rooms for the officer

	A	B	C	D	E	F	G	H	I	K	L	M	N	O	P	R	S
size	0,027 ha	0,028 ha	0,039 ha	0,046 ha	0,026 ha	per. 1: 0,113 ha per. 2: 0,71 ha	0,03 ha	0,084 ha	0,06 ha	per. 1: 0,16 ha per. 2: 0,08 ha	per. 1: 0,07 ha per. 2: 0,13 ha	0,3 ha	0,045 ha	0,2 ha	per. 1: 0,15 ha per. 2: 0,22 ha	0,029 ha	0,03 ha
fortification	stone	stone	stone	stone	turf	turf	turf	turf	timber	irregular /timber	timber	timber/ stone	timber	stone	timber/ stone	stone	stone
gates	1	2	2	2	2	1	2	1	2	1	1	1	1	2	2	per. 1: 2 per. 2: 1	1
ditches	none	none	none	none	1	1	1	1	2	1 / 2	2	1	2	none	1	1	1
internal structures	per. 1: 1 per. 2: 2	per. 1: 1 later 2	2	1	2	2	4	2	2	per. 1: tents ? per. 2: u-shaped	u-shaped	2	u-shaped	2	2	2	u-shaped
barrack blocks	1 block	1 block	2 blocks	1 blocks	1 or 2 blocks	2 blocks	3 blocks small	2 blocks	1 block	per. 1: 10 tents		2		2	2	2	2
storage	per. 2: 1 ?	1						1	1			1			1		
other		ovens, hearths	oven	hearth	per. 1: 2 ovens per. 2–3: 2 hearths	per. 1–2: latrine per. 3: hearths	4 hearths, 4 ovens	hearth, latrine	oven, forge, latrine	per. 1: 3 ovens, well ?	per. 1: cistern, per. 2: cistern	hearths			3 cisterns, 2 cellars		2 ovens
soldiers appr. *		8	32	8	8	32	24	80	12+	80	40 / 80				60–80	20–30	10–20
date	122– c400	122–400	122– c400	122–	122–180	122–200	122–140	140–160	40–85	80 – ?	90–160	100–210	135–	150–260	160–260	?	180–260

Table 19.1. Structures of milecastles and fortlets

* information calculated by the authors

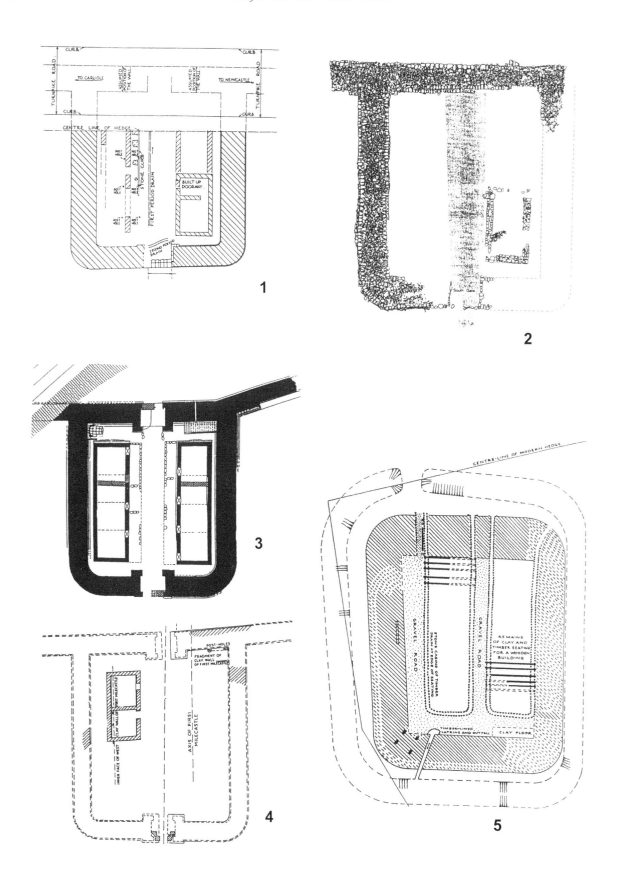

Fig. 19.1. Ground plans of fortlets. 1. A MC 9 (Chapel House; Birley 1930). 2. B MC 35 (Sewingshields; Haigh and Savage 1984) 3. C MC 48 (Poltross Burn; Gibson and Simpson 1911). 4. D MC 54 (Randylands; Simpson and Richmond 1935). 5. F MF 5 (Cadurnock; Simpson and Hodgson 1947)

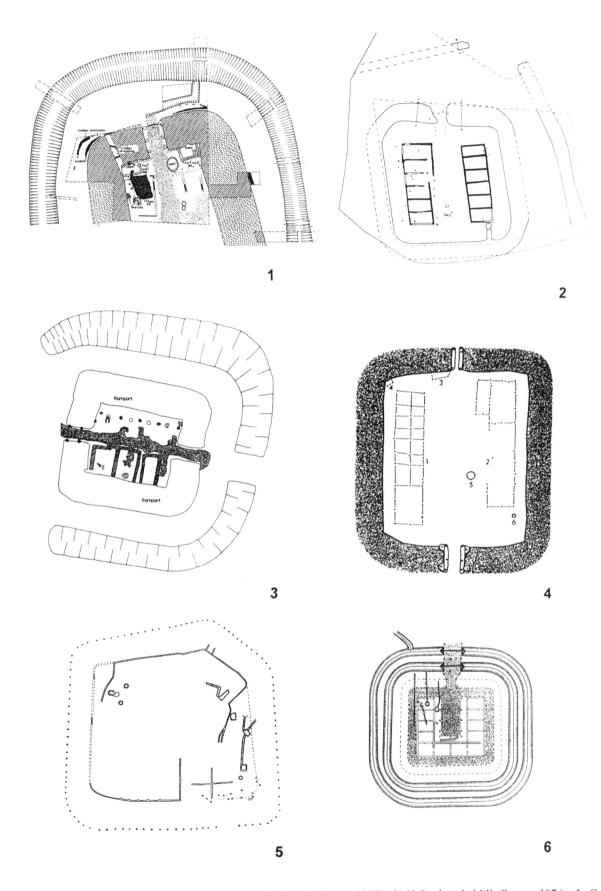

Fig. 19.2. Ground plans of fortlets. 1. E MF 1 (Biglands; Potter 1977). 2. H Barburgh Mill (Breeze 1974). 3. G MF 21 (Swarthy Hill; Turnbull 1998). 4. I Nersingen (Mackensen 1987). 5. K Saalburg Schanze A (Schallmayer 1997). 6. K Saalburg Schanze B (Schallmeyer 1997)

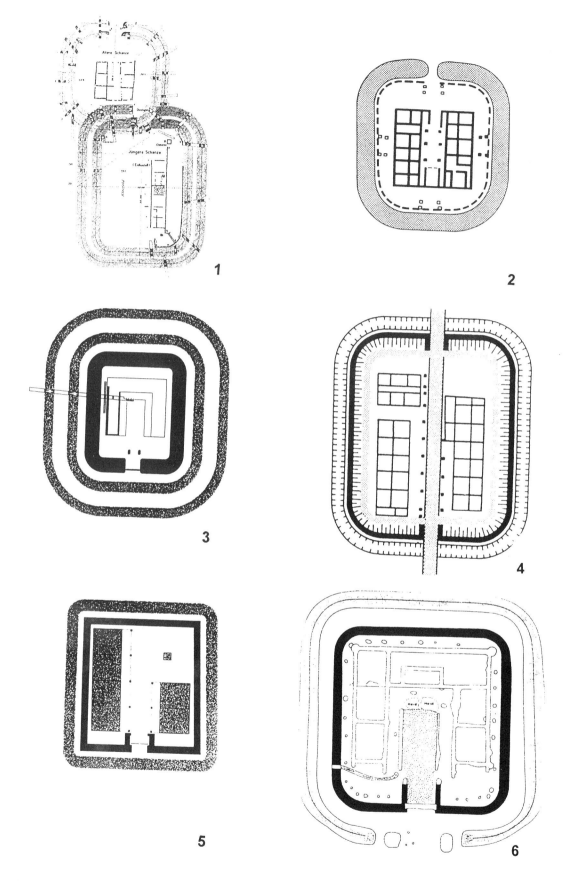

Fig. 19.3. Ground plans of fortlets. 1. L Kemel 1 and 2 (Fabricius 1936; Oelmann and Schleiermacher 1936). 2. M Degerfeld (Jorns and Meier-Arndt 1967; Simon 1968). 3. N Neuwirtshausen (Czysz 1977; 1979; 1989). 4. P Haselburg (Conrady 1931a; Nuber 1976). 5. R Holzheimer Unterwald (Seitz 1991a; 1991b). 6. S Rötelsee (Planck 1986)

(Degerfeld and Haselburg). Rooms for storage seem to be more easily recognisable in this type of fortlet, and may be indicated by rooms of smaller size (Barburgh Mill), different shape or the planning of the interior (Nersingen and Degerfeld), or even by a separate building (Haselburg). Hearths do not appear in all fortlets. At Nersingen, for instance, no hearths at all were recorded. The fortlet in Nersingen, however, like Rötelsee, contained a large central oven, which was situated immediately adjacent to the main road, whereas ovens are mostly recovered in the intervallum beside the gate or in one of the corners of the fortification, *e.g.* milecastle 35 (Sewingshields), milecastle 48 (Poltross Burn), milefortlet 1 (Biglands) and Haselburg. Only very few of the fortlets in Britain or Germany contained pits used for storage or to deposit the rubbish, a feature so common in many larger military fortifications. Two pits were recorded in milecastle 50 Turf Wall (High House) and a large pit lay beside the Wall gateway in milecastle 79 (Solway House), (Simpson *et al* 1935; Richmond and Gillam 1952). This does not differ from the evidence in Upper Gemany, where larger pits were recorded only in the officer's quarter in Degerfeld and in both building-blocks in Haselburg. In his report on Nersingen Michael Mackensen has already referred to this peculiarity (Mackensen 1987, 47), assuming that the rubbish was regularly removed and dumped outside the fortlet.

The question of how the soldiers organised their water supply cannot be answered at all the sites. In some places like in milefortlet 1 (Biglands), Kemel period 2 or in Haselburg a well or a cistern was located next to the main road or beside one of the gates. We know even less about the sewage systems. Michael Mackensen interpreted a very lightly constructed shed beside the rear gate in Nersingen as a latrine (Mackensen 1987, 49). Since he had no evidence for a pit or drain there, he assumed that a bucket was used which was removed and emptied regularly. A latrine with a proper sewage drain was identified in the south-west corner of milecastle 50 Turf Wall (High House) (Simpson *et al* 1935) and at Barburgh Mill.

Traces of a timber structure excavated in one of the corners in Nersingen were interpreted as a base for a staircase leading to the wall-walk. Other sites have produced evidence for staircases: milecastles 48 (Poltross Burn), 50 (High House) and 79 (Solway House) on Hadrian's Wall (Gibson and Simpson 1911; Simpson *et al* 1935; Richmond and Gillam 1952).

In the report on the excavation of the fortlet at Barburgh Mill, consideration was given to the nature of the garrison. Several contemporary and adjacent forts did not have sufficient buildings within them to hold a complete unit and it was therefore suggested that the soldiers at Barburgh Mill were a complete century drawn from one of these forts. However, the relevant documentary evidence was also examined. The rosters of 219 and 222 of the *cohors XX Palmyrenorum milliaria equitata* stationed at Dura

Europos on the Euphrates record many men away from base serving at as many as 9 outposts in those years (Breeze 1993a, 506–8). The detachments vary in size but two are close to the number of men who might have been based at Barburgh Mill. All detachments contained both infantry and cavalry drawn, apparently at random, from many of the centuries and *turmae* of the unit. The conflicting nature of the archaeological and documentary evidence was noted. Attention was drawn to the discovery of harness pieces, but they were not thought to be conclusive evidence for the presence of cavalry as the officer in charge might have retained a horse at the site.

The arrangement of the barrack-blocks has also been discussed by Egon Schallmayer who suggested (Schallmayer 2001) that it often seems to be the case that a barrack-block for a century was divided and arranged on both sides of the road. Soldiers came from the neighbouring auxiliary forts and *numeri* forts and differ between 12 (Nersingen) and 80, a whole century.

Fortlets often seem to represent an essential part of the first building phase on a newly established frontier line. This is the case in the construction of the early *Limes* along the Danube in southern Germania Superior and Raetia, where smaller fortifications, for example Nersingen or Burlafingen, were part of the very first building activities in late Tiberian and early Claudian times (Mackensen 1987, 127–8; Dietz 1995, 74–8). Interpretation of the function of these two fortlets differs widely. The fortlet at Burlafingen, where a strong fortification but no recognisable internal structures were found, had a very short life. The soldiers based there might have supervised the building of the *Limes* road along the south bank of the Danube (Mackensen 1987, 127). Nersingen lasted for more than 30 years and controlled the traffic on a crossing point over the Danube. There are other places in Upper Germany where forts like Altenstadt, Saalburg or Stockstadt have produced earlier fortifications of much smaller size, often called 'Schanzen'. Although none of them have been investigated more recently or in detail, it is clear that the size and structure of these sites are very similar to fortlets such as Nersingen and Burlafingen. This can be demonstrated, for example, at Altenstadt on the Wetteraulimes, where the first timber-built fortification is an enclosure of 0.3 ha with one gate and ditch (Schönberger 1962, 78–82; Schönberger and Simon 1983, 60). In the Taunus area both so-called 'Schanzen' next to the later Saalburg fort belong to the same type. After reviewing and re-interpreting the archaeological evidence of the old excavation reports at the Saalburg, Schallmayer was able to reconstruct both building phases (Schallmayer 1997). Whereas the first fortified installation (Schanze A) is completely irregular in shape, the following period (Schanze B) clearly shows a fortlet with an internal U-shaped structure of the block type (Fig. 19.2.5 and 19.2.6). According to Schallmayer, the earlier fortlet, where no traces of building activities have been found, provided room for 10 tents and some extra space for horses next to a well (Figure 19.4.1). The two earlier fortlets beside the later fort at Kemel also need to be included here. All of these small military installations are earth-and-timber structures which were surrounded by one or two ditches; Schönberger excavated parts of the palisade and a corner tower in Altenstadt but nothing is known about the internal structures and buildings of these sites.

Although there are very few finds associated with these fortlets, which makes it difficult to date them, Schönberger argued on the basis of his excavations in Altenstadt that this building phase started at the end of the first century in the time of Domitian (Schönberger and Simon 1983). At the same time, or maybe slightly later, many *numeri* forts appear on the Odenwaldlimes; for example, the 0.56 ha fort at Hesselbach (Baatz 1973), in the Taunus area at Marienfels, Zugmantel, Saalburg and Kapersburg, and on the Wetteraulimes at Inheiden, Oberflorstadt and Altenstadt. These newly enlisted units with 100 to 150 soldiers were especially designed for guarding the outer frontier line (Reuter 1999, 407; Baatz 2000, 19). Some of the old fortlets were replaced by *numeri* forts (Altenstadt and Saalburg) or, from AD 135 onwards, by larger, regular-sized auxiliary forts. Nearly everywhere these later forts were built over or very close to the abandoned early fortlets. The garrisons of the early fortlets would presumably have been provided by the forts situated in the hinterland of the frontier. This is not so different from the first plan for Hadrian's Wall, when milecastles and turrets were built at the same time as the Wall itself, whereas the core of the troops still remained in their forts on the Stanegate or in the hinterland. Only later did the army start to build forts along the line of the Wall too.

In the mid-second century, when the *Limes* in Germania Superior and Raetia was moved to the outer lines, fortlets of similar type were erected at regular spaces all along the line of the frontier. Together with the towers they became a standard feature whose function in the frontier system is not entirely clear yet but which presumably related to frontier control. In contrast to the larger *numeri* forts, the garrisons of fortlets could not operate as independent tactical units although many contained accommodation, which might have housed an officer or even administrative staff.

On Hadrian's Wall it has been suggested that the role of the soldiers based in the milecastles was to guard the gate through the Wall at that point and maintain observation over the frontier (Figure 19.4.2), for which duty they were supplemented by their comrades in the turrets to each side (Breeze and Dobson 2000, 33–41).

Finds

If we try to compare the finds assemblages from turrets on Hadrian's Wall, which have been usefully brought together (Allason-Jones 1988) with those from fortlets in Germany and the milecastles of Hadrian's Wall and from the two well known *numeri* forts in Hesselbach in the Odenwald (Baatz 1973) and Ellingen in Raetia (Zanier 1992), we can see some interesting and significant differences (see Table 19.2).

The majority of artefacts from fortlets fall into the categories of weapons and other military equipment, personal accessories and pottery, mostly table- and kitchenware. Whereas weapons, mostly spearheads, and other military equipment and jewellery, mostly brooches, are common finds in turrets, there is no indication at all of items connected with horses. This is in contrast to the finds from fortlets, where at least five out of thirteen sites have produced one or even two to three pieces, mostly strap-fittings or pendants, *e.g.* milecastle 48 (Poltross Burn), Barburgh Mill and Nersingen, Kemel, Degerfeld (Figure 19.5). A further item of horse equipment, a harness strap junction with a Celtic scroll motif, was also found in the fortlet at Kinneil on the Antonine Wall (Webster 1996).

The largest quantity of finds from fortlets were implements and pottery to prepare the soldiers' meals (jugs, plates, bowls, mortaria, knifes and millstones). In this respect it seems slightly surprising that samian ware is so well represented, considering the size of the installations. In milecastle 48 (Poltross Burn) even a fragment of a handle from a bronze *patera* came to light. Weapons, jewellery, kitchen- and tableware, gaming-boards and counters appear equally frequently inside turrets, fortlets and larger forts. There is, however, a contrast between forts and fortlets when it comes to storage facilities. While larger forts always produce storage pits and all kinds of storage vessels (*dolia* and *amphorae*), such installations and vessels are often missing in fortlets. The same is the case with furniture, a second category of storage facilities. Fortlets have produced only a very limited amount of metal fittings, like clasps, handles, locks or keys, which are integral parts of boxes or larger trunks and are quite common finds on most other larger military sites. Fittings of furniture do not occur in the finds recovered from turrets on Hadrian's Wall (Allason-Jones 1988). This lack of evidence does not seem to be a mere accident but indicates a characteristic feature of the finds assemblages. It seems that there was no need to provide storage facilities for personal equipment or food at turrets/towers and little need to provide them at fortlets, maybe because the soldiers were only detached to these places for a limited/short period of time, though a study of the pottery assemblages from turrets and forts show that the former had a higher percentage of jars and a lower percentage of bowls and dishes (Evans 1993, 99, 112). If soldiers were sent to the turrets and fortlets (milecastles) from the forts along the Wall or from the hinterland, one would expect them to keep the majority of their belongings at their main base, in their home-fort. On Hadrian's Wall the second building in a milecastle, where it exists, has been interpreted as being provided for storage (Birley 1930). In fact we have seen that most of the fortlets do have some extra space – in Degerfeld even a third extra building, but it might be different goods, like trade-goods or building material,

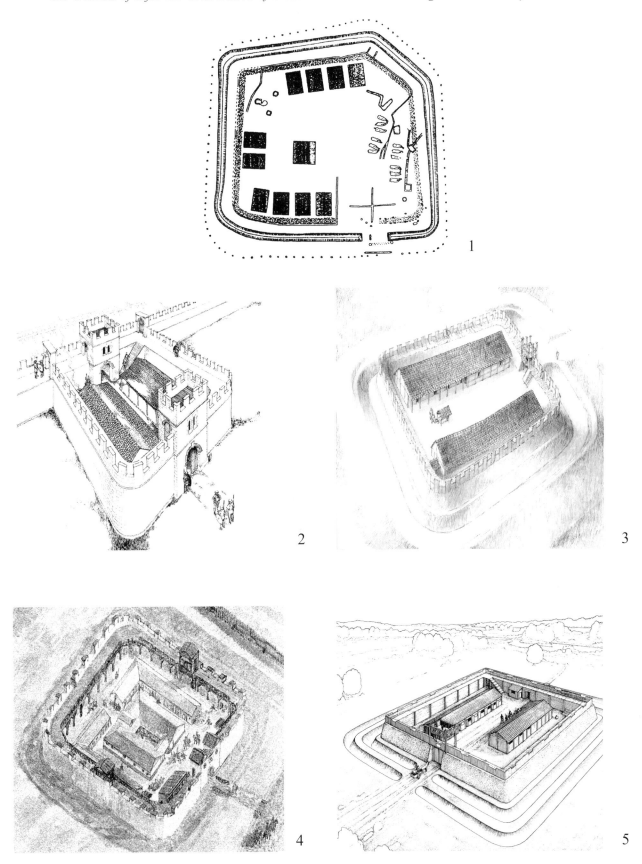

Fig. 19.4. Reconstruction of fortlets. 1. K Saalburg Schanze A. 2. milecastle on Hadrian's Wall. 3. H Barburgh Mill. 4. M Degerfeld. 5. I Nersingen

which were stored there. This interpretation is strongly supported at the Saalburg, where Egon Schallmayer and Britta Rabold believe that a forum-like building replaced the younger fortlet (Schanze B) and was mainly erected for trading purposes. It is conveniently situated by the main road opposite and across the road from the contemporary *numerus* fort (Rabold 1997; Schallmayer 2001).

The archaeological evidence that appears to suggest that soldiers did not stay long in fortlets seems to be at odds with the documentary evidence. The two rosters of *cohors XX Palmyrenorum milliaria equitata* dating to 219 and 222 indicate that many soldiers were outposted from their parent unit for three years or more (Breeze 1993a, 506–8). However, another factor may be brought into play. Some of the outposts manned by the soldiers of the *cohors XX Palmyrenorum* were far removed from the parent fort at Dura, in one case by as many as 250 km. This might account for soldiers staying away from their base for periods as long as three years or more. On the other hand, where fortlets were closer to the parent fort, the aim might have been to seek a quicker turnover of staff; this would certainly be more in the spirit of Trajan's request not to allow soldiers to stay away from the colours (Pliny, *Letters* 10, 20).

The lack of medical or cosmetic instruments can be explained by similar arguments. Although very few examples from turrets and fortlets are known, they appear in much larger quantities inside forts. If we consider that one of the principal functions of milecastles and some fortlets lay in the control of traffic across the border, which means that the soldiers also had to look after customs, the lack of writing implements seems strange. Not a single seal box nor any *spatulae* or inkstand has come to light, and only Nersingen and Degerfeld have produced a single *stilus* each while part of a wooden writing tablet was found at milecastle 50 (High House) on the turf section of Hadrian's Wall (Simpson *et al* 1935). In milecastle 35 (Sewingshields) a lead seal was found. Roger Tomlin has suggested that the obverse reads *C(ohors) (Prima) T(hracum)* or *T(ungrorum)* while the reverse mentions *Ae(lius) Sec(undus)* (Allason-Jones 1984). When this lack is compared with the category of games, where counters and fragments of gaming-boards are a small but regular element in many places, both in turrets and fortlets (in addition to the sites in the tables, a gaming board was found at milecastle 79 (Solway House) on Hadrian's Wall, for example; Richmond and Gillam 1952), there is a temptation to assume that there were more leisure time activities than hard work. Although there is a reasonable number of tools, these are mostly knifes, which can be used for a variety of purposes. Milecastle 35 (Sewingshields) has produced a reaping-hook and a spindle-whorl,

Table 19.2. Finds from milecastles and fortlets

A MC 9 (Chapel House; Birley 1930)
B MC 35 (Sewingshields; Haigh and Savage 1984)
C MC 48 (Poltross Burn; Gibson and Simpson 1911)
D MC 54 (Randylands; Allason-Jones and Bennett and Welsby 1984)
E MF 1 (Biglands; Potter 1977)
F MF 5 (Cadurnock; Simpson and Hodgson 1947)
G MF 21 (Swarthy Hill; Turnbull 1998)
H Barburgh Mill (Breeze 1974)
I Nersingen (Mackensen 1987)

K Saalburg (Schallmayer 1997)
L Kemel (Fabricius 1936; Oelmann and Schleiermacher 1936)
M Degerfeld (Jorns and Meier-Arndt 1967; Simon 1968)
N Neuwirtshausen (Czysz 1979; Czysz 1989)
O Hönehaus (Conrady 1931b)
P Haselburg (Conrady 1931a; Nuber 1976)
R Holzheimer Unterwald (Seitz 1991a, 1991b)
S Rötelsee (Planck 1986)
T Hesselbach (Baatz 1973)
U Ellingen (Zanier 1992)

	A	B	C	D	E	F	G	H	I	L	M	O	P	T	U
weapons/militaria	x	xxx	xx	xx		xx	x		xx	x	xxx	xx		xx	xxx
horse-harness			xx					xx	x	xx	xx				xxx
pers. accessories	x	xxx	xxx		xx	x	x	xx	xxx		xxx			x	xxx
game		xx			x	xx				x	x				xx
furniture		xx			x					x					xxx
med.-cosmet. instruments			xx								xx				xxx
writing implements									x		x				xx
tools		x	x			xx	x	x	x			xx	xxx	xx	xx
fittings		xxx	xx		xx	xx		x	xx	xx		xx		x	xxx
industry		xxx													xx
religious practices	x	x									x	x	x		
samian ware	xxx	xxx	xxx	xx	x		xxx		xx	xx	xxx	xx	xxx	xxx	xxx
kitchen/tableware	xxx	xxx	xxx	xxx	x	xxx	xxx	xxx	xxx	xxx	xxx	xxx		xxx	xxx
storage vessels, amphorae		xxx				x					xx	xx		xxx	xxx
milling-stones		xxx		xx										x	xx

x single find xx 2–5 finds xxx more than 5 finds

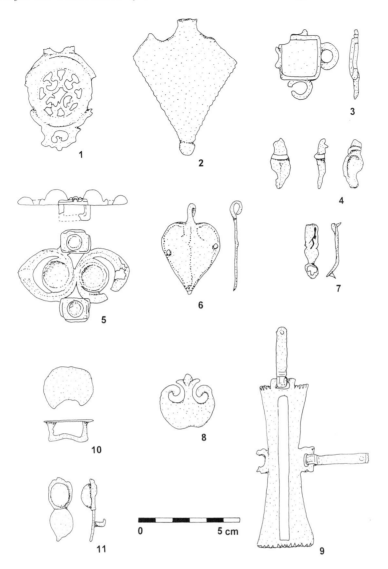

Fig. 19.5. Horse-harness from fortlets. 1–2. MC 48 (Poltross Burn), fitting, pendant. 3–4. Barburgh Mill, strap junction, strap fitting. 5. Kinneil, strap junction. 6–7. Nersingen, pendant, strap fitting. 8–9. Kemel, nose-band, fitting. 10–11. Degerfeld, fitting, pendant

the latter perhaps the only item at all which might be related to the presence of females in fortlets. There are no obviously feminine objects found in turrets either (Allason-Jones 1988, 218). To compare the quantity of fittings, like nails, studs, hooks or bars, is often difficult. At some sites, like milecastle 35 (Sewingshields), for example, they seem to exist in large quantities. Others, like milecastle 9 (Chapel House) or the milefortlet 21 (Swarthy Hill) on the Cumbrian Coast, have not produced a single piece. This might be related to the less attractive material, mostly iron, or to the conditions of preservation.

Evidence for industrial activities is equally rare within fortlets and turrets. The only exceptions are Nersingen, where a forge was excavated, and milecastle 35 (Sewingshields), where a complete crucible and several fragments of clay moulds have been found and indicate a metal-workshop, possibly set up after the fortlet was abandoned

by the troops. Although we know that all sorts of workshops are mostly located outside military installations, in the civil settlements or the small towns in the hinterland (Gschwind 1997), some smaller workshops and associated finds also turn up in forts. It is possible that the main purpose of the industrial activity in fortlets was in repairing damaged pieces rather than in producing new ones.

Only a very few items, mostly altars, can be associated with religious practices. An altar, whose inscription was completely damaged, is known from Haselburg (CIL III 6595). A small inscribed altar in the form of a little house was found in the fortlet at Hönehaus, although it is not clear whether it was brought there later (Wiegels 1971). Altars have been found at or near several mile-castles on Hadrian's Wall (19, 37, 42, 45, 49, 52, 55, 59, 60 and 73: see Breeze 2003), but no religious items are clearly associated with turrets.

Conclusions

The evidence of the small finds found in milecastles and fortlets indicates a less permanent and more fluctuating nature to their garrisons. Their finds assemblages come closer to the spectrum of small finds from turrets than to those from *numeri* forts with their permanent garrisons, though fortlets do produce rather more fittings and furniture items than turrets, implying that soldiers stayed there longer. The main exception relates to horse harness, which on Hadrian's Wall has never been recorded in connection with turrets. The presence of horses, and therefore of cavalry, in fortlets possibly related to the necessity to keep contact with the regiments in the forts, whereas the manning of turrets/towers might have been organised differently, the soldier here being sent out from milecastles and fortlets rather than directly from forts. The presence of the horse equipment also raises questions concerning the function of the buildings within the fortlets/milecastles. Did one building or one room serve as a stable? At Barburgh Mill, there was an outer enclosure protected by a ditch, and it is not impossible that horses were retained here (Breeze 1974, 139–41), while the Vallum offered protection for the environs of the milecastles on Hadrian's Wall. The suggestion that cavalry were based in some fortlets finds support in the documentary evidence which indicates that the detachments drawn from the *cohors XX Palmyrenorum*, based at Dura Europos on the Euphrates in the early third century, were mixed groups of infantry and cavalry.

We believe that this discussion of small finds from fortlets has indicated the value of such studies, integrating structural and architectural evidence, small finds and sculpture, and documentary and literary sources, in order to provide a more rounded picture of life on the frontiers, including the nature and origin of the garrisons of these small installations and therefore their functions; we hope that it will stimulate further such analyses.

Acknowledgements

We are most grateful to Richard Hingley and Steve Willis for allowing us to include this paper in the conference proceedings and to Lindsay Allason-Jones for helpful discussion.

Bibliography

Allason Jones, L. (1984) The small objects. In D. Haigh and M. Savage, Sewingshields. *Archaeologia Aeliana* 5th ser. 12, 74–147.

Allason Jones, L. (1988) 'Small finds' from Turrets on Hadrian's Wall. In J. C. Coulston (ed.) *Military Equipment and the Identity of Roman Soldiers.* Proceedings of the Fourth Roman Military Equipment Conference, 197–233. Oxford.

Allason Jones, L. (2002) Chapter 11: Review of Roman small finds research. In C. Brooks, R. Daniels and A. Harding (eds) *Past Present and Future. The archaeology of northern England.* Proceedings of a Conference held in Durham in 1996, 113–19. Durham.

Allason Jones, L., Bennett, J. and Welsby, D. (1984) The finds from milecastle 54, Randylands. *Archaeologia Aeliana* 5th ser. 12, 228–35.

Allison, P. M. (1999) Introduction. In P. M. Allison (ed.) *The Archaeology of Household Activities.* London and New York, Routledge.

Baatz, D. (1973) *Kastell Hesselbach.* Limesforschungen 12. Berlin, Gebrüder Mann Verlag.

Baatz, D. (2000) *Der Römische Limes. Archäologische Ausflüge zwischen Rhein und Donau.* Berlin, Gebrüder Mann Verlag.

Birley, E. (1930) Excavations on Hadrian's Wall west of Newcastle upon Tyne in 1929. *Archaeologia Aeliana* 4th ser. 7, 143–74.

Bishop, M. C. and Coulston, J. C. N. (1993) *Roman Military Equipment.* London, Batsford.

Böhme, A. (1972) Die Fibeln der Kastelle Saalburg und Zugmantel. *Saalburg-Jahrbuch* 32, 1–112.

Breeze, D. J. (1974) The Roman fortlet at Barburgh Mill, Dumfriesshire. *Britannia* 5, 130–62.

Breeze, D. J. (1993a) The garrisoning of Roman fortlets. In D. J. Breeze and B. Dobson *Roman Officers and Frontiers.* Mavors Roman Army Researches 10, 505–10. Stuttgart, Franz Steiner Verlag.

Breeze, D. J. (1993b) The ownership of arms in the Roman army. In D. J. Breeze and B. Dobson *Roman Officers and Frontiers.* Mavors Roman Army Researches 10, 571–73. Stuttgart, Franz Steiner Verlag.

Breeze, D. J. (2003) Auxiliaries, legionaries, and the operation of Hadrian's Wall. In J. J. Wilkes (ed.) *Documenting the Roman Army. Essays in honour of Margaret Roxan*, London, University College, 47–51.

Breeze, D. J. and Dobson, B. (2000) *Hadrian's Wall.* London, Penguin.

Conrady, W. (1931a) *Strecke 7. Von Miltenberg am Main bis zum Haghof bei Welzheim.* Der Obergermanisch-raetische Limes Abteilung A IV (Haselburg), 70–2. Berlin and Leipzig, Verlag Otto Peters.

Conrady, W. (1931b) Strecke 7. *Von Miltenberg am Main bis zum Haghof bei Welzheim.* Der Obergermanisch-raetische Limes Abteilung A IV (Hönehaus), 83–4. Berlin and Leipzig, Verlag Otto Peters.

Crow, J. G. (1989) Milecastle 39 – Castle Nick. In C. Daniels *The Eleventh Pilgrimage of Hadrian's Wall*, 52–3. Kendal.

Czysz, W. (1977) Archäologische Nachuntersuchungen am Kleinkastell Neuwirtshaus bei Hanau. *Neues Magazin für Hanauische Geschichte* 6, Nr. 5, 121 ff.

Czysz, W. (1979) Der römische Limes zwischen Kinzig und Main. *Archäologische Denkmäler in Hessen* 3.

Czysz, W. (1989) Das Kleinkastell Neuwirtshausen. In D. Baatz and F.-R. Herrmann *Die Römer in Hessen*, 337–40. Stuttgart, Theiss Verlag.

Daniels, C. (1978) *Handbook to the Roman Wall.* 13th edition. Newcastle upon Tyne.

Davies, R. (1989) *Service in the Roman Army.* Edited by D. Breeze and V. Maxfield. Edinburgh.

Dietz, K.-H. (1995) Okkupation und Frühzeit. In W. Czysz, K.-H. Dietz, T. Fischer and H.-J. Kellner *Die Römer in Bayern*, 18–99. Stuttgart, Theiss Verlag.

Erdrich, M. (2001) *Rom und die Barbaren.* Römisch-germanische Forschungen 58. Mainz.

Erdrich, M. Giannotta, K. M. and Hanson W. S. (2000) Traprain Law: native and Roman on the northern frontier. *Proceedings of the Society of Antiquaries of Scotland* 130, 441–56.

Evans, J. (1993) Pottery functions and finewares in the Roman north, *Journal of Roman Pottery Studies* 9, 95–118.

Fabricius, E. (1936) *Strecke 2. Der Limes von der Lahn bis zur Aar.* Der Obergermanisch-raetische Limes Abteilung A Band I (Kemel), 78–82. Berlin and Leipzig, Verlag Otto Peters.

Feugère, M. (2002) *Weapons of the Romans.* Tempus.

Fischer, T. (2002) Waffen und militärische Ausrüstung in zivilem Kontext – grundsätzliche Erklärungsmöglichkeiten. *Jahresbericht Gesellschaft Pro Vindonissa* 2001, 13–18.

Förtsch, R. (1993) *Archäologischer Kommentar zu den Villen-briefen des Jüngeren Plinius.* Beiträge zur Erschliessung hellenistischer und kaiserzeitlicher Skulptur und Architektur 13. Mainz.

Fox, A. and Ravenhill, W. L. D. (1966) Early Roman outposts on the North Devon coast: Old Burrow and Martinhoe. *Proceedings of Devonshire Archaeology Exploration Society* 24, 3–39.

Gibson, J. P. and Simpson F. G. (1911) The milecastle on the Wall of Hadrian at the Poltross Burn. *Transactions of the Cumberland and Westmorland Archaeological and Antiquarian Society* 2nd ser. 11, 390–461.

Göldner, H. (1998) Schaurig ist's übers Moor zu gehen. Untersuchungen an einer römischen Sumpfbrücke bei Bickenbach. *Denkmalpflege und Kulturgeschichte* 1998, 40–1.

Gschwind, M. (1997) Bronzegießer am raetischen Limes. *Germania* 75, 607–38.

Haigh, D. and Savage, M. (1984) Sewingshields. *Archaeologia Aeliana* 5th ser. 12, 33–147.

Hunter, F. (2001) Roman and native in Scotland: new approaches. *Journal of Roman Archaeology* 14, 289–309.

Jobey, I. (1979) Housesteads Ware – a Frisian tradition on Hadrian's Wall. *Archaeologia Aeliana* 5th ser. 7, 127–43.

Jorns, W., and Meier-Arndt, W. (1967) Das Kleinkastell Degerfeld bei Butzbach, Kr. Friedberg (Hessen). *Saalburg-Jahrbuch* 24, 12–32.

Mackensen, M. (1987) *Frühkaiserzeitliche Kleinkastelle bei Nersingen und Burlafingen an der oberen Donau.* Münchner Beiträge zur Vor- und Frühgeschichte 41. München, C. H. Beck'sche Verlagsbuchhandlung.

Maxfield, V. A. (1986) Pre-Flavian forts and their garrisons. *Britannia* 17, 59–72.

Nuber, H. U. (1976) Ausgrabungen im römischen Kleinkastell Haselburg. *Nachrichtenblatt Denkmalpflege Baden-Württemberg* 5, 64 ff.

Oelmann, F. and Schleiermacher, W. (1936), *Die Einzelfunde (Kemel). Der* Obergermanisch-raetische Limes Abteilung A I, 106–22. Berlin and Leizig, Verlag Otto Peters.

Planck, D. (1986) Kleinkastell Rötelsee. In Ph. Filtzinger, D. Planck and B. Cämmerer *Die Römer in Baden Württemberg*, 617–18. Stuttgart, Theiss Verlag.

Potter, T. (1977) The Biglands milefortlet and the Cumberland coast defences. *Britannia* 8, 149–73.

Rabold, B. (1997), Kaufhaus, *forum*, Villa oder was? In E. Schallmayer (ed.) *Hundert Jahre Saalburg. Vom römischen Grenzposten zum europäischen Museum*, 166–69. Mainz, Verlag Philipp von Zabern.

Reuter, M. (1999) Studien zu den *numeri* des Römischen Heeres in der Mittleren Kaiserzeit. *Bericht der Römisch-German-ischen Kommission* 80, 357–569.

Richmond, I. A. and Gillam, J. P. (1952) Report of the Cumberland Excavation Committee for 1947–49. 3. Mile-castle 79 (Solway). *Transactions of the Cumberland and Westmorland Archaeological and Antiquarian Society* 2nd ser. 52, 17–40.

Schallmayer, E. (1997) Kastelle am Limes. In E. Schallmayer (ed.) *Hundert Jahre Saalburg. Vom römischen Grenzposten zum europäischen Museum*, 106–18. Mainz, Verlag Philipp von Zabern.

Schallmayer, E. (2001) Kleinkastelle. In T. Fischer (ed.) *Die römischen Provinzen. Eine Einführung in ihre Archäologie*, 120–21. Stuttgart, Theiss.

Schönberger, H. (1962) *Neuere Grabungen am obergermani-schen und rätischen Limes.* Limesforschungen 2, 69–137. Berlin.

Schönberger, H. and Simon, H. G. (1983) *Die Kastelle in Altenstadt.* Limesforschungen 22. Berlin.

Seitz, G. (1991a) Neue Forschungen am nördlichen Wetterau-Limes. Das Kastell Holzheimer Unterwald. *Wetterauer Geschichtsblätter* 40, 235–44.

Seitz, G. (1991b) Neue Forschungen am nördlichen Wetterau-limes. Das Kastell Holzheimer Unterwald. In V. Rupp (ed.) *Archäologie in der Wetterau.* Friedberg.

Simon, H. G. (1968) Das Kleinkastell Degerfeld in Butzbach, Kr. Friedberg (Hessen) Datierung und Funde. *Saalburg-Jahrbuch* 25, 5–64.

Simpson, F. G. and Hodgson, K. S. (1947) The coastal mile-fortlet at Cardurnock. *Transactions of the Cumberland and Westmorland Archaeological and Antiquarian Society* 2nd ser. 47, 78–125.

Simpson, F. G., and Richmond, I. A. (1935) Report of the Cumberland Excavation Committee for 1934. 5. Randylands Milecastle, 54. *Transactions of the Cumberland and Westmorland Archaeological and Antiquarian Society* 2nd ser. 35, 236–44.

Simpson, F. G., Richmond, I. A., and St. Joseph, K. (1935) Report of the Cumberland Excavation Committee for 1934. 2. The turf-wall milecastle at High House. *Transactions of the Cumberland and Westmorland Archaeological and Antiquarian Society* 2nd ser. 35, 220–29.

Spradley, K. (2001) *Small Finds: Problems and Possibilities.* Proceedings of the 10th Annual Theoretical Roman Archae-ology Conference 2000, 104–11.

Swan, V. (1999) The Twentieth Legion and the history of the Antonine Wall reconsidered. *Proceedings of the Society of Antiquaries of Scotland* 129, 399–480.

Swift, E. (2000) *Regionality in Dress Accessories in the Late Roman West.* Montagnac, Editions Monique Mergoil.

Turnbull, P. (1998) Excavation at Milefortlet 21. *Transactions of the Cumberland and Westmorland Archaeological and Antiquarian Society* 2nd ser. 98, 61–106.

Webster, G. (1996) Harness strap junction. In G. B. Bailey and J. Cannel, Excavations at Kinneil fortlet on the Antonine Wall, 1980–81. *Proceedings of the Society of Antiquaries of Scotland* 126, 318–20.

Wiegels, R. (1971) Ein römisches Inschriftenhäuschen aus dem Kleinkastell Hönehaus (Odenwald). *Germania* 51, 543–52.

Zanier, W. (1992) *Das römische Kastell Ellingen.* Limes-forschungen 23. Berlin.

20 Silver for the Barbarians: Interpreting Denarii Hoards in North Britain and Beyond

Fraser Hunter

Introduction

Hoards of Roman denarii from north of Hadrian's Wall have excited interest since the sixteenth century. They are usually linked to historical references to conflict on the northern frontier in the reigns of Commodus and Severus (*e.g.* Robertson 1978). However, this is only one aspect of the phenomenon. The recent discovery of two denarii hoards on an Iron Age site in north-east Scotland has prompted a reappraisal of how these hoards arrived in native hands and how they may have been used.

Denarii hoards from Birnie

The recent finds come from an unenclosed Iron Age settlement at Birnie, near Elgin in Moray, some 300 km north of Hadrian's Wall. They were excavated in 2000 and 2001 following the discovery of a scatter of 18 denarii by a metal-detectorist in 1996. Aerial photographs (Jones *et al.* 1993, 69, pl. VIII) revealed the presence of later prehistoric roundhouses in the same field, presenting a tremendous chance to investigate the connection between

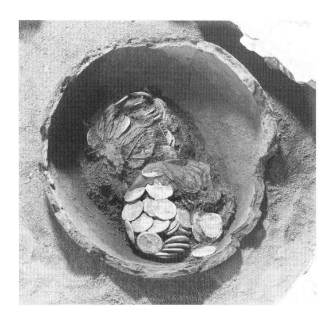

Fig. 20.1. Hoard of denarii found at Birnie (Moray) in 2001, contained in two leather pouches within an Iron Age pot. © *National Museums of Scotland*

a hoard and a settlement. The two hoards were buried in Iron Age pots less than 10 m apart in the heart of the settlement. The site was a long-lived one, and details of the sequence await radiocarbon dating, but results to date indicate it was occupied during the Roman Iron Age. An interim account can be found in Hunter (2002). Study of the coins by Nick Holmes (NMS) is in progress: initial results indicate that both hoards consist of just over 300 denarii and date to the period AD 193–97, with perhaps a few years between them (Fig. 20.1).

The wider picture

To put the Birnie finds in context, all coin hoards north of Hadrian's Wall up to AD 250 have been considered. Systematic study, notably by Anne Robertson (1975, 1978, 2000), has put the subject on a firm footing. The Scottish examples were considered in detail by her in 1978: her 29 hoards can now be expanded to 45, with eight new finds and eight additional antiquarian records from Scotland and north Northumberland (some known to Robertson but not viewed as certain hoards). This provides a reasonable dataset for analysis: 38 are denarii hoards, three aurei hoards, two bronze and two uncertain. They are summarised in Appendix 1, where references to individual hoards may be found.

While the size varies considerably, from a mere handful to almost 2000, a typical denarii hoard would contain several hundred coins. In five instances the hoards were said to include non-numismatic material, although only the jewellery from the probable scattered hoard at Usan (Angus) survives. Find circumstances vary: some are clearly associated with Roman sites, others (as at Birnie) with Iron Age sites, while many are apparently isolated finds. This question of their final deposition is discussed further below. The container also varies, with Roman vessels of pottery, glass, bronze and perhaps stone; Iron Age pots; and cloth and leather bags. These latter were probably most common, as around half had no surviving container. The updated distribution (Fig. 20.2) is less skewed to the east coast than previous commentators have suggested; even when hoards from Roman sites are discounted, there is a spread in south and central Scotland as well, with a few scattered (and often uncertain) examples further afield.

This article will focus primarily on those hoards not

certainly associated with Roman sites, and consider their life cycle upon leaving the Roman world: why did they move beyond the frontier, how were they used there and how and why were they finally deposited? The necessary initial step, however, is to assess the quality of the data.

Source criticism

Discoveries of Roman coin hoards have a long pedigree (Fig. 20.3). Roman finds have always been of particular interest to antiquarians, and the classical training of the average minister or lord made him a reasonably reliable observer of Roman coins. As a result, from the 18th century onwards we have some details of most hoards, and in a number of cases quite a good list of emperors. The rise in discoveries comes with agricultural and industrial expansion *c.*1750–1850, while metal-detecting and excavation finds have sustained matters in recent years.

The date of the latest coin in a hoard is of course simply a *terminus post quem* for the date of deposition, with its reliability depending on both burial and recovery circumstances (Abdy 2002, 7–9): in particular, how representative a sample of contemporary coinage were the coins, and how well were they recorded. Sadly, the quality of information is highly variable. As Fig. 20.4 shows, we can be fairly confident about the latest emperor with little more than half of the hoards. With many older discoveries there are uncertainties over whether the latest emperor was correctly identified (especially as they may be represented by only one or two coins), or whether hoards ending in 'coins of Antoninus' are really of Antoninus Pius or a later emperor with similar titles (such as the later Antonines or Caracalla). The problem is seen in Fig. 20.5, where hoard terminal dates are categorised by data quality: the large number of poorly-recorded hoards apparently of Antoninus Pius is worrying. Furthermore, several of the 'early' finds only appear so because of the poor records, while there is an absence of old finds of post-Severan hoards, perhaps because a few late issues could be easily overlooked. This cautions against interpretations relying on too much chronological precision. In general, however, the well-recorded hoards confirm the basic trends.

Hoard size is also an issue. The coins of the reigning emperor were always in a minority during his reign, peaking some 20–30 years after his death (Robertson 1978, 189–190); in a small hoard, coins of the current emperor may be absent altogether. Robertson's figures (1978, 190–2) for a selection of Scottish hoards show the coins of the latest emperor ranging from 2.7 to 6.1% of the total, while in the Edston (Peeblesshire) hoard this figure was only 1% (Holmes and Hunter 1997). Thus the hoards with Trajanic end-dates, all linked to Roman sites, are small and were deposited during the Antonine period.

Interpreting the patterns is further complicated because we have hoards deposited by both Romans and natives. If we isolate those certainly connected to Roman sites, clear

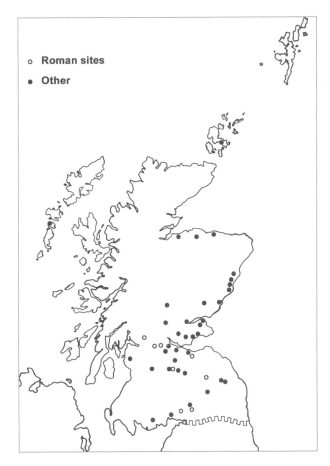

Fig. 20.2. Distribution of Roman coin hoards north of Hadrian's Wall to AD 250

patterns emerge (Fig. 20.6). Hoards associated with Roman sites can be correlated with the periods of occupation. By contrast, those hoards without Roman associations peak after the Antonine occupation, as has been noted before (*e.g.* Hanson and Maxwell 1983, 141–2). The breadth of this peak is worth noting, however: broadly similar numbers from Antoninus Pius to Severus, with a smaller quantity of post-Severan ones. Again the question of data quality rears its head. If we remove poorly-recorded hoards and those with fewer than 20 coins, the peak becomes much sharper, from Commodus to Severus Alexander (Fig. 20.7) – but we now have only nine hoards in the sample (from originally 37 in non-Roman contexts), so they may not be representative. This leaves something of a quandary: do we take the pattern from the small number of well-recorded hoards, or (with due reservations) accept the potentially longer timescale suggested by the larger number with poorer quality data? At present it seems safe to say that the phenomenon of denarii hoards on non-Roman sites certainly ran from the reigns of Commodus to Severus Alexander, but there is a good chance that some batches of coin came north earlier, at least in the reign of Marcus Aurelius.

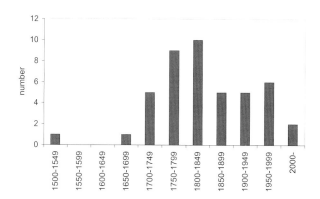

Fig. 20.3. Discovery dates of Roman coin hoards shown in Fig. 20.2. Where the find date is not known the date of first publication has been used

Fig. 20.4. Record quality for the hoards under study

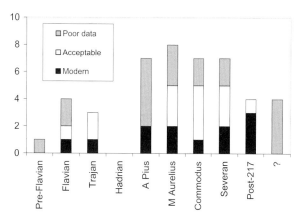

Fig. 20.5. Terminal dates of the hoards, categorised by data quality. Hoards of AD 69 have been categorised with Flavian ones, those of AD 193 with Severan ones

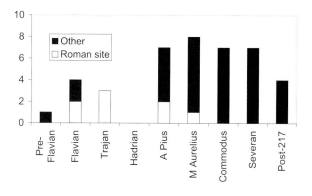

Fig. 20.6. Terminal dates subdivided into Roman and non-Roman associations

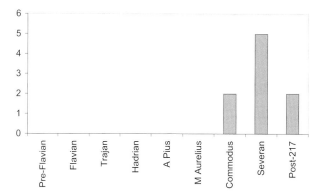

Fig. 20.7. Terminal dates of the best-recorded hoards (non-Roman associations, over 20 coins)

Coins beyond the frontier: dates and motives

Robertson (1978) separated these hoards into four chronological clusters, but they are better treated as the same phenomenon – trying to split them up by emperor forces a historical filter over the data which is unwarranted, especially given the dating uncertainties mentioned earlier. They are best seen as a unitary spread from *c.*160/180 to *c.* 230. The chronological pattern of hoards without Roman associations can usefully be compared to northern English hoards and to the general British picture (Fig. 20.8): data are from Robertson (2000), using all hoards without discriminating for data quality. There are marked differences, with the rest of Britain rising from Hadrian to a peak under Marcus Aurelius and then dropping off sharply, before rising again after Severus. Northern England shows a more pronounced peak from Hadrian to Marcus Aurelius than the overall UK pattern. Neither matches the peak north of Hadrian's Wall, however, which focuses in Commodan and Severan times. This is significantly different from the pattern within the province.

How should this be interpreted? Commentators generally start from the historical sources: references to warfare early in the reign of Commodus, to Virius Lupus buying peace around AD 197, and to the politics and warfare of the Severan campaigns create a strong temptation to interpret the coin hoards in terms of these events. For instance, Robertson (2000, xxvi) commented that the Commodan hoards 'may well have been lost in the warfare at the beginning of Commodus' reign' and notes that the 'Scottish hoards ending with Severan coins can certainly be linked with Severus' campaigns in the north'. Indeed, in her 1978 paper she tries to fit as many hoards as possible into a Severan phase, arguing, for instance, that

the peace payments to the Maeatae cleaned out the Roman banks, and that hoards with earlier terminal dates should be seen as Severan (Robertson 1978, 192). This is special pleading – we should take the data at face value and interpret them as they stand unless there are good reasons not to. Here the historical sources have constrained past interpretations. Given the likely spread of dates the hoards should not be tied solely to specific historical events or campaigning armies: they are better seen as gifts or bribes to powerful local people or groups which were part of a general and long-running policy. This has been suggested before, and argued most persuasively by Todd (1985) for the Falkirk (Stirlingshire) hoard; it should be applied more widely to all these hoards. The evidence at Birnie of hoards in direct association with an Iron Age settlement is best explained as just such a 'gift'. They could also represent the outcome of raids on the province, although the dual hoards at Birnie and the existence of a selective range of other materials (see Hunter forthcoming) is more consistent with a deliberate Roman policy.

It seems that the historical sources can be as much a constraint as a support – while they provide a general model, it is far from the total story. This is confirmed by a consideration of the wider European picture. The Scottish hoards are not unique: they form part of a pattern that stretches from Ireland to Russia. Lind's (1981) survey of the Continental material provides a convenient baseline for wider study. His catalogue is comprehensive for Sweden, and for other areas lists hoards with at least 20 denarii. Detailed regional studies have confirmed the broad patterns he identified (*e.g.* Berger 1992, 133–50).

There are strong similarities in the overall trends across northern Europe, with differences in detail. In all areas there is a marked concentration from Marcus Aurelius to

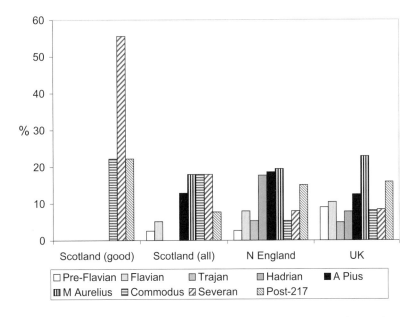

Fig. 20.8. Hoard dates for Scotland compared to northern England and the general British pattern (using data from Robertson 2000). Sample size (l to r): 9, 32, 113, 345

Severus, dropping off sharply thereafter (Fig. 20.9). In Scotland and Germany the peak appears broader, with a significant number of hoards of Antoninus Pius. The sparse Irish examples also fit this pattern (Bateson 1971), while Germany shows an earlier Augustan phase. In Poland, the former USSR and Scandinavia the pattern is much more focussed on Commodus and Severus. The overall focus on the late second and early third century is, however, essentially similar. The hoards from Scotland should thus be seen not as responses to peculiarly British historical events, but as reflecting a long-lived and widespread Roman policy of 'diplomatic gifts' to peoples beyond the frontier which was applied across northern Europe for a period of over 50 years. In other words, it was part of a process rather than tied to a series of historical events. Of course this was a twin policy of military might allied to diplomatic guile which has a long pedigree (cf. Gordon 1949; Howgego 1992, 5–6; Austin and Rankov 1995, 147–9), but the military has been overplayed and the diplomatic underplayed in interpreting the Scottish hoards.

This is not to suggest that there was a blanket policy applied irrespective of local circumstances. Apart from differing local uses of the coins (which will be considered below), the subtle differences in the date profiles noted above point to regional variations within the broad policy framework. The evidence from Friesland (Netherlands) is a good example: while there are two small denarii hoards ending in 180 and 194, fitting the general patterns, there is also a Hadrianic hoard and a series of antoniniani hoards ending in 253–73 which are unparalleled in other areas (van der Vin 1996).

Why do the hoards stop? Berger (1996, 59) has related it to a policy decision by Severus to stop paying subsidies, while Erdrich (2000) has noted for parts of Germany a general lack of earlier third century material which might

suggest policy changes around this time. This is not so pronounced in Scotland, however, where there is a range of finds broadly datable to the late second / early third century, albeit in lower quantities (Holmes and Hunter 2001, 174–5). Moreover, it is clear from the graphs and from specific Scottish examples like Edston and Falkirk that it does run through and beyond the Severan period. If the policy changed this was more likely in the 230s. Could it be the economics of the situation? With the continual devaluation of the denarius and the introduction of the antoninianus, Roman silver may have been a less desirable commodity and the nature of diplomatic gifts could have changed. The question remains unresolved.

Use of the coins

What use was made of these denarii in an Iron Age context? There was no circulating monetary economy in Scotland outwith Roman sites: finds from native sites are few and show a strong preference for silver and (where available) gold, rather than bronze small change (Robertson 1975, 418). Indeed, Roman coinage is generally seen as having little impact (Nash Briggs 1995, 251–2). If not to buy things, what were the denarii for?

They are often interpreted as bullion to be converted into ornaments. As Todd (1985) pointed out, however, there is an almost total lack of silver ornaments in the late second to third century. It is only from the late fourth century onwards that silver jewellery starts to appear in any appreciable quantity, and this can best be related to the renewed supply of silver from *hacksilber* hoards. It is, of course, possible that silver ornaments were manufactured but have not entered the surviving archaeological record. Extensive analysis of crucibles by Andrew Heald (at the National Museums of Scotland), however, has provided

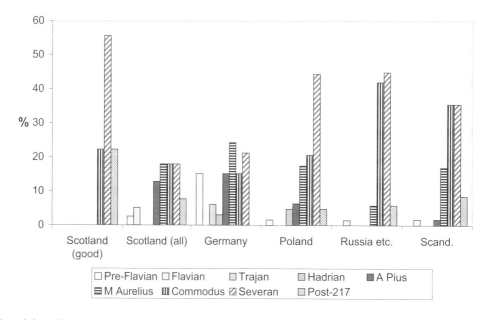

Fig. 20.9. Hoard dates beyond the northern frontiers (from data in Lind 1981). Sample size (l to r): 9, 32, 33, 63, 69, 59

no evidence of silver-working until the post-Roman period – except on Traprain Law, with its late Roman *hacksilber* hoard (Curle 1923). So what was the silver used for?

I suggest it functioned not as money in a market economy sense but as a special-purpose coinage, much as Celtic coins did earlier in southern Britain. When reviewing the lack of Celtic coinage in northern Britain (Hunter 1997b) I suggested three factors in the adoption of coinage: the stimulus of a coin-using culture; selection of only certain aspects of this external coinage; and, initially, restricted use of coins for special purposes. This is the pattern found in the early phases of Celtic coinage in both Gaul and southern Britain, where Greek and subsequently Roman coins provided the models. I argued that there was no stimulus in the north to use coins because contacts with the south were concerned primarily with the exchange of a restricted range of prestige goods, and coins had no role in this.

This changed with the Roman invasions, as the presence of the Romans provided a stimulus to coin use: by the mid to late second century peoples in Scotland had been exposed intermittently to coinage for around a century. There was therefore likely to be some familiarity with it. The high-value component of this coinage was preferentially selected (Robertson 1975, 418) – much as early Celtic coinages were based on precious metals. Can we then carry the analogy further and suggest that denarii functioned like early Celtic coins? These are seen as restricted-use coinage, valued as a means of storing wealth, displaying status, paying mercenaries and sealing alliances (*e.g.* Nash 1978, 7; Haselgrove 1979, 202); perhaps with these denarii we could add dealing with Romans. While little of this can yet be proved, I feel it may give us more realistic insights into the potential uses of these coins. There is certainly other evidence that prestige goods were a key part of social interaction at the time, as seen in the metalwork (MacGregor 1976). This was primarily personal ornaments, but doubtless a role could have been found for this new medium of display and social interaction. It may have functioned over a wider social range than existing prestige goods, as coins by their very nature could be more readily divided or accumulated at a range of scales.

It is worth considering the Scandinavian evidence here. Hedeager has suggested a role for denarii in the Germanic sphere as tokens for 'limited and specialised transactions' which acted as the interface between a fully monetary economy and a 'primitive' one (Hedeager 1988). This is a more restricted role than that proposed for Scotland, but in either scenario one obvious question is how long such denarii could have been used for. Was this a short-lived use which did not exceed the period of ready supply from the Romans or, once received, did they continue in use through the third century and even beyond? Lind's (1988) detailed assessment of the Swedish hoards points to a long life-cycle for them once they left the Roman world. Where denarii come from burials in Scandinavia, the burial is

often several centuries later than the coin; in hoards, they are regularly found in association with late Roman solidi (Lind 1988; Nielsen 1988). In contrast to the Scottish (and German) hoards, however, the Scandinavian denarii tend to be very worn because of this extended use. This also contributes to the regional differences in the hoard pattern mentioned earlier. Denarii arriving in Scandinavia formed part of a wider secondary circulation pool for up to several hundred years which homogenised the disparate batches of coins. When a hoard was withdrawn it thus reflected a sample of the total coins then in circulation, not the coins at the date they arrived. If the latest coins in circulation were Commodan and Severan then most of the hoards would end in these issues, biasing the whole graph to the last phases of contact. As this model would predict, the biggest hoards are all very similar since they are most representative of the whole coin pool (Lind 1988, fig 3). This seems a more coherent explanation than Lind's rather contorted attempts to link the hoards to a horizon of payoffs following Gothic attacks in the 240s (Lind 1988, 209–210; cf. Berger 1996, 58).

The lack of wear on the latest Scottish coins indicates they did not spend long in people's pouches, and the same is true in north-west Germany (Berger 1996, 58). Does this invalidate the idea of secondary circulation as special-purpose coins? Not necessarily, if their use was restricted to a shorter period (perhaps a century or so for the sake of argument) and/or if their movements were restricted and took place largely in bulk rather than as single coins. Nash (1978, 7) has suggested a similar picture for early Gaulish coins: their lack of wear suggests they spent much of their life immobile rather than circulating. In this case we would see less homogenisation, with the chronological pattern reflecting more accurately the dates when the coins arrived. Indeed, the suggested accumulation of the Falkirk hoard as a series of groups of coins over perhaps 70 years provides a possible example of this. Prior to the Birnie finds, only three of the substantial hoards (>100 coins) from Scotland had complete coin lists, of which two (Edston and Falkirk) were anomalous in Romano-British terms. Various reasons have been suggested for this (Reece 1980; Robertson 1982; Todd 1985; Holmes and Hunter 1997); now the local circulation and specific use of the coins may be added. The movement of these coins outwith the empire in a society where their use was different from the more monetarised province might be expected to lead to compositional differences, arising from differences in supply frequency, circulation rate, use, and so on. These need not be marked in every case, however: the north-west German hoards show a similar composition to neighbouring hoards within the Empire (Berger 1996, 57).

There is some supporting evidence for the idea of movement of denarii from the record of stray finds and Iron Age site finds compared to Roman site finds. The Roman site finds tie closely to the occupation periods, and the Iron Age site finds seem to follow this, although the sample is very small. The strays do not, however –

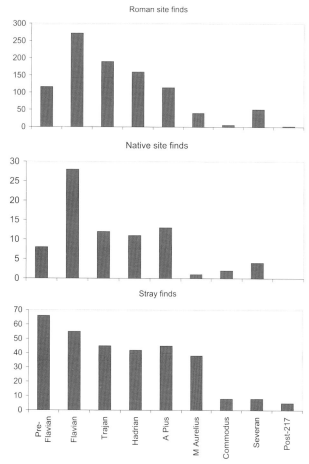

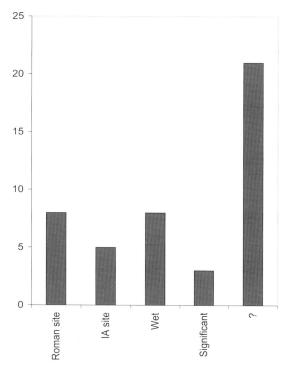

Fig. 20.10. Chronological distribution of Roman coins from Roman sites, Iron Age sites and stray finds. Data from Robertson (1983), Bateson (1989), and Bateson and Holmes (1997; 2003)

Fig. 20.11. Hoard find circumstances

there was clearly some post-Antonine coinage circulating, and this may well be the 'leakage' from hoards which were dipped into and saw active social use (Fig. 20.10).

Some support for this secondary life of denarii may be adduced from coin moulds. Three moulds for fake denarii are known from Scotland; in two instances the issues they represent are at odds with the normal ones on counterfeiters' moulds south of the border (Holmes and Hunter 2001). Could this be because the Scottish "market" was more concerned with the presence of silver coins than with the numismatics of them?

Contexts and motives for burial

Historically the tendency has been to see coin hoards as buried for safekeeping but, as Aitchison (1988) has noted, they may equally have been votive offerings. The contexts in which they were buried may give us some clues to the motives behind their burial. Sadly, few have detailed contextual information, but many can be broadly categorised: from or close to a site (Roman or native); in a wet location; in a significant/unusual location; and, most commonly, from an unknown location or one with no obvious significance (Fig. 20.11). With any further hoard finds it is imperative that the find-spot is archaeologically investigated, on a scale which allows it to be contextualised: as the work at Birnie has shown, this is vital if we are to understand such finds. Without putting hoards in a setting, they are little better than nineteenth century stray finds, and study of the findspots should be standard for new discoveries.

This varied locational evidence hints at a range of motives, including both safekeeping and votive deposits. If we consider Roman sites, the hoard from the foundation trench of the headquarters building at Elginhaugh (Midlothian) and the plated coins from the well at Bar Hill (Dunbartonshire) are both *prima facie* cases of votive hoards. With other finds linked to Roman sites, such as the aurei hoard from Broomholm (Dumfriesshire) and the bronze hoard from near Castledykes (Lanarkshire), there is nothing about their location to suggest that they are anything but security hoards, although the records are too poor to be sure. Of the finds from native sites, the small hoard from Aitnock (Ayrshire) was in destruction deposits and may have been part of a ritual marking the end of the site's use. The motive behind the Edston hoard, close to a large rock near a hillfort, is uncertain, and with the Birnie hoards it is still too early to assess. The final one, from Lingrow (Orkney), is so scattered that little can be said of it. These hoards do indicate, however, a clear connection with Iron Age sites.

There is a greater likelihood of votive intent with those hoards from wet locations – primarily bogs and mosses, with one from the banks of a river and another from the shores of the Tay (in a location with other hints of Roman-period votive activity; Hunter 1996, 117–18). Such wet locations are often seen as ritually significant liminal areas, and were often places where retrieval would be difficult. Caution is required: there are safekeeping hoards from wet locations, as Randsborg (2002) has demonstrated with more recent material, and he rightly warns against too rigid a dichotomy between votive and safekeeping, since the deposition of a hoard may have several motives. In the local Iron Age context such watery deposits are commonplace, however, and are best seen as regional traditions of votive hoards (Hunter 1997a). The Roman coin hoards can be interpreted in the same light. Indeed, the coin hoard distribution closely mirrors the main areas of Iron Age hoarding and may reflect this existence of a depositional habit as much as any historical connection with the Caledonii and Maeatae (cf. Robertson 1978, 192).

The coin hoards span areas with different Iron Age hoarding traditions. Those from south of the Forth fit into a context where exotic material was readily incorporated into local practices. In north-east Scotland this was not the case: here hoards show a strong dominance of the local at the expense of the imported. Prestige metalwork deposits exhibit a strong dichotomy, with personal items of massive-tradition metalwork (MacGregor 1976; Ralston 1979, 482–4) being deposited in on-site contexts in contrast to communal items (such as vessels or the Deskford carnyx) being deposited off-site. The denarii hoards cut across this division, with some from settlements and others from off-site locations. This suggests an ambiguity over the nature of these exotic new prestige items. It seems they could be either personal or communal, or that access to them was less restricted than to traditional status items. Given the nature of coinage, which could be accumulated at various scales according to an individual or group's means and motives, this should not be surprising. Indeed, the very varying scales of deposition point to just such a range of social involvement. The person or group behind the Falkirk hoard (over 1,900 denarii) was operating on a very different level from the depositor of the Inchyra (Perthshire) hoard (eight denarii). This is reinforced by the deposit of two bronzes of Maximinus from Hallrule (Roxburghshire). These are not normally treated as a hoard since their value was minimal, but they had been placed 'in the cavity of a stone' (Tancred 1907) and may plausibly represent a small-scale, very personal offering. The same is doubtless true of an unknown and unknowable percentage of coin stray finds. A votive tradition of depositing coins would again find parallel with Celtic coins (Haselgrove 1996, 76).

To summarise, on Roman sites there is evidence for both safekeeping and votive hoards. Of the rest, some may be buried for safekeeping but a significant number are likely to be votive offerings which can be seen within an Iron Age hoarding tradition. While in the south of Scotland this fits an existing pattern, in the north-east their appearance represents a shift in previous habits.

Conclusions

The Birnie hoards provide us with our best-contexted examples of coin hoards beyond the frontier and should allow a much greater insight into the kinds of people receiving Roman coins and the ways they treated them. Things changed during the third century: silver coins stopped coming north, Celtic-style metalwork apparently ceased, and by the end of the century we have our first references to a new group, the Picts (Mann 1974, 40–1). Clearly there were changes (as yet opaque), especially within the societies north of the Forth, and it is tempting to see the appearance and disappearance of a new prestige good, denarii, having some role in this. This is a topic for further investigation. In the broader context, we must look beyond the specific historical sources for Roman Scotland and consider instead the wider picture in *barbaricum*, seeing the Scottish hoards as part of a more general pattern of gifts or subsidies beyond the frontier from Pius or Aurelius to Severus which continued on a lower level into the 230s. More speculatively, the use of these coins in Iron Age society could have been more complex than we give it credit for, functioning perhaps like early Celtic coinage as a specialised currency and prestige good. The role of Roman denarii in Iron Age societies was more active and more influential than is generally credited.

Acknowledgements

I am grateful to Nick Holmes for attempting to keep me on the numismatic straight and narrow, to Andrew Heald for access to his crucible research, and to him and David Clarke for comments. I am also indebted to useful discussion generated after the presentation of versions of this paper at the Durham conference and at a Roman Northern Frontiers Seminar in Edinburgh. Thanks are due to Craig Angus for Fig. 20.2.

Bibliography

Abdy, R. A. (2002) *Romano-British coin hoards*. Princes Risborough, Shire.

Aitchison, N. B. (1988) Roman wealth, native ritual: coin hoards within and beyond Roman Britain. *World Archaeology* 20.2, 270–84.

Austin, N. J. E. and Rankov, N. B. (1995) *Exploratio*. London, Routledge.

Bateson, J. D. (1971) The finding of Roman silver coins in the vicinity of the Giant's Causeway. *Ulster Journal of Archaeology* 34, 50–7.

Bateson, J. D. (1989) Roman and medieval coins found in Scotland, to 1987. *Proceedings of the Society of Antiquaries of Scotland* 119, 165–88.

Bateson, D. and Hall, M. (2002) Inchyra, Perthshire. In R. Abdy, I. Leins and J. Williams (eds) *Coin hoards from Roman Britain Volume XI*, 119–20. London, Royal Numismatic Society.

Bateson, J. D. and Holmes, N. M. McQ. (1997) Roman and medieval coins found in Scotland, 1988–95. *Proceedings of the Society of Antiquaries of Scotland* 127, 527–61.

Bateson, J. D. and Holmes, N. M. McQ. (2003) Roman and medieval coins found in Scotland, 1996–2000. *Proceedings of the Society of Antiquaries of Scotland* 133, 245–276.

Berger, F. (1992) *Untersuchungen zu Römerzeitlichen Münzfunden in Nordwestdeutschland.* Frankfurt, *Studien zu Fundmünzen der Antike* 9.

Berger, F. (1996) Roman coins beyond the northern frontiers: some recent considerations. In C. E. King and D. G. Wigg (ed.) *Coin Finds and Coin Use in the Roman World*, 55–61. Berlin, Mann Verlag.

Curle, A. O. (1923) *The Treasure of Traprain.* Glasgow, Maclehose.

DES *Discovery and Excavation in Scotland.* Edinburgh, Council for Scottish Archaeology.

Erdrich, M. (2000) *Rom und die Barbaren: Das Verhältnis zwischen dem Imperium Romanum und den Germanischen Stämmen vor seiner Nordwestgrenze von der späten römischen Republik bis zum Galischen Sonderreich.* Römisch-Germanische Kommission (Forschungen 58). Mainz.

Gordon, C. D. (1949) Subsidies in Roman Imperial Defence. *Phoenix* 3, 60–9.

Hanson, W. S. and Maxwell, G. S. (1983) *Rome's North West Frontier: the Antonine Wall.* Edinburgh, Edinburgh University Press.

Haselgrove, C. (1979) The significance of coinage in pre-Conquest Britain. In B. C. Burnham and H. C. Johnson (eds) *Invasion and Response: the case of Roman Britain.* BAR 73, 197–209. Oxford.

Haselgrove, C. (1996) Iron Age coinage: recent work. In T. C. Champion and J. R. Collis (eds) *The Iron Age in Britain and Ireland: recent trends*, 67–85. Sheffield, J. R. Collis Publications.

Hedeager, L. (1988) Money economy and prestige economy in the Roman Iron Age. In B. Hårdh, L. Larsson, D. Olausson and R. Petré (eds) *Trade and Exchange in Prehistory*, 147–53. *Acta Archaeologica Lundensia* 16. Lund.

Holmes, N. M. McQ. (forthcoming) Two denarius hoards from Birnie, Moray. *British Numismatic Journal.*

Holmes, N. M. McQ., and Hunter, F. (1997) Edston, Peeblesshire. In R. Bland and J. Orna-Ornstein (eds) *Coin Hoards from Roman Britain Volume X*, 149–68. London, British Museum.

Holmes, N. M. McQ. and Hunter, F. (2001) Roman counterfeiters' moulds from Scotland. *Proceedings of the Society of Antiquaries of Scotland* 131, 167–76.

Howgego, C. (1992) The supply and use of money in the Roman world. *Journal of Roman Studies* 82, 1–31.

Hunter, F. (1996) Recent Roman Iron Age metalwork finds from Fife and Tayside. *Tayside and Fife Archaeological Journal* 2, 113–25.

Hunter, F. (1997a) Iron Age hoarding in Scotland and northern England. In A. Gwilt and C. Haselgrove (eds.) *Reconstructing Iron Age Societies*, 108–33. Oxford, Oxbow.

Hunter, F. (1997b) Iron Age coins in Scotland. *Proceedings of the Society of Antiquaries of Scotland* 127, 513–25.

Hunter, F. (2002) Birnie: buying a peace on the northern frontier. *Current Archaeology* 181, 12–16.

Hunter, F. (2005) Rome and the creation of the Picts. In Z. Visy (ed.) *Limes XIX: Proceedings of the XIXth Congress of Roman Frontier Studies held in Pécs, Hungary, September 2003*, 235–244. Pécs, University of Pécs.

Jardine, W. (1866) Address of the President. *Transactions of the Dumfriesshire and Galloway Natural History and Antiquarian Society* 1863–4, 1–28.

Jones, B., Keillar, I. and Maude, K. (1993) The Moray Aerial Survey: discovering the prehistoric and protohistoric landscape. In W. D. H. Sellar (ed.) *Moray: Province and People*, 47–74. Edinburgh, Scottish Society for Northern Studies.

Lind, L. (1981) *Roman denarii found in Sweden 2. Catalogue text.* Stockholm, Almqvist and Wiksell.

Lind, L. (1988) *Romerska denarer funna i Sverige.* Stockholm, Förlaget Rubicon.

Macdonald, G. (1918) Roman coins found in Scotland. *Proceedings of the Society of Antiquaries of Scotland* 52, 203–76.

MacGregor, M. (1976) *Early Celtic Art in North Britain.* Leicester, Leicester University Press.

Mann, J. C. (1974) The northern frontier after A.D. 369. *Glasgow Archaeological Journal* 3, 34–42.

Nash, D. (1978) Settlement and coinage in central Gaul *c.* 200–50 B.C. British Archaeological Reports International Series 39. Oxford.

Nash Briggs, D. (1995) Coinage. In M. Green (ed.) *The Celtic World*, 244–53. London, Routledge.

Nielsen, S. (1988) Roman denarii in Denmark – an archaeological approach. *Nordisk Numismatisk Årsskrift 1987–88*, 147–69.

Ralston, I. B. M. (1979) The Iron Age (*c.* 600 BC – AD 200). B, Northern Britain. In J. V. S. Megaw and D. D. A. Simpson (eds) *Introduction to British Prehistory*, 446–96. Leicester, Leicester University Press.

Randsborg, K. (2002) Wetland hoards. *Oxford Journal of Archaeology* 21.4, 415–8.

Reece, R. (1980) Coins and frontiers: the Falkirk hoard reconsidered. In W. S. Hanson and L. J. F. Keppie (eds) *Roman Frontier Studies 1979*, 119–29. BAR I 71. Oxford.

Robertson, A. S. (1975) The Romans in North Britain: the coin evidence. In H. Temporini (ed.), *Aufstieg und Niedergang der Römisches Welt II.3*, 364–426. Berlin.

Robertson, A. S. (1978) The circulation of Roman coins in North Britain: the evidence of hoards and site-finds from Scotland. In R. A. G. Carson and C. M. Kraay (eds) *Scripta Nummaria Romana*, 186–216. London, Spink.

Robertson, A. S. (1982) The Falkirk (1933) hoard of over 1900 denarii: a review in the light of recent research. In S. Scheers (ed.) *Studia Paulo Naster Oblata I: Numismatica Antiqua*, 207–26. Leuven, Peeters.

Robertson, A. S. (1983) Roman coins found in Scotland, 1971–82. *Proceedings of the Society of Antiquaries of Scotland* 113, 405–48.

Robertson, A. S. (2000) *An Inventory of Romano-British Coin Hoards.* London, Royal Numismatic Society.

Tancred, G. (1907) *Rulewater and its people.* Edinburgh, Constable.

Todd, M. (1985) The Falkirk hoard of denarii: trade or subsidy? *Proceedings of the Society of Antiquaries of Scotland* 115, 229–32.

Van der Vin, J. (1996) Roman coins in the Dutch province of Friesland. In C. E. King and D. G. Wigg (eds) *Coin Finds and Coin Use in the Roman World*, 357–71. *Studien zu Fundmünzen der Antike* 10. Berlin, Mann Verlag.

Appendix.

Roman coin hoards to AD 250 north of Hadrian's Wall (known to the writer as of January 2003). Alternative names are given in brackets. The 'quality' column reflects the reliability of the record: 1 is recorded to modern standards, 2 acceptable, 3 poor. Italicised entries are certainly or probably associated with a Roman site: the precise location of the Broomholm hoard is unknown, but there is a fort on the farm; Kirkintilloch was found just south of the Antonine Wall; Endrick Water lies close to Drumquhassle fort; Carstairs is close to the Castledykes complex. Of the others, the Benbecula account is a very strange one, and the Milton of Buittle and Burnswark finds are not certainly hoards. The Lingrow finds were scattered and are not certainly a hoard, but they are taken as one here since they would represent an exceptional quantity of site finds for a northern site. Where a number only is given in the reference column, this is the hoard's number in Robertson 2000. Pre-1975 counties and four-figure grid references only are used.

Findspot	County	Quality	Discovery date	Latest emperor recorded	Latest date	Metal	Quantity	Container	Associations	Context	NGR	Reference
Silver Burn (Petercoulter)	Aberdeen	3	pre 1726	?	?	AR	a great quantity			moss	NJ 84 04	966
Glamis (Green Cairn)	Angus	3	pre 1707	Galba	68–69	AR	great quantities	urn		tumulus	NO 38 48	50
Usan	Angus	1	1996–9	M Aurelius	175–176	AR	3		intaglio, Au ring	?	NO 72 54	DES 1996, 12; 1998, 11; 1999, 12
Aitnock	Ayr	1	1901–02	A Pius	145–161	AR	4	wrapped		dun	NS 28 51	184
Deskford	Banff	3	pre 1726	A Pius	138–161	AR	at least 27			?	NJ 51 61	198
Broomholm	*Dumfries*	2	*1782*	*Domitian*	*81–96*	*AV*	*6*			?	*NY 37 81*	*97*
Burnswark	*Dumfries*	2	*c 1725*	*Trajan*	*98–117*	*AR*	*4*			*Roman camp*	*NY 18 79*	*125*
Lochar Moss	Dumfries	3	pre 1864	Republican	82 BC	AR	15–16			peat bog	NY 0 7	Jardine 1866, 18
Bar Hill	*Dunbarton*	1	*1902*	*Marcus Caesar*	*140–144*	*AR/copies*	*13*			*Roman fort*	*NS 71 76*	*206*
Kirkintilloch	*Dunbarton*	2	*1893*	*Faustina II*	*161–176*	*AR*	*min 47*		*Fe spear, nail*	?	*NS 66 74*	*282*
Craigiehill (Leuchars)	Fife	3	1808	Severus	193–211	AR	almost 100	jar		?	NO 45 24	376
East Wemyss	Fife	1	2000	Elagabalus	218–222	AR	6			?	NT 33 97	Bateson & Holmes 2003
Leven	Fife	3	1519	?	?	AV/AR	?	Ae vessel		?	NO 37 00	1886
Pitcullo (Leuchars)	Fife	2	1781	Commodus	177–192	AR	19			?	NO 41 19	345
Benbecula	Inverness	3	1808	Severus	193–211	AR	a few pieces	'a Roman urn'	skeleton	sand bank		Robertson 1983, 417
Cowie Moss (Fetteresso)	Kincardine	2	1843	Severus	193–211	AR	?	?		moss	NO 85 91	367
Fawsyde (Bervie, Kineff)	Kincardine	3	19th century	A Pius	138–161	?	?	?box	2 Ae bars, clamp (?box fittings)	?	NO 84 77	228
Megray	Kincardine	2	1852	Severus	202–210	AR	>200	urn		?	NO 88 88	368
Portmoak (Kirkness)	Kinross	2	1851	Severus	196–7	AR	>600	?bag	Fe sword, Ag ornament	bog	NT 18 98	369
Rumbling Bridge (Briglands)	Kinross	1	1938–57	Commodus	186–7	AR	180			bank of River Devon	NT 02 99	335
Milton of Buittle	Kirkcudbright	2	pre 1794	Commodus	177–192	AR	3			?	NX 81 64	Macdonald 1918, 243

Appendix, cont.

Bracco (Shotts)	Lanark	2	1842	Commodus	177–192	AR	several hundred	cloth bag		moss	NS 83 66	346
Carstairs	*Lanark*	*3*	*1781*	*A Pius*	*138–161*	*AE*	*c. 100*			*?*	*NS 94 45*	*266*
Lanark	Lanark	3	1847	A Pius	138–161	AR	?			cairn	NS 91 44	185
Torfoot (Strathaven)	Lanark	3	1803	Crispina	178–188	AR	c. 400	square glass bottle		foot of rising ground	NS 64 39	347
Edinburgh	Midlothian	3	pre 1741	Faustina II	161–176	AR	a good many	"urn"		stone structure?	NT 20 70	283
Elginhaugh	*Midlothian*	*1*	*1986*	*Vespasian for Domitian*	*77–78*	*AR*	*45*			*Roman fort*	*NT 32 67*	*63*
Birnie 1	Moray	1	1996–2000	Severus	194–7	AR	317	IA pot		IA site	NJ 21 59	Hunter 2002 Holmes forthcoming
Birnie 2	Moray	1	2001	Pertinax	193	AR	310	IA pot		IA site	NJ 21 59	Hunter 2002 Holmes forthcoming
Nairn	Nairn	3	pre 1780	?	?	AR	?	urn		?	NH 87 56	1870
Downham	N'umberland	3	c 1830	?	?	AR	a large quantity	jar/vase		?	NT 86 33	1784A
Mindrum	N'umberland	3	1826	M Aurelius	161–180	AR	500–700	Ae flagon		?	NT 84 32	274
Lingrow	Orkney	2	1870–1	Crispina	178–188	AR	6	scattered		broch outworks	HY 43 09	349
Edston	Peebles	1	1994	Elagabalus	218–222	AR	290			rock near hillfort	NT 23 40	Holmes & Hunter 1997
Greatlaws (Skirling)	Peebles	3	c 1825	A Pius	138–161	?	?			?	NT10 40	186
Drummond Castle (Muthill)	Perth	3	pre 1672	Commodus	177–192	AR	> bushel		Au ring	?	NN 80 15	348
Inchyra	Perth	1	1993	M Aurelius for Commodus	178	AR	8			foreshore of Tay	NO 18 20	Bateson & Hall 2002
Taymouth (Kenmore)	Perth	2	1755	M Aurelius	161–180	AR	12–14	box?		near hill crest	NN 80 42	236
Hallrule (Rulewater)	Roxburgh	2	pre 1907	Maximinus	235–238	AE	2	cavity in stone		in cavity in stone	NS 59 14	Macdonald 1918, 239
Newstead	*Roxburgh*	*1*	*1986*	*Trajan*	*103–111*	*AR*	*4*	*?*		*Roman fort*	*NT 57 34*	*126*
Wauchope Bridge	Dumfries	3	1782	Otho	69	AV	3?			?in a small holm	NY 36 85	51
Endrick Water (Drymen)	*Stirling*	*2*	*1771*	*Trajan*	*100*	*AV*	*2*			*in an old quarry*	*NS 47 87*	*Macdonald 1918, 245*
Falkirk	Stirling	1	1933	Severus Alexander	230	AR	1934	Roman jar		in face of small hill	NS 89 80	415
Linlithgow (Burgh Muir)	W Lothian	3	1781	M Aurelius	161–180	AR	c. 300	earthen urn		?	NT 02 78	268
West Calder (Crosswood Hill)	W Lothian	2	1810	M Aurelius	161–180	AR	some			moss 5' below surface	NT 03 56	267

Index